Reuben Asbury Reese

The True Doctrine of Ultra Vires in the Law of Corporations

Reuben Asbury Reese

The True Doctrine of Ultra Vires in the Law of Corporations

ISBN/EAN: 9783337811440

Printed in Europe, USA, Canada, Australia, Japan

Cover: Foto ©Suzi / pixelio.de

More available books at **www.hansebooks.com**

THE

TRUE DOCTRINE OF ULTRA VIRES

IN

THE LAW OF CORPORATIONS

BEING

A CONCISE PRESENTATION OF THE DOCTRINE IN ITS
APPLICATION TO THE POWERS AND LIABILITIES
OF PRIVATE AND MUNICIPAL CORPORATIONS

BY

REUBEN A. REESE, Esq.
OF THE COLORADO BAR

CHICAGO
T. H. FLOOD AND COMPANY
1897

COPYRIGHT, 1897,
BY
T. H. FLOOD & CO.

STATE JOURNAL PRINTING COMPANY,
PRINTERS AND STEREOTYPERS,
MADISON, WIS.

TO THE

HON. THOMAS J. BALLINGER,

OF TEXAS,

WHOSE MASTERFUL ABILITIES AS A LAWYER,

UNIMPEACHABLE INTEGRITY AS A MAN,

AND

UNSWERVING LOYALTY AS A FRIEND,

MAKE HIS

ACQUAINTANCE AN HONOR AND HIS COMPANIONSHIP

A DELIGHT,

AS A SLIGHT ACKNOWLEDGMENT

OF THE

HIGH REGARD IN WHICH HE IS HELD BY THE AUTHOR,

THIS VOLUME

IS RESPECTFULLY INSCRIBED.

PREFACE.

The aim and purpose of this volume is to set forth in a concise and practical way the established principles of the Doctrine of *Ultra Vires* in its application to the acts and contracts of corporations both public and private. By the title — "The *True* Doctrine of *Ultra Vires*" — no reflection is meant to be made upon other writers who have heretofore treated the subject in works on corporation law, although, in some respects, the views herein expressed are diametrically opposed to those of some modern law writers who have casually discussed the various phrases of this doctrine. In whatever features, however, this brief exposition of the subject differs from its presentation by others, comparison as to the number and character of authorities cited to sustain the propositions laid down is respectfully invited. In style and composition neither classical precision, stilted phraseology, nor laborious efforts at "fine writing," has been attempted, the main object being to furnish a brief and practical compendium of the doctrine of *ultra vires* for the practicing attorney; and it is believed the work, though purposely condensed, may for that reason be all the more useful to him for ready reference. The difficulties to be overcome in classifying and arranging, under separate headings, the several branches of the subject, and at the same time avoid discussing in detail the general law of corporations, which has already been fully considered by many eminent commentators, are quite apparent, and this in some measure may account for the fact that no American treatise on the doctrine has ever been published. The obstacles to be surmounted in the preparation of a work of this character will, it is to be hoped, insure to the writer the kind indulgence of the profession.

R. A. R.

COLORADO SPRINGS,
March 4, 1897.

CONTENTS.

CHAPTER I.
CREATION AND CONSTRUCTION OF CORPORATE CHARTERS.

PART I.
CREATION OF CHARTERS.

Section. Page.
1. Introductory 1
2. A corporation a legal entity 2
3. Creation of chartered corporations 2
4. What acceptance of charter implies 7
5. Distinction between natural and artificial persons . . 8
6. Distinction between corporation and partnership . . . 9
7. Distinction between corporations under general and special act 10

PART II.
CONSTRUCTION OF CHARTERS.

8. General rule of construction 12
9. Corporations have only powers given by charters . . . 13
10. Rule peculiarly applicable to corporation organized under general laws 16
11. *Ultra vires* questions decided by law of organization . 17
12. Province of court in construing corporate powers . . 20
13. Powers construed as incidental to those expressly given 21
14. Discretion of corporations 22
15. Miscellaneous incidental powers 22

CHAPTER II.
THE DOCTRINE OF ULTRA VIRES.
THE DOCTRINE GENERALLY.

16. Introductory 25
17. *Ultra vires* — Senses in which term used 26

Section.		Page.
18.	Principles of doctrine plain	28
19.	Two propositions of doctrine settled	28
20.	Chronological review of doctrine	30
21.	Head v. Providence Ins. Co.	30
22.	People v. Utica Ins. Co.	31
23.	New York Firemen's Ins. Co. v. Sturges	31
24.	Bank of United States v. Dandridge	32
25.	Beach v. Fulton Bank	32
26.	Bank of Augusta v. Earle	32
27.	Barry v. Merchants' Exchange	33
28.	Perrine v. Chesapeake, etc. Canal Co.	34
29.	Hood v. New York, etc. R. Co.	34
30.	Pearce v. Madison, etc. R. Co.	37
31.	Bissell v. Michigan, etc. R. Co.	39
32.	Monument Nat. Bank v. Globe Works	41
33.	Miners' Ditch Co. v. Zellerbach	42
34.	Franklin Co. v. Lewistown Institute for Savings	43
35.	Thomas v. Railroad Co.	43
36.	Davis v. Old Colony R. Co.	45
37.	Central Transp. Co. v. Pullman's Palace Car Co.	46
38.	Lucas v. White Line Transp. Co.	51
39.	The doctrine as construed by English courts — Colman v. Eastern Counties Ry. Co.	55
40.	East Anglian Co. v. Eastern Counties Ry. Co.	57
41.	Ashbury, etc. Ry. Co. v. Riche	58
42.	Attorney-General v. Great Eastern Ry. Co.	64
43.	Small et al. v. Smith et al.	65
44.	Baroness Wenlock v. River Dee, etc.	65
45.	Trevor v. Whitworth	66

CHAPTER III.

CONTRACTS OF CORPORATIONS.

THE DOCTRINE APPLIED TO CONTRACTS GENERALLY.

46.	Introductory	67
47.	Application of doctrine to contracts generally	68
48.	Province of court in applying doctrine	69
49.	Tendency of courts to disregard statutory enactments	70
50.	As to incidental contractual powers	72
51.	Irregularity no defense to liability on corporate contracts	73

Section.	Page.
52. When charter prescribes mode of contracting, must be strictly pursued	74
53. All persons bound to take notice of limits of corporate powers	75
54. Why corporations not liable on *ultra vires* contracts	76
55. Distinction between *ultra vires* and illegal contracts	77
56. Prohibited contracts regarded as illegal and void	79
57. Unauthorized contracts none the less illegal because ignored by courts	80

CHAPTER IV.
THE DOCTRINE APPLIED TO EXECUTED CONTRACTS.

58. Estoppel — Defense of *ultra vires* to executed contracts	83
59. Same subject	84
60. Same subject — Corporation similar to one under legal disability	85
61. Performance by innocent party to contract *ultra vires* a corporation	86
62. Position of United States supreme court on alleged rule	89
63. San Antonio v. Mehaffey	91
64. Railway Co. v. McCarthey	93
65. Hitchcock v. Galveston	94
66. Jones v. Guaranty Co.	97
67. National Bank v. Mathews	97
68. Central Transp. Co. v. Pullman Car Co.	98

CHAPTER V.
ACTIONS ON ULTRA VIRES CONTRACTS.

69. General rule as to actions on illegal contracts	100
70. *Ultra vires* as defense to actions — General rule	102
71. Court must be satisfied of legality of contract	104
72. Actions on executed *ultra vires* contracts	105
73. Actions in courts of equity and at law	107
74. *Quantum meruit* — Relief on *ultra vires* contracts	113
75. Relief on contracts *ultra vires* and under statute of frauds	116

CHAPTER VI.
ADOPTION AND RATIFICATION OF CONTRACTS.

76. General doctrine of ratification stated	119
77. Nature and effect of ratification	120

Section.		Page.
78.	*Ultra vires* contracts of corporations cannot be ratified	121
79.	Ratification by corporation of acts of promoters	123

CHAPTER VII.
THE DOCTRINE APPLIED TO INCIDENTAL POWERS OF CORPORATIONS.

80.	Introductory	126
81.	Power to acquire real property	127
82.	Devise to corporations	131
83.	*Jus disponendi* in corporations	131
84.	Power to sell implies power to mortgage	133
85.	Power of bank to hold real estate	134
86.	Power to acquire by eminent domain	135
87.	Alienation by deed	136
88.	Conveyance by agent	137
89.	Acknowledgment to corporate deeds	137
90.	Affixing seal to deeds	138
91.	Assignment for benefit of creditors	138
92.	Power to act as trustee	139
93.	Trust must be within scope of corporate powers	140
94.	Cannot be compelled to execute repugnant trust	140
95.	Power to take by bequest	141
96.	Power to borrow money	142
97.	Test to determine if transaction is borrowing	144
98.	Instances of implied power to borrow	144
99.	Power to loan money	146
100.	Power as to negotiable notes	147
101.	Power as indorsee	149
102.	Power of savings bank to make negotiable paper	149
103.	Power as to discount and purchase	149
104.	Liability on accommodation paper	151
105.	Power to pledge securities	151

CHAPTER VIII.
POWERS AND LIABILITIES AS TO CAPITAL STOCK.

106.	Introductory — Nature and purpose of capital stock	152
107.	Capital stock as a trust fund	153
108.	Limitation on doctrine that capital stock a trust fund	155
109.	Power to increase capital stock	156

Section.		Page.
110.	Consent of stockholders necessary to increase capital stock	157
111.	Power of national bank to increase capital stock	158
112.	Irregularity in executing power as affecting stockholders	160
113.	Power to reduce capital stock	160
114.	Reduction of capital stock in England	161
115.	Power to issue new stock	161
116.	Powers as to special stock	162
117.	Power to issue shares at discount	163
118.	Power to issue preferred stock	164
119.	Liability on *ultra vires* issue of preferred stock	165
120.	Power to deal in own stock	167
121.	Power to purchase stock of other corporations	169
122.	Instances where power denied	169
123.	Power of foreign corporation to purchase stock of domestic company	171
124.	Power to declare dividends	171
125.	Power to pledge future calls	172
126.	Liability on dividends declared	173
127.	Liability on illegal stock	174

CHAPTER IX.

THE DOCTRINE APPLIED TO RAILROAD CORPORATIONS.

128.	General power to make contracts	175
129.	Contracts to carry beyond own line	176
130.	Traffic agreements between railroads	177
131.	Pooling contracts	178
132.	Railroad bonds — Definition	180
133.	Power to issue bonds	181
134.	Formalities prescribed must be strictly pursued	181
135.	Negotiability of railroad bonds	182
136.	Power to guaranty bonds of another company	183
137.	Power to lease road and franchises	184
138.	*Ultra vires* lease will not be set aside at suit of lessor	189
139.	Instances where power to lease denied	189
140.	Power to mortgage property	190
141.	Power to mortgage franchises	191
142.	Consolidation and amalgamation — Definition	192
143.	Powers of corporations to consolidate	194

Section.	Page.
144. Effect of consolidation	195
145. Effect of interstate consolidation	198
146. Rights and liabilities of consolidated company	199
147. Consolidation as affecting stockholders	200
148. Consolidation as affecting taxation	202
149. Trusts and illegal combinations	203

CHAPTER X.

THE DOCTRINE IN ITS RELATION TO DIRECTORS AND OTHER OFFICERS AND AGENTS OF CORPORATIONS.

150. Introductory	207
151. Distinction between corporate acts and unauthorized acts of directors	207
152. Test to distinguish acts of directors from corporate acts	209
153. Directors as trustees	210
154. General powers of directors	211
155. Instances of directors' powers	211
156. General liability of directors	212
157. Power of bank directors	213
158. Liability of bank directors	214
159. Powers and liabilities of bank president	215
160. Powers and duties of bank cashier	216
161. Instances of cashier's powers	217

CHAPTER XI.

THE DEFENSE OF ULTRA VIRES AS TO TORTIOUS ACTS OF OFFICERS AND AGENTS.

162. General rule as to liability of corporation for torts	219
163. Liability for tortious acts of agent	221
164. Authority of agent in fixing liability	223

CHAPTER XII.

POWERS AND LIABILITIES OF FOREIGN AND DE FACTO CORPORATIONS.

165. General powers of foreign corporations	225
166. The absence of prohibitory legislation presumes a tacit adoption of foreign laws	226

Section.		Page.
167.	Contractual powers similar to domestic corporations	227
168.	De facto corporations estopped to deny corporate existence	227

CHAPTER XIII.
THE DOCTRINE OF ULTRA VIRES APPLIED TO MUNICIPAL CORPORATIONS.

169.	Introductory — Nature of municipal corporations	231
170.	Exercise of municipal powers	232
171.	Ordinances — Power to enact	233
172.	Nature and effect of ordinances	234
173.	Ministerial and judicial ordinances distinguished	235
174.	Effect of *ultra vires* ordinances	236
175.	Instances of *ultra vires* ordinances	236
176.	Ordinances must be reasonable	237
177.	Courts cannot interfere with discretion of municipality	239
178.	Courts may restrain passage of *ultra vires* ordinances	240
179.	Powers as to taxation	240
180.	Power to tax may be revoked	241
181.	Power can be exercised only for public purposes	242
182.	Taxation and power to license distinguished	243
183.	Power to exercise right of eminent domain	244
184.	Distinction between eminent domain and taxation	244
185.	Powers as to property	245
186.	Powers of divided municipality	247
187.	Powers of extinguished municipalities	248

CHAPTER XIV.
GENERAL POWERS AS TO CONTRACTS.

188.	Introductory — General rule as to contracts	249
189.	The mode prescribed must be strictly pursued	252
190.	*Ultra vires* contracts by officers	254
191.	Implied municipal contracts	256
192.	When estoppel not applicable	257
193.	When estopped to deny irregularity	258
194.	Ratification of *ultra vires* contracts	258
195.	Contracts of compromise and arbitration	259
196.	Limitation on contracting indebtedness	260
197.	Instances where increase denied	262
198.	Equity will enjoin illegal creation of debt	263

CHAPTER XV.

PARTICULAR POWERS AND LIABILITIES OF MUNICIPAL CORPORATIONS.

Section. Page.
199. Exclusive control over streets 265
200. When estopped to deny existence of street 266
201. Power to grade and improve streets 266
202. Discretionary powers as to improvement 268
203. Liability for consequential damages 269
204. Liability for accidents upon streets 271
205. Instances of liability for defective streets 273
206. Notice to authorities required 274
207. Sewers — General powers as to 275
208. Discretion in selecting system 276
209. Duty to provide sewer outlet 277
210. City not insurer of condition of sewer 277
211. Liability for injury from defective sewer 278
212. Power to abate nuisances 279
213. Liability as to nuisances 280
214. Powers as to quarantine regulations 282
215. Powers as to public wharves 283
216. Exclusive privileges to gas and water companies . . . 284
217. Contracts as to gas and water supply 285
218. Power to regulate rates 285
219. Liability for damages owing to inadequate water supply 286
220. Doctrine of *respondeat superior* 287
221. Distinction between public *quasi*-corporations and municipal corporations 289
222. Not liable for damages arising from *ultra vires* acts of officers 291

CHAPTER XVI.

POWERS AND LIABILITIES AS TO MUNICIPAL SECURITIES.

223. Power to issue bonds 295
224. Purposes for which bonds may be issued 296
225. Instances where power denied 297
226. Formality in execution as affecting liability 298
227. Irregularity as affecting liability 298
228. Effect of recitals in bonds 299

Section.		Page.
229.	Who are *bona fide* holders	301
230.	Power to issue bonds not implied from power to borrow .	302
231.	Limitation on indebtedness as affecting legality of bonds	303
232.	Invalid bonds cannot be ratified	305
233.	Liability cannot be avoided by reorganization	306
234.	Liability in *assumpsit* on invalid bonds	307
235.	Illegal issue of bonds may be enjoined	308
236.	Municipal-aid bonds	309
237.	Power must be specially granted	309
238.	Power to subscribe to railroad stock	311
239.	Limitation on amount of subscription	312
240.	Levying tax to pay subscription	313

TABLE OF CASES CITED.

References are to sections.

A.

Abbey, Metropolitan Concert Co. v., 139.
Abbott, Elliott v., 160, 161.
Abbott v. Johnstown, etc. R. Co., 137.
Abbott v. Omaha Smelting Co., 3.
Abbott v. Packet Co., 70.
Abbott, Society, etc. v., 107.
Abbott, Thompson v., 144, 146, 186, 188.
Abel, March v., 71.
Aberdeen, State Board v., 191.
Aberdeen R. Co. v. Blaikie, 153.
Academy, Moss v., 96.
Academy of Music v. Flanders Bros., 168.
Ackerman v. Halsey, 158.
Acres, Lake Erie R. Co. v., 163.
Adams, Anthony v., 213, 222.
Adams v. Farnsworth, 191.
Adams, Haven v., 87.
Adams, Tash v., 175.
Adams, Valparaiso v., 203.
Adams Co., Quincy Bridge Co. v., 145.
Adams Express Co. v. Wilson, 129.
Addlestone Co., In re, 117.
Adriance v. Roome, 52.
Ætna Bank v. Charter Oak Ins. Co., 9, 136.
Ætna Ins. Co., Middleport v., 240.
Agar v. Insurance Co., 160.
Agnew v. Brall, 195.
Agricultural Association, Taylor v., 96.
Aicardi v. State, 8.
Akron, McCombs v., 220.

B

Alabama, etc. Co. v. Central Association, 70, 96.
Alabama R. Co., Jordon v., 162.
Alabama R. Co. v. Smith, 53.
Alabama R. Co., Waddill v., 53.
Albany, People v., 212.
Albany Co., Laramie Co. v., 86.
Albert Association Co., In re, 137.
Albert Lea, Graham v., 205.
Albright v. Town Council, 188.
Alden v. Minneapolis, 203.
Aldrich, Lumbard v., 81.
Aldrich v. Tripp, 222.
Alers, Sherwood v., 70.
Alexander v. Brown, 77.
Alexander v. Cauldwell, 154, 194.
Alexander, Mathews v., 173.
Alexander v. O'Donnell, 69.
Alexander v. Relfe, 163.
Alexander, Richmond Factory Co. v., 3.
Alexander v. Tolleston Club, 81.
Allegheny City, Amey v., 239.
Allegheny City v. McClurkan, 70, 74.
Allen, Camden v., 224.
Allen, Chouteau v., 105, 194.
Allen v. Galveston, 170.
Allen v. Herrick, 127.
Allen v. Inhabitants, etc., 224.
Allen v. Joy, 181, 225.
Allen v. Lafayette, 233.
Allen, Page v., 198.
Allen, Phillips v., 212.
Allerton, Railway Co. v., 109, 110.
Alley v. Inhabitants, etc., 170.
Allison, Bank of Hindustan v., 127.
Allison v. Railroad Co., 235.

TABLE OF CASES CITED.

References are to sections.

Almada & Tirito Co., In re, 117.
Almy, Salem Nat. Bank v., 51, 168.
Alton, Sturtevant v., 188, 201.
Alvis, Sheward v., 53, 70.
American Academy v. Howard, 94.
American Com. Co. v. Humboldt M. Co., 136.
American Ins. Co., Judah v., 14.
American Ins. Co., Miller v., 74.
American Preserves Trust v. Manufacturing Co., 69, 148.
American Tube Works v. Boston Mach. Co., 116.
American, etc. Soc., Wade v., 92.
American, etc. Union v. Yount, 81.
Amery, Rex v., 3.
Ames, British Am. Land Co. v., 166.
Amey v. Allegheny City, 239.
Amherst, Merrick v., 225.
Ammon, Miller v., 69.
Amy, Pendleton v., 227.
Amy, St. Joseph Township v., 227.
Anderson, Bliss v., 53.
Anderson v. City, 175.
Anderson, Smith v., 153.
Anderson v. Township of Santa Ana, 238.
Andover, Gassett v., 191.
Andover v. Grafton, 230.
Andover, Jenkins v., 224.
Andreas, Craig v., 69.
Androscoggin R. Co. v. Auburn Bank, 105.
Androscoggin R. Co., Evansville R. Co. v., 129.
Anglo-Cal. Bank, Mahoney Min. Co. v., 96, 98.
Anita, Davis v., 176.
Anthony v. Adams, 213, 222.
Anthony v. County of Jasper, 226.
Anthony v. Household Mach. Co., 116.
Appeal of City of Erie, 196, 197.
Appleton, Hayes v., 170.
Archer v. Terre Haute R. Co., 9.
Ardesco Oil Co. v. N. A. Min. Co., 83, 91.
Argenti v. San Francisco, 188, 190, 191, 192.
Arkansas, Curran v., 107.

Armstrong, Beaver v., 135.
Armstrong v. Brunswick, 212, 213.
Armstrong, St. Louis v., 194.
Armstrong, Winters v., 109, 111.
Arn v. City of Kansas, 211.
Arnot v. Erie R. Co., 129, 136.
Arrighi, Jefferson Co. v., 194.
Arthur v. Bank, 91.
Arthur v. Griswold, 158.
Ash, Conservators v., 3.
Ashbury, Glass v., 170.
Ashbury Ry. Co. v. Riche, 41, 42, 43, 44, 45, 52, 53, 72, 78, 137.
Ashley v. Port Huron, 211.
Ashton-under-Lynn, Bateman v., 70.
Ashville Division, etc. v. Aston, 81.
Aspinwall, Eaton v., 106.
Aspinwall, Knox Co. v., 135, 190, 193, 227, 228.
Aspinwall v. Sacchi, 106.
Assurance Co., In re, 168.
Aston, Ashville Div. etc. v., 81.
Atchison, etc. R. Co. v. Commissioners, 146.
Atchison, etc. R. Co. v. Denver, etc. Co., 131.
Atchison, etc. R. Co. v. Fletcher, 136.
Athenæum, etc. Co. v. Tooley, 74.
Athens City Water Works, Fowler v., 217.
Atkinson v. Marietta, etc. R. Co., 9.
Atlanta, Cooper v., 222.
Atlanta, Fulla v., 203.
Atlanta, Wells v., 177, 188, 217.
Atlantic, etc. R. Co. v. State, 144.
Atlantic City Water Works v. Atlantic City, 216, 217.
Atlas Bank v. Nahant Bank, 74.
Attorney-General v. Boston, 145.
Attorney-General v. Great Eastern Ry., 42, 43, 44, 47.
Attorney-General v. Insurance Co., 100.
Attorney-General v. Stevens, 168.
Attorney-General v. Wilson, 153.
Atwater, First Cong. Soc. v., 92.
Atwood, De Camp v., 91.
Aubert v. Walsh, 69.
Auburn Bank, Androscoggin R. Co. v., 105.

TABLE OF CASES CITED. xix

References are to sections.

Auburn Plank Road Co. v. Douglas, 8.
Augusta, Walsh v., 196.
Augusta, Williams v., 212.
Augusta, Wright v., 219.
Auerbach v. Le Sueur Mill Co., 81, 100.
Aukland v. Westminster Board, 53.
Aurora v. Cobshire, 200.
Aurora, Faulkner v., 204.
Aurora v. West, 135, 237.
Aurora Agl. Soc. v. Paddock, 77, 84.
Austin, Berrick v., 161.
Austin, Doyle v., 181.
Austin v. Mundy, 175.
Australian, etc. Co. v. Mounsey, 96, 98.
Averhill, Moss v., 56, 100.
Averhill, Rochester Sav. Bank v., 9.

B.

Backman v. Charleston, 194.
Bacon, Holt v., 161.
Badger v. Bank, 160, 161.
Badger, Partridge v., 83, 96, 100.
Bagshaw v. Eastern Counties Ry. Co., 53.
Bagshaw v. Eastern Union Ry. Co., 9, 70.
Bailey v. M. E. Church, 53.
Bailey, Padrick v., 176.
Bailey, State v., 142, 143, 147.
Baird v. Bank, 81.
Baker v. Boston, 222.
Baker, City of Madison v., 211.
Baker, Dixon v., 211.
Baker, Niagara County Bank v., 103.
Baker, Shawneetown v., 195.
Baker, Whitman M. Co. v., 47, 81.
Bakersfield Association v. Chester, 51, 168.
Baldwin, Farmers' & M. Bank v., 103.
Balfour v. Ernest, 148.
Ball, Savage v., 100.
Ballard, Bradley v., 58, 96.
Ballou, Litchfield v., 233.
Ballston Bank v. Marine Bank, 161.

Baltimore v. Baltimore, etc. Co., 47.
Baltimore v. Eschbach, 190, 201, 222.
Baltimore v. Gill, 196, 198.
Baltimore, Horn v., 201.
Baltimore v. Musgrove, 190.
Baltimore v. Radicke, 176, 178.
Baltimore, etc. R. Co. v. Glenn, 166.
Baltimore, etc. R. Co., Mayor, etc. v., 128.
Baltimore, etc. R. Co. v. Schumacher, 129.
Bangor, Darling v., 202.
Bangor, Smith v., 205.
Bangor Savings Bank v. Stillwater, 233.
Bangor & Slate Co., In re, 118.
Banigan, Bard v., 119.
Bank, Arthur v., 91.
Bank, Badger v., 160, 161.
Bank, Baird v., 81.
Bank v. Bruce, 120.
Bank v. Chillicothe, 96.
Bank v. Colby, 144.
Bank, County of Moultrie v., 197.
Bank, Dabney v., 91.
Bank, Dana v., 87.
Bank, Dater v., 83.
Bank, Farmers' & M. Bank v., 160.
Bank, Godbold v., 156.
Bank v. Haskill, 161.
Bank, Jones v., 168.
Bank, Lloyd v., 160.
Bank, Louisville v., 215.
Bank, Mackay v., 162.
Bank, McDonough v., 79.
Bank, Merrick v., 91.
Bank, Minor v., 160.
Bank, Norton v., 74.
Bank, People v., 170.
Bank, Pomeroy v., 144.
Bank, Potter v., 100.
Bank, Reese v., 124.
Bank, Ridgeway v., 96, 100.
Bank v. St. John, 156.
Bank, St. Louis v., 171.
Bank, Smith v., 161.
Bank, Spohr v., 168.
Bank, State v., 83.
Bank, Sturges v., 161.
Bank v. Transportation Co., 120.

TABLE OF CASES CITED.

References are to sections.

Bank, Union M. Co. v., 96.
Bank, Wild v., 160.
Bank, Williams v., 74.
Bank of Augusta v. Earle, 8, 9, 26. 28, 47, 52, 103, 156, 157, 165, 167.
Bank of Australasia v. Breillat, 96, 98.
Bank of British Columbia, Willamette v., 9, 53.
Bank of Columbia, Mechanics' Bank v., 161.
Bank of Columbia v. Paterson, 76, 77, 188.
Bank of England, Coles v., 124.
Bank of Gennessee v. Patchin Bank, 9.
Bank of Hindustan v. Allison, 127.
Bank of Hindustan, In re, 142.
Bank of Kentucky, Lewis v., 167.
Bank of Kentucky v. Schuylkill Bank, 79, 160.
Bank of Lyons v. Demon, 77.
Bank of Maryland, State v., 100.
Bank of Michigan v. Niles, 81, 85.
Bank of Pennsylvania v. Comm., 8, 9, 12.
Bank of Pennsylvania v. Reed, 161.
Bank of St. Paul v. Dana, 14.
Bank of Sonoma County v. Fairbanks, 225.
Bank of United States v. Dandridge, 13, 24, 28, 50, 76, 151, 154, 157, 160.
Bank of United States v. Fleckner, 21, 77, 103, 160.
Bank of United States v. Owens, 69.
Bank of Virgennes v. Warren, 160.
Banking Co. v. Jersey City, 178.
Banking Co., Leggett v., 84.
Banks v. Poitiaux, 83.
Baptist Society, Chambers v., 94.
Barber, Erie Co. Iron Works v., 162.
Barber, Montgomery Co. v., 188.
Barber Asphalt Pav. Co. v. Gogreve, 189.
Barber Asphalt Pav. Co. v. Hunt, 189.

Barbour v. Ellsworth, 222.
Barclay Coal Co., Morris R. Co. v., 131.
Bard v. Banigan, 119.
Bard v. Poole, 166, 167.
Barker v. Hoff, 69.
Barker v. Insurance Co., 100.
Barker District v. Valley District, 186.
Barlow, Whitney Arms Co. v., 55, 56, 58, 61, 63, 64, 66, 68.
Barnes v. District of Columbia, 220.
Barnes v. Lacon, 237.
Barnes v. Ontario Bank, 96, 98, 160, 161.
Barnett v. Denison, 229.
Barney, Frothingham v., 122.
Baroness Wenlock v River Dee, 44.
Barr v. City of Kansas, 204.
Barr, Hatch v., 87, 90.
Barrington v. Neuse River, 86.
Barritt v. New Haven, 203.
Barrow, etc. Co., In re, 114.
Barry v. Merchants' Exchange, 27, 83, 84, 96, 100, 106, 124.
Bartholomew, etc. Co. v. Beatty, 168.
Bartlett, Spring Valley Water Works v., 235.
Bartlett v. Viner, 55.
Barwick v. English, etc. Bank, 162.
Bass, White v., 69.
Bassett, Granger v., 124, 126.
Bassett, Holbrook v., 96.
Batelle v. Northwestern Cement Co., 79.
Bateman v. Ashton-under-Lynn, 70.
Bateman, City Bank v., 77.
Bateman v. Covington, 215.
Bateman v. Mayor, 50, 189.
Bates, Savings Bank v., 91.
Bates County v. Winter, 190.
Bauerle, Wilkinson v., 91.
Baumgartner v. Hasty, 212.
Bay St. Louis, Chandler v., 230.
Bayonne, Paret v., 195.
Beach v. Fulton Bank, 25.
Beacher, Tyler v., 181.
Beale, Robinson v., 120.

TABLE OF CASES CITED. xxi

References are to sections.

Bean v. Joy, 195.
Bear River Co., Blen v., 194.
Bear River Co., Shaver v., 77.
Bearden v. Madison, 172.
Beardstown, etc. R. Co. v. Metcalf, 84.
Beasley, Mayor, etc. v., 176.
Beatty v. Bartholomew, etc. Co., 168.
Beatty v. Insurance Co., 47.
Beaty v. Knowler, 8, 12, 47.
Beaufort Co., Satterthwaite v., 177.
Beaver v. Armstrong, 135.
Becker v. Keokuk Water Works, 219.
Beckwith, Mount Pleasant v., 186, 187.
Beckwith, Winslow Mfg. Co. v., 88.
Beecher, Tyler v., 225.
Beekman v. Saratoga Ry. Co., 86.
Beers v. Phœnix Glass Co., 96, 160.
Belding v. Pitkin, 69.
Bell, State v., 173.
Bell, Weir v., 158.
Bell Tel. Co., St. Louis v., 170.
Bell's Gap Ry. Co. v. Christy, 79.
Bellamy Mfg. Co., Dispatch Co. v., 77.
Belleville, St. Louis, etc. Co. v., 192.
Bellevue, Town of Depere v., 186.
Bellmeyer v. Marshalltown, 9.
Belmont v. Erie Ry. Co., 53.
Belmont, Frost v., 79.
Beman v. Rufford, 137.
Bennett v. Filyaw, 129.
Bennett v. Peninsular S. Co., 129.
Bennett, Watson v., 161.
Bennington Ins. Co., Isham v., 90.
Benson v. Heathorn, 153.
Bentley v. County Commissioners, 170.
Bentz, St. Louis v., 212.
Bergen v. Clarkson, 173, 174.
Bergen v. Fishing Co., 91.
Bergen County, Merchants' Bank v., 226, 229.
Bergman v. St. Paul, etc. Ass'n, 53.
Bernal, Parker v., 122.
Bernerly, Trumpler v., 86.
Berrick v. Austin, 161.

Berry, New Decatur v., 214.
Berry, Pneumatic Gas Co. v., 76.
Berry, Railroad Co. v., 144.
Berry v. Yates, 121.
Bever, Clark v., 115.
Bevers, State v., 190.
Bigelow v. Randolph, 219.
Bigler v. Mayor, etc., 189.
Bill v. Western Union Tel. Co., 139.
Billings, Providence Bank v., 8.
Binney's Case, 83.
Biscoe, Ringas v., 91.
Bishmeyer v. Evansville, 219.
Birch v. Cropper, 117.
Bird v. Bird's Pat. Co., 33, 78.
Birkshire, etc. R. Co., Winchester v., 137.
Birmingham Gas Co., Smith v., 162.
Birmington v. Wallis, 69.
Bishop v. Brainerd, 143.
Bishop v. Centralia, 200.
Bishop, Wright v., 235.
Bissell, Blanchard v., 171.
Bissell v. Jeffersonville, 193.
Bissell v. Kankakee, 181, 225.
Bissell v. Mich. S. R. Co., 31, 38, 55, 61.
Bissell v. Spring Valley Township, 226.
Black v. Columbia, 219.
Black v. Delaware Canal Co., 53, 70, 72, 137, 143.
Black v. United Companies, 8.
Blackburne v. Selma, etc. R. Co., 81.
Blackburne Bldg. Soc. v. Cunliffe, etc. Co., 96, 97.
Blackshire v. Homestead, 87.
Blackstone Canal, Farnum v., 96.
Blaikie, Aberdeen R. Co. v., 153.
Blair, Fogg v., 115.
Blair v. Insurance Co., 100.
Blake, Great Western R. Co. v., 129.
Blake v. Mayor, 170.
Blalock v. Kernesville Mfg. Co., 120.
Blanchard v. Bissell, 171.
Blanchard's Factory v. Warner, 81.
Bland, Robinson v., 75.

TABLE OF CASES CITED.

References are to sections.

Blanke, Egmann v., 120.
Blasdell v. Fowler, 69.
Blazier v. Miller, 117.
Blen v. Bear River Co., 194.
Bliss v. Anderson, 53.
Bloodgood, Utica Ins. Co. v., 75.
Bloom, Slee v., 107.
Bloom v. Xenia, 170.
Blunt v. Walker, 81.
Board, etc., McDermott v., 172.
Board of Commerce v. Legg, 210.
Board of Education v. State, 225.
Boardman v. Hayne, 190.
Boardman v. Lake Shore R. Co., 124.
Boffinger, St. Louis v., 177.
Bogardus v. Trinity Church, 81.
Bolles, Commissioners v., 238.
Bolton v. San Antonio, 235.
Bond, Crawfordsville v., 209.
Boney, Louisville, etc. R. Co. v., 146.
Bonham, Susquehanna Canal Co. v., 141.
Bonner v. New Orleans, 135.
Boogher v. Life Association, 162.
Boom Co. v. Paterson, 86, 183.
Boonville, Hunt v., 203.
Booth v. Robinson, 96, 98, 122.
Bornham, Canal Co. v., 15.
Borough, etc. v. Fitzpatrick, 204.
Borough of Reading, Green v., 203.
Bornman, Penn v., 69.
Boston, Attorney-General v., 145.
Boston, Baker v., 222.
Boston, Brimmer v., 215.
Boston, Burrill v., 190.
Boston, Cavanagh v., 183, 212.
Boston, Child v., 208.
Boston, Dingley v., 212.
Boston, Fisher v., 219.
Boston, Hill v., 219.
Boston, Lowell v., 69, 179, 181, 225.
Boston, Nason v., 205.
Boston, Shaw v., 176.
Boston, Thayer v., 162, 222.
Boston Association, Roylston Market v., 170.
Boston Carpet Co., Howe v., 122.
Boston Mach. Co., American Tube Works v., 116, 127.

Boston, etc. R. Co. v. B. & M. Ry. Co., 8.
Boston, etc. R. Co., Lightner v., 146.
Boston, etc. R. Co., Middlesex R. Co. v., 137.
Boston, etc. R. Co. v. New York, etc. Co., 137.
Boston, etc. R. Co., State v., 81.
Boston, etc. R. Co., Troy, etc. R. Co. v., 9.
Boston Water Power Co., Dupee v., 83.
Bostwick, Brinkerhoff v., 156, 158.
Bostwick, Fishkill Sav. Inst. v., 77.
Bott v. Pratt, 172.
Boucher v. New Haven, 205.
Boulton v. Crowther, 203.
Bound v. Wisconsin Cent. R. Co., 197, 235.
Bousquet, Huthsing v., 190.
Bower, Corgill v., 158.
Bowes, Patterson v., 198.
Bowman, Eidman v., 110.
Bowman, Insurance Co. v., 101.
Bowman, Jackson v., 215.
Boyce v. Montauk Gas Co., 52.
Boyce, Wheeler Mfg. Co. v., 163.
Bradford, Grant Co. v., 175.
Bradford v. Mayor, 204, 206.
Bradley v. Ballard, 58, 96.
Bradley v. New York, etc. Co., 8.
Bradley v. South Carolina Phos. Co., 8.
Bradsall v. Clark, 173.
Brady v. Mayor, 70, 189, 190, 194, 201.
Brainerd, Bishop v., 143.
Brainerd, Moore v., 129.
Brainerd, New London v., 170, 175.
Brainerd v. Railroad Co., 135.
Brall, Agnew v., 195.
Branch v. Charleston, 148.
Branch v. Jessup, 9, 53, 137.
Branch, Tomlinson v., 146, 148.
Brandow, Dutch Church v., 95.
Brannen v. Loving, 159.
Breillat, Bank of Australasia v., 96, 98.
Bremond, International R. Co. v., 143.

TABLE OF CASES CITED. xxiii

References are to sections.

Brenham v. German Am. Bank, 224, 230.
Brenham v. Water Co., 170, 188.
Brewer Brick Co. v. Brewer, 181.
Briant, McCoy v., 170.
Bridenbecker v. Lowell, 161.
Bridge Co., East Hartford v., 199.
Bridge Co. v. Frankfort, 191.
Bridge Co. v. Land & Imp. Co., 8.
Bridge Co. v. Metz, 145.
Bridge Proprietors v. Hoboken, 8.
Bridgeport, Davidson v., 77.
Bridgeport, Gregory v., 188.
Bridgeport v. Railroad Co., 170, 177, 201.
Bridgeport Hydraulic Co., Nickerson v., 219.
Bridgewater Nav. Co., In re, 119.
Brueswick v. Mayor, etc., 171.
Briggs, Buckley v., 100.
Briggs v. Cape Cod Canal Co., 168.
Briggs, Chicago & A. Ry. Co. v., 8.
Briggs v. Penniman, 107.
Briggs v. Spaulding, 154, 156, 157, 158.
Brigham, Caine v., 100.
Brighton, People v., 86.
Brimmer v. Boston, 215.
Brinkerhoff v. Bostwick, 156, 158.
Brintnall v. Railroad Co., 129.
Brisham v. Delaware, etc. R. Co., 126.
Bristol v. Newchester, 186.
British Am. Land Co. v. Ames, 166.
British Cast-Plate Co. v. Meredith, 203.
British Life Ins. Co., In re, 122.
Briton, Police Jury v., 100, 223, 237.
Broadway Bank, Lionberger v., 91.
Broadway Co. v. Hankey, 216.
Broburg v. Des Moines, 205.
Brockport, West v., 219.
Brode v. Insurance Co., 100.
Brodhead v. Milwaukee, 225.
Brokaw v. New Jersey R. Co., 162, 164.
Bromley, Smith v., 69.
Bronson v. La Crosse R. Co., 53.
Bronson, Oberlin v., 175.
Brookfield, Cheeney v., 190.

Brooklyn v. City R. R., 215.
Brooklyn, Mills v., 202, 208.
Brooklyn G. R. Co. v. Slaughter, 9, 50.
Brooklyn R. Co., Stewart v., 163.
Brooks, Claiborne Co. v., 223, 237.
Broughton v. Pensacola, 233.
Broughton, Water Co. v., 50.
Brown, Alexander v., 77.
Brown, Duke v., 229.
Brown, Eastern R. Co. v., 162.
Brown, Jackson v., 84, 85.
Brown, Joint-stock Co. v., 122, 158.
Brown v. Lehigh Canal Co., 124.
Brown v. Mayor, 194.
Brown, Parkersburg v., 74, 181, 224.
Brown, Shrewsbury v., 191.
Brown, State v., 185.
Brown, Steamboat Co. v., 129.
Brown, Townsend v., 8.
Brown, Tuckerman v., 108.
Brown v. Vinalhaven, 213.
Browning v. Owen Co., 222.
Brownlee, Cashman v., 146.
Bruce, Bank v., 120.
Bruffett v. Great Western R. Co., 146.
Brunswick, Armstrong v., 212, 213.
Brunswick G. L. Co. v. United Gas Co., 137.
Bryan v. Chicago, etc. R. Co., 163.
Bryan v. M. & P. R. Co., 129.
Bryan v. Page, 191, 194.
Bryson v. Philadelphia, 215.
Buchanan v. Litchfield, 196, 224, 228, 232.
Buck, Logan City v., 170.
Buckeye Brewing Co., Easum v., 122.
Buckeye Marble Co. v. Harvey, 72, 74, 123.
Buckley v. Briggs, 100.
Buckley v. Prescott, 205.
Buena Vista Co., Carpenter v., 228.
Buffalo, Hodges v., 194.
Buffalo, Ketchum v., 100, 185, 188.
Buffalo, La Couteulx, 185.
Buffalo Ins. Co., Webster v., 52.
Buffalo Oil Co. v. Oil Co., 162.

TABLE OF CASES CITED.

References are to sections.

Buffalo R. R. Co., Soper v., 154.
Buffit v. Troy, etc. R. Co., 13, 128.
Buford v. Grand Rapids, 211.
Buford v. Keokuk Pack. Co., 83, 121.
Buhl, Richardson v., 148.
Building Association, Franz v., 168.
Building Association, Massey v., 101.
Bullions. Robertson v., 92.
Burch, Miller v., 212.
Burke, New Albany v., 115.
Burlington, French v., 196.
Burlington, Mills Co. v., 195.
Burlington, Rogers v., 225.
Burlington, Starr v., 172.
Burlington, etc. R. Co., Miller v., 163, 164.
Burmeister v. Howard, 172.
Burnham v. Webster, 160.
Burnham. Wells v., 189.
Burr v. Glass Co., 83, 100.
Burr v. McDonald, 88, 96.
Burrill v. Boston, 190.
Burroughs v. Railroad Co., 129.
Burt v. Rattle, 84, 119.
Burton's Appeal, 83, 87.
Butchers' Bank v. McDonald, 168.
Butler, Lexington v., 228.
Butts v. Cuthberson, 100.
Byrnes v. Cohoes, 209, 211.
Byrnes, Hutchins v., 87, 90.
Byron, Metropolitan Co., 98.

C.

Cabanniss, Danielly v., 177, 225.
Cabot v. Rome, 188, 217.
Cadwell, Utica Ins. Co. v., 75.
Cahous, Sewell v., 200.
Caine v. Brigham, 100.
Calais, Woodcock v., 213.
Caldwell, Louisville, etc. R. Co. v., 100.
Caledonia R. Co. v. Helensburg, 70, 79.
Calhoun, Kelly v., 89.
California Pac. R. Co. v. Low, 136.
Callenday v. Marsh, 203.
Calloway Min. Co. v. Clark, 81.
Camden v. Allen, 224.

Camden, Miss. etc. R. Co. v., 237.
Camden v. Mulford, 173, 174.
Camden, Simmons v., 203.
Camden, etc. R. Co., Elkins v., 131, 155.
Camden, etc. R. Co. v. Forsyth, 129.
Camden, etc. R. Co. v. May's Landing R. Co., 137.
Cameron, Chicago v., 53.
Cameron, Mathes v., 230.
Campbell v. Marietta R. Co., 137.
Campbell v. Montgomery, 202, 220.
Campbell, Nebraska v., 220.
Campbell's Case, 137, 147.
Canaan, Coates v., 200.
Canal Commissioners, Penn. Ry. v., 8, 12.
Canal Co., Black v., 143.
Canal Co. v. Borham, 15.
Canal Co., Briggs v., 168.
Canal Co., Conant v., 77.
Canal Co., Farnum v., 145.
Canal Co. v. Fulton Bank, 143, 148.
Canal Co., Gue v., 141.
Canal Co. v. Parnably, 220.
Canal Co. v. Valette, 83, 91, 96, 100.
Canal, etc. R. Co. v. St. Charles R. Co., 52.
Canney, Ossepee Mfg. Co. v., 74, 75, 81.
Canton, Leonard v., 170.
Canton v. Nist, 172.
Canton Masonic Society, Rockhold v., 7.
Cape Cod Canal Co., Briggs v., 168.
Cape May, Green v., 170, 194.
Capitol Bank, Pope v., 103.
Capitol City Water Co. v. Montgomery, 217.
Carey v. East Saginaw, 74.
Carey, Ottawa v., 170, 225.
Carey, Perin v., 93, 185.
Caroudelet, Taylor v., 212.
Carpenter v. Buena Vista Co., 228.
Carpentier, Oakland v., 215.
Carr v. Le Fevre, 135.
Carr v. Northern Liberties, 202, 203.

TABLE OF CASES CITED. XXV

References are to sections.

Carr v. Rogers, 61.
Carr, Sherman v., 170.
Carroll v. East St. Louis, 81.
Carroll, Farmers' L. & T. Co. v., 9, 14.
Carroll Co. v. Smith, 190.
Carter v. Howe Mach. Co., 162.
Carter v. Peck, 129.
Carter, Pontiac v., 203.
Carter, Wright v., 8.
Carthage, Cullen v., 170.
Case v. Kelly, 81, 85.
Casey v. Galli, 112.
Cashman v. Brownlee, 146.
Cass v. Manchester, etc. Co., 53.
Cass Co. v. Johnson, 227.
Catherman, Hilbish v., 181.
Caudy v. Knitting Co., 162.
Cauldwell, Alexander v., 154, 194.
Cavanagh v. Boston, 183, 212.
Cecil, Lamb v., 91.
Cedar County, Withelm v., 194.
Cemetery Association v. New Haven, 183.
Central Association, Alabama Ins. Co. v., 70, 96.
Central Bank v. Empire Stone Co., 9.
Central Bank, Merchants' Bank v., 77.
Central Gold Min. Co. v. Platt, 83.
Central Ry. Co. v. Coggin, 146.
Central Ry. Co. v. Collins, 9.
Central Ry. Co. v. Georgia, 141, 143, 144, 148.
Central Ry. Co., Low v., 9.
Central Ry. Co., Morris Canal Co. v., 8.
Central Ry. Co. v. Penn. R. Co., 121.
Central Ry. Co. v. Smith, 163.
Central Ry. Co., Stockton v., 137.
Central Trans. Co. v. Pullman Co., 9, 10, 12, 37, 52, 53, 54, 55, 68, 69, 70, 72, 74, 78, 137, 138.
Centralia, Bishop v., 200.
Centralia v. Krouse, 206.
Chadsey, Alvey v., 159.
Chaffee v. Granger, 188.
Chaffee v. Rutland R. Co., 124.
Chaffee Co. v. Potter, 53.
Chamberlin v. Evansville, 176.

Chamberlin v. Huguenot Mfg. Co., 51, 168.
Chambers v. Baptist Society, 94.
Chambers v. Falkner, 9, 53, 71, 99.
Chambers v. Manchester, etc. R. Co., 70, 134.
Chambers v. Satterlee, 203.
Chambers v. St. Louis, 81.
Champaign v. McInnes, 205.
Champlain Ry. Co. v. Valentine, 81.
Chandler v. Bay St. Louis, 230.
Chapin v. Greenlees, 120.
Chapin v. Vermont, etc. R. Co., 135.
Chapman v. Colby, 85.
Chapman v. Douglas Co., 74, 233.
Chapman, Walker v., 69.
Charles River Bridge Co. v. Bridge Co., 8, 9, 28.
Charleston, Backman v., 194.
Charleston, Branch v., 148.
Charleston, Butler v., 201.
Charleston, Feldman v., 181.
Charleston, Johnston v., 206.
Charlotte, Hill v., 202.
Charlotte, Wilson v., 177.
Charlton v. New Castle Ry. Co., 143.
Charter Oak Ins. Co., Ætna Bank v., 9.
Chase, Harvey v., 100.
Cheeney v. Brookfield, 190.
Chemical Bank v. Kohner, 161.
Chesapeake & Del. Ry., Perrine v., 8, 12, 28, 81.
Chesire, Smith v., 230.
Chesire Glass Co., Dorley v., 51, 168.
Chester, Bakersfield, etc. Ass'n v., 51, 168.
Chetlain v. Insurance Co., 120.
Chewacla Lime Works v. Dismukes, 70.
Cheyenne, Union Pac. Co. v., 177.
Chicago v. Cameron, 53.
Chicago, Clayburg v., 220.
Chicago v. Cleveland, 126.
Chicago v. Fowler, 204.
Chicago, Fuller v., 196.
Chicago, Garrison v., 196.
Chicago, Kinzie v., 47.
Chicago v. Laflin, 212.

TABLE OF CASES CITED.

References are to sections.

Chicago, Maher v., 94, 191.
Chicago v. McGiven, 205.
Chicago v. McGraw, 222.
Chicago v. Robbins, 206, 220.
Chicago. Schnell v., 192.
Chicago v. Stearns, 206.
Chicago v. Trotter, 176.
Chicago, Transportation Co. v., 81, 203.
Chicago, Tugman v., 176.
Chicago. Wheeler v., 191.
Chicago, etc. Coal Co. v. Hall, 146.
Chicago, etc. R. Co. v. Briggs, 8.
Chicago, etc. R. Co., Bryan v., 163.
Chicago, etc. R. Co., Chicago Co. v., 145.
Chicago, etc. R. Co., Craker v., 163.
Chicago, etc. R. Co., Ellerman v., 247.
Chicago, etc. R. Co., Hodgman v., 235.
Chicago, etc. R. Co. v. Howard, 96, 136.
Chicago, etc. R. Co. v. Lake Shore, etc. R. Co., 143.
Chicago, etc. R. Co. v. Marseilles, 120.
Chicago, etc. R. Co. v. Moffitt, 144, 146.
Chicago, etc. R. Co., Peck v., 145.
Chicago, etc. R. Co. v. People, 129.
Chicago, etc. R. Co. v. St. Anne, 240.
Chicago, etc. R. Co. v. Union Pac. R. Co., 19, 71.
Chicago, etc. R. Co., Wiggins Ferry Co., 129.
Chicago Gas Trust Co., People v., 121, 122, 137, 148.
Chichester, etc. R. Co., Taylor v., 52, 55, 56, 70.
Child v. Boston, 208.
Childs v. Smith, 3.
Chillicothe, Bank v., 96.
Chin Yan, Ex parte, 176.
China, Estes v., 213.
Chorn, Hadden v., 94.
Chouteau v. Allen, 105, 194.
Christian Union v. Yount, 166.
Christian University v. Jordon, 78.

Christopher v. Christopher. 189.
Christy, Bell's Gap Ry. Co. v., 79.
Chubb v. Upton, 106, 112.
Church v. City, 172.
Church, Donnelly v., 100.
Church v. Sterling, 77, 128.
Churchill, Frankfort Co. v., 79.
Cincinnati. Walker v., 170.
Cincinnati, Wheeler v., 170, 219.
Cincinnati Co. v. Rosenthal, 71.
Citizens' Bank v. Wiegand, 159.
Citizens' Building Ass'n v. Coriell, 156, 158.
Citizens' Gas Co. v. Elwood, 216.
Citizens', etc. R. Co., State Board v., 9.
Citizens' Savings Ass'n v. Topeka, 181.
Citizens' Water Co. v. Hydraulic Co., 216.
Citizens' Water Co., Sherwood v., 218.
City, Anderson v., 175.
City, Church v., 172.
City, Commissioners v., 209.
City of Aurora v. West, 237.
City of Eufaula v. McNab, 224.
City of Flora v. Nancy, 205.
City of Kahoka, Hill v., 233.
City of Kansas, Arn v., 211.
City of Kansas, Barr v., 204.
City of Louisville v. Bank, 215.
City of Madison v. Baker, 211.
City of Nevada, Norton v., 233.
City of New York, Brady v., 189.
City of Ohio v. New York, etc. R. Co., 124.
City of Paterson, State v., 235.
City of Raleigh, Tucker v., 96.
City of Toledo v. Cone, 169, 170.
City of Topeka v. Huntoon, 177.
City Bank v. Bateman, 77.
City Bank, Perkins v., 161.
City Council, Davis v., 202.
City Council v. Plank Road Co., 9, 70.
City Council, Stockton, etc. R. Co. v., 181.
City Council, Winter v., 239.
City Gas Co., Norwich Gas Co. v., 216, 218.
City Railroad. Brooklyn v., 215.
Claflin v. South, etc. R. Co., 132.

Claflin v. Hopkinton, 175.
Clapp v. Peterson, 120.
Claiborne County v. Brooks, 223, 237.
Clarendon, Lewis v., 237.
Clarendon Township, Young v., 223, 230, 237.
Clark v. Bever, 115.
Clark v. Bradsall, 173.
Clark, Calloway M. Co. v., 81.
Clark v. Davenport, 170.
Clark v. Des Moines, 230.
Clark v. Edgar, 158.
Clark v. Farmers' Mfg. Co., 100.
Clark v. Farrington, 14.
Clark v. Hancock, 223.
Clark, Harvester Co. v., 168.
Clark v. Iowa City, 135.
Clark v. Lyons Co., 194.
Clark v. Omaha R. Co., 137.
Clark v. School District, 100.
Clark, State v., 171, 176, 181.
Clark, Stoutmore v., 101, 168.
Clark v. Sutton, 203.
Clark v. Titcomb, 83, 96.
Clarkin, Natoma, etc. Co. v., 81.
Clarksburg, Richards v., 170.
Clarkson, Bergen v., 173, 174.
Clarksville, Gause v., 230.
Clason v. Milwaukee, 176.
Clay v. County, 237.
Clay v. Grand Rapids, 207.
Clayburg v. Chicago, 220.
Clayers, Vermont Ry. Co. v., 3.
Clearwater v. Meredith, 144, 147, 148.
Cleary, Marquette v., 202.
Cleburne, Coler v., 226.
Cleneay, Junction R. Co. v., 135.
Cleveland, Chicago v., 126.
Cleveland, Rhodes v., 211.
Cleveland v. St. Paul, 206.
Cleveland, State v., 172.
Cleveland, Western College v., 220.
Cleveland, Williams College v., 220.
Cleveland, etc. R. Co. v. Closser, 131.
Cleveland, etc. R. Co., Conn. L. Ins. Co. v., 135.
Cleveland, etc. R. Co., Mut. Ins. Co. v., 100.

Cleveland, etc. R. Co. v. Prewitt, 146.
Cleveland, etc. R. Co. v. Robbins, 126.
Cleveland, etc. R. Co., Zabriskie v., 9, 53, 76, 135.
Clinch v. Financial Corp., 142.
Clinton, Donelson v., 206.
Clinton v. Phillips, 176.
Clinton, Ross v., 211.
Clinton Water Works, Davis v., 219.
Close v. Glenwood Cemetery, 168.
Closser, Cleveland, etc. R. Co. v., 131.
Coal Float v. Jeffersonville, 176.
Coal Valley Co., Peoria, etc. R. Co. v., 9.
Coates v. Canaan, 200.
Coates v. Donnell, 91.
Coates, Gaines v., 216.
Cobourg, etc. Ry. Co., Coyley v., 146.
Cobshire, Aurora v., 200.
Cochran, Kennedy v., 69.
Coe, Pennock v., 8.
Coggeshill v. Pelton, 95.
Coggin v. Central R. Co., 146.
Cohen v. Wilkinson, 53.
Cohoes, Byrnes v., 209, 241.
Coit v. N. Car. Gold Co., 108, 115.
Coke Co., State v., 199.
Colby, Bank v., 144.
Colby, Chapman v., 85.
Cole, First Parish v., 92.
Cole, Inhabitants, etc. v., 81.
Cole v. La Grange, 181, 225.
Coles v. Bank of England, 124.
Coleman v. Columbia Oil Co., 120.
Coler v. Cleburne, 226.
College, State v., 83.
Collerne v. London Bldg. Soc., 120.
Collier, Ruggles v., 9.
Collins, Central Ry. Co. v., 9.
Collins v. Hatch, 212.
Colman v. Eastern Counties Ry. Co., 9, 39, 136.
Coloma v. Eavis, 227, 228.
Colorado Springs, Cornell v., 81.
Colter v. Doty, 15.
Columbia, Black v., 219.
Columbia Co., Flint v., 87.

TABLE OF CASES CITED.

References are to sections.

Columbia Oil Co., Coleman v., 120.
Columbus, etc. R. Co., McAuley v., 143.
Columbus, etc. R. Co. v. Powell, 146.
Colvin, Sheridan v., 177.
Combination Trust Co. v. Wild, 105.
Commanche Co. v. Lewis, 228.
Commercial Bank, Franklin Bank v., 121.
Commercial Bank v. Iola, 181, 225, 237.
Commercial Bank. Lathrop v., 81.
Commercial Bank v. Newport Mfg. Co.. 96, 100.
Commercial Hotel, Richwold v., 83, 91.
Commissioners, Atchison, etc. R. Co. v., 146.
Commissioners v. Bolles, 238.
Commissioners v. City, 209.
Commissioners, Comm. v., 179.
Commissioners v. Cox. 190.
Commissioners v. Gas Co., 176, 212.
Commissioners v. Goodrich, 212.
Commissioners, Haag v., 222.
Commissioners, Hadley v., 3, 12.
Commissioners, Inhabitants v., 86.
Commissioners v. January, 238.
Commissioners, Louisville v., 185.
Commissioners, Memphis R. Co. v., 141.
Commissioners, Moran v., 193.
Commissioners, Munn v., 96, 100.
Commissioners, People v., 189.
Commissioners, Pother v., 228.
Commissioners v. Railway Co., 96.
Commissioners, Reynolds v., 83.
Commissioners, State v., 148, 173, 185.
Commissioners v. Thayer, 227.
Commissioners v. Worcester, 312.
Commonwealth, Bank of Pennsylvania v., 8, 12.
Commonwealth v. Commissioners, 179.
Commonwealth, Erie Ry. Co. v., 8, 10, 12.
Commonwealth v. Franklin Canal Co., 12.
Commonwealth, Kepner v., 171.
Commonwealth v. Markham, 182.

Commonwealth v. Pittsburg, 100.
Commonwealth v. Smith, 83, 133, 134, 137.
Commonwealth, Society, etc. v., 3.
Commonwealth v. Steffee, 176.
Commonwealth, Williamsport v., 188.
Commonwealth v. Worcester, 176.
Compagnie Francaise v. Western Union Co., 121.
Conant v. Canal Co., 77.
Concord, Hubbard v., 205.
Concord, Hutchison v., 204.
Concord v. Robinson, 223, 228, 230, 237.
Concord, etc. R. Co.. Manchester, etc. R. Co. v., 130.
Concord, etc. R. Co., Pearson v., 122.
Cone v. Hartford, 207.
Cone, Toledo v.. 169, 170, 220.
Conery v. New Orleans Water Works, 177.
Congregational Church v. Trustees, 94.
Congress, etc. Co., Knowlton v., 109, 119.
Conn, Flash v., 166.
Connecticut, etc. Ins. Co. v. Cleveland, etc. R. Co., 100, 135.
Connecticut Sav. Bank v. Fiske, 96.
Conservators, etc. v. Ash, 3.
Converse, Green Co. v., 144.
Converse v. Norwich Trans. Co., 53.
Conybeare, New Brunswick Ry. v., 162.
Cook v. Milwaukee, 205, 220.
Cook v. Tullis, 77.
Cook Co. v. Hough. 81.
Coombs, Ft. Wayne v., 207, 209, 211.
Coon, People v., 195.
Cooper v. Atlanta. 222.
Cooper v. Corbin, 131.
Cooper v. Curtis, 161.
Coose, Sawyer v., 220.
Copley v. Grover & B. Co., 162.
Corbin, Cooper v., 131.
Corgill v. Bower, 158.
Cork, etc. R. Co.. In re. 96.
Coriell, Building Association v., 156, 158.

TABLE OF CASES CITED. xxix

References are to sections.

Corn Exchange Bank v. Coal Co., 77.
Cornell v. Colorado Springs, 81.
Cornell v. Guilford, 175.
Cornes, Gordon v., 225.
Corporation of Ireland, Guiness v., 118.
Corporation of Ireland, Knight v., 168.
Corrigan v. Gage, 176.
Corser v. Paul, 161.
Corwith, Galena v., 50.
Cory v. County of Somerset, 189.
Coughlin v. Gleason, 189.
Coulson v. Portland, 231.
Coulter, St. Paul v., 171, 212.
Council Bluffs, Dodge v., 166.
Council Bluffs, Everett v., 212.
Council Bluffs, Powers v., 220.
Council Bluffs v. Stewart, 196.
County, Clay v., 237.
County, People v., 230.
County Commissioners, Bentley v., 170.
County Commissioners v. Ducket, 220.
County of Daviess v. Huidekoper, 227.
County of Douglas, Chapman v., 233.
County of Jasper, Anthony v., 226.
County of Moultrie v. Bank, 197.
County of Randolph v. Post, 227.
County of Somerset, Cary v., 189.
Cousley, Screw Co. v., 79.
Coventry, Evans v., 120.
Covert v. Rogers, 91.
Covington, Bateman v., 215.
Covington, Harper v. 224.
Covington, Haynes v., 201.
Covington, Henderson v., 170, 175.
Cowan v. Milburne, 69.
Cowan v. West Troy, 189, 194.
Cowdrey, Galveston v., 141.
Cowell v. Springs Co., 166.
Cowgill v. Long, 238.
Cox, Lafayette v., 9.
Coyley v. Cobourg, etc. R. Co., 146.
Cozart v. Georgia, etc. R. Co., 52, 136, 137.
Craig v. Andreas, 69.

Craig v. Vicksburg, 135.
Craigie v. Hadley, 162.
Craker v. Chicago, etc. R. Co., 163.
Crane, Unity Ins. Co. v., 3.
Crawford v. Longstreet, 81.
Crawfordsville v. Bond, 209.
Creal v. Keokuk, 201.
Crescent City G. L. Co. v. New Orleans G. L. Co., 216.
Crescent City Ins. Co., New Orleans v., 219.
Creswell, Williams v., 166.
Crocker, Shaw v., 203.
Crompton, Pierce v., 167.
Crompton v. Zabriskie, 198.
Cropper, Birch v., 117.
Cross, Lumsden v., 225.
Crossett v. Janesville, 203.
Crowther, Boulton v., 203.
Crum's Appeal, 76.
Culbertson, Butts v., 100.
Culbertson v. Fulton, 197, 231.
Cullen v. Carthage, 170.
Cumberland, etc. Co., **Exchange Bank** v., 77.
Cumberland, etc. Co., **Hoffman**, etc. Co. v., 153.
Cumberland, etc. Co. v. Parish, 153.
Cunliffe v. Manchester, etc. R. Co., 53.
Cunliffe, B. & Co., Building Society v., 96, 97.
Cunliffe, Mayor, etc. v., 190, 222.
Curran v. Arkansas, 107.
Currier v. Lebanon Co., 120.
Curry v. Mt. Sterling, 86.
Curtis, Cooper v., 161.
Curtis, Farmers' L. & T. Co. v., 81.
Curtis v. Leavitt, 13, 74, 96, 98, 100.
Curtis, Medomak Bank v., 77.
Curtis v. Piedmont Co., 74.
Curtis v. Whipple, 224.
Curzon, Droitwich, etc. Co. v., 109, 113.

D.

Dabney v. Bank, 91.
Dalley, Wakeman v., 158.

TABLE OF CASES CITED.

References are to sections.

Dana v. Bank, 14, 87.
Danbury, etc. R. Co. v. Wilson, 9.
Dandridge, Bank of U. S. v., 13, 24, 28, 50, 76, 151, 154, 157, 160.
Dandridge, Steam Nav. Co. v., 201.
Danielly v. Cabanniss, 177, 225.
Danville, Small v., 213.
Danville Seminary, Nutt v., 7.
Darling v. Bangor, 202.
Darling v. Railroad Co., 129.
Darling v. St. Paul, 173.
Darnell, Coates v., 91.
Darst v. Gale, 58.
Darst v. People, 212.
Dartmouth College v. Woodward, 9, 21, 28, 50.
Dater v. Bank, 83.
Davenport, Clark v., 170.
Davenport, Davenport, etc. Co. v., 197.
Davenport, East Lincoln v., 238.
Davenport, Grant v., 198, 217.
Davenport, King v., 212.
Davenport v. Mayor, 204.
Davenport v. Ruckman, 220.
Davenport, Van Pelt v., 209, 211.
Davidson v. Bridgeport, 77.
Davidson, Hayward v., 81.
Davidson, Milne v., 172.
Davidson v. Ward, 158.
Davidson, Williams v., 170, 172.
Davidson v. Young, 192.
Daviess Co. v. Dickinson, 190, 224, 231.
Daviess Co. v. Huidekoper, 227.
Daviess Co., Ogden v., 229.
Davis v. Anita, 176.
Davis v. City Council, 202.
Davis v. Clinton Water Works, 219.
Davis v. Des Moines, 197.
Davis, De Russey v., 170.
Davis, Home Ins. Co. v., 166.
Davis, Littlewort v., 70.
Davis v. Mayor, 199.
Davis v. Montgomery, 213, 219.
Davis v. Old Colony R. Co., 36, 47, 53, 136, 137.
Davis v. Ren. & Sar. Ry. Co., 8.
Davis' Case, 96.
Dawson, Iron Co. v., 166.

Dawson, Revanna Nav. Co. v., 81, 95.
Day v. Mitford, 204.
Day v. Spiral Spring Co., 74.
Dayton v. Quigley, 176.
Dearborn, England v., 96.
Dean v. Todd, 177.
De Camp v. Atwood, 91.
De Camp v. Dobbins, 81.
Decatur, Hill v., 171.
Decker, Evansville v., 209.
Deering, Seele v., 213.
De Grand, Russell v., 71.
De Kay, Hackensack Water Co. v., 134, 135, 168.
Delamon, New Orleans, etc. Co. v., 141.
Delaware, etc. Co., Black v., 53, 70, 72, 137.
Delaware, etc. Co., Brisham v., 126.
Delaware, etc. Co. v. East Orange, 176.
Delaware, etc. Co. v. Penn. Coal Co., 77.
Delaware, etc. Co., Wasmer v., 137.
Delaware Bay, etc. R. Co., Joint Co. v., 8.
Delaware Tax Cases, 8, 145, 148.
Deming Co., Roberts v., 74.
Demon, Bank of Lyons v., 77.
Denike v. Lime Co., 143.
Denison, Barnett v., 229.
Denison, Simpson v., 130.
Denton v. Jackson, 3.
Denver, etc. R. Co. v. Atchison, etc. Co., 131.
Denver, etc. R. Co. v. Harris, 162.
Depere v. Bellevue, 186.
Deposit Association, Lamm v., 194.
Derby Fishing Co., Witte v., 15.
Derinzy v. Ottawa, 203.
De Russey v. Davis, 170.
De Ruyter v. St. Peter's Church, 83.
Des Moines, Broburg v., 205.
Des Moines, Clark v., 230.
Des Moines, Davis v., 197.
Des Moines, Des Moines Gas Co. v., 172, 177, 216.
Des Moines, Hauger v., 170.

References are to sections.

Des Moines, Van Horn v., 219.
Des Moines, etc. R. Co., Teachout v., 53.
De Sota, Land v., 233.
Des Plaines. Poyer v., 178.
Detroit. Dewey v., 202.
Detroit, Goodrich v., 50, 188.
Detroit v. Hosmer, 189.
Detroit, Mekellar v., 205.
Detroit, Wilkins v., 189.
Devian. Guenther v., 69.
Dewey v. Detroit, 202.
Dewitt v. San Francisco, 185.
Deyo v. Otoe Co., 237.
Dhlin, Insurance Co. v., 77.
Dickerman, Somerville v., 170, 195.
Dickinson, Daviess Co. v., 190, 224, 231.
Dickinson v. Poughkeepsie, 191.
Dickson v. United States, 82.
Dill v. Inhabitants, etc., 201.
Dill v. Wareham, 119.
Dingley v. Boston, 212.
Dingman v. People, 215.
Dinsmore v. Atlantic, etc. R. Co., 137.
Dimpfell v. Ohio R. Co., 78.
Dismukes, Chewacla Lime Works v., 70.
Dispatch Line v. Bellamy Mfg. Co., 77.
District of Columbia, Barnes v., 220.
District of Columbia, Johnson v., 208.
Dix v. Dummerston, 195.
Dix, West River, etc. Co. v., 183.
Dixon v. Baker, 211.
Dixon Co. v. Field, 53, 190, 228, 232.
Dixon Co., Hedges v., 73, 231.
Dobbins, De Camp v., 81.
Dodge, Council Bluffs v., 166.
Dodge, Houghton v., 77.
Dodge v. Woolsey, 53.
Donnally, Parker v., 159.
Donnell v. Lewis Co. Bank, 96.
Donnelly v. Church, 100.
Donohue, French v., 168.
Donovan v. Green, 237.
Dooley v. Chesire Glass Co., 51, 168.
Dore v. Milwaukee, 203.

Dorman v. Jacksonville, 203.
Doty, Cotter v., 15.
Dougherty v, Hunter, 159.
Douglas, Auburn Plank Road Co. v., 8.
Douglas, Niantic Sav. Bank v., 146.
Douglas v. Placerville, 198.
Douglas v. Virginia City, 50, 188.
Douglas, Weismer v., 181, 237.
Douglas Co., Chapman v., 74, 233.
Doulson v. Clinton, 206.
Dover & D. Ry. Co., McGregor v., 9, 55, 56, 70.
Dow, Memphis, etc. R. Co. v., 96.
Downey, Ill. Cent. R. Co. v., 164.
Downing v. Marshall, 82.
Downing v. Mt. Washington, etc. Co., 9, 47.
Doyle v. Austin, 181.
Doyle v. Migner, 3.
Drainage Commissioners, Elmore v., 221.
Drake v. Lowell, 204.
Drake v. Phillips, 198.
Dranesburg v. Jenkins, 237.
Drew, National Ex. Co. v., 162.
Drew, Northern Cent. Co. v., 146.
Drexel v. Town of Lake, 207.
Droitwich, etc. Co. v. Curzon, 109, 113.
Drury v. Inhabitants, 94.
Dry Docks Co. v. Hicks, 81.
Dubuque, Gelpcke v., 135, 227, 238.
Dubuque v. Maloney, 212.
Dubuque, Manderchid v., 203.
Dubuque, etc. R. Co. v. Litchfield, 9.
Duckett, County Commissioners v., 220.
Duckwall v. New Albany, 175.
Duke v. Brown, 229.
Dummer, Wood v., 107.
Dummerston, Dix v., 195.
Duncomb v. N. Y. etc. R. Co., 105.
Dunlap, Rabe v., 137.
Dunlap, Ryan v., 161.
Dunn, New Orleans, etc. v., 177.
Dupee v. Water Power Co., 83, 120.
Durango v. Pendleton, 201.
Durant v. Palmer, 206.
Durer v. Hudson Co. Ins. Co., 77.

xxxii TABLE OF CASES CITED.

References are to sections.

Dutch Church v. Brandow, 95.
Dutch Church, Van Houton v., 91.
Dyersburg, Norton v., 223, 230.

E.

Eakin v. St. Louis R. Co., 137.
Eagle Bank, Hooker v., 77.
Eagle Ins. Co., Strauss v., 9, 47, 50.
Earl of Shrewsbury v. North Stafford Ry. Co., 70, 79.
Earle, Bank of Augusta v., 8, 9, 26, 28, 47, 52, 103, 156, 157, 165, 167.
Earle, Taylor v., 122.
Early's Appeal, 120.
East Anglian Ry. v. Eastern Counties Ry., 9, 40, 53, 70, 72.
East Haddam Bank, Goodspeed v., 162, 164.
East Hartford, Bridge Co. v., 187, 199.
East Lincoln v. Davenport, 238.
East Montpelier, Montpelier v., 92.
East Oakland v. Skinner, 190, 224, 238.
East Orange, Delaware, etc. R. Co. v., 176.
East Portland, Baltimore v., 201, 222.
East River Bank v. Hoyt, 154.
East Saginaw, Carey v., 74.
East Saginaw, Stecket v., 201.
East St. Louis, Carroll v., 81.
East St. Louis, Gartside v., 178.
East St. Louis v. Gas Light Co., 188, 216.
East St. Louis v. St. John, 86.
East St. Louis v. Wehrung, 173.
East Tenn. etc. R. Co. v. Nelson, 129.
East Tenn. etc. R. Co. v. Rogers, 129.
East Warren, etc. L. Co., Senney v., 87.
Eastern, etc. R. Co., Bagshaw v., 9, 53, 70.
Eastern, etc. R. Co. v. Brown, 162.
Eastern, etc. R. Co., Coleman v., 9, 39.
Eastern, etc. R. Co. v. East Anglian, etc. Co., 9, 40, 53, 70, 72.

Eastern, etc. R. Co. v. Hawkes, 9, 52, 137.
Eastern, etc. R. Co., Lynch v., 235.
Eastern, etc. R. Co., March v., 124.
Eastern, etc. R. Co., Sturges v., 118.
Eastern Plank Road Co. v. Vaughan, 3.
Eastman v. Meredith, 219.
Easum v. Buckeye Brew. Co., 122.
Eaton v. Aspinwall, 106.
Eaton, Nelson v., 96.
Eaton v. Pacific Nat. Bank, 127.
Eaton, etc. R. Co. v. Hunt, 145.
Eau Claire, Smith v., 203.
Eavis, Coloma v., 227, 228.
Ebbw. Vale, etc. Co., In re, 109, 113.
Eby v. Guest, 120.
Eddy, Jeverin v., 206.
Edgar, Clark v., 158.
Edison E. L. Co. v. New Haven, etc. Co., 144.
Edwards v. Grand Junction R. Co., 77.
Edwards v. Midland Ry., 162.
Edwards, Springfield v., 196, 235.
Egmann v. Blanke, 120.
Eickemeyer, Sheldon Hat Co. v., 83, 106.
Eidman v. Bowman, 110.
Eldridge v. Smith, 141.
Elkhorn Bank, Rockwell v., 96, 100, 134.
Elkins v. Camden, etc. R. Co., 131, 155.
Ellerman v. Chicago, etc. R. Co., 47.
Elliott v. Abbott, 160, 161.
Elliott, Marietta, etc. R. Co. v., 9.
Elliott, Mayor v., 95.
Elliott v. Philadelphia, 219.
Elliott, Union Bank v., 91.
Ellsworth, Barbour v., 222.
Elmore v. Drainage Commission, 221.
Elmwood Township v. March, 238.
Elwood, Citizens' Gas Co. v., 216.
Ely v. Grand Rapids, 189.
Ely, Hooper v., 198.
Ely, N. Y. etc. Ins. Co. v., 12.
Emerson v. Newburg, 194.

TABLE OF CASES CITED. xxxiii

References are to sections.

Emery, Harper v., 225.
Emery v. Mariaville, 230.
Emery v. Ohio Candle Co., 148.
Emery, Pierce v.. 83, 91, 100.
Emmet v. Reed, 77.
Empire Assur. Corp.. In re, 142.
Empire Mfg. Co. v. Stewart, 167.
Empire Stone Co., Central Bank v., 9.
England v. Dearborn, 96.
English v. People, 181.
English Joint-Stock Co., Barwick v., 162.
Episcopal Society v. Episcopal Church, 77.
Erie, Grant v., 202, 219.
Erie, Schwingle v., 221.
Erie City Iron Works v. Barber, 162.
Erie R. Co., Arnot v., 129.
Erie R. Co., Belmont v., 53.
Erie R. Co., Comm. v., 8, 10, 12.
Erie R. Co., Heath v., 53.
Erie R. Co., McGregor v., 145, 167.
Erie R. Co., Pennsylvania v., 124.
Erie R. Co., Vance v., 162.
Eric R. Co., Woodruff v., 9.
Erie Trans. Co., Stewart v., 9, 53, 129, 130.
Ernest v. Balfour, 148.
Ernest v. Nichols, 120.
Errol, Rich v., 74, 75.
Eschbach, Baltimore v., 190, 201, 222.
Estelle v. Lake Crystal, 205, 206.
Estes v. China, 213.
Eufaula v. McNab, 185, 224.
Eureka Basin Co., In re, 181.
Eureka Flour Mills, Smith v., 47, 96, 100.
European. etc. R. Co. v. Poor, 153.
Evans v. Coventry, 120.
Evans, Holdworth v., 70.
Evansville, Bishmeyer v., 219.
Evansville, Chamberlin v., 176.
Evansville, Decker v., 209.
Evansville, Evansville R. Co. v., 177.
Evansville R. Co. v. Androscoggin, etc. Co., 129.
Evansville R. Co., Fisher v., 143.
Evening Journal Association v. McDermott, 162.

Everett v. Council Bluffs, 212.
Everhardt v. West Chester Ry. Co., 118.
Ewing, Lincoln Sav. Bank v., 92.
Ewing v. Robeson, 51, 168.
Ewing, Shiras v., 218.
Excelsior Co. v. Lacey, 156.
Exchange Bank, Rice v., 219.
Exchange Bank v. Sibley, 157, 158.
Exchange Bank, Smith v., 103.
Ex parte Chin Yan, 176.
Ex parte Frank, 175.
Ex parte Grady, 70.
Ex parte Maude, 117.
Ex parte Mayor, etc., 215.
Ex parte Scholbred, 72.
Ex parte Stanley, 125.
Ex parte Williams, 135.
Ex parte Williamson, 70, 98.
Export Co., Taylor v., 120.
Eyser v. Weissgarber, 74, 75.

F.

Fairbanks, Bank of Sonoma v., 225.
Falkner, Chambers v., 9, 53, 70, 99.
Fanning v. Schammel, 238.
Farmers', etc. Bank v. Baldwin, 103.
Farmers', etc. Bank v. Bank, 160.
Farmers', etc. Bank, John v., 101.
Farmers', etc. Bank v. Needles, 101.
Farmers', etc. Bank, Phelps v., 124.
Farmers', etc. Bank, Ridgeway v., 96, 100.
Farmers', etc. Bank v. Sherman, 77.
Farmers'. etc. Bank, Spohn v., 12.
Farmers', etc. Bank v. Transportation Co., 129.
Farmers' Ins. Co., Luthe v., 53.
Farmers' L. & T. Co. v. Carroll, 9, 14.
Farmers' L. & T. Co. v. Curtis, 81.
Farmers' L. & T. Co., Harmock v., 131.
Farmers' L. & T. Co. v. Insurance Co., 92.

c

TABLE OF CASES CITED.

References are to sections.

Farmers' L. & T. Co., Racine R. Co. v., 144, 145.
Farmers' L. & T. Co. v. St. Joseph, etc. R. Co., 74, 131.
Farmers' Mfg. Co., Clark v., 100.
Farnsworth, Adams v., 191.
Farnum v. Blackstone Canal, 96, 145.
Farrington, Clark v., 14.
Faulkner v. Aurora, 204.
Faure Elec. Co., In re, 154.
Fay v. Noble, 96, 100.
Fell v. Gas Co., 144.
Feital v. Middlesex R. Co., 129.
Feitsam v. Hay, 137.
Feldman v. Charleston, 181.
Ferguson v. Meredith, 144.
Ferris v. Ludlow, 109.
Festial v. King's College, 124.
Field, Dixon County v., 53, 190, 228, 232.
Field v. West Orange, 203, 211.
Fifth Ward Savings Bank v. First National Bank, 102, 159.
File Works, McLennon v., 136.
Filyaw, Bennett v., 129.
Financial Corporation, In re, 113.
Financial Corporation, Clinch v., 142.
Finnegan, Roddy v., 172.
Fireman's Ins. Co., Brode v., 100.
First Cong. Soc. v. Atwater, 92.
First National Bank v. Fricke, 77.
First National Bank v. Graham, 163.
First National Bank v. Pierson, 103.
First National Bank v. Salem Mill, 120.
First National Bank v. Savings Bank, 102, 159.
First National Bank, Weckler v., 9, 50.
First Parish, etc. v. Cole, 92.
Fish v. Mayor, 201.
Fisher v. Boston, 219.
Fisher v. Evansville R. Co., 143.
Fisher v. Harrisburg, 176, 207.
Fisher, Morris Canal Co. v., 135.
Fisher v. N. Y. etc. R. Co., 146.
Fisher, Schockley v., 91.
Fishing Co., Bergen v., 91.

Fishkill Savings Bank v. Bostwick, 77.
Fiske, Conn. Sav. Bank v., 96.
Fiske, State v., 173.
Fitchburg, Weare v., 205.
Fitzpatrick, Borough, etc. v., 204.
Flack v. Hughes, 235.
Flagg, People v., 201.
Flagg, Stone v., 3, 12.
Flanagan, Kansas City v., 170.
Flanders Bros., Academy of Music v., 168.
Flash v. Conn, 166.
Fleckner v. Bank, 21, 77, 103, 160.
Flemming, Louisville, etc. R. Co. v., 163.
Fletcher, Atchison, etc. Co. v., 136.
Flint v. Columbia Co., 87.
Fogg v. Blair, 115.
Fogg v. Railroad Co., 162.
Fond du Lac, Kane v., 195.
Foote, Newport Bridge Co. v., 203.
Foote v. Pike Co., 227.
Forbes v. Marshall, 96.
Formholz v. Taylor, 74, 75.
Forsyth, Camden, etc. R. Co. v., 129.
Fortier v. New Orleans Bank, 53.
Fort Scott, United States v., 196.
Fort Wayne v. Coombs, 207, 209. 211.
Fort Wayne, Grove v., 204.
Fort Wayne Elec. Co., Keokuk v., 137.
Fort Worth City Ry. v. Smith Bridge Co., 9.
Foster, Iowa Lumber Co. v., 120.
Foster v. Lookout Water Co., 219.
Foster, McPherson v., 231, 232.
Foundry Co., Stoddard v., 124.
Fowler v. Athens City Water Works, 219.
Fowler, Blasdell v., 69.
Fowler, Chicago v., 204.
Fowler v. Robinson, 107.
Fowler v. Scully, 69.
Fox v. New Orleans, 190.
Fox, State Bank v., 120.
Francis v. Troy, 170.
Frank, Ex parte, 176.
Frankenberg, Illinois Cent. R. Co. v., 129.
Frankfort, Bridge Co. v., 191.

References are to sections.

Frankfort Co. v. Churchill, 79.
Franklin Bank v. Commercial Bank, 121.
Franklin Bank v. White, 69, 74, 75, 119.
Franklin Bridge Co. v. Wood, 3, 12.
Franklin Canal Co., Comm. v., 12.
Franklin County, German Sav. Bank v., 238.
Franklin County v. Lewistown Inst., 9. 34, 53, 55, 70, 121.
Franklin County, Maupin v., 190.
Franklin Ins. Co. v. Hart, 79.
Franklin Wharf Co. v. Portland, 208, 213.
Franz v. Building Association, 168.
Fraser v. Ritchie, 120.
Frazee's Case, 175.
Frazier v. Wilcox, 83, 166.
Freeberg. Pitzman v., 237.
Freeman, Home v., 141.
Freeman v. Minn. etc. R. Co., 137.
Freeman, State v., 176.
Freher v. Geiseka, 74, 75.
French v. Burlington, 196.
French v. Donohue, 168.
Fricke, First Nat. Bank v., 77.
Fricke, Keithburg v., 238.
Frost v. Belmont, 79.
Frost v. Frostburg Coal Co., 168.
Frothingham v. Barney, 122.
Frye v. Tucker, 128.
Fuller v. Atlantic, 203.
Fuller v. Chicago, 196.
Fuller v. Heath, 196.
Fulton, Culbertson v., 197, 231.
Fulton v. Lincoln, 170.
Fulton Bank, Beach v., 25.
Fulton Bank, Sharon Canal Co. v., 143, 148.
Fulton County, Marsh v., 190, 191, 193, 194, 201, 224, 233.
Furnell v. St. Paul, 205.
Furniss v. Gilchrist, 96.

G.

Gabel v. Houston, 172.
Gage, Corrigan v., 176.
Gage v. Newmarket, 70.
Gaines v. Coates, 216.
Gale, Darst v., 58.
Gale v. Kalamazoo, 173, 215.
Galena v. Corwith, 50.
Gallatin Turnpike Co., Hopkins v., 88.
Galli, Casey v., 112.
Galveston, Allen v., 170.
Galveston v. Cowdrey, 141.
Galveston, Hitchcock v., 62, 65, 193, 196, 233.
Garrison v. Chicago, 196.
Gartside v. East St. Louis, 178.
Gas Co., Commissioners v., 176, 212.
Gas Co. v. Des Moines, 172.
Gas Co., East St. Louis v., 216.
Gas Co., Fee v., 144.
Gas Co., Grand Rapids, etc. Co. v., 199.
Gas Co., Indianapolis v., 172.
Gas Co. v. Light Co., 199, 216.
Gas Co. v. Manufacturing Co., 144.
Gas Co. v. Middleton, 199.
Gas Co. v. San Francisco, 171, 191.
Gas Co., State v., 215, 216, 218.
Gas Light Co. v. Gas Co., 199.
Gas Light Co., East St. Louis v., 188.
Gas Light Co., Indianapolis v., 217.
Gas Light Co. v. Saginaw, 199, 216.
Gas Light Co., State v., 218.
Gas Light Co. v. United Gas Co., 74.
Gas Light Co., Young v., 53.
Gassett v. Andover, 191.
Gates v. Hancock, 194.
Gatling Gun, In re, 114.
Gause v. Clarkville, 230.
Geiseka, Freher v., 74, 75.
Gelpcke v. Dubuque, 135, 227, 238.
Georg v. Nevada Central R. Co., 137.
Georgetown, Goszler v., 21, 203.
Georgetown, Perley v., 222.
Georgia, Railroad Co. v., 141, 143, 144, 148.
Georgia, etc. R. Co., Cozart v., 52, 136, 137.
Georgia, etc. R. Co., Wilkes v., 53.

xxxvi TABLE OF CASES CITED.

References are to sections.

German Am. Bank, Brenham v., 224, 230.
German Am. etc. Co., National Park Bank v., 136.
German M. Co., In re, 96.
German Savings Bank v. Franklin Co., 238.
German Savings Bank v. Wulfekehlen. 120.
Germantown Ins. Co., Dhlin v., v., 77.
Gettys, Kerchner v., 166.
Gibboney, Union Township v., 194.
Gibbs' Case, 96.
Gibbs, Mersey Docks v., 220.
Gibbs, Overend & G. Co. v., 154, 156.
Gibson v. Goldthwaite, 159.
Gifford v. Railroad Co., 198.
Gilchrist, Furniss v., 96.
Gildersleeve. Hinkley v., 9.
Gilham v. Wells, 176.
Gill, Baltimore v., 196, 198.
Gill, Mayor, etc. v., 177.
Gillette v. Missouri, etc. R. Co., 164.
Gilliam v. South, etc. R. Co., 163.
Gillison v. Charleston, 211.
Girard, Vidal v., 92, 93, 94.
Glasby v. Morris, 207.
Glasgow v. Rouse, 181.
Glass v. Ashbury, 170.
Glass Co., Beers v., 160.
Glass Co., Burr v., 100.
Gleason, Coughlin v., 189.
Gleason, Mills v., 194.
Glenn, Baltimore, etc. R. Co. v., 166.
Glenwood Cemetery, Close v., 168.
Glidden v. Striplen, 61.
Globe Works, Monument Bank v., 9, 32, 74, 100, 104, 162.
Godbold v. Bank, 156.
Goddard, Root v., 70.
Godfrey, Metropolitan Bank v., 85.
Goff v. Great Northern R. Co., 162.
Gogreve, Barber Paving Co. v., 189.
Gold Mining Co. v. National Bank, 76.

Gold Mountain Co., Morrison v., 79.
Goldsmith, London v., 205.
Goldthwaite, Gibson v., 159.
Goldworthy, Smith v., 113.
Gooch v. McGee, 86.
Goodrich, Commissioners v., 212.
Goodrich v. Detroit, 50, 188.
Goodspeed v. East Haddam Bank, 162, 164.
Goodwin v. Hardy, 124.
Goodwin v. Ramsey Co., 230.
Gordon v. Cornes, 225.
Gordon v. Preston, 84.
Gordon, Proprietors, etc. v., 77.
Gordon's Ex'rs v. Richmond, etc. Co., 119.
Gorrell v. Life Ins. Co., 96.
Goszler v. Georgetown, 21, 203.
Gottfried v. Miller, 91.
Goundie v. Water Co., 81.
Grady, Ex parte, 70.
Grafton, Andover v., 230.
Graham v. Albert Lea, 205.
Graham, Lake Co. v., 53.
Graham, National Bank v., 162, 163.
Grand Chute v. Winegar, 228.
Grand Junction, etc. Co., Edwards v., 77.
Grand Junction, etc. Co., Haven v., 135.
Grand Junction Water Works, Ware v., 53.
Grand Lodge v. Waddell, 70.
Grand Rapids, Buford v., 211.
Grand Rapids, Clay v., 207.
Grand Rapids, Ely v., 189.
Grand Rapids, McBride v., 189.
Grand Rapids, etc. Co. v. Grand Rapids, etc. Co., 170.
Grand Rapids Elec. Co. v. Gas Co., 199.
Grandjean, Slidell v., 9.
Granger v. Bassett, 124, 126.
Granger, Chaffee v., 188.
Grangers', etc. Ins. Co. v. Kamper, 3, 109.
Grant v. Davenport, 198, 217.
Grant v. Erie, 202, 219.
Grant Co. v. Bradford, 175.
Grant Co., Richardson v., 191.
Graves, Goszler v., 215.

TABLE OF CASES CITED. xxxvii

References are to sections.

Gray v. Jackson, 129.
Great Eastern Ry., Attorney-General v., 42, 43, 44, 47.
Great Luxemberg R. Co. v. Magnay, 153.
Great Northern R. Co., Goff v., 162.
Great Northern R. Co. v. Railway Co., 137.
Great Northern Ry. Co., South Yorkshire, etc. R. Co. v., 55, 70, 137.
Great Western Ry. v. Blake, 129.
Great Western Ry., Bruffett v., 146.
Great Western, etc. Ry. Co., Hoole v., 118.
Great Western, etc. Ry. Co., Midland Ry. Co. v., 130.
Great Western, etc. Ry. Co., Root v., 129.
Great Western, etc. Ry. Co. v. Rushout, 53.
Greeley v. Nashua Sav. Bank, 53.
Greeley v. People, 185.
Green v. Borough of Reading, 203.
Green v. Cape May, 170, 194.
Green, Donovan v., 237.
Green, Hutchison v., 155.
Green v. Omnibus Co., 162.
Green, State v., 146.
Green, Underwood v., 212.
Green Bay, etc. R. Co. v. Union S. S. Co., 9, 47, 53, 129, 136, 137.
Green County v. Converse, 144.
Green County, State v., 143.
Greenbush, Parr v., 190.
Greenville, Mauldin v., 231.
Greenville Compress v. Planters' Press, 72, 74, 143.
Greenville, etc. Co., Wiswall v., 9.
Greenwood v. Louisville, 219.
Greer, Pittsburg v., 220.
Gregory v. Bridgeport, 188.
Gregory v. Jersey City, 189.
Gregory v. Patchett, 70.
Greiner v. Ulery, 101.
Griffin v. New York, 206.
Grimes v. Hamilton, 195.
Griswold, Arthur v., 158.
Griswoldville, Ward v., 107.
Grove v. Fort Wayne, 204.

Grover & Baker Co., Copley v., 162.
Gruber v. Washington, etc. R. Co., 162, 163.
Guaga Iron Co. v. Dawson, 166.
Guaranty Co., Jones v., 66.
Gue v. Canal Co., 141.
Guenther v. Devien, 69.
Guest, Eby v., 120.
Guiness v. Corporation of Ireland, 118.
Gunness v. Land Corporation, 55, 56.
Gunter v. Leckey, 69.
Gurno, St. Louis v., 203.
Guthrie Co., Tracy v., 76.

H.

Haag v. Commissioners, 222.
Habersham, Jones v., 81, 93.
Hackensack, etc. Co. v. De Kay, 134, 135, 168.
Hackensack, etc. Co., Zabriskie v., 53.
Hackett v. Ottawa, 227, 229.
Hackettstown v. Swackhamer, 96.
Hadden v. Chorn, 94.
Haddersfield, Corporation of Ireland v., 86.
Hadley, Craigie v., 162.
Hadley v. Commissioners, 3, 12.
Hafford v. New Bedford, 219.
Hague v. Philadelphia, 194.
Hale v. Houghton, 217.
Hall, Chicago, etc. Coal Co. v., 146.
Hall v. Paris, 53, 74.
Hall, Skinner v., 129.
Hall v. Sullivan R. Co., 141.
Hall v. Swansea, 74.
Hallowell Bank v. Hamlin, 159.
Halsey, Ackerman v., 158.
Halstead v. Mayor, 175.
Ham, Railroad Co. v., 144.
Hamilton v. McLaughlin, 87.
Hamilton v. New Castle Ry. Co., 96, 100, 128.
Hamilton, Vail v., 9.
Hamilton Co., Grimes v., 195.
Hamlin, Hallowell Bank v., 159.
Hamm, McConnell v., 181.

TABLE OF CASES CITED.

References are to sections.

Hammett v. Philadelphia. 225.
Hammond v. Straus, 51, 168.
Hammonton, State v., 188.
Hams, New Orleans, etc. R. Co. v., 137.
Hancock, Clark v., 223.
Hancock, Gates v., 194.
Hancock v. Holbrook, 83.
Hancock, Howson v., 74, 75.
Handley v. Stutz, 107, 109, 110, 112, 117.
Hankey, Broadway Co. v., 216.
Hanmer, Peninsular Bank v., 77.
Hannauer Oil Works, Mallory v., 53, 70, 148.
Hanover Sav. Ass'n, Larwell v., 96.
Hansborough, Upton v., 51, 168.
Hanser, State v.. 173.
Hanson, Merchants' Bank v., 53.
Hanson v. Vernon, 181, 224.
Hapgood, Penn. Match Co. v., 79.
Harbeck v. Toledo, 183.
Harding, etc. v. Rockford, 223.
Hardy, Goodwin v., 124.
Hardy v. Merriweather, 100.
Hare v. London, etc. R. Co., 130.
Harmock v. Farmers' L. & T. Co., 131.
Harned. Manhattan B. Co. v., 127.
Harper v. Emery, 225.
Harrington, Webster v., 198.
Harris, Denver, etc. R. Co. v., 162.
Harris v. McGregor, 3.
Harris, People v., 185.
Harris v. Runnels, 69.
Harris v. San Francisco R. Co., 126.
Harrisburg, Fisher v., 176, 207.
Harrison v. State, 199.
Hart, Franklin Ins. Co. v., 79.
Hartford, Cone v., 207.
Hartford, Manchester v., 205.
Hartford, Portland Ry. Co. v., 235.
Hartford, etc. Co. v. Sprague. 145.
Hartford Bridge Co. v. East Hartford, 187.
Hartridge v. Rockwell, 120.
Hartwell, Jackson v., 15, 185.
Harvey v. Chase, 100.
Harvey, Marble Co. v., 72, 74, 123, 136.
Hasbrouck v. Milwaukee, 235.

Hascall v. Life Association, 100.
Haskell, Bank v., 161.
Haskell v. New Bedford, 208.
Hastelow v. Jackson, 69.
Hasty, Baumgartner v., 212.
Hat Co., Priest v., 168.
Hatch v. Barr, 87, 90.
Hatch, Collins v., 212.
Hauger v. Des Moines, 170.
Haven v. Adams, 87.
Haven v. Grand Junc. etc. R. Co., 135.
Hawkes, Eastern Counties Ry. Co. v., 9, 52, 137.
Hay, Feitsam v., 137.
Hayden, Leland v., 120.
Hayes v. Appleton, 170.
Hayes v. Holly Springs, 190, 224, 229.
Hayes v. Oshkosh, 219.
Hayne, Boardman v., 190.
Haynes v. Covington, 201.
Hayward v. Davidson, 81.
Haywood v. Pilgrim Society, 77.
Hazlehurst v. Savannah R. Co., 52, 121.
Head v. Providence Ins. Co., 21, 28, 37: 47, 50, 70, 170.
Heath v. Erie R. Co., 53.
Heath, Fuller v., 196.
Heathorn. Benson v., 153.
Heck v. McEwin, 3.
Hedges v. Dixon County, 73, 231.
Hedges v. Paquett, 156.
Hedley, Williams v., 69.
Heenrich v. Pullman Co., 163.
Heineberg, Page v.. 81.
Heland v. Lowell, 171, 172.
Helensburg, Caledonian Ry. v., 70, 79.
Helfrich v. Williams, 164.
Heller v. Sedalia, 219.
Hempsted, North Hempsted v., 187.
Henckes v. Minneapolis, 205.
Henderson v. Covington, 170, 175.
Henley, Mayor v., 220.
Henley, Warren v., 181.
Hennesy v. St. Paul, 53.
Henry Co., Redd v., 235.
Hensley v. People, 225.
Herkimer, Ind. etc. M. Co. v., 3.
Herley, Mayor v., 162.

References are to sections.

Herne Bay, Webb v., 134.
Herrick, Allen v., 127.
Heurson v. New Haven, 213.
Hewison v. New Haven, 204.
Hewitt v. School District, 223.
Hicks, Dry Docks Co. v., 81.
Hicks, Mott v., 96, 100.
Higert v. Green Castle, 205.
Hightower v. Thornton, 106.
Hilbert, St. Louis Carriage Co. v., 120.
Hilbish v. Catherman, 181.
Hildreth v. Lowell, 86.
Hill v. Boston, 219.
Hill v. Charlotte, 202.
Hill v. City of Kahoka, 233.
Hill v. Decatur, 177.
Hill v. Nisbet, 121.
Hill Mfg. Co. v. Railroad Co., 129.
Hill v. Memphis, 223, 229, 237.
Himmelmann v. Hoadley, 201.
Hines v. Lockport, 202.
Hinkley v. Gildersleeve, 9.
Hitchcock v. Galveston, 62, 65, 193, 196, 233.
Hitchins Bros. v. Maybard, 211.
Hoadley, Himmelmann v., 201.
Hoag, Sawyer v., 103.
Hoboken, Bridge Proprietors v., 8.
Hoboken, North Hudson Co. v., 182.
Hoboken, State v., 182.
Hodges v. Buffalo, 194.
Hodges v. Screw Co., 83, 122, 154, 156.
Hodgman v. Chicago, etc. R. Co., 235.
Hodgson v. Powers, 53.
Hoff, Baker v., 69.
Hoffman, Moore v., 178.
Hoffman, etc. Co. v. Cumberland, etc. Co., 153.
Hogie v. People's Association, 120.
Holbrook v. Bassett, 96.
Holbrook, Hancock v., 83.
Holdsworth v. Evans, 70.
Holland v. San Francisco, 9, 14.
Hollister, Salt Lake City v., 9, 53, 74, 163, 222, 233.
Holly Springs, Hayes v., 190, 224, 229.
Holmes v. Johnson, 69, 71.

Holmes v. Mead, 82.
Holmes, etc. Mfg. Co. v. Holmes, etc. Co., 121.
Holt v. Bacon, 161.
Holt, Wahl v., 129.
Holt v. Walworth, 107.
Holt v. Winfield Bank, 159.
Home v. Boston Carpet Co., 122.
Home v. Freeman, 141.
Home v. Keeler, 194.
Home Ins. Co., Seignouret v., 113.
Homestead, Blackshire v., 87.
Hood v. Lynn, 175.
Hood v. Railroad Co., 13, 29, 53, 129, 164.
Hooker v. Eagle Bank, 77.
Hoole v. Great Western R. Co., 118.
Hooper v. Ely, 198.
Hope v. International Co., 120.
Hopkins v. Swanson, 172.
Hopkins v. Turnpike Co., 88.
Hopkins, Yancey v., 190.
Hopkinton, Claflin v., 175.
Hopper v. Covington, 224.
Horn v. Baltimore, 201.
Horn v. People, 171.
Horton v. Thompson, 194.
Hosmer, Detroit v., 189.
Hoth, United States Bank v., 83, 100.
Hough v. Cook Co., 81.
Houghton v. Dodge, 77.
Houghton, Hale v., 217.
Housatonic R. Co., Bridgeport v., 170, 177.
House, Imhoff v., 74, 75.
House v. Montgomery Co., 204.
Household Mach. Co., Anthony v., 119.
Houston, Gabel v., 172.
Houston & T. C. R. Co. v. Shirley, 142, 144.
Hovelman v. Kansas City, etc. Co., 216.
Hovey v. Mayo, 177, 203.
Howard, American Academy v., 94.
Howard, Bermeister v., 172.
Howard, Chicago, etc. Co. v., 96, 136.
Howard, Railroad Co. v., 9.
Howard v. San Francisco, 219.

TABLE OF CASES CITED.

References are to sections.

Howard, Stein v., 115.
Howard, Thornton v., 94.
Howard, White v., 82.
Howe, In re, 93.
Howe, N. Y. Inst. v., 95.
Howe, Brown & Co., Tool Co. v., 84.
Howe Machine Co., Carter v., 162.
Howe Machine Co., Webster v., 104.
Howson v. Hancock, 74, 75.
Hoyle v. Plattsburg, etc. R. Co., 153.
Hoyt, East River Bank v., 154.
Hoyt, Reed v., 91.
Hoyt, Thompson v., 159.
Hubbard v. Concord, 205.
Hubbard v. Investment Co., 55.
Hubbardston, Stone v., 205.
Hudson, York, etc. R. Co. v., 153.
Hudson Co. Ins. Co., Durar v., 77.
Hughes, Flack v., 235.
Huguenot Mfg. Co., Chamberlin v., 51, 168.
Huidekoper, Daviess Co. v., 227.
Hull Glass Co., Smith v., 77.
Humboldt v. Long, 53.
Humboldt M. Co. v. Am. Com. Co., 136.
Humes v. Mayor, 203, 204.
Humphrey v. Patrons' Mer. Ass'n, 77, 168.
Hunt, Barber Asphalt Paving Co. v., 189.
Hunt v. Boonville, 203.
Hunt, Eaton, etc. Co. v., 145.
Hunt v. Knickerbocker, 69, 71.
Hunter, Dougherty v., 159.
Huntoon, City of Topeka v., 177.
Hurford v. Omaha, 170.
Hussey v. King, 164.
Hussey v. Norfolk R. Co., 162.
Hutchins v. Byrnes, 87, 90.
Hutchins, Lake Shore, etc. R. Co. v., 146.
Hutchinson v. Concord, 204.
Hutchinson v. Green, 155.
Huthsing v. Bousquet, 190.
Hutson v. Mayor, 204.
Hyde Park v. Oakwood, 183.
Hydes v. Joyes, 173.
Hydraulic Co., Citizens' Water Co. v., 216.

I.

Ice Co., Mott v., 164.
Illinois, Turnpike Co. v., 8.
Illinois Canal Co. v. St. Louis, 215.
Illinois Cent. R. Co. v. Downey, 164.
Illinois Cent. R. Co. v. Frankenberg, 129.
Illinois Cent. R. Co. v. Johnson, 129.
Imhoff v. House, 74, 75.
Ind. Car Co. v. Parker, 210.
Ind. etc. Co., Indianapolis v., 170, 188.
Ind. Roll. Mill Co. v. Railroad Co., 159.
Indiana, etc. R. Co., Ohio, etc. R. Co. v., 137.
Indianapolis v. Gas, etc. Co., 172, 217.
Indianapolis v. Ind. etc. Co., 170, 188.
Indianapolis v. Scott, 210.
Indianapolis v. Tate, 211.
Indianapolis Ins. Co., Ray v., 101.
Indianapolis, etc. M. Co. v. Herkimer, 2.
Indianapolis, etc. R. Co. v. Jones, 146.
Indianapolis, etc. R. Co., Mowrey v., 144.
Indianapolis, etc. R. Co., Smead v., 9, 96.
Inhabitants, etc., Allen v., 170, 224.
Inhabitants, etc. v. Cole, 81.
Inhabitants, etc. v. Commissioners, 86.
Inhabitants, etc., Dill v., 201.
Inhabitants, etc. v. Field, 211.
Inhabitants. etc., Morrison v., 134.
Inhabitants, etc. v. New Orleans, 177.
Inhabitants, etc., Prout v., 195.
Inman v. Tripp, 211.
In re Addleston Co., 117.
In re Albert Association Co., 137.
In re Assurance Co., 168.
In re Almada & Tirito Co., 117.
In re Bangor & State Co., 148.
In re Bank of Hindustan, 142.
In re Barrow, etc. Co., 114.

TABLE OF CASES CITED. xli

References are to sections.

In re Bridgewater Nav. Co., 119.
In re British Life Ins. Co., 122.
In re Building Society, 70.
In re Cork, etc. R. Co., 53, 73, 74, 96.
In re Corporation of Haddersfield, 86.
In re Ebbw. Vale, etc. Co., 109, 113.
In re Empire Assurance Corporation, 142.
In re Eureka Basin Co., 181.
In re Faure Elec. Co., 154.
In re Financial Corporation, 113.
In re Gatling Gun, 114.
In re German M. Co., 96.
In re Howe, 93.
In re Insurance Co., 120.
In re International Ins. Co., 96.
In re London, etc. R. Co., 120.
In re Marseilles, etc. Co., 120.
In re Mt. Washington, etc. Co., 86.
In re New York, etc. Co., 8.
In re Northern Coal Min. Co., 120.
In re Phœnix Co., 74.
In re Pyle Works, 125.
In re Quebrada Ry., 114.
In re Sage, 145.
In re Sankey Brook Coal Co., 125.
In re Sea Foam, etc. Ins. Co., 74.
In re Union Plate Glass Co., 114.
In re United Service Co., 120.
In re Washington Avenue, 225.
In re Weymouth Packet Co., 117.
Insurance Co., Ætna Nat. Bank v., 136.
Insurance Co., Agar v., 160.
Insurance Co., Attorney-General v., 100.
Insurance Co., Beatty v., 47.
Insurance Co., Blair v., 100.
Insurance Co., Chetlain v., 120.
Insurance Co., Farmers', etc. Co. v., 92.
Insurance Co., Jones v., 172.
Insurance Co., Kennebec Co. v., 166.
Insurance Co., Life & Fire Ins. Co. v., 162.
Insurance Co., Liverpool, etc. Co. v., 9.
Insurance Co., Maynard v., 162.
Insurance Co., McCullough v., 168.
Insurance Co., Mumford v., 100.
Insurance Co., Nichol v., 160.
Insurance Co., Ramsey v., 168.
Insurance Co., Smith v., 70.
Insurance Co., Southall v., 143.
Insurance Co., Susquehanna, etc. Co. v., 84.
Insurance Co., Vance v., 156.
Insurance Co., Williams v., 162.
International, etc. Co. v. Bremond, 143.
International, etc. Co., Hope v., 120.
International, etc. Co., Kentle v., 163.
International, etc. Co. v. United States, 77.
Investment Co., Hubbard v., 155.
Iola, Commercial Bank v., 181, 225, 237.
Iowa City, Clark v., 135.
Iowa Lumber Co. v. Foster, 120.
Iowa Mountain Bank v. Mercantile Bank, 162.
Irish v. Railroad Co., 129.
Iron R. Co. v. Ironton, 86.
Irvine v. Union Bank. 78.
Isham v. Bennington Ins. Co., 90.
Ithica, Saulsbury v., 205.
Ives v. Smith, 131.

J.

Jackson v. Bowman, 215.
Jackson v. Brown, 84, 85.
Jackson, Denton v., 3.
Jackson, Gray v., 129.
Jackson v. Hartwell, 15, 185.
Jackson, Hastelow v., 69.
Jackson's Adm'rs v. Plank Road Co., 124.
Jacksonville, Dorman v., 203.
Jacksonville v. McConnel, 47.
Jacksonville, Murphy v., 175.
Jacobs, Union Bank v., 96, 98, 100.
James v. Portage, 200.
Janesville, Crossett v., 203.
January, Commissioners v., 238.
Jasper County, Anthony v., 226.
Jefferson County v. Arrighi, 194.

TABLE OF CASES CITED.

References are to sections.

Jeffersonville, Bissell v., 193.
Jeffersonville, Coal Float v., 176.
Jeffersonville, Shallcross v., 175.
Jenkins v. Andover, 224.
Jenkins, Dranesburg v., 237.
Jermain v. Lake Shore R. Co., 124.
Jersey City, Banking Co. v., 178.
Jersey City, Gregory v., 189.
Jersey City, Keeney v., 189.
Jersey City, McConvill v., 175.
Jersey City, Roucde v., 227.
Jersey City, State v., 173, 174, 176, 235.
Jersey City, Trapshagen v., 207.
Jessup, Branch v., 9, 53.
Jeverin v. Eddy, 206.
Jewett v. New Haven, 219.
John v. Farmers' Bank, 101.
Johnson, Cass County v., 227.
Johnson v. Dispatch Co., 162.
Johnson v. District of Columbia, 208.
Johnson, Holmes v., 69, 71.
Johnson, Ill. Cent. R. Co. v., 129.
Johnson, Kean v., 137.
Johnson, Musser v., 87.
Johnson, Northern Bank v., 161.
Johnson v. Philadelphia, 215.
Johnson v. Shrewsbury, etc. R. Co., 71, 137.
Johnson v. Utica Water Works, 86.
Johnson, Wood v., 96, 100.
Johnson County v. McClintock, 235.
Johnston v. Charleston, 206.
Johnston, Meyer v., 142.
Johnston Harvester Co. v. Clark, 168.
Johnston, etc. R. Co., Abbott v., 137.
Joint Co. v. Delaware Bay Ry. Co., 8.
Joint-Stock Co. v. Brown, 122, 158.
Jones v. Bank, 168.
Jones v. Guaranty Co., 66.
Jones v. Habersham, 81, 93.
Jones v. Ind. etc. R. Co., 146.
Jones v. Insurance Co., 172.
Jones v. New Haven, 220.
Jones, Quincy v., 203.
Jones v. Richmond, 188.

Jones, Stewart v., 141.
Jones v. Terre Haute R. Co., 124.
Jones, Wetherell v., 55.
Jordon v. Alabama R. Co., 162.
Jordon, Christian Union v., 78.
Joy, Allen v., 181, 225.
Joy, Bean v., 195.
Joy v. St. Louis, 128, 146.
Joyes, Hydes v. 173.
Junction R. Co., Cleneay v., 135.
Junction R. Co., McCrary v., 53, 147.

K.

Kaine, St. Louis v., 172.
Kaist v. St. Paul, 203.
Kalamazoo, Gale v., 173, 215.
Kalamazoo, Shelden v., 162.
Kamper, Grangers' Ins. Co. v., 3, 107.
Kane v. Fond du Lac, 195.
Kankakee, Bissell v., 181, 225.
Kansas City v. Flanagan, 170.
Kansas City v. Kiley, 213.
Kansas, etc. Co., Hovelman v., 216.
Kean v. Johnson, 137.
Kean v. Van Reuth, 168.
Keeler, Howe v., 194.
Keeler, Mead v., 100.
Keeney v. Jersey City, 189.
Keithburg v. Frick, 238.
Keller v. Leavenworth, 230.
Kelley, Louisville R. Co. v., 163.
Kelley v. Milan, 223.
Kelly v. Calhoun, 89.
Kelly, Case v., 81, 85.
Kelly v. Mayor, etc., 96, 100.
Kelly v. Meeks, 170.
Kelly v. Milwaukee, 177.
Kendall Co., Post v., 190.
Kennebec Co. v. Insurance Co., 166.
Kennedy v. Cochran, 69.
Kennedy v. Phelps, 212.
Kennicott v. Supervisors, 228.
Kenosha, Paul v., 74, 191.
Kent v. Quicksilver M. Co., 96, 106, 124, 127.
Kentle, International, etc. Co. v., 163.
Keokuk, Creal v., 201.

References are to sections.

Keokuk v. Ft. Wayne Elec. Co., 137.
Keokuk v. Scroggs, 170.
Keokuk, etc. Bridge Co., Pittsburg, etc. R. Co. v., 9, 47, 52, 53, 54, 69, 74, 76.
Keokuk Packing Co., Buford v., 83, 121.
Keokuk, etc. R. Co., State v., 144.
Keokuk Water Works, Becker v., 219.
Kep, Utica Ins. Co. v., 69.
Kepner v. Commonwealth, 171.
Kerchner v. Gettys, 166.
Kernaghan v. Williams, 53.
Kernesville Mfg. Co., Blalock v., 120.
Kerr, Troy, etc. R. Co. v., 137.
Kersey Oil Co. v. Oil Creek R. Co., 139.
Ketchum v. Buffalo, 100, 185, 188.
Ketchum, N. Y. etc. Co. v., 79.
Keyser v. School District, 77.
Kiel, Morris v., 87.
Kiley, Kansas City v., 213.
Killam, Lawrence v., 188.
King v. Davenport, 212.
King, Hussey v., 164.
King v. Patterson, 124, 126.
King, Phillips Academy v., 92.
King, Trustees v., 95.
King, Warren v., 119.
King, Wood Hydraulic Co. v., 166.
King Mountain Min. Co., Nason v., 87.
King's College, Festial v., 124.
Kinmundy v. Mayham, 173.
Kinzie v. Chicago, 47.
Kip, N. Y. etc. R. Co. v., 86.
Kip v. Paterson, 176.
Kipp v. Mayor, 176.
Kirkham v. Russell, 170, 176.
Kneeland, Lathrop v., 109.
Kneeland v. Milwaukee, 189.
Kneeland, Tombigbie v., 165, 166.
Knickerbocker, Hunt v., 69, 71.
Knight v. Corporation, 168.
Knitting Co., Caudy v., 162.
Knowler, Beaty v., 8, 12, 47.
Knowlton v. Congress, etc. Co., 109, 110.

Knowlton, Spring Co. v., 69, 73, 138.
Knox Co. v. Aspinwall, 135, 190, 193, 227, 228.
Knox Ins. Co., Ogilvie v., 108.
Kohner, Chemical Bank v., 161.
Konrad v. Rogers, 185.
Krightly, Oliver v., 198.
Krouse, Centralia v., 206.
Krulevitz v. Railroad Co., 162.
Kyle v. Railroad Co., 129.

L.

Lacey, Excelsior Co. v., 156.
Lacey, Orr v., 70.
Lacon, Barnes v., 237.
La Crosse R. Co., Bronson v., 53.
Lafayette, Allen v., 233.
Lafayette v. Cox, 9.
Lafayette Ave. Bank v. St. Louis S. Co., 9.
Lafayette R. Co., Tippecanoe Co. v., 53, 78.
Laflin, Chicago v., 212.
La Grange, Cole v., 181, 225.
Laing v. Reed, 98.
Laing, Solomon v., 53, 121.
Laird v. De Sota, 233.
Lake, Terre Haute v., 201.
Lake County v. Graham, 53.
Lake County, Sutliff v., 53.
Lake Crystal, Estelle v., 205, 206.
Lake Erie Ins. Co., Valley R. Co. v., 121.
Lake Erie, etc. R. Co. v. Acres, 163.
Lake Erie, etc. R. Co., Paine v., 144, 146.
Lake Shore, etc. R. Co., Boardman v., 124.
Lake Shore, etc. R. Co. v. Hutchins, 146.
Lake Shore, etc. R. Co., Jermain v., 126.
Lake Shore, etc. R. Co., Sage v., 145.
Lake View v. Letz, 212.
Lamb v. Cecil, 91.
Lamb, Powder River, etc. Co. v., 74, 75.
Lambert, Thompson v., 96.
Lamm v. Deposit Association, 194.

xliv TABLE OF CASES CITED.

References are to sections.

Lamont, Thompson v., 84.
Lampkin, Nebraska City v., 203.
Lamson, Boom Co. v., 3.
Lancaster, Miller, etc. R. Co. v., 144.
Lancaster, Savanna R. Co. v., 96.
Lancaster, Steck v., 200.
Land v. Coffmann, 81.
Land Credit Co. v. Lord Fermoy, 158.
Land Corporation of Ireland, Gunniss v., 55, 56.
Land & Improvement Co., Bridge Co. v., 8.
Lane's Case, 110.
Langstone v. S. C. R. Co., 135.
Lanier, Southern Ins. Co. v., 14, 74.
Lansing v. Toolan, 202.
Laramie Co. v. Albany Co., 186.
Larned, Randolph, v., 141.
Larue, Minturn v., 170, 199.
Larwell v. Hanover Savings Bank, 96.
Lathrop, Commercial Bank v., 81.
Lathrop v. Kneeland, 109.
Laughton v. Hughes, 71.
Lauman v. Lebanon V. R. Co., 137, 142, 144, 147.
Law v. People, 196, 197, 231.
Lawrence v. Killam, 188.
Lawrence, Morrison v., 213, 222.
Layten, Osgood v., 108.
Lead Co., Mechanics' Association v., 100.
Leasure v. Life Insurance Co., 166.
Leavenworth, Keller v., 230.
Leavenworth v. Miller, 225.
Leavitt, Curtis v., 13, 74, 96, 98, 100.
Leavitt v. Palmer, 74.
Leazure v. Hillegas, 81.
Lebanon Co., Currier v., 120, 137, 142, 144.
Lebanon V. R. Co., Lauman v., 137, 142, 144, 147.
Leckey, Gunter v., 69.
Le Claire, Springfield v., 220.
Le Couteulx v. Buffalo, 185.
Lee, Morris v., 157, 158.
Lee, Thompson v., 238.
Leech, Waters v., 176.
Le Fevre, Carr v., 135.

Legg, Board of Commissioners v., 210.
Leggett v. Banking Co., 84.
Leggett v. New Jersey Mfg. Co., 8, 13.
Lehigh Canal Co., Brown v., 124.
Lehigh Water Co.'s Appeal, 216.
Lehman v. Tallassee Mfg. Co., 105, 135.
Leland v. Hayden, 120.
Leo v. Union Pacific R. Co., 105.
Leonard v. Canton, 170.
Lessee, etc., Runyan v., 81.
Leslie v. St. Louis, 86.
Le Sueur Mill Co., Auerbach v., 81.
Letz, Lake View v., 212.
Levy, Life Association v., 166.
Levy, Mayor v., 213.
Lewis v. Bank of Kentucky, 167.
Lewis v. Clarendon, 237.
Lewis, Commanche Co. v., 228.
Lewis County Bank, Donnell v., 96.
Lewistown Inst. etc., Franklin Co. v., 9, 34, 53, 55, 70, 121.
Lex, Whitman v., 95.
Lexington v. Butler, 228.
Life Association, Boogher v., 162.
Life Association, Hascall v., 100.
Life Association v. Levy, 166.
Life Association, Twiss v., 74.
Life, etc. Insurance Co., Gorrell v., 96.
Life Insurance Co. v. Insurance Co., 162.
Life Insurance Co., Leasure v., 166.
Light Co., Gas Co. v., 199.
Lightner v. Boston, etc. R. Co., 146.
Lincoln, Fulton v., 170.
Lincoln Co., U. P. R. Co. v., 235.
Lincoln, etc. R. Co., Peters v., 137.
Lincoln Savings Bank v. Ewing, 92.
Lionberger v. Broadway Bank, 91.
Lime Co., Denike v., 143.
Litchfield v. Ballou, 233.
Litchfield, Buchanan v., 196, 224, 228, 232.
Litchfield, Dubuque, etc. Co. v., 9.
Little v. O'Brien, 74, 75.

Little Rock, Vance v., 170.
Littlewort v. Davis, 70.
Livingston County v. Weider, 235.
Livingstone v. Temperance Society, 120.
Liverpool, etc. Co. v. Insurance Co., 9.
Llanelly Ry. v. London, etc. R. Co., 130.
Lloyd v. Bank, 160.
Loan Association v. Topeka, 179, 181, 224, 225, 238.
Loan Co., Marchand v., 79.
Lock Co. v. Railroad Co., 129.
Lockhart v. Van Alstyne, 124.
Lockport, Hines v., 202.
Lockwood, Peck v., 212.
Lockwood, Railroad Co. v., 9.
Lockwood v. St. Louis, 177.
Logan City v. Buck, 170.
Logan County Bank v. Townsend, 74.
Lombard, School District v., 230.
London v. Goldsmith, 205.
London, Stuart v., 77.
London Bldg. Soc., Collerne v., 120.
London Omnibus Co., Green v., 162.
London, etc. R. Co., Hare v., 130.
London, etc. R. Co., In re, 120.
London, etc. R. Co., Llanelly Ry. v., 130.
Long, Cowgill v., 238.
Long, Humboldt v., 53.
Longstreet, Crawford v., 81.
Lookout Water Co., Foster v., 219.
Lord v. Oconto, 170, 173.
Lord Fermoy, Credit Co. v., 158.
Los Angeles, Og v., 219.
Los Angeles, etc. R. Co., Smith v., 146.
Los Angeles Water Co. v. Los Angeles, 217.
Louisiana v. New Orleans, 204, 233.
Louisiana v. Wood, 191, 233.
Louisiana Light Co., New Orleans G. L. Co. v., 216.
Louisiana Ry., Richmond Ry. v., 8.

Louisiana State Bank v. Orleans Nav. Co., 47, 170.
Louisville v. Bank, 215.
Louisville v. Commissioners, 185.
Louisville, Greenwood v., 219.
Louisville, Murphy v., 201.
Louisville, Pollock v., 219.
Louisville v. University, 185.
Louisville v. Weible, 216.
Louisville, etc. R. Co. v. Boney, 146.
Louisville, etc. R. Co. v. Caldwell, 100.
Louisville, etc. R. Co. v. Flemming, 163.
Louisville, etc. R. Co. v. Kelly, 163.
Louisville, etc. R. Co. v. Louisville, 215.
Lovette v. Sawmill Association, 89.
Loving, Brannen v., 159.
Low v. Central Pac. R. Co., 9, 136.
Low, Smith v., 96.
Lowell v. Boston, 69, 179, 181, 225.
Lowell, Bridenbecker v., 161.
Lowell, Drake v., 204.
Lowell, Heland v., 171, 172.
Lowell, Hildreth v., 86.
Lowell, Proprietors, etc. v., 213.
Lucas v. Pitney, 96, 100.
Lucas v. White Line Transp. Co., 4, 9, 38, 52, 70.
Ludlow, Ferris v., 109.
Lumbard v. Aldrich, 81.
Lumber Co., Tenney v., 88.
Lumsden v. Cross, 225.
Luthe v. Farmers' Ins. Co., 53.
Lyde v. East Bengal R. Co., 53.
Lynch v. Eastern, etc. R. Co., 235.
Lynch v. New York, 208, 211.
Lynch, Sheidley v., 177.
Lynchburg, Peters v., 170.
Lynn, Hood v., 175.
Lyons County, Clark v., 194.

M.

M. & P. R. Co., Bryan v., 129.
Mabel, Titus v., 131.
Mabry, Shea v., 156.
Mackay v. Bank, 162.

TABLE OF CASES CITED.

References are to sections.

Maddox, Pollard v., 141.
Mad River R. Co., Weeden v., 77.
Madison, Bearden v., 172.
Madison, State v., 81, 185.
Madison, Weis v., 211.
Madison, etc. P. Rd. Co. v. Watertown, etc. Co., 9, 99. 136.
Madison. etc. R. Co., Pearce v., 9, 30, 52, 53, 70, 143, 148.
Magee v. Mokelumne, etc. Co., 96, 98, 100.
Magnay, Great Luxemburg R. Co. v., 153.
Maher v. Chicago, 74, 191.
Mahoney v. Mining Co., 168.
Mahoney v. State, 3.
Mahoney Min. Co. v. Anglo-Cal. Bank, 96, 98.
Maine Cent. R. Co. v. Maine, 144, 146, 148.
Mallett v. Simpson, 81.
Mallory v. Hannauer Oil Works, 53, 70, 148.
Maloney, Dubuque v., 212.
Manchester v. Hartford, 205.
Manchester, Ray v., 204.
Manchester, etc. Co., Cass v., 53.
Manchester Canal Co., Cunliffe v., 53.
Manchester, etc. R. Co., Chambers v., 70, 134.
Manchester, etc. R. Co. v. Concord, etc. R. Co., 130.
Manchester Water Co., Broughton v., 50.
Manderchid v. Dubuque, 200.
Manhattan Beach Co. v. Harned, 127.
Mankato, Phelps v., 200.
Mansfield v. Moore, 205.
Mansfield, State v., 81.
Manufacturing Co., Gas Co. v., 144.
Manufacturing Co., Railroad Co. v., 129.
Manufacturing Co., Smith v., 156.
Manufacturing Co., White v., 79.
Marble Co. v. Harvey, 136.
March v. Eastern, etc. R. Co., 124.
Marchand v. Loan Co., 79.
Marcy, Elwood Township v., 238.
Marcy v. Oswego, 53.
Marcy, Sumner v., 122.

Mariaville, Emery v., 230.
Marietta, etc. R. Co., Atkinson v., 9.
Marietta, etc. R. Co., Campbell v., 137.
Marietta. etc. R. Co. v. Elliott, 9.
Marine Bank, Ballston Bank v., 161.
Marion Co., State v., 170.
Markham, Comm. v., 182.
Marks v. Purdue University, 225.
Marquette v. Cleary, 202.
Marseilles, Chicago, etc. R. Co. v., 120.
Marseilles. etc. Co., In re, 120.
Marsh v. Callender, 203.
Marsh v. Fulton County, 190, 191, 193, 194, 201, 224. 233.
Marsh v. N. Y. etc. R. Co., 146.
Marshall, Downing v., 82.
Marshall, Forbes v., 96.
Marshall, Turquand v., 158.
Marshalltown, Bellmeyer v., 9.
Martin v. Mayor, 215.
Martin v. Mobile, etc. R. Co., 166.
Martin, Rochester Ins. Co. v., 9.
Martin, State v., 195.
Martin v. Webb, 160.
Marvin Safe Co. v. Ward, 219.
Maryland, Phil. etc. R. Co. v., 146, 148.
Mason, Greenville v., 186.
Mason v. M. E. Church, 93.
Mason v. Shawnee, 172.
Mason City, Noyes v., 203.
Massey v. Building Association, 101.
Mather v. Ottawa, 170, 225.
Mathes v. Cameron, 230.
Mathews v. Alexander, 173.
Mathews, National Bank v., 53, 67.
Mathews v. Skinner, 9.
Maude, Ex parte, 117.
Mauldin v. Greenville, 231.
Maund v. Monmouthshire Co., 162.
Maupin v. Franklin Co., 190.
Mawhood, Smith v., 55.
May, People v., 196.
Maybard, Hitchins Bros. v., 211.
Mayer, Western Union Ins. Co. v., 166.
Mayham, Kinmundy v., 173.

TABLE OF CASES CITED. xlvii

References are to sections.

Maynard v. Insurance Co., 162.
Mayo, Hovey v., 177.
Mayor v. Baltimore, etc. R. Co., 128.
Mayor, Bateman v., 50, 188.
Mayor v. Beasley, 176.
Mayor, Bigler v., 189.
Mayor, Blake v., 170.
Mayor, Bradford v., 204, 206.
Mayor, Brady v., 70, 194, 201.
Mayor, Brieswick v., 171.
Mayor, Brown v., 194.
Mayor v. Comak, 177.
Mayor v. Cunliffe, 190, 222.
Mayor, Davenport v., 204.
Mayor, Davis v., 199.
Mayor v. Elliott, 95.
Mayor, Fish v., 201.
Mayor v. Gill, 177.
Mayor, Halstead v., 175.
Mayor v. Henry, 220.
Mayor v. Herley, 162.
Mayor, Hovey v., 203.
Mayor, Humes v., 203, 204.
Mayor, Hutson v., 204.
Mayor, Kelly v., 96, 100.
Mayor, Kipp v., 176.
Mayor, Levy v., 213.
Mayor, Martin v., 215.
Mayor, Maximilian v., 219.
Mayor, McDonald v., 190, 194.
Mayor, McSpeden v., 191.
Mayor v. Moag, 170.
Mayor, Nichol v., 170.
Mayor, O'Meara v., 219.
Mayor, Paterson v., 185, 194.
Mayor, People v., 225.
Mayor, Presbyterian Church v., 215.
Mayor, Radcliffe's Ex'rs v., 208.
Mayor, Rae v., 188.
Mayor v. Railroad Co., 215.
Mayor v. Ray, 14, 119, 230, 237.
Mayor, Reinhard v., 205.
Mayor v. Reynolds, 190.
Mayor, Russell v., 220.
Mayor, Schanck v., 177.
Mayor, Scott v., 220.
Mayor v. Second Ave. R. Co., 182.
Mayor, Sharpless v., 224.
Mayor v. Sheffield, 200, 206.
Mayor, Smoot v., 220.
Mayor, State v., 176, 222.

Mayor, Stuyvesant v., 215.
Mayor, Tone v., 220.
Mayor, West v., 178.
Mayor, Whitney v., 178.
Mayor, Whyte v., 212.
Mayor v. Winfield, 176.
Maysfield, Stack v., 177.
Mazet v. Pittsburg, 189.
Mead, Holmes v., 82.
Mead v. Keeler, 100.
Mead v. New Haven, 222.
Mead v. N. Y. etc. R. Co., 143.
Mechanics' Association v. Lead Co., 100.
Mechanics' Bank v. Bank of Colorado, 161.
Mechanics' Bank v. Meriden Co., 121.
Mechanics' Bank v. N. Y. etc. R. Co., 109.
Mechanics' Ins. Co., Barker v., 100.
Medical College Case, 3.
Medomak Bank v. Curtis, 77.
Meeker v. Winthrop Ins. Co., 139.
Meeks, Kelly v., 170.
Mehaffey, San Antonio v., 62, 68, 227.
McKellar v. Detroit, 205.
Memphis v. Dean, 53.
Memphis, Hill v., 223, 230, 237.
Memphis, Trigally v., 171.
Memphis v. Water Co., 216.
Memphis, etc. R. Co. v. Dow, 96.
Memphis, etc. R. Co., People's R. R. v., 215.
Memphis, etc. R. Co. v. Railroad Commissioner, 141, 144.
Menard Co., West v., 90.
Menser v. Risdon, 173.
Mercantile Bank, Iowa M. Bank v., 162.
Mercer v. Pittsburg, etc. Co., 183.
Merchants' Bank v. Bergen Co., 226, 229.
Merchants' Bank v. Central Bank, 77.
Merchants' Bank v. Randolph, 161.
Merchants' Bank v. State Bank, 160, 162.
Merchants' Exchange, Barry v., 27, 83, 84, 96, 100, 106, 124.

TABLE OF CASES CITED.

References are to sections.

Merchants' Nat. Bank v. Hanson, 53.
Meredith, Cast-plate Co. v., 203.
Meredith, Clearwater v., 144, 147, 148.
Meredith, Eastman v., 219.
Meredith, Ferguson v., 144.
Meridan Agency Co., Mutual Association v., 122.
Meriden Co., Savings Bank v., 121.
Merrick v. Amherst, 225.
Merrick v. Bank, 91.
Merrick v. Reynolds Eng. Co., 51, 168.
Merrick v. Van Santford, 166.
Merrill v. Monticello, 223, 224, 230.
Merrill v. Plainfield, 198.
Merrill v. Portland, 204.
Merrimack, etc. R. Co., Richards v., 84, 100, 141.
Merriweather, Hardy v., 100.
Mersey Docks v. Gibbs, 220.
Metcalf, Beardstown, etc. Co. v., 84.
Methodist Episcopal Church, Bailey v., 53.
Methodist Episcopal Church, Mason v., 92.
Metropolitan Bank v. Godfrey, 85.
Metropolitan, etc. Co. v. Abbey, 139.
Metropolitan, etc. Co. v. Byron, 98.
Metz, Bridge Co. v., 145.
Metzker, Petersburgh v., 47, 170.
Meyer v. Johnston, 142.
Meyer v. Porter, 235.
Miami County, Moran v., 227, 228.
Michener v. Philadelphia, 207.
Michigan, etc. R. Co., Bissell v., 31, 38, 55, 61.
Michigan, etc. R. Co., Swartout v., 168.
Michigan, etc. R. Co., Williston v., 124.
Middleport v. Ætna Ins. Co., 240.
Middlesex R. Co. v. Boston, etc. R. Co., 137.
Middlesex R. Co., Feital v., 129.
Middleton, Ohio, etc. R. Co. v., 77.
Middleton, Gas Co. v., 199.
Midland, etc. Ry. Co., Edwards v., 162.
Midland R. Co. v. Great Western R. Co., 130.
Migner, Doyle v., 3.
Migret v. Supervisors, 238.
Milan, Kelley v., 223.
Milbank v. N. Y. etc. R. Co., 121.
Milbourne, Cowan v., 69.
Milhau v. Sharp, 215.
Mill Co., Auerbach v., 100.
Miller v. American Ins. Co., 74.
Miller v. Ammon, 69.
Miller, Blazier v., 171.
Miller v. Burch, 212.
Miller v. Burlington, etc. R. Co., 163, 164.
Miller, Gottfried v., 91.
Miller, Leavenworth v., 225.
Miller v. Milwaukee, 188.
Miller, National Trust Co. v., 70, 72, 78, 137.
Miller v. Newberg Coal Co., 168.
Miller v. Norristown, 203.
Miller v. St. Paul, 205.
Miller & Miss. R. Co. v. Lancaster, 144.
Milliard v. St. Francis, etc. Academy, 100.
Mills v. Brooklyn, 202, 208.
Mills v. Gleason, 194.
Mills v. Northern R. Co., 53.
Mills County v. Burlington, 195.
Milne v. Davidson, 172.
Milnor v. N. Y. etc. R. Co., 167.
Milwaukee, Brodhead v., 225.
Milwaukee, Clason v., 176.
Milwaukee, Cook v., 205.
Milwaukee, Dart v., 203.
Milwaukee, Hasbrouck v., 235.
Milwaukee, Kelly v., 177.
Milwaukee Kneeland v., 189.
Milwaukee, Miller v., 188.
Milwaukee, Owens v., 203.
Milwaukee, Schultz v., 204.
Milwaukee, Tyson v., 203.
Milwaukee, Yates v., 112.
Milwaukee Gas Light Co., State v., 216.
Miner v. N. Y. etc. R. Co., 9.
Miners' Ditch Co. v. Zellerbach, 9, 33, 83, 87.
Mining Co., Mahoney v., 168.
Minneapolis, Alden v., 203.
Minneapolis, Henckes v., 215.

References are to sections.

Minneapolis, etc. R. Co., Snell v., 53.
Minnesota, etc. R. Co., Freeman v., 137.
Minor v. Bank, 160.
Minturn v. Larue, 170, 199.
Mississippi, etc. R. Co. v. Camden, 237.
Mississippi, etc. R. Co. v. Lancaster, 144.
Missouri, etc. R. Co., Gillette v., 164.
Mitchell v. Rome, 203.
Mitchell, St. Andrew's Bay Co. v., 52.
Mitford, Day v., 204.
Moag, Mayor v., 170.
Mobile v. Watson, 233.
Mobile v. Yuelle, 212.
Mobile Bank, Reed v., 135.
Mobile, etc. R. Co., Martin v., 166.
Mobile, etc. R. Co. v. Tallman, 96.
Mobile, etc. R. Co., Warren v., 146.
Moffitt, Chicago, etc. R. Co. v., 144, 146.
Mohawk Bridge Co. v. Utica, etc. Co., 8, 216.
Mokelumne, etc. Co., Magee v., 96, 98, 100.
Monmouth, Parsons v., 194.
Monmouthshire Co., Maund v., 162.
Monroe Co., Wall v., 230.
Monument Nat. Bank v. Globe Works, 9, 82, 74, 100, 104, 162.
Montague v. School District, 100.
Montauk Gas Co., Boyce v., 52.
Montgomery, Campbell v., 202, 220.
Montgomery, Capital City W. W. Co. v., 217.
Montgomery, Davis v., 213, 219.
Montgomery v. Montgomery, etc., 53.
Montgomery, State v., 235.
Montgomery, Studebaker v., 168.
Montgomery Co. v. Barber, 188.
Montgomery Co., House v., 204.
Monticello, Merrill v., 223, 224, 230.
Montpelier v. East Montpelier, 92.

Moore, Fitchburg R. Co. v., 162.
Moore v. Hoffman, 178.
Moore, Mansfield v., 205.
Moore v. New York, 191, 193.
Moore, Rapho v., 206, 210.
Moor's Heirs v. Moor's Devisees, 81, 82.
Moran v. Commissioners, 193.
Moran v. Miami Co., 227, 228.
Morch v. Abel, 71.
Morgan, Staten v., 141.
Morris, Glasby v., 207.
Morris v. Kiel, 87.
Morris v. Lee, 157, 158.
Morris Canal Co. v. Central R. Co., 8.
Morris Canal Co. v. Fisher, 135.
Morris, etc. R. Co. v. Barclay Coal Co., 131.
Morris, etc. R. Co. v. Sussex, etc. R. Co., 8, 10, 130, 131.
Morrison v. Gold Mountain Co., 79.
Morrison v. Inhabitants, etc., 174.
Morrison v. Lawrence, 213, 222.
Morrison, McMahon v., 144.
Morrow v. Nashville, 115.
Morse v. Brainerd, 129.
Morse, Smith v., 215.
Moses v. Ocoee Bank, 109.
Moss v. Academy, 96.
Moss v. Averill, 56, 100.
Moss, McCullough v., 78, 100.
Moss v. Oakley, 100.
Moss v. Rossie L. Min. Co., 77.
Mott v. Hicks, 96, 100.
Mott v. Ice Co., 103.
Mott, Shotwell v., 95.
Moulton, Wheelock v., 90.
Moultrie Co. v. Bank, 197.
Moundeville, Ohio Iron Works v., 225.
Mounsey, Australia, etc. Co. v., 96, 98.
Mount Hermon School, Nims v., 162.
Mount Pleasant v. Beckwith, 186, 187.
Mount Sterling, Curry v., 86.
Mount Washington, etc. Co., Downing v., 9, 47.
Mount Washington, etc. Co., In re, 86.

D

TABLE OF CASES CITED.

References are to sections.

Mowrey v. Indiana, etc. R. Co., 144.
Mueller. Seeger v., 192.
Mulford, Camden v., 173, 174.
Mullen, Selma v., 170.
Mulligan v. Railway Co., 129.
Mumford v. Insurance Co., 100.
Mundy, Austin v., 175.
Munn v. The Commission, 96, 100.
Munson v. Railroad Co., 79.
Murdock, McDonough v., 93.
Murphey v. Louisville, 201.
Murphy v. Jacksonville, 175.
Murphy v. Peoria, 202.
Murphy, Sullivan v., 100.
Murphy's Flushing Co., Union Water Co. v., 64.
Murray, Ottawa R. Co. v., 77.
Murray, People v., 233.
Musgrove, Baltimore v., 190.
Musser v. Johnson v., 87.
Mutual, etc. Ass'n v. Meridan Agency Co., 122.
Mutual Life Ins. Co. v. McElway, 109.
McAlpine v. Union Packing Co., 146.
McAuley v. Columbus R. Co., 143.
McBride v. Grand Rapids, 189.
McCann, State v., 225.
McCartee v. Orphans' Asylum, 81, 82, 95.
McCarthey, Railway Co. v., 62, 63, 64, 68.
McCaslin v. State, 190.
McClintock, Johnson Co. v., 235.
McClure v. Oxford Township, 229, 235.
McClurken, Allegheny City v., 70, 74.
McCombs v. Akron, 220.
McConnell v. Hamm, 181.
McConnell, Jacksonville v., 47.
McConvill v. Jersey City, 175.
McCoy v. Briant, 170.
McCracken v. San Francisco, 170, 191, 194.
McCray v. Junction R. Co., 53, 147.
McCreery, People v., 181.
McCullough v. Moss, 78, 100.
McCullough v. Talldega Ins. Co., 77, 168.

McCune, People v., 238.
McCurdy v. Rogers, 190.
McDermott v. Board, 172.
McDermott, Evening Journal Association v., 162.
McDonald, Bank v., 168.
McDonald, Burr v., 88, 96.
McDonald v. Mayor, 190, 194.
McDonough v. Bank, 79.
McDonough v. Murdock, 93.
McElway, Mutual Life Ins. Co. v., 109.
McEwin, Heck v., 3.
McGee, Gooch v., 86.
McGinnity v. New York, 206.
McGirr, Richmond v., 177.
McGiven, Chicago v., 205.
McGraw, Chicago v., 222.
McGregor v. Dover & D. R. Co., 9, 55, 56, 70.
McGregor v. Erie, etc. R. Co., 145, 167.
McGregor, Harris v., 3.
McGuire v. Rapid City, 201.
McInnis, Champaign v., 205.
McIntire v. McLain Ditch Co., 3.
McKnight v. New Orleans, 217.
McLain Ditch Co., McIntire v., 3.
McLaughlin, Hamilton v., 87.
McLennan v. File Works, 136.
McMahon v. Morrison, 144.
McMasters v. Reed, 47, 100.
McMillan v. Railroad Co., 129, 137.
McNab, Eufaula v., 185, 224.
McPherson v. Foster, 231, 232.
McQuade, Van Dyke v., 156.
McSpeden v. Mayor, 191.

N.

Nagle, Wright v., 199.
Nahant Bank, Atlas Bank v., 74.
Nancy, City of Flora v., 205.
Narragansett Bank v. Silk Co., 100.
Nash v. St. Paul, 194.
Nashua, etc. R. Co., Smith v., 128.
Nashua Savings Bank, Greeley v., 53.
Nashville, Morrow v., 115.
Nason v. Boston, 205.
Nason v. King Mountain M. Co., 87.

TABLE OF CASES CITED.

References are to sections.

Nassau Co., Petersborough R. Co. v., 50.
National Bank, Gold Min. Co. v., 76.
National Bank v. Graham, 162.
National Bank v. Mathews, 53, 67.
National Bank v. Whitney, 53.
National Bank v. Young, 104.
National, etc. Co. v. Clarkin, 81.
National Docks v. Railroad Co., 168.
National Exchange Co. v. Drew, 162.
National Iron Co. v. Bowman, 101.
National Park Bank v. German, etc. Co., 136.
National Trust Co. v. Miller, 70, 72, 78, 137.
Naugatuck R. Co. v. Button Co., 53.
Nauvoo v. Ritter, 227.
Navigation Co., Louisiana Bank v., 170.
Nebraska, Campbell v., 220.
Nebraska City v. Lampkin, 203.
Nebraska Dist. Co., State v., 55.
Needles, Farmers' Bank v., 101.
Nelson, East Tenn. etc. R. Co. v., 129.
Nelson v. Eaton, 96.
Nesbit v. Riverside District, 228.
Neuse River, Barrington v., 86.
Nevada Cent. R. Co., George v., 137.
New Albany v. Burke, 115.
New Albany, Duckwall v., 175.
New Bedford, Halford v., 219.
New Bedford, Haskell v., 208.
New Bedford, Pierce v., 204.
New Bedford, Wilson v., 211.
New Bedford, etc. R. Co. v. Old Colony R. Co., 146.
New Brunswick, Parker v., 173.
New Brunswick Ry. Co. v. Conybeare, 162.
New Decatur v. Berry, 214.
New Haven, Barritt v., 203.
New Haven, Boucher v., 205.
New Haven, Cemetery Association v., 183.
New Haven, Heurson v., 213.
New Haven, Hewison v., 204.
New Haven, Jewett v., 219.

New Haven, Jones v., 220.
New Haven, Mead v., 222.
New Haven E. L. Co., Edison, etc. Co. v., 144.
New Jersey, Williams v., 180.
New Jersey Mfg. Co., Leggett v., 8, 13.
New Jersey, etc. R. Co., Brokaw v., 162, 164.
New Jersey, etc. R. Co. v. Strait, 146.
New London v. Brainerd, 170, 175.
New Orleans, Bonner v., 135.
New Orleans, Crescent City Ins. Co. v., 219.
New Orleans, Fox v., 190.
New Orleans, Inhabitants v., 177.
New Orleans, Louisiana v., 204, 233.
New Orleans, McKnight v., 217.
New Orleans v. Phillipi, 212.
New Orleans, Seibrecht v., 50, 188, 190.
New Orleans v. Southern Bank, 194.
New Orleans, United States v., 179.
New Orleans v. Water Co., 180.
New Orleans Bank, Fortier v., 53.
New Orleans, etc. Co. v. Delamon, 141.
New Orleans, etc. Co. v. Dunn, 177.
New Orleans, etc. Co. v. Dry Docks Co., 122.
New Orleans G. L. Co., Crescent City, etc. Co. v., 216.
New Orleans G. L. Co. v. Louisiana L. Co., 216.
New Orleans, etc. R. Co. v. Harnes, 137.
New Orleans Water Co. v. Rivers, 216.
New Orleans Water Works, Conery v., 177.
New Orleans Water Works, Tammany Water Works v., 216.
New York, Brady v., 189, 190.
New York, Griffin v., 206.
New York, Lynch v., 208, 211.
New York, McGinnity v., 206.
New York, Moore v., 191, 193.

TABLE OF CASES CITED.

References are to sections.

New York, Peterson v., 77.
New York, Reinhard v., 172.
New York, Wiggins v., 177.
New York, etc. Canal Co. v. Fulton Bank, 148.
New York Inst. v. Howe, 95.
New York, etc. Ins. Co. v. Ely, 12.
New York, etc. Ins. Co. v. Sturges, 23.
New York, etc. R. Co., Boston, etc. R. Co. v., 137.
New York, etc. R. Co., Bradley v., 8.
New York, etc. R. Co., Buffet v., 13.
New York, etc. R. Co., City of Ohio v., 124.
New York, etc. R. Co., Duncomb v., 105.
New York, etc. R. Co., Fisher v., 146.
New York, etc. R. Co., Hood v., 13, 29, 53.
New York, etc. R. Co. v. Ketchum, 79.
New York, etc. R. Co. v. Kip, 86.
New York, etc. R. Co., Marsh v., 146.
New York, etc. R. Co., Mead v., 143.
New York, etc. R. Co., Mechanics' Bank v., 109.
New York, etc. R. Co., Milbank v., 121.
New York, etc. R. Co., Milnor v., 167.
New York, etc. R. Co., Minor v., 9.
New York, etc. R. Co. v. Nickals, 124.
New York, etc. R. Co. v. Schuyler, 109.
New York, etc. R. Co. v. Winans, 9.
New South Wales Coal Co., Payne v., 79.
Newark, State v., 81.
Newark, Stoudinger v., 207.
Newburg, Emerson v., 194.
Newburg, Smith v., 170, 194.
Newburg Coal Co., Miller v., 168.
Newburg Petroleum Co. v. Weare, 166.
Newcastle R. Co., Charleston v., 143.

Newcastle R. Co., Hamilton v., 96, 100, 128.
Newcastle R. Co. v. Simpson, 119.
Newchester, Bristol v., 186.
Newell v. Smith, 129.
Newmarket, Gage v., 70.
Newport Bridge Co. v. Foote, 203.
Newport Co., Widrig v., 158.
Newport Mfg. Co., Commercial Bank v., 96, 100.
Niagara County Bank v. Baker, 103.
Niantic Savings Bank v. Douglas, 146.
Nichol v. Insurance Co., 160.
Nichol v. Mayor, 170.
Nichols, Ernest v., 120.
Nickals, N. Y. etc. R. Co., v. 124.
Nickerson v. Hydraulic Co., 219.
Niles, Bank of Michigan v., 81, 857.
Niles Water Works v. Niles, 189, 196.
Nims v. Mount Hermon School, 162.
Nisbet, Hill v., 121.
Nist, Canton v. 172.
Noble, Fay v., 96. 100.
Norfolk R. Co., Hussey v., 162.
Norfolk R. Co., Norwich v., 52, 55, 56, 70.
Norfolk R. Co. v. Shaw, 141.
Normand v. Otoe Co., 198.
Norristown, Miller v., 203.
Norristown v. Thayer, 204. 210.
North, Silver Lake Bank v., 166, 167.
North American Coal Co., Talmage v., 47, 52.
North American Min. Co., Ardesco Oil Co. v., 83, 91.
North Carolina Gold Co., Coit v., 108, 115.
North Hempsted v. Hempsted, 187.
North Hudson Co. v. Hoboken, 182.
North River, etc. Co., People v., 137, 148.
North River, etc. Co., Wylde v., 129.
North Side Ry. v. Worthington, 7.

References are to sections.

North Stafford Ry., Earl, etc. v., 70, 79.
North Yarmouth v. Skillings, 186.
Northern Bank v. Johnson, 161.
Northern Bank v. Porter, 226.
Northern Bank v. Trustees, 228.
Northern Cent. R. Co. v. Drew, 146.
Northern Coal M. Co., In re, 120.
Northern Liberties, Carr v., 202, 203.
Northern Liberties, Pray v., 224.
Northern Mo. R. Co., Powell v., 146.
Northern T. Co. v. Chicago, 81.
Northwestern Cement Co., Batelle v., 79.
Northwestern Pack. Co. v. Shaw, 53, 74.
Northwestern Ry., Shrewsbury Ry. v., 55, 70, 129, 137.
Norton v. Bank, 74.
Norton v. City of Nevada, 233.
Norton, Commercial Bank v., 160.
Norton v. Dyersburg, 223, 230.
Norwich v. Norfolk R. Co., 52, 55, 56, 70.
Norwich Gas Co. v. City Gas Co., 216, 218.
Norwich Transp. Co., Converse v., 53.
Noyes v. Mason City, 203.
Noyes v. Railroad Co., 129.
Nugent v. Supervisors, 143, 146.
Nunnemacher, Ohio Ins. Co. v., 9.
Nutt v. Danville Seminary, 7.
Nutting v. Railroad Co., 129.

O.

Oakland v. Carpentier, 215.
Oakland Bank v. Wilcox, 159.
Oakley, Moss v., 100.
Oakwood, Hyde Park v., 183.
Oberlin, Bronson v., 175.
O'Brien, Little v., 74, 75.
O'Brien v. St. Paul, 211.
Occum Co. v. Sprague Mfg. Co., 9, 137.
Ocean Dry Dock Co., New Orleans Co. v., 122.
Ocoee Bank, Moses v., 109.

O'Connor v. Pittsburg, 203.
Oconto, Lord v., 170, 173.
O'Donnell, Alexander v., 69.
Og v. Lansing, 219.
Ogden v. Daviess County, 229.
Ogdensburg, Urquhart v., 202.
Ogdensburg, etc. R. Co. v. Vermont, etc. R. Co., 9.
Ogilvie v. Knox Ins. Co., 108.
Ogle, Roberts v., 212.
Ohio, Shields v., 143, 144.
Ohio Candle Co., Emery v., 148.
Ohio Iron Works v. Moundeville, 225.
Ohio, etc. Ins. Co. v. Nunnemacher, 9.
Ohio, etc. Ins. Co. v. Trust Co., 74.
Ohio, etc. R. Co., Dimpfell v., 78.
Ohio, etc. R. Co. v. Ind. etc. R. Co., 137.
Ohio, etc. R. Co. v. Middleton, 77.
Ohio, etc. R. Co. v. Wheeler, 145.
Oil Co., Buffalo Oil Co. v., 162.
Oil Co. v. Railway Co., 81.
Oil Creek R. Co., Kersey Oil Co. v., 139.
Oil Creek R. Co., Root v., 146.
Olcott, Sutherland v., 109, 113.
Olcott v. Tioga R. Co., 100.
Old Colony R. Co., Davis v., 9, 36, 47, 53.
Old Colony R. Co., New Bedford, etc. Co., 146.
Oliver v. Krightly, 198.
Olney v. Chadsey, 159.
Omaha, Hurford v., 170.
Omaha R. Co., Clark v., 137.
Omaha Smelting Co., Abbott v., 3.
O'Meara v. Mayor, 219.
Oneida Bank v. Ontario Bank, 74, 119.
Onstott v. People, 238.
Ontario Bank, Barnes v., 96, 98, 160, 161.
Ontario Bank, Oneida Bank v., 74, 119.
Ontario, etc. R. Co., Rome, etc. R. Co. v., 146.
Ooregum G. Min. Co. v. Roper, 117.
Opinions of Judges, 181.
Oregon Ry. v. Oregonian Ry., 3, 8, 9, 10, 12, 53, 69, 72, 78, 137, 138.

TABLE OF CASES CITED.

References are to sections.

Orleans v. Pratt, 228.
Orleans Navigation Co., Louisiana State Bank v., 47.
Orphans' Asylum, McCartee v., 81, 82, 95.
Orr v. Lacey, 70.
Orton, Southern Pac. Co. v., 81.
Osawkie Township, State v., 225.
Osborne, Toll Bridge Co. v., 9.
Osborne v. Tunis, 90.
Osgood v. Layten, 108.
Oshkosh, Hayes v., 219.
Ossepee Mfg. Co. v. Canney, 74, 75, 81.
Oswego, Marcy v., 53.
Otoe County, Deyo v., 237.
Otoe County, Normand v., 198.
Ottawa v. Carey, 170, 225.
Ottawa, Derinzy v., 203.
Ottawa, Hackett v., 227, 229.
Ottawa, Mather v., 170, 225.
Ottawa R. Co. v. Murray, 77.
Ouachita Co. v. Wolcott, 230.
Overend & Gurney Co. v. Gibbs, 154, 156.
Overseers v. Overseers, 186.
Owen County, Browning v., 222.
Owens, Bank of U. S. v., 69.
Owens v. Milwaukee, 203.
Oxford Ins. Co. v. Spradley, 96, 100.
Oxford, etc. R. Co., Rogers v., 53.
Oxford Township, McClure v., 229, 235.

P.

Pacific Nat. Bank, Eaton v., 127.
Pacific Postal Tel. Co. v. Western Union, etc., 53.
Pacific R. Co. v. Seeley, 85.
Packer v. Railway Co., 8, 9.
Packet Co., Abbott v., 70.
Paddock, Aurora Ag'l Soc. v., 77, 84.
Page v. Allen, 198.
Page, Bryan v., 191, 194.
Page v. Heinberg, 81.
Page v. St. Louis, 177.
Paine v. Lake Erie, etc. Co., 144, 146.

Paine v. Spratley, 170.
Palmer, Durant v., 206.
Palmer, Leavitt v., 74.
Palmer, Pritts v., 81.
Palmer, Railroad Co. v., 144.
Pangborn v. Westlake, 69.
Paquet, Hedges v., 156.
Paret v. Bayonne, 195.
Paris, Hall v., 53, 74.
Paris Rink Co., Spiller v., 79.
Parish, Cumberland, etc. Co. v., 153.
Parish v. Wheeler, 129.
Parker v. Bernal, 122.
Parker v. Donnally, 159.
Parker, Ind. Car Co. v., 210.
Parker v. New Brunswick, 173.
Parker, Wetmore v., 93.
Parker, Williams v., 116.
Parkersburg v. Brown, 74, 181, 224.
Parkersburg Gas Co. v. Parkersburg, etc. Co., 170, 199, 216.
Parks, People v., 181.
Parnably, Canal Co. v., 220.
Parr v. Greenbush, 190.
Parsons v. Monmouth, 194.
Partridge v. Badger, 83, 96, 100.
Passaic, State v., 170.
Patapsco Guano Co., Peebles v., 162.
Patchett, Gregory v., 70.
Patchin Bank, Bank of Gennessee v., 9.
Paterson, Bank of Columbia v., 76, 77, 188.
Paterson, Boom Co. v., 86, 183.
Paterson v. Bowers, 198.
Paterson, King v., 124, 126.
Paterson, Kip v., 176.
Paterson v. Mayor, 185, 194.
Paterson, Rye v., 212.
Paterson, State v., 173, 235.
Patrons' Merc. Ass'n, Humphrey v., 77, 168.
Paul, Corser v., 161.
Paul v. Kenosha, 74, 191.
Payne v. N. S. W. Coal Co., 79.
Payson v. Stoever, 110.
Payson, Turnbull v., 127.
Peacock, Talladega Ins. Co. v., 100.
Pearce v. Madison, etc. R. Co., 9, 30, 52, 53, 70, 143, 148.

TABLE OF CASES CITED.   lv

References are to sections.

Pearson v. Concord, etc. R. Co., 122.
Peaslee. Trustees v., 15, 93.
Peay, Whitney v., 74.
Peck, Carter v., 129.
Peck v. Chicago, etc. R. Co., 145.
Peck v. Lockwood, 212.
Pedrick v. Bailey, 176.
Peebles v. Patapsco Guano Co., 162.
Peet v. Railway Co., 129.
Pell, Talmage v., 121.
Pelton, Coggeshell v., 95.
Pendleton v. Amy, 227.
Pendleton, Durango v., 201.
Peninsular Bank v. Hanmer, 77.
Peninsular S. Co., Bennett v., 129.
Penn v. Bornman, 69.
Pennington, Town of Durango v., 189.
Pennock v. Coe, 8.
Pennsylvania v. Erie R. Co., 124.
Pennsylvania Coal Co., Del. Canal Co. v., 77.
Pennsylvania Match Co. v. Hapgood, 79.
Pennsylvania R. Co. v. Canal Commissioners, 8, 12.
Pennsylvania R. Co. v. St. Louis. etc. R. Co., 9, 53, 72, 74, 136, 137, 138.
Pennsylvania R. Co., Central R. Co. v., 121.
Pennsylvania R. Co. v. Perry, 129.
Penobscot Boom Co. v. Lamson, 3.
Pensacola. Broughton v., 233.
Pensacola Tel. Co. v. Western Union Co., 166.
People v. Albany, 212.
People v. Bank, 170.
People v. Brighton, 86.
People v. Chicago Gas Trust Co., 55, 121, 122, 137, 148.
People v. Chicago, etc. R. Co., 129.
People v. Commissioners, 189.
People v. Coon, 195.
People v. County, 230.
People, Darst v., 212.
People, Dingley v., 215.
People, English v., 181.
People, Flagg v., 201.
People, Greeley v., 185.
People v. Harris, 185.

People, Hensley v., 225.
People, Horn v., 171.
People, Law v., 196, 197, 231.
People v. May, 190.
People v. Mayor, 225.
People v. McCreery, 181.
People v. McCune, 238.
People v. Murray. 233.
People v. Onstott, 238.
People v. Parks, 181.
People v. Ragg, 225.
People v. San Francisco, 195, 201.
People v. Selfridge, 3.
People v. Smith, 183.
People v. Special Sessions, 171.
People, St. Louis Bridge Co. v., 207.
People v. Sugar Refining Co., 137, 148.
People v. Swift, 194.
People v. Troop, 176.
People v. Trustees, 186.
People, Turnpike Co. v., 9.
People v. Utica Ins. Co., 9, 12, 22.
People v. Weber, 170.
People's Association, Hagie v., 120.
People's Railroad v. Memphis, etc. R. R. Co., 215.
Peoria, Murphy v., 202.
Peoria, etc. R. Co. v. Coal Valley Co., 9.
Peoria, etc. R. Co. v. Thompson, 131.
Perin v. Carey, 93, 185.
Perkins, City Bank v., 161.
Perkins v. Railroad Co., 129.
Perkins, South Ottawa v., 224.
Perkinson v. St. Louis, 190.
Perley v. Georgetown, 222.
Perrine v. Ches. & Del. Ry., 8, 12, 28, 81.
Perry, Penn. R. Co. v., 129.
Perry v. Waterproof Co., 77.
Perry's Case, 158.
Peru. Wilkinson v., 235.
Peters v. Lincoln, etc. R. Co., 137.
Peters v. Lynchburg, 170.
Petersborough R. Co. v. Nassau Co., 50.
Petersburg v. Metzker, 47, 170.
Peterson, Clapp v., 120.
Peterson v. New York, 77.

TABLE OF CASES CITED.

References are to sections.

Phelps v. Farmers' Bank, 124.
Phelps, Kennedy v., 212.
Phelps v. Mankato, 200.
Philadelphia, Bryson v., 215.
Philadelphia, Elliott v., 219.
Philadelphia, Hague v., 194.
Philadelphia, Hammett v., 225.
Philadelphia, Johnson v., 215.
Philadelphia, Michener v., 207.
Philadelphia, Reilly v., 194.
Philadelphia v. Ridge Ave. etc. Co., 146.
Philadelphia, Savings Fund v., 215.
Philadelphia, Sharpless v., 181.
Philadelphia, Sower v., 171.
Philadelphia. etc. R. Co. v. Maryland, 146, 148.
Philadelphia, etc. R. Co. v. Quigley, 162.
Philadelphia, etc. R. Co., Taylor v., 98.
Phillipi, New Orleans v., 212.
Phillips v. Allen, 212.
Phillips, Clinton v., 176.
Phillips, Drake v., 198.
Phillips v. Railroad Co., 129.
Phillips Academy v. King, 92.
Phœnix Co., In re, 74.
Phœnix Glass Co., Beers v., 96.
Picard v. Pullman Car Co., 9.
Pickering v. Stephenson, 53, 154.
Piedmont Co., Curtis v., 74.
Pierce v. Crampton, 167.
Pierce v. Emery, 83, 91, 100.
Pierce v. New Bedford, 204.
Pieri v. Shieldsboro, 212.
Pierson, First Nat. Bank v., 103.
Pike Co., Foote v., 227.
Pilgrim Society, Haywood v., 77.
Pilkin, Belding v., 69.
Pimental v. San Francisco, 191.
Pine Grove Township v. Talcott, 238.
Pipes, St. Louis, etc. R. Co. v., 129.
Pinto Co. Case, 137.
Pitney, Lucas v., 96, 100.
Pittsburg, Commonwealth v., 100.
Pittsburg v. Green, 220.
Pittsburg, Mazet v., 180.
Pittsburg, O'Connor v., 203.
Pittsburg, etc. Co., Mercer v., 183.

Pittsburg. etc. R. Co. v. Keokuk, etc. Co., 9, 47, 52, 53, 54, 69, 74, 76.
Pittsburg, etc. R. Co., Shawmut's Bank v., 129.
Pittsford, Taft v., 9, 70, 201.
Pitzman v. Freeberg, 237.
Placerville, Douglas v., 198.
Plainfield, Merrill v., 198.
Plank Road Co., City Council v., 9, 70.
Plank Road Co., Jackson's Adm'rs v., 124.
Planters' Bank v. Sharp, 77.
Planters' Bank v. Whittle, 91.
Planters' Press, Greenville Compress v., 72, 74, 143.
Platt, Central G. Min. Co. v., 83.
Platt v. Union Pac. R. Co., 105.
Plattsburg, etc. R. Co., Hoyle v., 153.
Plattsmouth, Read v., 224.
Plume Co., Union Hardware Co. v., 74.
Plymouth B. Co. v. Berry, 76.
Poitiaux. The Banks v., 81, 83.
Police Jury v. Britton, 100, 223, 237.
Pollard v. Maddox, 141.
Pollock v. Louisville, 219.
Pomeroy v. Bank, 144.
Pontiac v. Carter, 203.
Poole, Bard v., 166, 167.
Poole v. West Point, etc. Ass'n, 110.
Poor. European, etc. R. Co. v., 153.
Pope v. Capitol Bank, 103.
Port Huron, Ashley v., 211.
Port Huron, Thomas v., 74.
Portage, James v., 200.
Porter, Meyer v., 235.
Porter, Northern Bank v., 226.
Portland, Coulson v., 231.
Portland, Franklin Wharf Co. v., 208, 213.
Portland, Merrill v., 204.
Portland v. Richardson, 206.
Portland L. & M. Co. v. East Portland, 201.
Portland, etc. R. Co. v. Hartford, 235.

TABLE OF CASES CITED. lvii

References are to sections.

Post, County of Randolph v., 227.
Post, Kendall Co. v., 190.
Potter v. Bank, 100.
Potter, Chaffee Co. v., 53.
Potter v. Commissioners, 228.
Poughkeepsie, Dickinson v., 191.
Powder River, etc. Co. v. Lamb, 74, 75.
Powell, Columbus, etc. R. Co. v., 146.
Powell v. Northern Mo. R. Co., 146.
Powers v. Council Bluffs, 220.
Powers, Hodgson v., 53.
Poyer v. Des Plaines, 178.
Pratt, Bott v., 172.
Pratt, Orleans v., 228.
Pratt v. Pratt, 53.
Pratt v. Railroad Co., 129.
Pratt v. Short, 74.
Pratt v. Topeka Bank, 161.
Presbyterian Church v. Mayor, etc., 215.
Prescott, Buckley v., 205.
Preston, Gordon v., 84.
Preston v. Railroad Co., 77.
Price v. Quincy, 196.
Price v. St. Louis Ins. Co., 137.
Priest v. Hat Co., 168.
Pritts v. Palmer, 81.
Proctor, Rutland, etc. R. Co. v., 129.
Proprietors, etc. v. Gordon, 77.
Proprietors, etc., Lowell v., 213.
Proprietors, etc., Royce v., 81.
Proprietors, etc., Woodbridge v., 77.
Prout v. Inhabitants, etc., 195.
Providence, Simmons v., 203.
Providence Bank v. Billings, 8.
Providence Ins. Co., Head v., 21, 28, 37, 47, 50, 70, 170.
Pullman v. Upton, 112.
Pullman Co., Heinrich v., 163.
Pullman Car Co., Central Trans. Co. v., 9, 10, 12, 37, 52, 53, 54, 55, 68, 70, 72, 74, 78, 137, 138.
Pullman Southern Car Co., Pickard v., 9.
Purdue University, Marks v., 225.
Putnam, Smith v., 155.
Pyle Works, In re, 125.

Q.

Quebrada Ry., In re, 114.
Quicksilver Min. Co., Kent v., 96. 106, 124, 127.
Quigley, Dayton v., 176.
Quigley, Philadelphia, etc. R. Co. v., 162, 222.
Quin v. City of Baltimore, 201.
Quincy v. Jones, 203.
Quincy, Price v., 196.
Quincy Bridge Co. v. Adams County, 145.

R.

Rabb, Trenton, etc. Co. v., 203.
Rade v. Dunlap, 137.
Racine, Teegarden v., 177.
Racine R. Co. v. Farmers' L. & T. Co., 144, 145.
Radcliff's Ex'rs v. Mayor, 208.
Radecke, Baltimore v., 176, 178, 212.
Rae v. Mayor, 188.
Ragg, People v., 225.
Railroad Association, Crawford v., 129.
Railroad Commissioners, Railroad Co. v., 144.
Railroad Co., Allison v., 235.
Railroad Co. v. Berry, 144.
Railroad Co., Bound v., 235.
Railroad Co., Brainerd v., 135.
Railroad Co., Bridgeport v., 170, 177, 201.
Railroad Co., Brintnall v., 129.
Railroad Co., Burroughs v., 129.
Railroad Co., Darling v., 129.
Railroad Co., Davis v., 136, 137.
Railroad Co., Fogg v., 162.
Railroad Co. v. Georgia, 141, 143, 144.
Railroad Co., Gifford v., 198.
Railroad Co., Hill Mfg. Co. v., 129.
Railroad Co., Hood v., 129, 164.
Railroad Co. v. Howard, 9.
Railroad Co., Ind. Roll. M. Co. v., 159.
Railroad Co., Irish v., 129.
Railroad Co., Krulevitz v., 162.
Railroad Co., Kyle v., 129.

TABLE OF CASES CITED.

References are to sections.

Railroad Co., Lock Co. v., 129.
Railroad Co. v. Lockwood, 9.
Railroad Co. v. Manufacturing Co., 129.
Railroad Co. v. Mayor, 215.
Railroad Co., McMillan v., 129, 137.
Railroad Co., Mohawk Bridge Co. v., 216.
Railroad Co., Mulligan v., 129.
Railroad Co., Munson v., 79.
Railroad Co., National Docks v., 168.
Railroad Co., Noyes v., 129.
Railroad Co., Nutting v., 129.
Railroad Co., Oil Co. v., 81.
Railroad Co. v. Palmes, 144.
Railroad Co., Peet v., 129.
Railroad Co., Perkins v., 129.
Railroad Co., Phillips v., 129.
Railroad Co., Pratt v., 129.
Railroad Co., Preston v., 177.
Railroad Co. v. Quigley, 222.
Railroad Co. v. Railway Co., 199.
Railroad Co., Ranger v., 162.
Railroad Co., Richards v., 84, 100.
Railroad Co., Ryan v., 156.
Railroad Co., Salem v., 212.
Railroad Co., State v., 144.
Railroad Co., State Board v., 191.
Railroad Co., Stevens v., 193.
Railroad Co., Tench v., 162.
Railroad Co., Thomas v., 35, 47, 52, 53, 55, 69, 70, 71, 72, 78, 119, 128, 137.
Railroad Co., Titus v., 159.
Railroad Co., Transportation Co. v., 129.
Railroad Co., Tucker Canal Co. v., 216.
Railroad Co. v. Union R. Co., 64.
Railroad Co. v. Vance, 9.
Railroad Co., Walker v., 162.
Railroad Co., West Guillimbury v., 198.
Railroad Co., Whitfield v., 162.
Railroad Co., Whitney v., 224.
Railroad Co., Woodward v., 129.
Railroad Co., Wright v., 172.
Railway Co. v. Allerton, 109, 110.
Railway Co., Coleman v., 136.
Railway Co., Commissioners v., 96.
Railway Co., Great Northern R. Co. v., 137.

Railway Co. v. McCarthey, 62, 64, 68.
Railway Co., Railroad Co. v., 199.
Railway Co. v. Redmond, 7.
Raleigh, Tucker v., 96.
Ramsay County, Goodwin v., 230.
Ramsey v. Insurance Co., 168.
Randall, Toppenden v., 69.
Randall v. Van Vechten, 77, 158.
Randolph, Bigelow v., 219.
Randolph v. Larned, 141.
Randolph County v. Post, 227.
Ranger v. Railroad Co., 162.
Rapho v. Moore, 206, 210.
Rapid City, McGuire v., 201.
Rattle, Burt v., 84.
Ray v. Ind. Ins. Co., 101.
Ray v. Manchester, 204.
Ray, Mayor v., 74, 119, 230, 237.
Read v. Plattsmouth, 225.
Redd v Henry County, 235.
Reddish, Cottage Co. v., 100.
Redmond, Railway Co. v., 7.
Redmond, South Wales R. Co. v., 128, 130.
Reed, Bank of Pennsylvania v., 161.
Reed, Emmett v., 77.
Reed v. Hoyt, 91.
Reed, Laing v., 98.
Reed, McMasters v., 47, 100.
Reed v. Mobile Bank, 135.
Reed v. Richmond, 3.
Reed v. Savings Bank, 162.
Reese v. Bank, 124.
Reeves v. Wood Co., 86.
Regents Canal Co., Ware v., 53.
Reichwold v. Commercial Hotel, 83, 91.
Reilly v. Philadelphia, 194.
Re International Ins. Co., 96.
Reinhard v. Mayor, 204.
Reinhard v. New York, 172.
Relfe, Alexander v., 163.
Rensselaer & Saratoga R. Co. v. Davis, 8.
Republic Ins. Co. v. Swigert, 120.
Requa v. Rochester, 204, 206, 220.
Rex v. Amery, 3.
Reynolds v. Commissioners, 83.
Reynolds, Mayor, etc. v., 190.
Reynolds v. Shreveport, 203.
Reynolds v. Stark Co., 81.

References are to sections.

Reynolds Eng. Co., Merrick v., 51, 168.
Rhodes v. Cleveland, 211.
Rice, Exchange Bank v., 219.
Rich v. Erral, 74, 75.
Rich v. Southern Pac. Co. 135.
Rich v. State Nat. Bank, 77.
Richards v. Clarksburg, 170.
Richards v. Merrimack R. Co., 84, 100, 141.
Richards v. Supervisors of Lyon Co., 196.
Richards v. Warren Co., 190.
Richardson v. Buhl, 148.
Richardson, Portland v., 206.
Richardson v. Sibley, 9, 53, 137.
Richardson Co. v. Grant, 191.
Riche, Ashbury R. Co. v., 9, 41, 42, 43, 44, 45, 52, 53, 72, 78, 137.
Richmond, Jones v., 188.
Richmond v. McGirr, 177.
Richmond, Reed v., 3.
Richmond, Thomas v., 73, 138, 172, 190.
Richmond, Wade v., 198.
Richmond Factory Co. v. Alexander, 3.
Richmond, etc. Co., Gordon's Ex'rs v., 119.
Richmond, etc. R. Co. v. Louisiana, etc. R. Co., 8.
Richmond, etc. R. Co. v. Snead, 100.
Ridge Avenue, etc. R. Co. v. Philadelphia, 146.
Ridgway v. Bank, 96, 100.
Ridley v. Plymouth Baking Co., 77.
Ringas v. Biscoe, 91.
Risdon, Menser v., 173.
Ritchie, Fraser v., 120.
Ritter, Nauvoo v., 227.
Rivanna Nav. Co. v. Dawson, 81, 95.
River Dee, etc. Co., Baroness Wenlock v., 44.
Rivers, New Orleans Water Co. v., 216.
Riverside District, Nesbit v., 228.
Robbins v. Chicago, 206, 220.
Robbins, Cleveland R. Co. v., 126.
Roberts v. Deming Co., 74.
Roberts v. Ogle, 212.

Roberts v. Van Buskirk, 129.
Robertson v. Bullions, 92.
Robertson v. Rockford, 144.
Robeson, Ewing v., 51.
Robie v. Sedgwick, 81.
Robinson v. Beale, 120.
Robinson v. Bland, 75.
Robinson, Booth v., 96, 98, 122.
Robinson, Comm. v., 176.
Robinson, Concord v., 223, 228, 230, 237.
Robinson, Ewing v., 168.
Robinson v. Smith, 156, 158.
Robinson v. St. Louis, 188.
Rochester, Requa v., 204, 206, 220.
Rochester, Smith v., 219, 222.
Rochester Ins. Co. v. Martin, 9.
Rochester Sav. Bank v. Averhill, 9.
Rock River Bank v. Sherwood, 9.
Rockford, Robertson v., 144.
Rockford, etc. Co., Harding v., 223.
Rockford R. R. Co. v. Sage, 79.
Rockhold v. Canton Masonic Society, 7.
Rockwell v. Elkhorn Bank, 96, 100, 134.
Rockwell, Hartridge v., 120.
Rocky Mountain National Bank, Union G. M. Co. v., 77.
Roddy v. Finnegan, 172.
Rogers v. Burlington, 225.
Rogers, Carr v., 61.
Rogers, Covert v., 91.
Rogers, East Tenn. R. Co. v., 129.
Rogers, Konrad v., 185.
Rogers, McCurdy v., 190.
Rogers v. Oxford, etc. R. Co., 53.
Rogers, St. Joseph Township v., 228, 238.
Rogers, Tapsham v., 194.
Rogers Locomotive Works v. Southern R. Ass'n, 136.
Rome v. Cabot, 188, 217.
Rome, Mitchell v., 203.
Rome, etc. R. Co. v. Ontario, etc. Co., 146.
Roome, Adriance v., 52.
Root v. Goddard, 70.
Root v. Great Western R. Co., 129.
Root v. Oil Creek, etc. Co., 146.
Roper, Ooregum M. Co. v., 117.

TABLE OF CASES CITED.

References are to sections.

Ropes, Salem Mill-dam Co. v., 109, 113.
Rosenthal, Cincinnati Co. v., 71.
Ross v. Clinton, 211.
Rossie L. M. Co., Moss v., 77.
Rouede v. Jersey City, 227.
Rouse, Glasgow v., 181.
Routerberg, Banking Co. v., 99.
Rowell v. Williams, 220.
Royal Bank v. Turquand, 160.
Royce, Proprietors Claremont Bridge v., 81.
Roylston v. Roylston, etc. Co., 188.
Roylston Market v. Boston Association, 170.
Ruckman, Davenport v., 220.
Rudolph, Merchants' Bank v., 161.
Rufford, Beman v., 137.
Ruggles v. Collier, 9.
Runnels, Harris v., 69.
Runyan v. Lessee, etc., 81.
Rush v. Steamboat Co., 51, 168.
Rushout, Great Western R. Co. v., 53.
Rusk v. Walsh, 69.
Russell v. De Grand, 71.
Russell, Kirkham v., 170, 176.
Russell v. Mayor, 220.
Russell, St. Louis v., 186.
Russell v. Tapping, 81, 85.
Rutland, etc. R. Co., Chaffee v., 124.
Rutland, etc. R. Co. v. Proctor, 129.
Rutland, etc. R. Co., Stevens v., 9, 129.
Rutland, etc. R. Co. v. Thrall, 118.
Ryan v. Dunlap, 161.
Ryan v. Railroad Co., 156.
Rye v. Paterson, 212.

S.

S. & F. Ry. Co., Whiting v., 224.
Sacchi, Aspinwall v., 106.
Safford v. Wycoff, 100.
Safety Dep. L. Co. v. Smith, 79.
Sage v. Lake Shore, etc. R. Co., 145.
Sage, Rockford R. Co. v., 79.
Sage, Welch v., 135.

Saginaw, Gas Light Co. v., 199, 216.
Sailor, Savings Association v., 161.
Salem v. Railroad Co., 212.
Salem Mill-dam Co. v. Ropes, 109, 113.
Salem Mills, First Nat. Bank v., 120.
Salem Nat. Bank v. Almy, 51, 168.
Salisbury Mfg. Co., Treadwell v., 83, 133.
Salt Lake City v. Hollister, 9, 53, 74, 163, 222, 233.
San Antonio, Bolton v., 235.
San Antonio v. Mehaffey, 62, 63, 68, 227.
Sanford Tool Co. v. Howe, Brown & Co., 84.
San Francisco, Argenti v., 188, 190, 191, 192.
San Francisco, De Witt v., 185.
San Francisco, Gas Co. v., 171, 191.
San Francisco, Holland v., 9, 14.
San Francisco, Howard v., 219.
San Francisco, McCracken v., 170, 191, 194.
San Francisco, People v., 195, 201.
San Francisco, Pimental v., 191.
San Francisco, Water Works v., 218.
San Francisco, Wheeler v., 129.
San Francisco, Zottman v., 201.
San Francisco Dock Co., Vandell v., 9.
San Francisco R. Co., Harris v., 126.
Sangamon Co. v. Springfield, 191.
Sanger v. Upton, 107, 112.
Sankey Brook Coal Co., In re, 125.
Santa Ana Township, Anderson v., 238.
Santa Clara Female Academy v. Sullivan, 166.
Santwood v. St. John, 129.
Saratoga, etc. R. Co., Beekman v., 86.
Saratoga, etc. R. Co., Weed v., 129.
Sargent v. Webster, 83, 91.
Satterlee, Chambers v., 203.
Satterthwaite v. Beaufort Co., 177.

TABLE OF CASES CITED. lxi

References are to sections.

Saulsbury v. Ithica, 205.
Sault Ste. Marie R. Co. v. Van Duzen, 194.
Savage v. Ball, 100.
Savanna v. Speers, 208.
Savanna R. Co., Hazelhurst v., 52, 121.
Savanna R. Co. v. Lancaster, 96.
Savings Association v. Sailor, 161.
Savings Association v. Topeka, 237.
Savings Bank v. Bates, 91.
Savings Bank v. Reed, 162.
Savings Fund v. Philadelphia, 215.
Sawmill Association, Lovett v., 89.
Sawyer v. Coose, 220.
Sawyer v. Hoag, 108.
Schammel, Fanning v., 238.
Schank v. Mayor, 177.
Schenck, Supervisors v., 227.
Schenley v. Commissioners, 173.
Schnell v. Chicago, 192.
School District, Clark v., 100.
School District, Hewitt v., 223.
School District, Keyser v., 77.
School District v. Lombard, 230.
School District, Montague v., 100.
School District, Williams v., 225.
School District, Wilson v., 194.
Schrauber, Treadway v., 170, 192.
Schultz v. Milwaukee, 204.
Schumaker, Baltimore, etc. R. Co. v., 129.
Schuyler, New York, etc. R. Co. v., 109.
Schuylkill Bank, Bank of Kentucky v., 77, 160.
Schwingle, Erie v., 220.
Scott, Indianapolis v., 210.
Scott v. Mayor, 220.
Scott, Utica Ins. Co. v., 74, 75.
Scoville v. Thayer, 109, 110.
Scranton, Torrey v., 203.
Screw Co., Hodges v., 83, 122, 154, 156.
Scroggs, Keokuk v., 170.
Scudder v. Trenton, etc. Co., 183.
Scully, Fowler v., 69.
Sea Foam Ins. Co., In re, 74.
Second Ave. R. Co., Mayor v., 182.
Sedalia, Hellen v., 219.
Sedgwick, Robie v., 81.
Seeger v. Mueller, 192.

Seele v. Deering, 213.
Seeley, Pacific R. Co. v., 85.
Seibrecht v. New Orleans, 50.
Seignouret v. Home Ins. Co., 113.
Seip, Slayden v., 155.
Selfridge, People v., 3.
Selma v. Mullen, 170.
Selma, etc. R. Co., Blackburne v., 81.
Senney v. East Warren, etc. L. Co., 87.
Sewell v. Cahous, 200.
Sewell v. St. Paul, 222.
Sewell's Case, 110.
Shaffner v. St. Louis, 183.
Shallcross v. Jeffersonville, 175.
Sharon, Terrett v., 198.
Sharon Canal Co. v. Fulton Bank, 143, 148.
Sharp, Milhan v., 215.
Sharpe, Planters' Bank v., 77.
Sharpe v. Teese, 69.
Sharpless v. Mayor, etc., 224.
Sharpless v. Philadelphia, 181.
Shaver v. Bear River M. Co., 77.
Shaw v. Boston, 176.
Shaw v. Crocker, 203.
Shaw v. Norfolk Ry., 141.
Shaw v. Packet Co., 53, 74.
Shawmut's Bank v. Pittsburg, etc. R. Co., 129.
Shawnee, Mason v., 172.
Shawnee Bank, West St. Louis Bank v., 160.
Shawneetown v. Baker, 195.
Shea v. Mabry, 156.
Shea, Southern Exp. Co. v., 129.
Sheffield, Mayor v., 200, 206.
Sheidley v. Lynch, 177.
Sheldon v. Kalamazoo, 162.
Sheldon Hat Co. v. Fickmeyer, 83, 106.
Sheridan v. Colvin, 177.
Sherlock v. Winnetka, 185.
Sherman v. Carr, 170.
Sherman, Farmers', etc. Bank v., 77.
Sherman, State v., 144.
Sherwood v. Alvis, 53, 70.
Sherwood, Rock River Bank v., 9.
Shetucket Co., Stoddard v., 126.
Sheward v. Citizens' Water Co., 218.

TABLE OF CASES CITED.

References are to sections.

Shields v. Ohio, 143, 144.
Shields, St. Louis v., 101.
Shieldsboro, Pieri v., 212.
Shiras v. Ewing, 218.
Shirley, Houston, etc. R. Co. v., 142, 144.
Shockley v. Fisher, 91.
Shore v. Wilson, 94.
Short, Pratt v., 74.
Shotwell v. Mott, 95.
Shreveport, Reynolds v., 203.
Shrewsbury v. Brown, 191.
Shrewsbury, etc. Ry., Johnson v., 71, 137.
Shrewsbury, etc. Ry. v. Northwestern Ry., 55, 70, 128, 137.
Sibley, Exchange Bank v., 157, 158.
Sibley, Richardson v., 9, 53, 137.
Siebrecht v. New Orleans, 188, 190.
Silk Co., Narragansett Bank v., 100.
Silliman, Wiley v., 223.
Silver Lake Bank v. North, 166, 167.
Simmons v. Camden, 203.
Simmons v. Providence, 203.
Simmons v. Troy Iron Works, 53, 70.
Simpson v. Denison, 130.
Simpson, Mallett v., 81.
Simpson, Newcastle Ry. v., 110.
Simpson v. Westminster Co., 137.
Sims, Visalia, etc. Gas Co. v., 137.
Singer v. St. Louis R. Co., 134.
Skillings, North Yarmouth v., 186.
Skinker, Mathews v., 9.
Skinner, East Oakland v., 190, 224, 238.
Skinner v. Hall, 129.
Skinner, White v., 158.
Slaughter, Brooklyn Bridge Co. v., 9.
Slaughter, Gravel Co. v., 50.
Slayden v. Seip, 155.
Slee v. Bloom, 107.
Slidell v. Grandjean, 9.
Small v. Danville, 213.
Small v. Smith, 43.
Smead v. Ind. etc. R. Co., 9, 96.
Smelser v. Turnpike Co., 168.
Smith v. Alexander, etc. Co., 53.

Smith v. Anderson, 153.
Smith v. Bank, 161.
Smith v. Birmingham Gas Co., 162.
Smith v. Bromley, 69.
Smith, Carroll Co. v., 190.
Smith, Central Ry. Co. v., 163.
Smith v. Chesire, 230.
Smith, Childs v., 3.
Smith, Comm. v., 83, 133, 134, 137.
Smith v. Eau Claire, 203.
Smith, Eldridge v., 141.
Smith v. Eureka Flour Mills, 47, 96, 100.
Smith, Exchange Bank v., 103.
Smith v. Goldworthy, 113.
Smith v. Hall Glass Co., 77.
Smith v. Insurance Co., 70.
Smith v. Ives, 131.
Smith v. Los Angeles, etc. R. Co., 146.
Smith v. Low, 96.
Smith v. Manufacturing Co., 156.
Smith v. Mawhood, 55.
Smith v. Morse, 215.
Smith v. Nashua, etc. R. Co., 128.
Smith v. Newburg, 170, 194.
Smith, Newell v., 129.
Smith, People v., 183.
Smith v. Putnam, 155.
Smith, Robinson v., 156, 158.
Smith v. Rochester, 219, 222.
Smith, Safety Dep. Co. v., 79.
Smith, Small v., 43.
Smith v. State, 77.
Smith v. St. Louis Ins. Co., 137.
Smith, Van Co. v., 160.
Smith v. Washington, 201, 203.
Smith, Western, etc. Co. v., 146.
Smith Bridge Co., Fort Worth City R. Co. v., 9.
Smoot v. Mayor, 220.
Smyth v. Bangor, 205.
Snead, Richmond, etc. R. Co. v., 100.
Snell v. Minneapolis, etc. R. Co., 53.
Snyder v. Studebaker, 101.
Society, etc. v. Abbott, 107.
Society, etc. v. Comm., 3.
Solomons v. Laing, 53, 121.
Somerset Co., Cory v., 189.
Somerville v. Dickerman, 170, 195.

TABLE OF CASES CITED. lxiii

References are to sections.

Soper v. Buffalo R. Co., 154.
South Ottawa v. Perkins, 224.
South Carolina Phos. Co., Bradley v., 8.
South, etc. R. Co., Claflin v., 132.
South, etc. R. Co., Gilliam v., 163.
South, etc. R. Co. v. Great Mt. Ry. Co., 55, 70, 137.
South, etc. R. Co., Langstone v., 135.
South, etc. R. Co. v. Redmond, 128, 130.
Southall v. Insurance Co., 143.
Southern Bank, New Orleans v., 194.
Southern Exp. Co. v. Shea, 129.
Southern Life Ins. Co. v. Lanier, 14, 74.
Southern Pac. Co. v. Orton, 81.
Southern Pac. Co., Rice v., 135.
Southern Pac. Co., Tex. Pac. R. Co. v., 131.
Southern R. Ass'n, Locomotive Works v., 136.
Sower v. Philadelphia, 171.
Spaulding, Briggs v., 154, 156, 157, 158.
Spears, Savanna v., 208.
Special Sessions, People v., 171.
Spering's Appeal, 147, 153, 154, 156, 158.
Spiller v. Paris Rink Co., 79.
Spiral Springs Co., Day v., 74.
Spohr v. Farmers' Bank, 12, 168.
Spradley, Oxford Ins. Co. v., 96, 100.
Sprague v. Hartford Ins. Co., 145.
Sprague Mfg. Co., Occum Co. v., 9, 137.
Spratley, Paine v., 170.
Spring Co., Cowell v., 166.
Spring Co. v. Knowlton, 69, 73, 138.
Springfield v. Edwards, 196, 235.
Springfield v. Le Claire, 220.
Springfield, Sangamon County v., 191.
Springfield, Stanton v., 205.
Spring Valley Township, Bissell v., 226.
Spring Valley Water Works v. Bartlett, 235.

Spring Valley Water Works v. San Francisco, 218.
Stace & Worth's Case, 109.
Stack v. Maysville, 177.
Standard Oil Co., State v., 12, 148.
Standifer v. Swann, 88.
Stanton v. Springfield, 205.
Stark v. United States Pottery Co., 77.
Stark Co., Reynolds v., 81.
Starr v. Burlington, 172.
State, Aicardi, v., 8.
State, Atlantic, etc. R. Co. v., 144.
State v. Bailey, 142, 143, 147.
State v. Baltimore, etc. R. Co., 146.
State v. Bank, 83.
State v. Bank of Maryland, 100.
State v. Bell, 173.
State v. Bevers, 190.
State, Board of Education v., 225.
State v. Boston, etc. R. Co., 81.
State v. Brown, 185.
State v. City of Palestine, 235.
State v. Clark, 171, 176, 181.
State v. Cleveland, 172.
State v. Coke Co., 199.
State v. College, 83.
State v. Commissioners, 148, 185.
State v. Fisk, 173.
State v. Freeman, 176.
State v. Gas Co., 215, 216, 219.
State v. Gaslight Co., 218.
State v. Green Co., 143, 146.
State v. Hanser, 173.
State v. Hammonton, 188.
State, Harrison v., 199.
State v. Hoboken, 182.
State v. Jersey City, 173, 174, 176, 235.
State v. Keokuk, etc. R. Co., 144.
State v. Madison, 81, 185.
State, Mahoney v., 3.
State v. Mansfield, 81.
State v. Marion Co., 170.
State v. Martin, 195.
State v. Mayor, 176.
State v. Milwaukee G. L. Co., 216.
State v. Montgomery, 235.
State v. McCann, 225.
State, McCaslin v., 190.
State v. Nebraska Dis. Co., 55.
State v. Newark, 81, 173.

TABLE OF CASES CITED.

References are to sections.

State v. Osawkie Township, 225.
State v. Passaic, 170.
State v. Paterson, 173.
State v. Railroad Co., 144.
State v. Sherman, 144.
State v. Smith, 77.
State v. Standard Oil Co., 12, 148.
State v. Stebbins, 47.
State v. Swearingen, 177.
State v. Trenton, 173.
State v. Tryon, 172.
State v. White, 175.
State v. Williams, 172.
State, Zimmer v., 144.
State Bank v. Fox, 120.
State Bank, Merchants' Bank v., 160, 162.
State Bank v. Wheeler, 161, 162.
State Board, etc. v. Citizens' Ry. Co., 9, 191.
State National Bank, Rich v., 77.
Staten v. Morgan, 141.
Steam Navigation Co. v. Dandridge, 201.
Steamboat Co. v. Brown, 129.
Steamboat Co., Rush v., 51, 168.
Stearns, Chicago v., 205.
Stebbins, State v., 47.
Steck v. Lancaster, 200.
Stecket v. East Saginaw, 201.
Steele v. Boston, 204.
Steffee, Comm. v., 176.
Stein v. Howard, 115.
Stephenson, Pickering v., 53, 154.
Sterling, Church v., 77, 128.
Sterling v. Thomas, 206.
Stevens, Attorney-General v., 168.
Stevens v. Railroad Co., 9, 198.
Stewart v. Brooklyn R. Co., 162.
Stewart, Council Bluffs v., 196.
Stewart, Empire Mfg. Co. v., 167.
Stewart v. Erie, etc. R. Co., 9, 53, 129, 130.
Stewart v. Jones, 141.
Stillwater, Bangor Savings Bank v., 233.
Stimson, Thomaston Bank v., 85.
Stockdale v. Wayland School District, 231.
Stockford v. St. Louis, 203.
Stockton v. Central Ry. Co., 137.
Stockton, etc. R. Co. v. City Council, 181.

Stoddard v. Foundry Co., 124.
Stoddard v. Shetucket Co., 126.
Stoever, Payson v., 110.
Stone v. Hubbardston, 205.
Stoudinger v. Newark, 207.
Stoutmore v. Clark, 101, 168.
Stowe v. Flagg, 3, 12.
Strait, New Jersey, etc. Ry. Co. v., 146.
Straus, Hammond v., 51, 168.
Strauss v. Eagle Ins. Co., 9, 47, 50.
Striplen, Glidden v., 61.
Stuart v. London, etc. R. Co., 77.
Studebaker v. Montgomery, 168.
Studebaker, Snyder v., 1, 118.
Sturge v. Eastern. etc. R. Co., 118.
Sturges v. Bank, 161.
Sturges, Firemen's Ins. Co. v., 23.
Sturtevant v. Alton, 188, 201.
Stutz, Handley v., 107, 109, 110, 112, 117.
Stuyvesant v. Mayor, 215.
Sugar Ref. Co., People v., 137, 148.
Sullivan v. Murphy, 100.
Sullivan v. Santa Clara Academy v., 81, 166.
Sumner v. Marcy, 122.
Sunbury & Erie Ry., Packer v., 8, 9.
Supervisors, Kennicutt v., 228.
Supervisors, Migret v., 238.
Supervisors, Nugent v., 143, 146.
Supervisors v. Schenck, 227.
Supervisors, Wells v., 237.
Supervisors of Lyon County, Richards v., 196.
Susquehanna Bridge Co. v. Insurance Co., 84.
Susquehanna Canal Co. v. Bonham, 141.
Sussex, etc. R. Co. v. Morris, etc. R. Co., 8, 10, 130, 131.
Sutherland v. Olcott, 109, 113.
Sutliff v. Lake Co., 53.
Sutton v. Clark, 203.
Swackhamer, Hackettstown v., 96.
Swann, Standifer v., 88.
Swansea, Hull v., 74.
Swanson, Hopkins v., 172.
Swartout v. Michigan, etc. R. Co., 168.
Swearingen, Scott v., 177.

TABLE OF CASES CITED. lxv

References are to sections.

Sweet v. Wabash, 175.
Swift, People v., 194.
Swigert, Republic Ins. Co. v., 120.
Syracuse, Weston v., 196.
St. Andrews Bay Co. v. Mitchell, 52.
St. Anne, Chicago, etc. R. Co. v., 240.
St. Charles R. Co., Canal, etc. R. Co. v., 52.
St. Clair County Turnpike Co. v. People, 9.
St. Clara Academy v. Sullivan, 81.
St. Francis Academy, Milliard v., 100.
St. John, Bank v., 156.
St. John, East St. Louis v., 86.
St. John, Santwood v., 129.
St. Joseph, Thurston v., 211.
St. Joseph, etc. R. Co., Farmers' L. & T. Co. v., 74, 131.
St. Joseph Township v. Amy, 227.
St. Joseph Township v. Rogers, 228, 238.
St. Louis v. Armstrong, 194.
St. Louis v. Bank, 171.
St. Louis v. Bell Tel. Co., 170.
St. Louis v. Bentz, 212.
St. Louis v. Buffinger, 177.
St. Louis, Chambers v., 81.
St. Louis v. Gurno, 203.
St. Louis Illinois Canal Co. v., 215.
St. Louis, Jay v., 128, 146.
St. Louis v. Kaime, 172.
St. Louis, Leslie v., 86.
St. Louis, Lockwood v., 177.
St. Louis, Page v., 177.
St. Louis, Perkins v., 190.
St. Louis, Robinson v., 188.
St. Louis, Russell v., 186.
St. Louis, Shaffner v., 183.
St. Louis v. Shields, 101.
St. Louis, Stockford v., 203.
St. Louis v. Webber, 9.
St. Louis Bridge Co. v. People, 207.
St. Louis Carriage Co. v. Hilbert, 120.
St. Louis Gas Light Co. v. St. Louis, 168.
St. Louis Ins. Co., Price v., 137.
St. Louis Ins. Co., Smith v., 137.

St. Louis, etc. R. Co. v. Bellville, 192.
St. Louis, etc. R. Co., Eakin v., 137.
St. Louis, etc. R. Co., Penn. etc. R. Co. v., 9, 53, 72, 74, 136, 137, 138.
St. Louis, etc. R. Co. v. Pipes, 129.
St. Louis, etc. R. Co., Singer v., 134.
St. Louis, etc. R. Co. v. Terre Haute, etc. R. Co., 53, 73, 138.
St. Louis Stoneware Co., Lafayette Bank v., 9.
St. Paul, Cleveland v., 206.
St. Paul v. Coulter, 171, 212.
St. Paul, Darling v., 173.
St. Paul, Furnell v., 205.
St. Paul, Hennesy v., 53.
St. Paul, Kaist v., 203.
St. Paul, Miller v., 205.
St. Paul, Nash v., 194.
St. Paul, O'Brien v., 211.
St. Paul, Sewell v., 222.
St. Paul v. Traeger, 170.
St. Paul, etc. Ass'n, Bergman v., 53.
St. Peter's Church, De Ruyter v., 83.
St. Tamany Water Works v. New Orleans Water Works, 216.

T.

Taft v. Pittsford, 9, 70, 201.
Tainter v. Worcester, 219.
Talcott, Pine Grove Township v., 238.
Talldega Ins. Co., McCullough v., 77.
Talldega Ins. Co. v. Peacock, 100.
Tallassee Mfg. Co., Lehman v., 105, 135.
Tallman, Western Bank v., 128.
Talmage v. North American Coal Co., 47, 52.
Talmage v. Pell, 121.
Talman, Mobile, etc. R. Co. v., 96.
Tash v. Adams, 175.
Tate, Indianapolis v., 211.
Taxpayer v. Tenn. etc. R. Co., 237.
Taylor v. Agricultural Association, 96.

E

References are to sections.

Taylor v. Carondelet, 212.
Taylor v. Chichester, etc. R. Co., 52, 55, 56, 70.
Taylor v. Earle, 122.
Taylor v. Export Co., 120.
Taylor v. Formholz, 74, 75.
Taylor v. Phil. etc. R. Co., 98.
Taylor v. Yonkers, 205.
Taylor Mfg. Co., American Pres. Trust v., 69, 148.
Teachout v. Des Moines, etc. R. Co., 53.
Teegarden v. Racine, 177.
Teese, Sharpe v., 69.
Temperance Society, Livingstone v., 120.
Tench v. Railroad Co., 162.
Tennessee v. Whitworth, 148.
Tennessee, etc. R. Co., Taxpayer v., 237.
Tennessee, etc. R. Co., Winston v., 235.
Tenney v. Lumber Co., 88.
Terre Haute v. Lake, 201.
Terre Haute, etc. R. Co., Archer v., 9.
Terre Haute, etc. R. Co., Jones v., 124.
Terre Haute, etc. R. Co., St. Louis, etc. R. Co. v., 53, 73, 138.
Terrett v. Sharon, 198.
Texas & Pac. R. Co. v. Southern Pac. Co., 131.
Thayer v. Boston, 162, 222.
Thayer, Commissioners v., 227.
Thayer, Norristown v., 204, 210.
Thayer, Scoville v., 109, 110.
The Banks v. Poiteaux, 81.
The Commission, Munn v., 96, 100.
The Hartford Bridge Co. v. East Hartford, 187.
The Liberty Bell, 175.
Thomas, County of Scotland v., 146.
Thomas v. Port Huron, 74.
Thomas v. Railroad Co., 35, 47, 52, 55, 69, 70, 71, 72, 78, 119, 128, 137, 138.
Thomas v. Richmond, 73, 138, 172, 190.
Thomas, Sterling v., 205.
Thomaston Bank v. Stimpson, 83.

Thompson v. Abbott, 144, 146, 186.
Thompson, Horton v., 194.
Thompson, Hoyt v., 159.
Thompson v. Lambert, 96.
Thompson v. Lamont, 84.
Thompson v. Lee, 238.
Thompson, Peoria, etc. R. Co. v., 131.
Thompson v. Waters, 9, 81.
Thornton, Hightower v., 106.
Thornton v. Howe, 94.
Thrall, Rutland Ry. v., 118.
Thurston v. St. Joseph, 211.
Tioga R. Co., Olcott v., 100.
Tippecanoe Co. v. Lafayette R. Co., 53, 78.
Tippets v. Walker, 159.
Titcomb, Clark v., 83, 96.
Titus v. Mabee, 131.
Titus v. Railroad Co., 159.
Todd, Dean v., 177.
Todd v. Troy, 210.
Toledo v. Case, 220.
Toledo, Harbeck v., 183.
Toledo Ins. Co., White's Bank v., 9, 47, 100.
Toll Bridge Co. v. Osborn, 9.
Tolleston Club, Alexander v., 81.
Tombigbee v. Kneeland, 165, 166.
Tomlinson v. Branch, 146, 148.
Tone v. Mayor, 220.
Toolan, Lansing v., 202.
Tooley, Athenæum, etc. Co. v., 74.
Topeka, Citizens' Savings, etc. v., 181, 237.
Topeka v. Huntoon, 177.
Topeka, Loan Association v., 179, 181, 224, 225, 238.
Topeka Bank, Pratt v., 161.
Tappenden v. Randall, 69.
Topping, Russell v., 81, 85.
Topsham v. Rogers, 194.
Torrey v. Scranton, 203.
Touche v. Warehousing Co., 79.
Town Council, Albright v., 188.
Town of Depere v. Bellevue, 186.
Town of Durango v. Pendleton, 201.
Town of Durango v. Pennington, 189.
Town of Lake, Drexel v., 207.
Town of Middleport v. Ætna Ins. Co., 240.

TABLE OF CASES CITED. lxvii

References are to sections.

Townsend v. Brown, 8.
Townsend, Logan Co. Bank v., 74.
Tracy v. Guthrie Co., 76.
Traeger, St. Paul v., 170.
Transportation Co., Bank v., 120.
Transportation Co. v. Chicago, 203.
Transportation Co., Farmers' Bank v., 129.
Transportation Co., Railroad Co. v., 129.
Trapshagen v. Jersey City, 207.
Treadway v. Schrauber, 170, 190.
Treadwell v. Salisbury Mfg. Co., 83, 133.
Trenton, State v., 173.
Trenton, etc. Co., Scudder v., 183.
Trevor v. Whitworth, 45, 117, 120.
Trigally v. Memphis, 171.
Trinity Church, Bogardus v., 81.
Tripp, Aldrich v., 222.
Tripp, Inman v., 211.
Troop, People v., 176.
Trott v. Warren, 194.
Trotter, Chicago v., 176.
Troupe's Case, 77.
Troy, Francis v., 170.
Troy, Todd v., 210.
Troy Iron Works, Simmons v., 53, 70.
Troy, etc. R. Co. v. Boston, etc. R. Co., 9.
Troy, etc. R. Co., Buffet v., 13, 128.
Troy, etc. R. Co. v. Kerr, 137.
Trumpler v. Bernerly, 86.
Trust Co., Ohio Ins. Co. v., 74.
Trustees, Congregational Church v., 94.
Trustees v. King, 95.
Trustees, Northern Bank v., 228.
Trustees v. Peaslee, 15, 93.
Trustee, People v., 186.
Trustees, Walsh v., 3.
Tryon, State v., 172.
Tuckahoe Canal Co. v. Railroad Co., 216.
Tucker v. City of Raleigh, 96.
Tucker, Fry v., 128.
Tuckerman v. Brown, 108.
Tugman v. Chicago, 176.
Tullis, Cook v., 77.
Tunis, Osborn v., 90.
Turnbull v. Payson, 127.

Turner, Vrooman v., 219.
Turner, Webster v., 83.
Turnpike Co. v. Illinois, 8.
Turnpike Co., Smelser v., 168.
Turquand v. Marshall, 158.
Turquand, Royal Bank v., 160.
Twiss v. Life Association, 74.
Tyler v. Beacher, 181, 225.
Tyson v. Milwaukee, 203.

U.

Ulery, Greiner v., 101.
Underwood v. Green, 212.
Union Bank v. Elliott, 91.
Union Bank, Irvine v., 76.
Union Bank v. Jacobs, 96, 98, 100.
Union Gold Min. Co. v. Rocky Mountain Nat. Bank, 77.
Union Hardware Co. v. Plume Co., 74.
Union Min. Co. v. Bank, 96.
Union Pac. R. Co. v. Cheyenne, 177.
Union Pac. R. Co., Chicago, etc. R. Co. v., 19, 71.
Union Pac. R. Co., Leo v., 105.
Union Pac. R. Co. v. Lincoln Co. 235.
Union Pac. R. Co., McAlpine v. 146.
Union Pac. R. Co., Platt v., 105.
Union Pac. R. Co., Whipple v. 146.
Union Plate Glass Co., In re, 114.
Union R. Co. v. Railroad Co., 64.
Union Steamboat Co., Green Bay, etc. R. Co. v., 9, 47, 53, 129, 136, 137.
Union Tool Co., Utley v., 3.
Union Township, Gibonney v., 194.
Union Trust Co. v. Ill. etc. Co., 138.
Union Trust Co., Whiting v., 77.
Union Water Co. v. Memphis, etc. Co., 64.
United Companies, Black v., 8.
United Gas Co., Gas Light Co. v., 74, 137.
Union Service Co., In re, 120.
United States, Dickson v., 82.

TABLE OF CASES CITED.

References are to sections.

United States v. Ft. Scott, 106.
United States, International Co. v., 77.
United States v. New Orleans, 179.
United States Bank v. Hoth, 83, 100.
United States Pat. Co., Stark v., 77.
Unity Ins. Co. v. Cram, 3.
University, Louisville v., 185.
University v. Yarrow, 94.
Upton, Chubb v., 106, 112.
Upton v. Hansborough, 51, 168.
Upton, Pullman v., 112.
Upton, Sanger v., 107, 112.
Upton v. Tribilcock, 112.
Upton, Webster v., 106, 112.
Upton, Whittenton Mills v., 9, 53, 148.
Urquhart v. Ogdensburg, 202.
Utica Ins. Co. v. Bloodgood, 75.
Utica Ins. Co. v. Caldwell, 75.
Utica Ins. Co. v. Kep, 69.
Utica Ins. Co., People v., 9, 12, 22.
Utica, etc. Co., Mohawk Bridge Co. v., 8.
Utica Water Works, Johnson v., 86.
Utley v. Union Tool Co., 3.

V.

Vail v. Hamilton, 9.
Valentine, Champlain R. Co. v., 81.
Valette, Canal Co. v., 83, 91, 96, 100.
Valley District, Barker District v., 186.
Valley Railroad Co. v. Insurance Co., 121.
Valparaiso v. Adams, 203.
Van Alstyne, Lockhart v., 123.
Van Buskirk, Roberts v., 129.
Van Co., Smith v., 160.
Van Duzen, Sault Ste. Marie R. Co. v., 194.
Van Dyke v. McQuade, 156.
Van Horn v. Des Moines, 219.
Van Houton v. Dutch Church, 94.
Van Pelt v. Davenport, 209, 211.

Van Reuth, Kean v., 168.
Van Santford, Merrick v., 166.
Van Vechten, Randall v., 77, 158.
Vance v. Erie, etc. R. Co., 162.
Vance v. Insurance Co., 156.
Vance v. Little Rock, 170.
Vance, Railroad Co. v., 9.
Vandall v. San Francisco D. Co., 9.
Vaughan, Eastern Plank Road Co. v., 3.
Vermont, etc. R. Co., Chapin v., 135.
Vermont, etc. R. Co. v. Clayers, 3.
Vermont, etc. R. Co., Ogdensburg, etc. R. Co. v., 9.
Vermont, etc. R. Co., White v., 135.
Vernon, Hanson v., 181, 224.
Vicksburg, Craig v., 135.
Vidal v. Girard, 92, 93, 94.
Vinalhaven, Brown v., 213.
Vincent, Walker v., 87.
Viner, Bartlett v., 55.
Virginia City, Douglas v., 50, 188.
Visalia, etc. Gas Co. v. Sims, 137.
Vrooman v. Turner, 219.

W.

Wabash, Sweet v., 175.
Wabash, St. Louis, etc. R. Co. v. Ham, 144.
Waddill v. Alabama R. Co., 53.
Waddill, Grand Lodge v., 70.
Wade v. American, etc. Society, 92.
Wade v. Richmond, 198.
Wahl v. Holt, 129.
Wakeman v. Dalley, 158.
Walker, Blount v., 81.
Walker v. Chapman, 69.
Walker v. Cincinnati, 70.
Walker v. Railroad Co., 163.
Walker v. Tippets, 158.
Walker v. Vincent, 87.
Wall v. Monroe County, 230.
Wallis, Birmington v., 69.
Walsh, Aubert v., 69.
Walsh v. Augusta, 196.
Walsh, Rusk v., 69.
Walsh v. Trustees, 3.
Walworth v. Holt, 107.

TABLE OF CASES CITED. lxix

References are to sections.

Ward v. Davidson, 158.
Ward v. Griswoldville, 107.
Ward v. Johnson, 96, 100.
Ward, Marvin Safe Co. v., 219.
Ware v. Grand Junction, etc. Co., 53.
Ware v. Regents Canal Co., 53.
Wareham, Dill v., 119.
Warehousing Co., Touche v., 79.
Warner, Blanchard's Factory v., 81.
Warner, Whitewell v., 77, 91.
Warren, Bank of Virgennes v., 160.
Warren v. Henley, 181.
Warren v. King, 119.
Warren v. Mobile, etc. R. Co., 146.
Warren, Trott v., 194.
Warren Bridge, Charles River Bridge Co. v., 8, 9, 28.
Warren County, Richards v.. 190.
Washington, Smith v., 201, 203.
Washington, Weightman v., 220.
Washington Avenue, In re, 225.
Washington, etc. R. Co., Gruber v., 162, 163.
Wasmer v. Delaware, etc. R. Co., 187.
Waterbury Button Co., Naugatuck R. Co. v., 53.
Water Co., Brenham v., 170, 188.
Water Co., Goundie v., 81.
Water Co., Memphis v., 216.
Water Power Co., Dupee v., 83, 120.
Waterproof Co., Perry v., 77.
Waters v. Leech, 171.
Waters, Thompson v., 9, 81.
Watertown, etc. Co., Madison, etc. Co. v., 9.
Watertown, etc. Co., Plank Road Co. v., 96, 136.
Water Works, New Orleans v., 180.
Watson v. Bennett, 161.
Watson, Mobile v., 233.
Watts' Appeal, 84, 100.
Wayland School District, Stockdale v., 231.
Weare v. Fitchburg, 205.
Weare, Petroleum Co. v., 166.
Webb v. Herne Bay, 134.
Webb, Martin v., 160.

Webber, St. Louis v., 9.
Weber, People v., 170.
Webster, Buffalo Ins. Co. v., 52.
Webster, Burnham v., 160.
Webster v. Harrington, 198.
Webster v. Howe Machine Co., 104.
Webster, Sargent v., 83, 91.
Webster v. Turner, 83.
Webster v. Upton, 106, 112.
Weckler v. First National Bank, 9, 50.
Weed, Combination Trust Co. v., 105.
Weed v. Saratoga, etc. R. Co., 129.
Weeden v. Mad River, etc. Co., 77.
Weet v. Brockport, 219.
Wehrung, East St. Louis v., 173.
Weible, Louisville v., 216.
Weider, Livingston Co. v., 235.
Weightman v. Washington, 220.
Weir v. Bell, 158.
Weis v. Madison, 211.
Weisner v. Douglas, 181, 237.
Weissgerber, Eyser v., 74, 75.
Weith v. Wilmington, 170.
Welch v. Sage, 135.
Wells v. Atlanta, 177, 188, 217.
Wells v. Burnham, 189.
Wells, Gillham v., 176.
Wells v. Supervisors, 237.
West, Aurora v., 135, 237.
West Chester Ry. Co., Everhardt v., 118.
West Guillimbury v. Railroad Co., 198.
West v. Mayor, 178.
West v. Menard Co., 90.
West Orange, Field v., 203.
West Point, etc. Ass'n, Poole v., 110.
West River, etc. Co. v. Dix, 183.
West St. Louis Bank v. Shawnee Bank, 160.
West Troy, Cowan v., 189, 194.
Western Bank v. Tallman, 128.
Western College v. Cleveland, 170, 202, 219.
Western Cottage Co. v. Reddish, 100.
Western News Co. v. Wilmarth, 162.
Western Screw Co. v. Cousley, 79.

References are to sections.

Western Union Tel. Co., Bell v., 139.
Western Union Tel. Co., Compagnie Francaise v., 121.
Western Union Tel. Co. v. Mayer, 166.
Western Union Tel. Co., Pacific P. Tel. Co. v., 53.
Western Union Tel. Co., Pensacola, etc. Co. v., 166.
Western Union Tel. Co. v. Smith, 146.
Western Union Tel. Co., Williams v., 124.
Westinghouse Mach. Co. v. Wilkinson, 7, 9.
Westlake, Pangborn v., 69.
Westminster Board, Aukland v., 53.
Westminster Co., Simpson v., 137.
Weston v. Syracuse, 196.
Wetherell v. Jones, 55.
Wetmore v. Parker, 93.
Weymouth Packet Co.. In re, 117.
Wheeler v. Chicago, 191.
Wheeler v. Cincinnati, 170, 219.
Wheeler, Ohio, etc. R. Co. v., 145.
Wheeler, Parish v., 129.
Wheeler v. San Francisco, 129.
Wheeler, State Bank v., 161, 162.
Wheeler, etc. Mfg. Co. v. Boyce, 163.
Wheelock v. Moulton, 60.
Whipple, Curtis v., 224.
Whipple v. Union Pac. R. Co., 146.
White v. Bass, 69.
White v. Franklin Bank, 69, 74, 75, 119.
White v. Howard, 82.
White v. Manufacturing Co., 79.
White v. Skinner, 158.
White, State v., 175.
White v. Vermont, etc. R. Co., 135.
White v. Yazoo City, 202, 203.
White Line Trans. Co., Lucas v., 4, 9, 38, 52, 70.
White's Bank v. Toledo Ins. Co., 9, 47, 100.
Whitewater Valley, etc. Co. v. Valette, 83, 91, 96, 100.
Whitewell v. Warner, 91.
Whitfield v. Railroad Co., 162.

Whiting v. S. & F. R. Co., 224.
Whiting v. Union Trust Co., 77.
Whitman M. Co. v. Baker, 47, 81.
Whitney v. Mayor, 178.
Whitney, National Bank v., 53.
Whitney v. Peay, 74.
Whitney v. Wyman, 51, 56, 79, 168.
Whitney Arms Co. v. Barlow, 55, 56, 58, 61, 63, 64, 66, 68.
Whittenton Mills v. Upton, 9, 53, 148.
Whittle v. Derby Fish Co., 15.
Whittle, Planters' Bank v., 91.
Whitwell v. Warner, 77.
Whitworth, Tennessee v., 148.
Whitworth, Trevor v., 45, 117, 120.
Whyte v. Mayor, 212.
Widrig v. Newport Co., 158.
Wilcox, Oakland Bank v., 159.
Wild v. Bank, 160.
Wiggins v. New York, 177.
Wiggins Ferry Co. v. Railroad Co., 129.
Wiley v. Silliman, 223.
Wilkes v. Georgia, etc. R. Co., 53.
Wilkins v. Detroit, 189.
Wilkinson v. Bauerle, 91.
Wilkinson, Cohen v., 53.
Wilkinson v. Peru, 235.
Wilkinson, Westinghouse Mach. Co. v., 7, 9.
Willamette Co. v. Bank, 9, 53.
Willey v. Greenbush, 230.
Williams, Ex parte, 135.
Williams v. Augusta, 212.
Williams v. Bank, 74.
Williams v. Creswell, 166.
Williams v. Davidson, 170, 172.
Williams v. Hedley, 60.
Williams, Helfrich v., 164.
Williams v. Insurance Co., 162.
Williams, Kernaghan v., 53.
Williams v. New Jersey, 180.
Williams v. Parker, 116.
Williams, Rowell v., 220.
Williams v. School District, 225.
Williams, State v., 172.
Williams v. Western Union Co., 124.
Williams College v. Cleveland, 220.
Williamson, Ex parte, 98.
Williamsport v. Comm., 188.

TABLE OF CASES CITED. lxxi

References are to sections.

Williston v. Michigan R. Co., 124.
Wilmington, Weith v., 170.
Wilson, Adams Exp. Co. v., 129.
Wilson, Attorney-General v., 153.
Wilson v. Charlotte, 177.
Wilson, Danbury, etc. R. Co. v., 9.
Wilson v. New Bedford, 211.
Wilson v. School District, 194.
Wilson, Shore v., 94.
Winans, York, etc. R. Co. v., 9, 128, 137.
Winchester v. Birkshire, etc. R. Co., 137.
Windsor Mfg. Co., Beckwith v., 88.
Winegar, Grand Chute v., 228.
Winfield, Mayor v., 176.
Winnetka, Sherlock v., 185.
Winston, Tenn. etc. R. Co. v., 235.
Winter, Bates Co. v., 190.
Winter v. City Council, 239.
Winters v. Armstrong, 109, 111.
Winthelm v. Cedar Co., 194.
Winthrop Ins. Co., Meeker v., 139.
Wiegand, Citizens' Bank v., 159.
Wisconsin Cent. R. Co., Bound v., 197.
Wiswall v. Greenville, etc. Co., 9.
Wittee v. Derby Fishing Co., 15.
Wolcott, Ouachita Co. v., 230.
Wood v. Dummer, 107.
Wood County, Reeves v., 86.
Wood Hydraulic Co. v. King, 166.
Wood, Louisiana v., 191, 233.
Woodbridge v. Proprietors, etc., 77.
Woodcock v. Calais, 213.
Woodruff v. Erie R. Co., 9.
Woodward, Dartmouth College v., 9, 21, 28, 50.
Woolsey, Dodge v., 53.
Worcester, Commissioners v., 176, 212.
Worcester, Tainter v., 219.
Workingmen's Banking Co. v. Routerberg, 99.
Worthington, North Side Ry. Co. v., 7.
Wright v. Augusta, 219.
Wright v. Bishop, 235.
Wright v. Carter, 8.
Wright v. Nagle, 199.
Wright v. Railroad Co., 172.
Wulfekehlen, German Savings Bank v., 120.
Wyandotte v. Zeitz, 188.
Wycoff, Safford v., 100.
Wylde v. North River, etc. Co., 129.
Wyman, Whitney v., 51, 56, 79, 168.

X.

Xenia, Bloom v., 170.

Y.

Yancey v. Hopkins, 190.
Yarrow, University v., 94.
Yates, Berry v., 121.
Yates v. Milwaukee, 212.
Yazoo City, White v., 202, 203.
Yonkers, Taylor v., 205.
York, etc. R. Co. v. Hudson, 153.
York, etc. R. Co. v. Winans, 128, 137.
Young v. Clarendon Township, 223, 230, 237.
Young, Davidson v., 192.
Young v. Gaslight Co., 53.
Young, National Bank of Republic v., 104.
Yount, American Christian Union v., 81, 166.

Z.

Zabriskie v. Cleveland, etc. R. Co., 9, 53, 76, 135.
Zabriskie, Crompton v., 198.
Zeitz, Wyandotte v., 188.
Zellerbach, Miners' Ditch Co. v., 9, 33, 83, 87.
Zimmer v. State, 144.
Zottman v. San Francisco, 201.
Zulueta's Case, 120.

THE DOCTRINE OF ULTRA VIRES

IN

THE LAW OF CORPORATIONS.

CHAPTER I.

CREATION AND CONSTRUCTION OF CORPORATE CHARTERS.

PART I.

CREATION OF CHARTERS.

§ 1. Introductory.
  2. A corporation a legal entity.
  3. Creation of chartered corporations.
  4. What acceptance of charter implies.
  5. Distinction between natural and artificial persons.
  6. Distinction between corporation and partnership.
  7. Distinction between corporations under general and special act.

§ 1. *Introductory.*— As the doctrine of *ultra vires* can be legitimately applied only to the acts of a corporation *as such*, acting by and through its authorized agents or representatives, it might be well to here state, upon the threshold of the subject, the position taken in these pages regarding the general character and attributes of this much anathematized creature of the law, which has occasioned so much legal investigation and has called forth at times such vigorous judicial condemnation.

§ 2. *A corporation a legal entity.*— It will be assumed, in the examination of the doctrine to be hereafter discussed, that a corporation, both under the common law and as now organized and created under our state laws, is a legal entity, separate and distinct from the members who compose it; that in the corporation — the creature of the law — is vested all the property and powers of the company; that it can only be affected by such acts and agreements as are done or executed on its behalf by its corporate agencies, *acting within the legitimate scope of its chartered powers;* and that no acts or contracts by the officers or agents of the company beyond the scope of its powers, as prescribed and designated in its charter or articles of association, can be ascribed to the corporation — the legal entity — though done and concurred in by each and all of the stockholders. It would seem from a careful examination of the authorities and adjudications that the foregoing propositions as to the nature of a corporation would go unchallenged; but, unfortunately, there is now in this country a newer growth of corporation lawyers and authors, fostered and fashioned in the same school, who would confuse the subject by regarding the rights, duties and powers of a corporation as identical with the rights, duties and powers of the individuals composing it. To recognize such an anomalous position would clearly nullify, in a great measure, the whole doctrine of *ultra vires.*

§ 3. *Creation of chartered corporations.*— Corporations can now be created and exist only by virtue of legislative enactment.[1] And to create a corporation by legislative act no express words are requisite; any words de-

---
[1] Stowe v. Flagg, 72 Ill. 397; Hadley v. Commissioners, 105 Mass. 526; Franklin Bridge Co. v. Wood, 14 Ga. 80.

scriptive of the legislative purpose are sufficient.[1] The manner in which private corporations may be organized is now usually prescribed by most of the states of the Union by general laws, the constitutions, with perhaps few exceptions, prohibiting special acts of incorporation. But the authority to organize corporations under general laws rather than by special act of the legislature is not intended to work any material change in their nature or character. The legislatures of the respective states have prescribed methods for the creation of corporations which were unknown to the common law, endowing them with special powers of management and limitations as to liability, and providing at the same time that all the world should have notice who were the persons authorized to manage and control the corporation and bind all the stockholders thereof by requiring the charter to be recorded, certified by the directors and made accessible to all. Under general incorporation law, when the instrument specifying the objects, conditions and name of the association, and whatever else the law may require, has been approved by the proper officers and enrolled according to law, the persons so associating become a corporation according to the objects and conditions and vested with the powers and privileges contained and specified in the instrument. These become their charter, and have the same force and effect in law as if they were specifically granted by special act.[2] Powers and privileges specified in such instrument, however, which contravene or are beyond the provisions of the statute are null and

[1] Rex v. Amery, 1 Term Rep. 575; Conservators v. Ash, 10 B. & C. 349; Grangers' Ins. Co. v. Kamper, 73 Ala. 325; Mahoney v. State Bank, 4 Ark. 620; Denton v. Jackson, 2 John. Ch. 325; Walsh v. Trustees, etc., 96 N. Y. 427.
[2] Society, etc. v. Commonwealth, 52 Pa. St. 125.

void,¹ and all acts done in pursuance of such provisions will be void.² But whatever be the mode prescribed by the act under which incorporation is had, substantial compliance with all its provisions is required before the corporation can be said to be *in esse*.³ A corporation created according to the rules of the common law must be governed by it in its mode of organization, in the manner of exercising its powers and in the use of the capacities conferred; when created in disregard of those rules, however, the existence, powers, capacities, and the mode of exercising them, must depend upon the law of its creation.⁴ The charter and not the organization under it creates the subscribers a corporation, at least so far as to render contracts for or against the corporation valid.⁵ A corporation, being an artificial creation, is the very thing it is made by the statute which brought it into being, and nothing more.⁶ In *Grangers' Life & Health Insurance Company v. Kamper, supra*, the court, in discussing the manner of organizing corporations under statutory enactments, said: "The mode of incorporation the statutes have

---

¹ Heck v. McEwin, 76 Tenn. 97; Eastern Plank Road Co. v. Vaughan, 14 N. Y. 546; Grangers', etc. Ins. Co. v. Kamper, 73 Ala. 325; Medical College Case, 3 Whart. (Pa.) 445.

² Eastern Plank Road Co. v. Vaughan, *supra*.

³ Harris v. McGregor, 29 Cal. 124; People v. Selfridge, 52 Cal. 331; McIntire v. McLain Ditching Co., 40 Ind. 104; Indianapolis, etc. Min. Co. v. Herkimer, 46 id. 142; Reed v. Richmond St. Ry. Co., 50 id. 342; Richmond Factory Co. v. Alexander, 61 Me. 351; Grangers' Life, etc. Asso. v. Kamper, 73 Ala. 325; Oregon Ry. v. Oregonian Ry., 130 U. S. 1; Utley v. Union Tool Co., 11 Gray (Mass.), 139; Doyle v. Mizner, 42 Mich. 332; Abbott v. Omaha Smelt. Co., 4 Neb. 416; Unity Ins. Co. v. Cram, 43 N. H. 636; Childs v. Smith, 55 Barb. (N. Y.) 45, 53.

⁴ Penobscot Boom Co. v. Lamson, 16 Me. 224.

⁵ Vermont Ry. Co. v. Clayes, 21 Vt. 30.

⁶ Oregon Ry. Co. v. Oregonian Ry., Co., *supra*.

carefully prescribed. The persons proposing to be incorporated must file and cause to be recorded in a designated public office a declaration in writing stating the name of the corporation, the objects for which it was formed, the amount of capital stock, the number of shares into which it is divided, the names of the stockholders, and the number of shares each may hold. The office and effect of the declaration the statutes do not leave in doubt; when recorded, the persons signing it and their successors become a body corporate by the name stated therein and with the powers conferred by law. It is an acceptance by the corporators, under the name designated, for the objects expressed, of the corporate powers and capacity the law confers, and a statement of the principal constituents of the corporation — the amount of the capital stock, the names of the stockholders and the quantity of interest each has in the capital stock. There is no authority of law for introducing more into it, and if more be introduced it is mere surplusage, not adding to or detracting from the force of the declaration. A controlling purpose, it may be supposed, in authorizing or compelling the creation of private corporations under general law, is to secure uniformity and equality of corporate powers, functions and privileges; that all corporations of the same class, formed for like purposes, should possess the same capacities and properties, and exercise and enjoy the same franchises and privileges. Unless it was intended to work a radical change in the nature and character of these artificial beings, the mere creatures of the law, and to subvert the whole theory which has prevailed in reference to them, it cannot have been contemplated that they should for themselves create powers and privileges by declaration or reservation, whether the declaration or reservation is expressed in the articles of incorporation, or in the constitution or by-laws ordained by the corporators for their government. Such declarations or reservations would soon become more liberal and diverse than was the liberality and diversity of the grants of corporate powers by special legislative enactment — the evil it was intended to remove. Of every corporation formed under the general law, the law itself becomes the charter, defines and enumerates the powers which are to be exercised, the nature and extent of corporate franchises and privileges. The declaration of incorporation, the constitution and by-laws adopted by corporate government, do not form the charter or define or enumerate the corporate powers. These are the acts of the corporators. The charter is the grant from the sovereign power of the state, and by that source only can be varied or enlarged. The expression in a declaration of incorporation that it is the intention and privilege to increase the capital stock or the number of shares, or to invest the corporators with any other powers not enumerated in the statute, whenever deemed proper and expedient, is vain and nugatory; it does not authorize an increase of capital at the mere will of the company in such mode as it elects. The power must be found in the law from which corporate existence is derived, or must be conferred by a subsequent law, the provisions of which must be observed in the exercise of the power. The implied or incidental powers corporations may rightfully exercise never have been extended to changes in the constitution or membership of the corporate body, or changes of the purposes for which the corporation was created. They have been confined to such powers as would enable the corporation to exercise properly its express powers."[1]

[1] In Oregon Ry. Co. v. Oregonian Ry. Co., 130 U. S. 1, Mr. Justice Miller, in speaking of the organization of modern corporations, said:

"A corporation in this country, whatever it may have been in

§ 4.] CREATION OF CHARTERS. 7

§ 4. *What acceptance of charter implies.*— A corporation, as we have seen,[1] exists and exercises its franchises only by virtue of a grant from the legislative power. "The granting and acceptance of a charter in the case of England at the time when the crown exercised the right of creating such bodies, can only have an existence under the express law of the state or sovereignty by which it is created. And these powers, where they do not relate to municipal corporations exercising authority conferred solely for the benefit of the public, and in some sense parts of the body politic of the state, have in this country, until within recent years, always been conferred by special acts of the legislative body under which they claim to exist. But the rapid growth of corporations which have come to take a part in all or nearly all of the business operations of the country, and especially in enterprises requiring large aggregations of capital and individual energy, as well as their success in meeting the needs of a vast number of most important commercial relations, have demanded the serious attention and consideration of law makers. And while valuable services have been rendered to the public by this class of organizations, which have stimulated their formation by numerous special acts, it came at last to be perceived that they were attended by many evils in their operation as well as much good, and that the hasty manner in which they were created by the legislatures, sometimes with exclusive privileges, often without due consideration and under the influence of improper motives, frequently led to bad results."

"Whether it was this consideration, or merely the desire to fix some more universal rule by which the rights and powers of private corporations, or those for pecuniary profit, should come into existence, it is certain that not many years ago state constitutions which were formed or remodeled came to have in them provisions for the formation of corporations under general laws, and prohibiting such creations by special enactment."

"Outside of the powers conferred and the privileges granted to those organizations by the statutes under which they exist, they are, in all the states of the Union which have the common law as the foundation of their jurisprudence, governed by that common law; and it is the established rule of the federal court, and, with

---

[1] § 3.

private corporations for pecuniary profit are based on the theory that the prosecution of the business proposed will be a benefit to the public, and that the investment of capital therein will result in pecuniary profit to the stockholders; and it is an undertaking on the part of the corporation and all of its stockholders that, in consideration of the grant of power, the capital shall be used for the prosecution of the purpose named in the charter, and no other. There is also an undertaking on the part of the corporation with each stockholder that the capital he invests shall be put to no other use, and subject to no other hazard, than that contemplated by the powers expressed in the charter, and that those things which are within the scope or objects of the corporation shall be done in the manner pointed out in the charter and the laws governing its action."

§ 5. *Distinction between a natural and artificial person.*— The distinction between a natural person and one of statutory creation — an artificial person — may be said

some exceptions, in the states in which that common law prevails, as well as of Great Britain, from which it is derived, that such a corporation *can exercise no power or authority which is not granted to it by the charter under which it exists or by some other act of the legislature which granted that charter.*

"Any authority for the exercise of corporate powers, derived from the general laws of a state, must be in accordance with the constitution of that state and its statutes upon that subject. A constitutional provision that corporations shall not be created by special laws, but may be formed under general laws, implies that no private corporation can be created thereafter until such general law has been enacted, and that it thereupon became the fundamental law of the state in regard to all corporations formed under it. It is idle to say, therefore, as has been contended, that any corporation could assume to itself powers of action by the mere declaration in its articles or memorandum that it possessed them."

[1] Lucas v. White Line Trans. Co., 70 Iowa, 541.

to be this: A natural person is not confined in the exercise of his capacities to any particular acts or business, but may do any act or enter into any contract not prohibited by law. An artificial person may do no acts nor enter into any contracts except such as are authorized by law; the one's powers being inherent whilst the powers of the other are conferred. In the transaction of business enterprises a natural person's powers are unlimited in regard to the mode of their exercise, and he may also embark in any occupation deemed advisable or advantageous; whilst an artifical person is necessarily restricted to the business and the mode of its exercise prescribed in the charter or laws of its creation. Much of the conflict encountered in the opinions of judges and text-writers may be directly traced to a disregard of this irreconcilable distinction, which no amount of specious argument can successfully overcome. That this distinction is technical and based, in a measure, on the fictitious character of the artificial person created by the legislature, in no wise changes the rule of construction regarding the respective powers of each. The natural person is born with inherent powers — the artificial person has its powers to achieve; and, having so achieved them through the aid of the law, it is entitled to protection *by* the law and held to the obeyance *of* the law.

§ 6. *Distinction between corporations and partnerships.* The principles of the law upon which the liability of corporations and joint-stock companies is founded are very clear and well settled, though not always in practice steadily kept in view. The law in ordinary partnerships, so far as relates to the power of one partner to bind the others, is a branch of the law of principal and agent. It is elementary that each member of a complete partnership is liable for himself, and, as agent for the rest, binds them upon all contracts made in the course of the ordinary scope of the partnership business. Any restrictions upon the authority of each partner imposed by mutual agreement among themselves could not affect third persons, unless such persons had notice of them; then they could take nothing by contract which those restrictions forbade. A corporation by common law could only bind itself by contract under the common seal. It is obvious that the law governing ordinary partnerships would be inapplicable to a company consisting of a great number of individuals who contribute to the common stock. To allow each one to bind the other by any contract which he thought fit to enter into, even within the scope of the corporate business, would soon lead to the utter ruin of the contributors.

§ 7. *As to distinction between corporations organized under general laws and special acts.*— In ascertaining the scope of the powers of corporations, the only difference between one organized under general law and one created by special statute is that in the former the court will look to the certificate of the promoters or incorporators, while in the latter but to the special statute. The rule, however, in construing the instrument is necessarily the same.[1] In both kinds of private corporations their powers are such as are specifically enumerated and such others as are incidental or necessary to carry the express powers into effect. They may not exercise any other powers than these.[2]

[1] Rockhold v. Canton Masonic, etc. Soc., 129 Ill. 440; Nutt v. Danville Seminary, 129 Ill. 403.

[2] Westinghouse Machine Co. v. Wilkinson, 79 Ala. 312; North Side Railway Co. v. Worthington, 30 S. W. Rep. 1058 (Tex., 1895); and see

cases cited in § 9, *post*. In North Side Ry. Co. v. Worthington, *supra*, the court, in discussing the difference between corporations created under general and special acts, said: "It occurs to us that in determining the powers of a corporation a distinction should be observed between such as are created by special charters and such as come into existence by virtue of authority conferred by a general law. A charter is in the nature of a contract, and it may be that in construing a special charter we should construe it in the light of the special circumstances attending the enterprise which was intended to be promoted; as, in case of a railroad, its connection with other lines of transportation whether by water or land, or its terminus at a seaport. The last-mentioned circumstance seems to have had a controlling influence upon the court in the case of Railway Co. v. Redmond, 10 C. B. (N. S.) 675, already cited. For example, if the legislature had the power to grant and had granted a special charter to the City Company, and it had appeared that a street railway was necessary to the success of the corporation, and that this fact was known, it may be the power to construct or at least to aid the construction of the street railway would have been implied. But this corporation having been created under a general law, we do not see that it can claim the right, by reason of its peculiar surroundings, to exercise a power which another like corporation could not exercise by reason of different circumstances. Our constitution provides that corporations shall be created only by general laws, and it would seem that one purpose of the provision was to prevent the legislature from granting to one company special powers or special privileges. At all events the general law, as we think, should be construed as a general rule, conferring upon each member of each particular class of corporations precisely the same powers."

Part II.

CONSTRUCTION OF CHARTERS.

§ 8. General rule of construction.
9. Corporations have only powers given by charter.
10. Rule peculiarly applicable to corporations organized under general laws.
11. Ultra vires questions decided by law of organization.
12. Province of court in construing corporate powers.
13. Powers construed as incidental to those expressly given.
14. Discretion of corporations.
15. Miscellaneous — Incidental powers.

§ 8. *General rule of construction.*— In all cases of legislative grants to private corporations the well-established rule of construction is this: That grants to private corporations shall be construed strictly against the grantees; and to prevail they must be express and clear beyond a doubt; a doubt defeats the power. What is not granted in clear and unequivocal language is withheld.[1] The object is to protect the public against improvident grants and grants made by implication without clear intention. They will not be sustained by doubtful words; ambiguity vitiates them. But this rule is qualified by another: That such grant, and the statute making it, must receive

---

[1] 2 Dwarris on Stat. 750; 2 Redf. Rys. 445, 446; C. & A. Ry. Co. v. Briggs, 2 Zabr. (N. J.) 623, 641, 647; Townsend v. Brown, 4 Zabr. (N. J.) 80, 87; Leggett v. New Jersey Mfg. Co., 1 N. J. Eq. 541; Bridge Co. v. Land & Imp. Co., 13, N. J. Eq. 81, 94; Joint Co. v. R. & Del. Bay Ry. Co., 1 C. E. Green (N. J.), 321; Morris Canal Co. v. Central Ry. Co., 10 N. J. Eq. 419; Morris & Essex Ry. Co. v. Sussex Ry. Co., 20 N. J. Eq. 542; Packer v. Sunbury, etc. L. Co., 19 Pa. St. 211; Bank of Penn. v. Comm., 19 Pa. St. 144; Penn. Ry. Co. v. Canal Comm'rs. 21 Pa. St. 9; Comm. v. Franklin Canal Co., 21 Pa. St. 125; Comm. v. Erie Ry. Co., 27 Pa. St. 339; Beaty v. Knowler, 4 Pet. 168.

a reasonable construction, and not be so construed as to defeat the intention of the legislature, and that the ambiguity must be such as is not removed by the settled rules of construction.[1]

§ 9. *Corporations have only powers given by charter.*— A corporation has, therefore, according to the foregoing rule of construction, no powers whatever except those given by its charter or law under which it is incorporated, either directly or as incidental to its purposes and existence.[2] This rule is very clearly stated by Mr. Justice

[1] Black v. United Cos., 7 C. E. Green (N. J.), 130; s. c., 9 C. E. Green (N. J.), 445; Providence Bank v. Billings, 4 Pet. (U. S.) 514: Charles River Bridge Co. v. Warren Bridge, 11 Pet. (U. S.) 420; Bank of Augusta v. Earle, 13 Pet. (U. S.) 519; Perrine v. Ches. & Del. Ry. Co., 9 How. (U. S.) 172; Richmond Ry. Co. v. Louisiana Ry. Co., 13 How. (U. S.) 71; Pennock v. Coe, 23 How. (U. S.) 117; Rice v. Railroad Co., 1 Black (U. S.), 358; Delaware Tax Case, 18 Wall. (U. S.) 206; Aicardi v. The State, 19 Wall. (U. S.) 635; Turnpike Co. v. Illinois, 6 Otto (U. S.), 63; Bradley v. South Carolina Phos. Co., 1 Hughes (U. S.), 72: Bradley v. N. Y. etc. Co., 21 Conn. 294: Boston, etc. Ry. Co. v. B. & M. Ry. Co., 5 Cush. (Mass.) 375; Mohawk Bridge Co. v. Utica, etc. Co., 6 Paige (N. Y.), 554; Auburn Plank Road Co. v. Douglas, 9 N. Y. 444; Ren. & Sar. Ry. v. Davis. 43 N. Y. 137; In re N. Y. & N. H. R. R., 46 N. Y. 546; Briggs v. C. & A. R. R., 2 Zab. (N. J.) 623; Wright v. Carter, 3 Dutch. (N. J.) 76; Bridge Prop. v. Hoboken Co., 2 Beas. (N. J.) 81: s. c., 1 Wall. 116; Packer v. Sunbury, etc. Ry. Co., 19 Pa. St. 218; Bank v. Comm., 19 Pa. St. 144; Penn. R. R. v. Canal Comm'rs, 21 Pa. St. 9; St. Clair Co. Turnpike Co. v. People, 82 Ill. 174.

[2] Dartmouth College v. Woodward, 4 Wheat. (U. S.) 636; City Council v. Plank Road Co., 31 Ala. 76: Holland v. San Francisco, 7 Cal. 361; Occum Co. v. Sprague Mfg. Co., 34 Conn. 529; Ohio Ins. Co. v. Nunnemacher, 15 Ind. 294; Thompson v. Waters, 25 Mich. 214; Rochester Ins. Co. v. Martin, 13 Minn. 59; Ruggles v. Collier, 43 Mo. 353; Downing v. Mt. Washington, etc. Co., 40 N. H. 230; People v. Utica Ins. Co., 15 John. (N. Y.) 358; Farmers' L. & T. Co. v. Carroll, 5 Barb. (N. Y.) 613: White's Bank v. Toledo Ins. Co., 12 Ohio St. 601; Lafayette v. Cox, 5 Ind. 38; Green Bay, etc. Ry. Co. v. Union S. Co.,

Miller in *Thomas v. Railroad Co.*, 101 U. S. 71, as follows: "The powers of corporations organized under legislative statutes are such, and such only, as those statutes confer. Conceding the rule applicable to all statutes,

107 U. S. 98; Bank of Augusta v. Earle, 13 Pet. (U. S.) 519; Miners' Ditch Co. v. Zellerbach, 37 Cal. 543; Vandall v. San Francisco Dock Co., 40 Cal. 83; Bellmeyer v. Marshalltown, 44 Iowa, 564; Weckler v. First Nat. Bank, 42 Md. 581; St. Louis v. Webber, 44 Mo. 547; Mathews v. Skinker, 62 Mo. 329; Brooklin Gravel Road Co. v. Slaughter, 33 Ind. 185; East Anglian Ry. Co. v. Eastern Counties Ry. Co., 11 C. B. 775; Ogdensburg, etc. R. Co. v. Vermont, etc. Ry. Co., 63 N. Y. 176; Davis v. Old Colony Ry. Co., 131 Mass. 258; Troy & Boston Ry. Co. v. Boston, etc. R. Co., 86 N. Y. 117; Hinkley v. Gildersleeve, 19 Grant, Ch. (U. Can.) 212; Archer v. Terre Haute, etc. R. Co., 102 Ill. 495; Pearce v. Madison, etc. R. Co., 21 How. (U. S.) 441, and cases cited; Taft v. Pittsford, 28 Vt. 286; Franklin Co. v. Lewistown Inst., 68 Me. 43; Rock River Bank v. Sherwood, 10 Wis. 230; Miner v. N. Y. etc. R. Co., 53 N. Y. 363; Monument Bank v. Globe Works, 101 Mass. 57; Lafayette Sav. Bank v. St. Louis Stoneware Co., 4 Mo. App. 276; Central Bank v. Empire Stone Co., 26 Barb. (N. Y.) 23; Madison, etc. Plank Road Co. v. Watertown, etc. Co., 7 Wis. 59; Ætna Bank v. Charter Oak L. Ins. Co., 50 Conn. 167; Bank of Genesee v. Patchin Bank, 13 N. Y. 319; Woodruff v. Erie Ry. Co., 25 Hun, 246; Chambers v. Falkner, 65 Ala. 448; Wiswall v. Greenville, etc. Co., 3 Jones, Eq. (N. C.) 183; Toll Bridge Co. v. Osborn, 35 Conn. 7; Zabrieskie v. Cleveland, etc. Co., 23 How. (U. S.) 381; Vail v. Hamilton, 85 N. Y. 453; Rochester Sav. Bank v. Averell, 96 N. Y. 467; Railroad Co. v. Howard, 7 Wall. (U. S.) 392; State Board v. Citizens' R. Co., 47 Ind. 407; Low v. Cent. Pac. R. Co., 52 Cal. 53; Stewart v. Erie Transp. Co., 17 Minn. 372; Whittenton Mills v. Upton, 10 Gray (Mass.), 582; Richardson v. Sibley, 11 Allen (Mass.). 65; Ashbury R. R. Co. v. Riche, 7 H. L. 653; Stevens v. Rutland, etc. Co., 29 Vt. 545; Danbury, etc. R. Co. v. Wilson, 22 Conn. 435; Coleman v. Eastern Counties Ry. Co., 10 Beav. 1; Bagshaw v. Eastern Counties Ry. Co., 7 Hare, 114; McGregor v. Deal & D. R. Co., 18 Q. B. 618; Eastern Counties Ry. Co. v. Hawkes, 5 H. L. 331; Smead v. Ind. P. & C. Ry. Co., 11 Ind. 104; Marietta & Cin. R. Co. v. Elliott, 10 Ohio St. 57; Atkinson v. Marietta, etc. R. Co., 15 Ohio St. 21; Straus v. Eagle Ins. Co., 5 Ohio St. 59; Peoria & R. I. R. Co. v. Coal Valley Co., 68 Ill. 489; Railroad Co. v. Vance, 96 U. S. 450; Pennsylvania Co. v. St. Louis Co., 118 U. S. 290; Oregon Ry. Co. v. Oregonian

that what is fairly implied is as much granted as what is expressed, it remains that the charter of a corporation is the measure of its powers, and that the enumeration of these powers implies the exclusion of all others." The proposition laid down by the learned justice in that case is sustained by the great weight of authority, both in this country and in England. The foregoing rule as to the construction of corporate powers was also forcibly expressed and upheld by Mr. Justice McCay in *Central Railroad Co. v. Collins,* 40 Ga. 582, in the following language: "Corporations are too apt to forget this fundamental law of their being. In the daily habit of transacting business in the name of the company as though it were an individual, they are apt to slide into the notion that a corporation *is* an individual in all respects, so far as business matters are concerned.

"But a corporation is a mere creature of the law, and only exists at all *for the purposes declared in its charter, and has absolutely no powers but those which the law confers upon it.* It is a creature of the law, and in the very nature of things is just what the law makes it, no more, no less; and by the word 'law' here, I do not mean the

Ry. Co., 130 U. S. 1; Same v. Same, 145 U. S. 54; New York, etc. R. Co. v. Winans, 17 How. (U. S.) 30; Branch v. Jessup, 106 U. S. 468; Salt Lake City v. Hollister, 118 U. S. 256; Willamette Co. v. Bank of British Columbia, 119 U. S. 191; Pittsburg, etc. R. Co. v. Keokuk, etc. Co., 131 U. S. 371; Charles River Bridge v. Warren Bridge, 11 Pet. (U. S.) 420; Dubuque, etc. R. Co. v. Litchfield, 23 How. (U. S.) 66, 88, 89; Slidell v. Grandjean, 111 U. S. 412; Pickard v. Pullman Sou. Car Co., 117 U. S. 34; Railroad Co. v. Lockwood, 17 Wall. 357; Liverpool, etc. Co. v. Insurance Co., 129 U. S. 397; Central Transp. Co. v. Pullman Car Co., 139 U. S. 24; Fort Worth City Co. v. Smith Bridge Co., 151 U. S. 294; Green Bay, etc. Co. v. Union Steamboat Co., 107 U. S. 98, 100; Central Ry. Co. v. Collins, 40 Ga. 582; Lucas v. White Line Transp. Co., 70 Iowa, 541; Westinghouse Mach. Co. v. Wilkinson, 79 Ala. 312.

general law which regulates the powers of persons, but the act of incorporation, the charter, the constitution."

§ 10. *Rule peculiarly applicable to corporations organized under general laws.*— The rule of construction under consideration is peculiarly applicable to articles of association framed under general laws, which are a substitute for a legislative charter, and which assume and define the powers of the corporation, without any supervision of the legislature or of any public authority.[1] It has been truly said that " the frequency of cases requiring the construction of charters excites some surprise, when it is considered that an act of incorporation is, and always must be, interpreted by a rule so simple that no man, whether layman or lawyer, can misunderstand or misapply it. That which a corporation is authorized to do by its charter or act of incorporation it may do; beyond that, all its acts are *ultra vires* and illegal, and the power must be given in plain words or by necessary implication. All powers not given in this direct and unmistakable manner are withheld."[2] " If you assert that a corporation had certain privileges, show us the words of the legislature conferring them. Failing in this, you must give up your claims. A doubtful charter does not exist; because whatever is doubtful is decisively against the corporation."[3]

[1] Oregon Ry. v. Oregonian Ry., 130 U. S. 26, 27; Central Trans. Co. v. Pullman Co., 139 U. S. 24; Commonwealth v. The Erie, etc. Ry. Co., 27 Pa. St. 339.

[2] Mr. Justice Miller, in Oregon Ry. v. Oregonian, etc. Ry. Co., 130 U. S. 26.

[3] Commonwealth v. The Erie & N. E. Ry. Co., 27 Pa. St. 351. In the discussion of this question the court, in Morris & Essex R. R. Co. v. Sussex Ry. Co., 20 N. J. Eq. 542, says: "The act under which a corporation is framed gives an imperative rule of construction con-

§ 11.] CONSTRUCTION OF CHARTERS. 17

§ 11. *Questions of ultra vires decided by law of organization.*— "It must then be carefully borne in mind," says Mr. Brice, "that questions of *ultra vires* relating to the express powers of corporations will have to be decided

cerning corporate powers. And where it is provided in such act that no corporation shall possess or exercise any corporate powers except those expressly given in the charter, and such as shall be necessary to the exercise of the powers so enumerated, its powers must be controlled by that act. It is quite apparent from the language of the statutes of the various states on the subject of corporate powers and privileges that the legislatures intended to interdict, as a matter of public policy, the exercise of any powers except such as are referred to in those acts. Whether without those enactments the common law would fully reach up to that measure upon any implication that powers not so granted or implied are prohibited, it is here unnecessary to consider. The common-law powers of corporations as ably discussed by commentators of the last century are not germane to modern corporations, and the attempt made by some modern writers to apply the common-law principles to statutory creations tends only to mislead, and can serve no purpose save to lend apparent dignity and weight to an alleged theory which has no foundation in fact. To determine the powers of a corporation under the act of its creation, it is sufficient that the terms of the enactment are plain and its meaning cannot be misunderstood; and when a corporation exercises powers outside of those permitted by that act, it is an exercise of power not only authorized, but is against an express enactment."

So Mr. Justice Miller, in Oregon Ry. v. Oregonian Ry., 130 U. S. 1, says:

"The construction of corporate powers should undoubtedly be reasonable, and so as to accomplish and not defeat the purpose and true intent of the charter in its full spirit and scope; and all contracts bearing upon the purposes for which it was organized that the exigencies of the business contemplated and authorized would reasonably require would be within the scope of the company's powers. There are many reasons not now useful to mention why, in justice to the state, the public, and the stockholders, and the very stability of the corporate body, the legislature should be jealous of its grants of franchises, and seek to confine them within definite limits, and to disallow any corporate act outside of them. The leg-

upon a consideration of the exact language used in the law of its organization, while such as concern their implied powers will be determined by the *ratio decidendi* to be gathered from an examination of numerous conflicting decisions. What is the business which may be undertaken by a corporation will be determined in each par-

islature has a policy in this matter, and contracts in contravention of it must be held to be illegal and of no binding obligation. . . . It is to be remembered that when a statute making a grant of property, or of powers or of franchises, to private individuals, or a private corporation, becomes the subject of construction as regards the extent of the grant, the universal rule is that, in doubtful points, the construction shall be against the grantees and in favor of the government or the general public. Nothing passes by implication. Therefore if the articles of association of a corporation, instead of being a mere adoption by the corporators themselves of the declaration of their own purposes and powers, had been an act of the legislature conferring such powers on the corporation, they would be subject to the rule above stated, and to rigid construction in regard to the powers granted. How much more, then, should the rule be applied, and with how much more reason should a court, called upon to determine the powers granted by these articles of association, construe them rigidly, with the stronger leaning in doubtful cases in favor of the public and against the private corporation.

"We have to consider, when such articles become the subject of construction, that they are in a sense *ex parte;* their formation and extension — what shall be put into them as well as what shall be left out — do not take place under the supervision of any official authority whatever. They are the production of private citizens, gotten up in the interest of the parties who propose to become corporators, and stimulated by their zeal for the personal advantage of the parties concerned rather than the general good. These articles, when signed by the corporators, acknowledged before any justice of the peace or notary public, and filed in the office of the secretary of state and the clerk of the proper county, become complete and operative. They are, so far as framed in accordance with law, a substitute for legislation, put in the place of the will of the people of the state, formerly expressed by acts of the legislature. Neither the officer who takes such acknowledgment, nor those who file the articles, have any power of criticism or rejection. The duty of the first

ticular instance by a reference to, and an examination of, the powers actually given to a corporation, read in connection with the business or other purposes for which it has been instituted. That it may carry on such primary business is plain — the difficulty arises in determining what is to certify to the fact, and of the second to simply mark them filed as public documents, in their respective offices.

"These articles, many of which have been heretofore considered of a public character, sometimes affecting the rights of the public very largely and very seriously, do not commend themselves to the judicial mind as a class of instruments requiring or justifying any very liberal construction. Where the question is whether they conform to the authority given by statute in regard to corporate organizations, it is always to be determined upon just construction of the powers granted them, with a due regard for all the other laws of the state upon that subject, and the rule stated above.

"Another important consideration to be observed, peculiarly applicable to the acts of corporations formed by the corporators themselves, declaring what business they are about to pursue, and the powers which they purpose to exercise in carrying it on, is, that while the thing to be done may be lawful in a general way, there are and must be limitations upon the means by which it is to be done or the purpose carried out, which the articles of incorporation cannot remove or violate. A company might be authorized by its articles to establish a large manufactory in a particular locality, and might be held to be a valid corporation with sufficient powers to prosecute the business described; but such articles, although mentioning the particular place, would not empower the company, in the exercise of the powers thus conferred, to carry on a business injurious to the health or comfort of those living in that vicinity.

"Instances might be multiplied in which powers described in general terms as belonging to the objects of the parties who thus became incorporated would be valid; but the corporation carrying out this general purpose would not be authorized to exercise the powers necessary for so doing in any mode which the law of the state would not justify in any private person or any unincorporated body. The manner in which these powers shall be exercised, and their subjection to the restraint of the general laws of the state and its general principles of public policy, are not in any sense enlarged by inserting in the articles of association the authority to depart therefrom."

other secondary matter, incidental to such primary business and necessary for the commodious and prolific carrying on and development of the same, are within the scope of its powers."[1]

§ 12. *Province of courts in construing corporate powers.*— Powers manifestly doubtful should never be recognized by judicial construction. If not given by plain words or by necessary implication, it should be declared not to exist.[2] Nor is it the province of the court to enlarge the powers of a corporation beyond the limitations of the charter because circumstances have changed. The court's province is to expound the law as it stands, not to determine whether larger powers would not have been given if the legislature had anticipated events which have since happened.[3] It is not sufficient that the officers or a majority of the stockholders of a private corporation believe its interests may be advanced by the exercise of additional powers.[4] What the state has not given to it can only be obtained by virtue of legislative enactment.[5] The exercise of corporate franchises, being restrictive of individual rights, cannot be extended beyond the letter and spirit of the act of incorporation.[6] And the specific grant of cer-

---

[1] Green's Brice's Ultra Vires, ch. III, p. 64.
[2] Bank of Pennsylvania v. Comm., 19 Pa. St. 144; Pennsylvania R. Co. v. Canal Comm'rs, 21 Pa. St. 9; Comm. v. Franklin Canal Co., 21 Pa. St. 117; Comm. v. Erie Ry. Co., 27 Pa. St. 339; Spohn v. Farmers' Bank, 13 Norris (Pa.), 432.
[3] Perrine v. Ches. & Del. Canal Co., 9 How. (U. S.) 172.
[4] State v. Standard Oil Co., 49 Ohio St. 137; Beaty v. Knowler, 4 Pet. (U. S.) 152, 168.
[5] Stowe v. Flagg, 72 Ill. 397; Hadley v. Commissioners, 105 Mass. 526; Franklin Bridge Co. v. Wood, 14 Ga. 80.
[6] Oregon Ry. v. Oregonian Ry., 130 U. S. 1; Central Trans. Co. v. Pullman Palace Car Co., 138 U. S. 54; Beaty v. Knowler, 4 Pet. (U. S.) 152.

tain powers in a charter is an implied prohibition of other and distinct powers.[1]

§ 13. *Powers construed as incidental to those expressly given.*— The powers of a corporation are, strictly speaking, twofold: those that are derived from express grant, and those that are incident and necessarily appertain to it, whether expressed in the grant or not.[2] An incidental power is one that is directly and incidentally appropriate to the execution of the specific grant, and not one that has a slight or remote relation to it.[3] For example, the power to make by-laws, to make and use a common seal, and the right to sue, are incident to every corporation.[4] In modern times it has been usual to embrace all these incidental powers in the act of incorporation, so that it may now be considered the general rule that the powers of a corporation are regulated and defined by the act which gives it existence. It has been a matter of much doubt and misapprehension as to whether the power to borrow money, to make bills and notes and other similar contracts are powers incident to a corporation. These and other powers, usually deemed incidental powers of corporations, will be hereafter considered. Whatever may be the incidental or implied powers of aggregate corporations by the common law, and the modes by which those powers are to be carried into operation, corporations created by statute must depend both for their powers and the mode of exercising them upon the true construction of the statute itself.[5]

[1] People v. Utica Ins. Co., 15 Johns. 358; New York Ins. Co. v. Ely, 2 Cow. (N. Y.) 678.
[2] See cases cited to § 9.
[3] Hood v. N. Y. Ry. Co., 22 Conn. 1; Buffet v. Troy, etc. R. Co., 40 N. Y. 168; Curtis v. Leavitt, 15 N. Y. 9.
[4] Leggett v. The N. J. Mfg. Co., 1 N. J. Eq. 541.
[5] Bank of United States v. Dandridge, 12 Wheat. (U. S.) 64.

§ 14. *Discretion of corporation in exercise of powers.*— Where a power is conferred by charter and the mode of exercising prescribed, the provisions are said to be dependent; but where a grant of power is clearly defined and no mode prescribed for its exercise, it is for the corporation to adopt such mode as in its judgment will secure the purpose contemplated.[1] On questions as to dealing in a corporate capacity with third persons, companies must be limited by their respective charters; but on those relating to the mere manner of getting into operation — of becoming prepared to act — a liberal construction is to be adopted.[2] But when an act of incorporation prescribes the mode in which a power given by the charter shall be executed, the corporation can execute it in no other mode.[3] A corporation, however, has a reasonable discretion in the selection of any of the means usual or proper at the time or place, or in the view of the circumstances, to accomplish the object of its incorporation.[4] Although a corporation may not transact business other than that for which it was chartered, yet it should be made clearly to appear that an act or contract was not within its powers before a court will so decide it.[5]

§ 15. *Miscellaneous incidental powers.*— A corporation cannot be a trustee for purposes foreign to its institution.[6] Nor can it exercise the power of creating perpetuities, unless that right be expressly granted.[7] A corporation

---

[1] Holland v. San Francisco, 7 Cal. 361; Southern Life Ins. Co. v. Lanier, 5 Fla. 110.
[2] Judah v. American Live Stock Ins. Co., 4 Ind. 333.
[3] Farmers' L. & T. Co. v. Carroll, 5 Barb. (N. Y.) 613.
[4] Clark v. Farrington, 11 Wis. 306.
[5] Dana v. Bank of St. Paul, 4 Minn. 385.
[6] Trustees v. Peaslee, 15 N. H. 317; Jackson v. Hartwell, 8 Johns. 422.
[7] Cotter v. Doty, 5 Ohio, 393.

may not, by resolution or otherwise, donate its property to a new corporation,[1] nor grant away its rights and franchises which are necessary to the existence and maintenance of the object for which it was created.[2] But corporations authorized by charter to contract in a prescribed mode may, nevertheless, by practice render themselves liable on instruments in a different mode.[3]

[1] Polar Star Lodge v. Polar Star Lodge, 16 La. Ann. 53.
[2] Canal Co. v. Borham, 9 Watts & S. (Penn.) 27. And see cases cited in note to § 137, *post*.
[3] Wittee v. Derby Fishing Co., 2 Conn. 260.

CHAPTER II.

THE DOCTRINE OF ULTRA VIRES.

THE DOCTRINE GENERALLY.

§ 16. Introductory.
17. *Ultra vires* — Senses in which used.
18. Principles of doctrine plain.
19. Two propositions of doctrine settled.
20. Chronological review of doctrine.
21. Head v. Providence Ins. Co.
22. People v. Utica Ins. Co.
23. New York Firemen Ins. Co. v. Sturges.
24. Bank of United States v. Dandridge.
25. Beach v. Fulton Bank.
26. Bank of Augusta v. Earle.
27. Barry v. Merchants' Exchange.
28. Perrine v. Chesapeake, etc. Canal Co.
29. Hood v. New York, etc. R. Co.
30. Pearce v. Madison, etc. R. Co.
31. Bissell v. Michigan, etc. R. Co.
32. Monument National Bank v. Globe Works.
33. Miners' Ditch Co. v. Zellerbach.
34. Franklin Co. v. Lewiston Institution.
35. Thomas v. Railroad Co.
36. Davis v. Old Colony R. Co.
37. Central Transp. Co. v. Pullman Co.
38. Lucas v. The White Line Transp. Co.
39. The doctrine as construed by English courts — Colman v. Eastern Counties Ry. Co.
40. East Anglian Co. v. Eastern Counties Ry. Co.
41. Ashbury Co. v. Riche.
42. Attorney-General v. The Great Eastern Ry. Co.
43. Small et al. v. Smith et al.
44. Baroness Wenlock v. The River Dee.
45. Trevor v. Whitworth et al.

§ 16. *Introductory.*— It has been amply demonstrated that in financial and commercial circles as in the animal kingdom, the law of natural selection dominates the world — the weak succumb to the strong — the fight is to the most powerful. That aggressive element to be found in human nature, which sometimes prompts mankind to shape his end regardless of the rights of his fellowmen, has caused the enactment of wholesome laws to restrain this innate tendency of the desire of gain within the bounds of reason and justice, and to protect those who by nature and circumstance are unable to successfully defend their just and legal rights against the wanton assaults of an abnormal greed, or the unavoidable consequences of a superior natural sagacity. For the purpose, then, of securing to all men equal rights before the law, impartial tribunals have been established, endowed with authority to determine the rights, and power to redress the wrongs, of every citizen, and to uphold the dignity of and command respect for the legislative departments of government. This inordinate greed, fed, fattened and intensified by growing success, finds a fitting embodiment and is strikingly magnified in the management and workings of our modern corporations. These public-spirited associations, though often alleged to be *soulless*, have proved themselves *not* to be altogether *sightless*, for they have readily seen and promptly taken advantage of every opportunity which a combination of capital, skill and industry has afforded, to strengthen their advantageous positions and to increase their doubtful possessions. This unbridled pruriency for illegitimate commercial procreation, stimulated by successful efforts in the aggregation of wealth and power at the expense of the public weal, has led corporations to overstep the boundaries designated in their charters within which they are to confine their acts and undertakings, and to enter upon the private preserves reserved for individual industry. To this tendency of corporations to attempt the exercise of unauthorized powers, and to usurp privileges which have not been granted them, must be attributed the evolution by the courts of the wholesome doctrine of *ultra vires*.

§ 17. *Ultra vires — Senses in which term is used.*— Few subjects have elicited more discussion or excited more general interest in the profession than that disturbing element in the law of corporations known as the "Doctrine of *Ultra Vires*." The term "*ultra vires*" is the modern legal nomenclature for acts of a corporation which exceed or are beyond the powers conferred by law upon the legal entity, acting through any of its instrumentalities.[1] The expression "*ultra vires*" has been used in different senses, to express either that the act of the directors or officers is in excess of their authority as agents of the corporation, or that the act of the majority of the stockholders is in violation of the rights of the minority, or that the act has not been done in conformity with the requirements of the charter, or the act is one which the corporation itself has not the capacity to do, as being in excess of the corporate powers. This subject has been discussed both by the courts of this country and England in an able and exhaustive manner. For a time there was an element of uncertainty appearing in the views expressed by the courts, as to whether or not the doctrine should be applied only to the acts of a corporation, as such, or whether it should not also be applied to acts of the directors or officers which were in excess of the authority given them in the management of the internal affairs of the company. In the former sense only is the

[1] Pomeroy's Spec. Perf., § 56.

doctrine legitimately applicable. This rather ambiguous conception of the doctrine led the courts into many avenues of technical reasoning, and precipitated discussions of the principles of the law governing the relations of principal and agent, of trustee and *cestui que trust*, and principles governing other questions of like nature, which do not properly belong to the doctrine in its application to chartered corporations. As was said by a learned judge in the case of *Camden, etc. R. Co. v. May's Landing, etc. Co.*, 48 N. J. L. 530: " The indiscriminate use of this expression with respect to cases different in their nature and principles has led to considerable confusion, if not misapprehension. Where an act done by directors or officers is simply beyond the powers of the executive department of the corporation — the agency by which the corporation exercises its functions — and not of the corporation itself, it may be made valid and binding by the action of the board of directors, or by the approval of the stockholders. Where the act done by the directors is not in excess of the powers of the corporation itself, but is simply an infringement upon the rights of the stockholders, it may be made binding upon the latter by ratification, or by consent implied by acquiescence. Where the infirmity of the act does not consist in a want of corporate power to do it, but in the disregard of formalities prescribed, it may or may not be valid as to third persons dealing *bona fide* with the corporation, according to the nature of the formality not observed, or the consequences the legislature has imposed upon non-observance. These are all cases depending upon legal principles not peculiarly applicable to corporations, and the use of the phrase '*ultra vires*' tends to confusion and misapprehension. In its legitimate use the expression '*ultra vires*' should be applied only to such acts as are beyond the powers of the corporation itself."[1]

§ 18. *Principles of the doctrine plain.*— The principles upon which the doctrine of *ultra vires* is predicated are apparently simple and elementary, being plain even to a wayfarer; yet, in construing corporate powers and duties under charters and statutory enactments, much doubt and no little confusion has certainly arisen. This uncertainty and confusion, however, has not arisen, it is respectfully submitted, by reason of any misapprehension of the correct construction which should be placed upon this doctrine, but rather from a growing tendency of the courts of this country — a spreading of the granger element in our state courts — to disregard purely legal rights and the rules of law controlling them, unwisely tempering their questionable judgments with even more questionable and unstrained mercy, and basing their findings upon the equitable rights of the parties, whatever may be the cause of action, as they appear to the particular court having jurisdiction of the subject-matter; the application of the doctrine being dependent, in a great measure, upon the temperament and discretion of the judge before whom the defense of *ultra vires* is urged. While this manner of adjusting legal complications may be commendable in a certain sense, it cannot be regarded as judicial wisdom by those who desire the fountains of legal jurisprudence maintained in all their pristine purity and vigor, undefiled by the wanton influence of class prejudice, or the natural flow thereof diverged by the misguided inspiration of political zeal.

§ 19. *Two propositions as to the doctrine settled.*— It has been well said by a learned justice that "the doc-

[1] Depue, J., dissenting.

trine of *ultra vires* has been thoroughly sifted within the last thirty years — its extent and limitations clearly defined. Two propositions are settled. One is that a contract by which a corporation disables itself from performing its functions and duties undertaken and imposed by its charter is, unless the state which created it consents, *ultra vires*. A charter not only grants rights; it also imposes duties. An acceptance of those rights is an assumption of those duties. As it is a contract which binds the state not to interfere with those rights, so, likewise, it is one which binds the corporation not to abandon the discharge of those duties. It is not like a deed or patent, which vests in the grantee or patentee not only title but full power of alienation, but it is more — it is a contract whose obligations neither party, state nor corporation, can, without the consent of the other, abandon. The other is that the powers of a corporation are such, and such only, as the charter confers; and an act beyond the measure of those powers, as either expressly stated or fairly implied, is *ultra vires*. A corporation has no natural or inherent rights or capacities. Created by the state, it has such powers as the state has seen fit to give it — only this and nothing more. And so when it assumes to do that which it has not been empowered by the state to do, its assumption of powers is void, the act is a nullity; the contract is *ultra vires*. These two propositions embrace the whole doctrine of *ultra vires*. They are its alpha and omega."[1] Were the two foregoing propositions steadily kept in view by the courts in applying this doctrine, the diversity of judicial opinion on this subject would be much less.

[1] Brewer, J., in Chicago, R. I. & P. R. Co. v. Union Pac. Ry. Co., 47 Fed. Rep. 15.

§ 20. *Chronological review of the doctrine.* — Before proceeding in detail to apply the doctrine of *ultra vires* to the different phases of corporate contracts and liabilities, and that the scope and effect of the same may the better be understood, it is deemed advisable to first give a brief chronological review of its advent and progress in the adjudications of the courts of this country and England. To this end the more leading cases where the doctrine has been discussed and applied will be considered.

§ 21. *Head v. Providence Ins. Co., 2 Cranch, 127 (1804).* — The principles which support the defense of *ultra vires* to unauthorized acts of corporations were first enunciated in this country by the supreme court of the United States in 1804, when, in the case of *Head v. Providence Ins. Co.*, Chief Justice Marshall, in discussing the source of corporate powers, expressed the views still held by that court. In that case an action was brought on two policies of insurance placed on merchandise on board Spanish brigs afterwards lost and destroyed. The learned justice there said: "Without ascribing to this body, which, in its corporate capacity, is the mere creature of the act to which it owes its corporate existence, all the qualities and disabilities annexed by the common law to the ancient institutions of this sort, it may correctly be said to be precisely what the incorporating act has made it, to derive all its powers from that act and be capable of exercising its faculties only in the manner which that act authorizes. With these bodies which have only a legal existence, the act of incorporation is an enabling act. It gives them all the powers they possess. It enables them to contract; and when it prescribes to them a mode of contracting, they must observe that mode, or the instrument no more creates a contract than if the body had never been incorporated." Upon the principles enunciated in this case rested the decisions of the *Dartmouth College Case*, 4 Wheat. 518; *Gozzler v. Corporation of Georgetown*, 6 Wheat. 593; *Fleckner v. Bank of United States*, 8 Wheat. 338, and many others at a later day.

§ 22. *People v. Utica Ins. Co.*, *15 John. 357* (*1818*).— That was a suit on information in the nature of *quo warranto* filed by the attorney-general against the defendant for exercising banking privileges without authority from the legislature, and judgment of ouster was rendered against the company. The court there said: "It was, however, contended on the argument that the right of carrying on banking operations was necessarily incident to the corporation, because not expressly prohibited, if they had surplus funds which they could spare for that purpose. But I cannot assent to this rule of construing a charter of incorporation for a specific object. Such an incorporated company have no rights except such as are specially granted and those that are necessary to carry into effect the purposes for which it was established. The specification of certain powers operates as a restraint to such objects only, and is an implied prohibition of the exercise of other and distinct powers. A contrary doctrine would be productive of mischievous consequences, especially with us, where charter privileges have been so alarmingly multiplied."

§ 23. *New York Firemen Ins. Co. v. Sturges*, *2 Cow. 664* (*1824*).— This was *assumpsit* against second indorsers on a promissory note, defendant company being one of the indorsers. In affirming the principle that corporations have no powers except such as are specially granted and those necessary to effect the powers so granted, it was held that a corporation having no power by the act of incorporation to discount notes, but created for the purpose of insurance, has no right to carry on the business of discounting.

§ 24. *Bank of United States v. Dandridge, 12 Wheat. 64 (1827).*— This was an action by the president, directors and company of the Bank of the United States upon a bond given to the bank to secure the faithful performance of the official duties of one of its cashiers. It was held that where a cashier is duly appointed, and permitted to act in his office for a long time, under the sanction of the directors, it is not necessary that his official bond should be accepted by the board of directors as satisfactory, according to the terms of the charter, in order to enable him to enter legally upon the duties of his office, or to make his sureties responsible for the non-performance of those duties.

§ 25. *Beach v. Fulton Bank, 3 Wend. 574 (1829).*— In this case it was held that a contract for the loan of money made with an incorporated company, as well as the security taken on such loan, is void, if the power to loan money is not expressly given, or necessarily incident to the powers granted to such company by its charter.

§ 26. *Bank of Augusta v. Earle, 13 Pet. 519 (1839).*— This was an action in the circuit court of the United States for the district of Alabama by the Bank of Augusta against the defendant, a citizen of Alabama, on a bill of exchange drawn at Mobile, Alabama, on New York, which had been protested for non-payment and returned to Mobile; the bill was made and indorsed for the pur-

§ 27.] THE DOCTRINE GENERALLY. 33

pose of being discounted by the agent of the bank, who had funds in his hands belonging to the plaintiff for the purpose of purchasing bills of exchange; the bill was discounted by the agent of the bank in Mobile for the benefit of the bank, with their funds. The question was as to the power of the bank to discount bills of exchange, and discussed the distinction between discounting and purchasing, and is a leading case on that subject.

§ 27. *Barry v. Merchants' Exchange, 1 Sandf. Ch. 280 (1844).*—The Merchants' Exchange was a corporation created with the power to purchase, hold and convey real estate, and to erect and build such an edifice or building as it might deem necessary or proper for the purposes of a public exchange in the city of New York. The question in this case was as to whether the corporation had power to borrow money in order to erect such a building, and to secure the repayment of the same by issuing bonds and by mortgaging its real estate. It was held that it had, the assistant vice-chancellor, who delivered the opinion of the court, saying: "While I have the honor of holding a seat in this tribunal I trust that no case of hardship, no argument founded upon broken faith, will influence me to treat any corporation (or persons participating with it) which has usurped powers not delegated to it or infringed any of its privileges with an indulgence inconsistent with the express injunctions of the law.

"Corporate privileges are generally obtained with a view to private interests, and they are ostensibly conferred to prosecute some single enterprise or to pursue some one separate or distinct branch of business. The innate tendency of the desire of gain, acting in these institutions upon a restricted franchise, is to enlarge the authority granted, and this leads to usurpation.

"The legislature of the several states has inundated the country with an infinity of corporations, created for almost every business and purpose known to a highly civilized and eminently commercial people, and I am fully satisfied that the interests of the public, as well as their own, will best be promoted by holding them to a strict accountability."

§ 28. *Perrine v. Chesapeake & Delaware Canal Co.*, 9 *How.* 172 (*1850*).— In this case it was held that where the charter of a corporation having provided for the payment of a certain toll by vessels not having merchandise on board, such vessel could not be excluded from the canal because they carried passengers; and not having been empowered by its charter to demand tolls on passengers, or on vessels by reason of their passengers, cannot exact such tolls. It is there said by Chief Justice Taney, who delivered the opinion of the court: "Now it is the well-settled doctrine of this court that a corporation created by statute is a mere creature of the law, and can exercise no powers except those which the law confers upon it or which are incident to its existence. *Head v. Providence Ins. Co.*, 2 Cranch, 127; *Dartmouth College v. Woodward*, 4 Wheat. 636; *Bank of United States v. Dandridge*, 12 Wheat. 64; *Charles River Bridge v. Warren Bridge*, 11 Pet. 544; *Bank of Augusta v. Earle*, 13 Pet. 587."

§ 29. *Hood v. The New York & N. H. R. Co.*, 22 Conn. 502 (*1853*).— In this case the powers of corporations are very clearly and accurately defined. It was a case where the agent of the railroad company, a corporation running their cars from New Haven to Plainville, sold the plaintiff a ticket for the fair at Collinsville, which was four miles beyond Plainville, from which last-named place passengers were being conveyed to Collinsville by means of sleighs or carriages upon runners, which stage line was owned by another company. Plaintiff was thrown out of the sleigh, and sustained severe injuries, and brought his action upon a *special contract* to carry him safely by railroad and stage from New Haven to Collinsville. The defendant pleaded want of power to make any such contract, and denied ever having made such contract. It was held that defendant was not estopped to claim that under their charter they had no power to enter into the alleged contract, and that it was not obligatory upon them. Mr. Justice Ellsworth, who delivered the opinion of the court, *inter alia*, said: "It is found that the defendants had no power to enter into the undertaking in question, and therefore, as a ground of claim, it must be agreed the undertaking merely is of no avail, for the reason that the directors, having no authority, did not in legal estimation make the contract for the company. The question is, are the defendants estopped setting up this in their defense? The statement of the case carries with it, on its very face, conviction to the mind that it cannot be so. The defendants estopped from denying that they have done what they never could have done! It is a question of power under the charter; and however individuals may be liable and estopped, who untruly hold themselves out as clothed with power, the defendants cannot be estopped on any such principle of law known to the court. The notion of an estoppel *in pais*, to which class, if any, this estoppel belongs, proceeds on the idea of acquiescence or consent; a contract expressly or impliedly given by the party claimed to be estopped. Of course there must be legal possibility or there can be no real or supposed acquiescence and consent, and where consent may be given silence may be sufficient proof that it is given. . . . If a corporation has the power to do a thing, and is in the habit of doing it in a particular way, it may bind itself to third persons, though it do not pursue the exact mode prescribed in the charter; for the mode is not exclusive but concurrent. . . . It being a question of power, silent acquiescence in the acts of subordinate agents does not make a stronger case; for if a formal contract is not obligatory on the company, one proved by inferior or circumstantial evidence certainly is not. The kind of evidence is quite immaterial. Should the directors of a savings bank, or of any bank, contract with a ship-builder for a steamship to navigate the ocean, would this contract bind the company? Certainly not; because the directors have no power to make it, nor would they have more were they to make such contracts from day to day. The legislature has absolutely marked the limit of this power, and they cannot exceed it under the charter; and if the directors, even with all the stockholders at their side, transcend the limits of the charter, and make contracts foreign to their business, they only act for themselves. The reason is, there can be no consent of the corporation. The consent of individual stockholders, however repeated, is not their consent, nor is it admissible proof to establish consent; so that, if it were true every stockholder had expressed his consent, it would make no difference in the case. If this is not so, there are no restrictions or limitations on chartered companies, and they may do anything the directors please which is not absolutely unlawful. The exercise of power is held to prove itself, which is absurd. . . . Were the charter a public one, it is agreed that the company would not be bound by such acts, however repeated; but in truth a private charter is not essentially different from a public one in this respect; for the plaintiff must have known that the defendants were incorporated by the legislature for the purpose of making or using only a railroad. The public know where the charter may be seen and what it contains. They hold that a principal that can give authority, whether a corporation or a person, may, when one assumes to act for him, and he does not object to it, be estopped denying his agency; but an infant is never estopped, nor a married woman, nor ought a body of stockholders to be, united as they are under a specific charter, especially when the directors have disregarded it and assumed to act according to their own pleasure. Could the company by legal possibility do the act, it would be otherwise. . . . We repeat that the directors and stockholders have no corporate powers or relations, and can give no consent, but what is within the appropriate business of the charter. Again, it is said that the defendants ought not to be permitted to call in question the acts of their agents. Why not as much as other principals whose agents transcend their authority and abuse their trust? If it is replied the directors have suffered this course of things for months when they could have arrested it at once, we ask whose agents they were? Certainly not of the innocent stockholders. *The directors represent them only while they act within the scope of the charter;* the charter is the measure of their power; and sad would it be if directors could trample upon this, and yet bind the stockholders as firmly as if they were acting within it. If the directors have done wrong, let them suffer the consequences."

§ 30. *Pearce v. Madison & Indiana R. Co., 21 How. 441 (1858).*— The first case, however, in the United States supreme court, where the doctrine of *ultra vires* was directly considered, was in the case of *Pearce v. Madison & Indiana R. Co., supra,* decided in 1858. It was there held that two corporations chartered by the state of Indiana to construct and manage distinct though connecting railroads had no power to consolidate themselves into one corporation, or to establish a steamboat line on the Ohio river to be run in connection with the railroad, and, therefore, were not liable on a promissory note sued on, which had been given by the officers of the consolidated line in payment of a steamboat. The opinion was delivered by Mr. Justice Campbell, and in defining the powers of corporations he used the following forcible and explicit language: "The rights, duties and obligations of the defendants are defined in the acts of the legislature of Indiana, under which they were organized, and reference must be had to these to ascertain the validity of their contracts. They empower the defendants respectively to do all that was necessary to construct and put into operation a railroad between the cities which are named in the acts of incorporation. There was no authority of law to consolidate these corporations and to place both under the same management, or to subject the capital of the one to answer for the liabilities of the other; and so the courts of Indiana have determined. But in addition to that act of illegality, the managers of these corporations established a steamboat line to run in connection with the railroad, and thereby diverted their capital from the objects contemplated by their charters and exposed it to perils for which they afforded no sanction. *Now, persons dealing with the managers of a corporation must take notice of the limitations imposed upon their authority by the act of incorporation.* These powers are conceded in consideration of the advantage the public is to receive from their direct and intelligent employment, and the public have an interest that neither the managers nor stockholders of the corporation shall transcend their authority."

§ 31. *Bissell v. Michigan Southern & Northern Indiana R. Co., 22 N. Y. 258 (1860).*— This was an action against two distinct railroad companies for a breach of their duty safely to carry the plaintiff, a passenger upon a train of cars, which they, by a contract between them, had united in running, and by reason of the negligence of their agents suffering a collision with another train, by which plaintiff's leg was broken. In the decision of the case it was held, by an almost unanimous court (Denio, J., dissenting), that where two corporations, chartered respectively by the states of Michigan and Indiana, with power to each to build and operate a railroad within its own state, have united in the business of transporting passengers over a third road in the state of Illinois, beyond the limits authorized by the charter of either, such corporations are jointly liable for injuries to a passenger resulting from the negligence of their employees. It was further held by the court that corporations, like natural persons, have power and capacity to do wrong; that they may, in their contracts and dealings, break over the restraints imposed upon them by their charters; and when they do so, their exemption from liability cannot be claimed on the mere ground that they have no attributes or faculties which render it impossible for them thus to act.

The interest in the *Bissell Case*, however, and the celebrity it has attained, have not arisen from the *decision* there rendered, but from the several propositions laid down by the learned judges who so exhaustively examined and discussed the various phases of the doctrine of *ultra vires* in its application to chartered corporations. The propositions laid down by Mr. Chief Justice Comstock (and he was alone in his contention) were, among others, the following: *First.* Corporations have no right to violate their charters, but they have capacity to do so, and to be bound by their acts where a repudiation of such acts would result in manifest wrong to innocent parties. *Second.* A corporation is more than an agent of the stockholders. Such bodies are clothed with the legal title to the property or funds which represent the capital, in trust, however, for the shareholders, who are the beneficial owners; and, like other trustees, it is possible for them to deal with capital in a manner and for purposes not authorized by their charters, and to be bound by such dealings. *Third.* The plea of *ultra vires*, according to its just meaning, imports, not that the corporation could not, and did not in fact, make the unauthorized contract, but that it ought not to have made it. Such a defense, therefore, necessarily rests upon the violation of trust or duty toward the shareholders, and is not to be entertained where its allowance will do a greater wrong to innocent third parties. The acquiescence of the shareholders in the abuse will prevent the interposition of such a plea. *Fourth.* Where a corporation has received the consideration of the unauthorized contract, and a restitution will not do complete justice, the remedy of the other party is not confined to a suit in disaffirmance of such contract, but may be directly upon it. So the contract will be enforced under any circumstances of controlling equity.

The propositions contended for by Mr. Justice Selden in the above case, in which Clerke, J., concurred, were set forth as follows: *First.* The powers and privileges of corporations are conferred, not for the private convenience of the corporators, but for public purposes and to promote the public interest. They are granted at the expense of the public, since they create advantages which persons unincorporated do not possess. The public benefit is treated as a compensation for the grant; and it would be an abuse of legislative power to make the grant except in contemplation of such benefit. *Second.* The legislature, in conferring corporate power, is presumed, in every instance, to have carefully considered the public interest, and to have granted just so much power as that interest requires. *Third.* If corporations are permitted to usurp powers not granted, it is done at the expense of the public. Sound policy, therefore, demands that they should be kept strictly within their chartered limits; and every contract made by them which exceeds those limits, like all other contracts in contravention of public policy, is illegal and therefore void. *Fourth.* It is a good defense for a corporation, when sued upon a contract, that, in making such a contract, it exceeded its corporate powers; this defense being allowed, not for the sake of the corporation, but for that of the public. The corporation would, however, be estopped from setting up the defense, in a case where the other party to the contract could not be presumed to be cognizant of the excess of power.

The arguments advanced by the two learned judicial combatants in support of their propositions will be hereafter noticed.

§ 32. *Monument National Bank v. Globe Works, 101 Mass. 57 (1869).*— It was held in this case that the note of a manufacturing corporation in the hands of a holder in good faith, for value, who took it before maturity and without knowledge that the maker had not received full consideration, could be enforced against the corporation, although it was made as an accommodation note. This on the ground that the corporation had power to make promissory notes, and the making of an accommodation note was only an abuse of that power, which abuse was, of course, unknown to the holder or purchaser for value.

§ 33. *Miners' Ditch Co. v. Zellerbach, 37 Cal. 543 (1869).* This case has been frequently cited as sustaining the propositions contended for by Chief Justice Comstock in the *Bissell Case, supra.* It holds directly the reverse. Chief Justice Sawyer, in delivering the opinion of the court, says: "From the cases cited it very clearly appears that the question, as between stockholders and the corporation, is a very different one from that which arises between the corporation itself and strangers dealing with it, and the principle established, when the contract arises between strangers and the corporation, is whether the act in question is one which the corporation is not authorized to perform under any circumstances, or one that may be performed by the corporation for some purposes, but may not for others. In the former case the defense of *ultra vires is available to the corporation as against all persons, because they are bound to know from the law of its existence that it has no power to perform the act.* But in the latter case the defense may or not be available, depending upon the question whether the party dealing with the corporation is aware of the intention to perform the act for an unauthorized purpose, or under circumstances not justifying its performance. And the test as between strangers, having no knowledge of an unlawful purpose, and the corporation is to compare the terms of the contract with the provisions of the law from which the corporation derives its powers, and, if the court can see that the act to be performed is necessarily beyond the powers of the corporation for any purpose, the contract cannot be enforced, otherwise it can. . . . Strangers are presumed to know the law of the land, and they are bound, when dealing with corporations, to know the powers conferred by their charters. These are open to their inspection, and it is easy to determine whether the act is within the scope of the general powers for that purpose."

§ 34. *Franklin Co. v. Lewiston Institution for Savings, 68 Me. 43 (1877).*— This was a case where the trustees of the Institution for Savings subscribed for $50,000 of the capital stock of the Continental Mills, and, having no money to pay for it, the Franklin Company, another corporation, paid that amount to the Continental Mills, taking the notes of the savings institution therefor and a certificate of the stock in their own name as collateral security for the payment of the notes. It was held, on suit brought to enforce payment, that the action of the trustees of the savings institution was *ultra vires;* that it was not within the authority of savings institutions, at a time when they have no funds for investment, to purchase stocks or other property not needed for immediate use, on credit, and thus create a debt binding upon the institution; that the Franklin Company, having participated in the illegal transaction, could not claim the privilege of a *bona fide* holder of commercial paper; and that the savings institution, having received no benefit from the transaction, was not estopped to set up the defense of *ultra vires.*

§ 35. *Thomas v. Railroad Co., 101 U. S. 71 (1879).*— In this case the doctrine of *ultra vires* was directly considered, and the previous decisions of that court reaffirmed. This case has perhaps been cited and approved by the courts of this country more than any other case bearing upon this doctrine. It was there decided that a lease for twenty years by a railroad company of its railroad, rolling stock and franchises, in consideration of being paid one-half of the gross sums collected from the operation of the road by the lessees during the term, and reserving to the lessor the right to terminate the lease and retake possession of the road at any time, paying to the lessee the value of the unexpired term, was void; and that the corporation upon terminating the lease and resuming possession when the lessees had been in possession five years, and the accounts of the parties for those years having been adjusted and paid, was not liable to an action by the lessees to recover the value of the unexpired term. Mr. Justice Miller, who delivered the judgment of the court, in the course of his learned opinion said: "The powers of corporations organized under legislative statutes *are such, and such only, as those statutes confer.* Conceding the rule applicable to all statutes, that what is fairly implied is as much granted as what is expressed, it remains that the charter of a corporation is the measure of its powers, and that the enumeration of those powers implies the exclusion of all others.

"There is another principle of equal importance, and equally conclusive against the validity of this contract, which, if not coming exactly within the doctrine of *ultra vires* as we have just discussed it, shows very clearly that the railroad company was without the power to make such a contract. That principle is that where a corporation, like a railroad company, has granted to it by a charter a franchise intended in a large measure to be exercised for the public good, the due performance of those functions being the consideration of the public grant, any contract which disables the corporation from performing those functions, which undertakes, without the consent of the state, to transfer to others the rights and powers conferred by the charter, and to release the grantees from the burden which it imposes, is a violation of the contract with the state, and is void as against public policy."

§ 36. *Davis v. Old Colony R. Co., 131 Mass. 258 (1879).* This was an action on an agreement signed by the Old Colony Railroad Company to guaranty plaintiffs against any deficiency that might arise toward defraying the expenses of a jubilee and musical festival to be held in Boston. The question in the case was whether it was within the powers of the railroad company to bind itself by such an agreement. It was held that it was not, although such agreement was made with the reasonable belief that the holding of the proposed festival would be of great pecuniary benefit to the corporation by increasing its proper business, and the festival was held and expenses incurred in reliance upon the guaranty. This case presents a most elaborate examination of the doctrine of *ultra vires*, some fifty-three cases bearing directly on the subject being examined. The opinion of the court was delivered by Chief Justice Gray (now associate justice of the United States supreme court), and is one of the strongest and most convincing opinions on this subject ever delivered in this country. In the course of his opinion the learned chief justice, *inter alia*, says:

"Upon full consideration of the elaborate arguments of counsel upon that question, the court is of the opinion that the agreement is *ultra vires*, and therefore no action can be maintained upon it against either defendant. . . .

"The corporation has power to do such business only as it is authorized by its act of incorporation to do, and no other. It is not held out by the government nor by the stockholders as authorized to make contracts which are beyond the purposes and scope of its charter. It is not vested with all the capacities of a natural person, or of an ordinary partnership, but with such only as its charter confers. If it exceeds its chartered powers, not only may the government take away its charter, but those who have subscribed to its stock may avoid any contract made by the corporation in clear excess of its powers. If it makes a contract manifestly beyond the powers conferred by its charter, and therefore unlawful, a court of chancery, on the application of a stockholder, will restrain the corporation from carrying out the contract; and a court of common law will sustain no action on the contract against the corporation. . . .

"The holding of a 'world's peace jubilee and international musical festival' is an enterprise wholly outside the objects for which a railroad corporation is established, and a contract to pay, or to guaranty the payment of, the expenses of such an enterprise, is neither a necessary nor an appropriate means of carrying on the business of the railroad corporation, is an application of its funds to an object unauthorized and impliedly prohibited by its charter, and is beyond its corporate powers. Such a contract cannot be held to bind the corporation, by reason of the supposed benefit which it may derive from an increase of passengers over its road, upon any grounds that would not hold it equally bound by a contract to partake in or to guaranty the success of any enterprise that might attract population or travel to any city or town upon or near its line."

§ 37. *Central Transportation Co. v. Pullman Palace Car Co., 139 U. S. 24 (1890).*— The doctrine of *ultra vires* has frequently come before the supreme court of the

United States for application and construction, and, when directly considered, the court has never wavered from the principles first enunciated by Chief Justice Marshall in 1804 in the case of *Head v. Providence Ins. Co.*, heretofore alluded to. In *Central Transportation Co. v. Pullman Palace Car Co., supra*, all the cases bearing upon this subject were cited, examined and re-affirmed. In that case the doctrine is given one of the most elaborate and complete discussions ever extended to the question, and the defense of *ultra vires* is examined in all its phases. To any but a prejudiced mind the opinion and adjudication in this case should forever set at rest the question as to what construction should be placed on the doctrine of *ultra vires* in this country. It was the province and privilege of Associate Justice Gray, who, as chief justice of the supreme court of Massachusetts, rendered such an elaborate opinion in the *Old Colony Railroad Company Case*, to deliver the opinion in this case, nor could it have been left to the elucidation of an abler mind. The facts of the case were substantially as follows: The Central Transportation Company was a corporation under the general laws of Pennsylvania, to exist for twenty years, with a certain capital stock, organized for "the transportation of passengers in railroad cars constructed and owned by the company" under certain patents, and carried on the business of manufacturing sleeping-cars under its patents, and of hiring or letting the cars to railroad companies by written contracts, receiving a revenue from the sale of berths and accommodations to passengers. Seven years after its incorporation, by special act of the legislature of Pennsylvania, the charter was extended for ninety-nine years, and the corporation was empowered by said special act to double its capital stock and to "enter into contracts with corporations of this or any other state for the leasing or hiring and transfer to them, or any of them, of its railway cars and other personal property." The corporation forthwith entered into an indenture with the Pullman Palace Car Company, a corporation by virtue of a special act of the legislature of Illinois, engaged in a similar business, by which it leased and transferred to that corporation all its cars, railroad contracts, patent rights and other personal property, moneys, credits and rights of action for the term of ninety-nine years, except so far as the contracts and patents should expire sooner, and covenanted not to "engage in the business of manufacturing, using or hiring sleeping-cars" while the lease should remain in force; and the lessee covenanted to pay all existing debts of the lessor, and to pay to the lessor annually a large sum of money during the term of ninety-nine years unless the indenture should be sooner terminated. Upon action brought by the Transportation Company to recover the amount due for the last three quarters, according to the terms of the lease, and after a most elaborate examination and discussion of the various decisions in this country and England, it was held that the contract of lease was unlawful and void because beyond the corporate powers of the lessor, and involving an abandonment of its duty to the public, and therefore no action could be maintained by the lessor upon the contract or to recover the sums thereby payable, even while the lessee had enjoyed the benefits of the contract. Mr. Justice Gray, in the course of his masterful opinion, says:

"The charter of a corporation, read in the light of general laws which are applicable, is the measure of its powers, and the enumeration of those powers implies the exclusion of all others not fairly incidental. All contracts made by a corporation beyond the scope of those powers are unlawful and void, and no action can be maintained upon them in the courts, and this upon three distinct grounds: the obligation of every one contracting with a corporation to take notice of the legal limits of its powers; the interest of the stockholders not to be subjected to risks which they have never undertaken; and, above all, the interest of the public that the corporation shall not transcend the powers conferred upon it by law. A corporation cannot, without the consent of the legislature, transfer its franchises to another corporation, and abnegate the performance of the duties to the public imposed upon it by its charter as the consideration for the grant of its franchise. Neither the grant of a franchise to transport passengers, nor a general authority to sell and dispose of property, empowers the grantee, while it continues to exist as a corporation, to sell or to lease its entire property and franchises to another corporation. These principles apply equally to companies incorporated by special charter from the legislature and to those formed by articles of association under general laws. . . .

" A contract of a corporation which is *ultra vires* in the proper sense, that is to say, outside the objects of its creation as defined in the law of its organization, and therefore beyond the powers conferred upon it by the legislature, is not voidable only, but wholly void and of no legal effect. The objection to the contract is not merely that the corporation ought not to have made it, *but that it could not make it*. The contract cannot be ratified by either party because it could not have been authorized by either. No performance on either side can give the unlawful contract any validity, or be the foundation of any right of action upon it.

" When a corporation is acting within the general scope of its powers conferred upon it by the legislature, the corporation, as well as the persons contracting with it, may be estopped to deny that it has complied with the legal formalities which were prerequisites to its existence or to its action, because such requisites might in fact have been complied with. But when the contract is beyond the powers conferred upon it by existing laws, neither the corporation nor the other party to the contract can be estopped by assenting to it, or by acting upon it to show that it was prohibited by those laws.

"A contract *ultra vires* being unlawful and void, not because it is in itself immoral, but *because the corporation, by the law of its creation, is incapable of making it,* the courts, while refusing to maintain any action upon the unlawful contract, have always striven to do justice between the parties, so far as could be done consistently with adherence to law, by permitting property or money, parted with on good faith of the unlawful contract, to be recovered back or compensation to be made for it.

"In such case, however, the action is not maintained upon the unlawful contract, nor according to its terms; but on an implied contract of the defendant to return, or failing to do that, to make compensation for, property or money which it has no right to retain. To maintain such action is not to affirm, but to disaffirm, the unlawful contract.

"The ground and the limits of the rule concerning the remedy, in the case of a contract *ultra vires*, which has been partly performed, and under which property has passed, can hardly be summed up better than they were by Mr. Justice Miller in a passage already quoted, where he said that the rule 'stands upon the broad ground that the contract itself is void, and that nothing which has been done under it, nor the action of the court, can infuse any vitality into it;' and that 'where the parties have so far acted under such a contract that they cannot be restored to their original condition, the court inquires if relief can be given independently of the contract, or whether it will refuse to interfere as the matter stands.' 118 U. S. 317."

§ 38. *Lucas v. The White Line Transportation Co., 70 Iowa, 541.*— This was an action to recover contribution as co-surety on a bond. The defendant was a corporation organized for the purpose of engaging in the "general freight and transfer business." By its secretary it joined the plaintiff in executing a bond of suretyship for L. and M. to the B. Co. Afterwards L. and M. failed, but they executed their note to plaintiff and defendant for the amount of the bond, in consideration of the payers assuming that amount of their indebtedness to the B. Co. Thereupon the defendant, by its president, joined plaintiff in a letter to the B. Co., assuming liability for the indebtedness of L. and M. to that amount. It also, by its officers and attorneys, joined plaintiff in an action on said note against L. and M. which was aided by attachment. Defendant refused to pay to the B. Co. any portion of the indebtedness thus assumed, and plaintiff paid the whole of it, and sought to recover contribution from the defendant company as a co-surety. It was held that defendant's original contract of suretyship was *ultra vires*, as was also its assumption of indebtedness by the letter signed by its president, and that the other acts of defendant's officers did not estop it from insisting on that fact as a defense, and that no recovery could be had. Rothrock, J., in delivering the opinion of the court, among other things, says:

"The corporation defendant is acting under the general incorporation laws of the state, and from the provisions of its articles and the statute it derives its powers.

A corporation exists and exercises its franchises only by virtue of a grant from the legislative power. The granting and acceptance of a charter in the case of private corporations for pecuniary profit are based on the theory that the prosecution of the business will be a benefit to the public, and that the investment of capital therein will result in pecuniary profit to the stockholders, and that it is an undertaking on the part of the corporation and all of its stockholders that, in consideration of the grant of power, the capital shall be used for the prosecution of the purpose named in the charter, and no other. There is also an undertaking on the part of the corporation with each stockholder that the capital he invests shall be put to no other use and subject to no other hazard than that contemplated by the powers expressed in the charter, and that those things which are within the scope or object of the corporation shall be done in the manner pointed out in the charter and the laws governing its action. But corporations and their officers do not always keep within their powers, and the application of the doctrine of *ultra vires* is often attended with very perplexing questions. By the application of a few plain rules, however, we may readily reach the proper answer to the question involved in this case. (1) Every person dealing with a corporation is charged with knowledge of its powers as set out in its recorded articles of incorporation. (2) Where a corporation exercises powers not given by its charter it violates the law of its organization, and may be proceeded against by the state, through its attorney-general, as provided by the statute, and the unanimous consent of all the stockholders cannot make illegal acts valid. The state has the right to interfere in such case. (3) Where a third party makes with the officers of a corporation an illegal contract beyond the powers of the corporation as shown by its charter, such third party cannot recover, because he acts with knowledge that the officers have exceeded their power, and between him and the corporation or its stockholders no amount of ratification by those unauthorized to make the contract will make it valid. (4) When the officers of a corporation make a contract with third parties in regard to matters apparently within their corporate powers, but which upon the proof of extrinsic facts (of which such parties had no notice) lie beyond their powers, the corporation must be held, unless it may avoid liability by taking timely steps to prevent loss or damage to such third parties; for in such cases the third party is innocent, and the corporation or stockholders less innocent for having selected officers not worthy of the trust reposed in them. . . . (6) When the corporation has permitted its officers to engage in *ultra vires* transactions, and in the prosecution of such transactions the officers commit a wrong or tortious act without the fault of the injured party, the corporation is estopped from taking advantage of the *ultra vires* character of the original undertaking. These rules do not cover all cases, but are sufficient to guide us in the determination of the question in this case.

"The case of *Bissell v. Michigan Southern & N. I. R. Co.*, 22 N. Y. 258, is relied upon by appellees as authority for holding corporations on *ultra vires* contracts. It is true that the opinion of Comstock, J., in that case, *appears not to be in accord with the well-established doctrine of ultra vires as applied to corporations;* but he says (page 272), 'I do not deny the validity of this excuse in many cases — I may say in all cases where it can be received without doing great injustice to others. If the person dealing with a corporation knows of the wrong done or contemplated, and he cannot show the acquiescence of the shareholder, he ought not to complain if he cannot enforce the contract. Aside from the law of corporations, agreements which involve or propose a violation of trust will not be enforced by the courts where no greater equities demand it.' In that case the defendant had constructed a railroad not authorized by their charter, and for some years had been operating the same, and made a contract to carry plaintiff over the road. He was injured in a collision occasioned by the negligence of defendant's employees. The plaintiff's cause of action did not arise out of the *ultra vires* contract to carry him, but out of the wrong done on the way, and to which wrong he was not a contributing party. This view is consistent with the sixth proposition above, and is the one in which Selden, J., sustained the right of recovery in a very able opinion in the same case, and *certainly in line with well-established authorities*, and in support of the doctrine of *ultra vires*. None of the other judges sustained the views of Comstock, J.; but all, except Denio, J., sustained the right of recovery. A different question would have been presented in that case if the plaintiff had sued to recover for failure of defendant to transport him according to agreement.

"In the case now before us the plaintiff seeks to recover contribution from the corporation as co-surety on the bond to the brewing company, and claims (1) that the contract of suretyship was within the defendant's corporate powers; and (2) that, if it were not within defendant's corporate powers, it had so acted on the contract as to now estop it from pleading *ultra vires*. It is claimed that the language of the articles of incorporation, defining the business to be 'the general freight and transfer business, and such other business as may not be inconsistent therewith,' is of such a general character as to cover almost any kind of business. This position, it seems to us, is not tenable, for the language itself implies that there may be business inconsistent with the general freight and transfer business. The name of the corporation indicated its principal business, and the language is equivalent to saying it may do such other business as is consistent with the freight and transfer business. 'Consistent' means standing together, or in agreement with. If the capital of the company is diverted into some other line of business entirely foreign to the freight and transfer business, it would be to the detriment of, and therefore not consistent with, the latter. But, whatever meaning may be attached to the language of the articles, it is quite certain it cannot include the contract of suretyship in question. The simple act of going security for another is out of the line of the prosecution of any business. It is a mere accommodation, and it cannot be assumed that the articles gave the officers of defendant any power to jeopardize its capital in any such venture. . . .

"It seems to us clear that the corporation defendant had no power to make the contract of suretyship in question; and, for the same reason, it is just as clear that the officers of the corporation had no power to sign the letter of May 27, purporting to assume the payment of the amount stipulated in the bond. Both instruments, so far as the defendant was concerned, were illegal and void, and no attempted ratification by parties having no power to make the original contract could make it valid, no matter how often such attempts were made."

§ 39. *The doctrine as construed by English courts— Colman v. Eastern Counties Ry. Co., 10 Beav. 1 (1846).* The first reported case touching the application of the doctrine of *ultra vires* in England was the case of *Col-*

man v. Eastern Counties Ry. Co., supra, where the question arose on a motion to dissolve a special injunction. The directors of a railway company, for the purpose of increasing the traffic, proposed to guaranty certain profits and to secure the capital of an intended steam packet company, who were to act in connection with the railway. It was held that such a transaction was not within their powers, and they were restrained and the injunction made perpetual. The Master of the Rolls, in his opinion, said:

"Joint-stock companies have funds so extensively large and exercise powers so extensive and so materially affecting the rights and interests of other persons and rights which the public or the subjects which her majesty have been accustomed to enjoy under the protection of the laws established in this kingdom, that to look upon a railway company in the light of a common partnership, and as subject to no greater vigilance than common partnerships are, would, I think, be greatly to mistake the functions which they perform, and the powers which they exercise of interference not only with the public, but the private rights of all individuals in this realm. We are to look upon these powers as given them in consideration for the benefit which, notwithstanding all other sacrifices, it is to be presumed and hoped, on the whole, will be obtained by the public. But it being to the interest of the public to protect the private rights of all individuals, and to defend them from all liabilities beyond those necessarily occasioned by the powers given by the several acts, those powers must always be carefully looked to; and I am clearly of opinion that the powers which are given by acts of parliament, like that now in question, extend no further than is expressly stated in the act, or is necessarily or properly required for carrying into effect the undertaking and works which the act has expressly sanctioned. . . . It has been stated that these things, to a small extent, have frequently been done since the establishment of railways; but, unless the acts so done can be proved to be in conformity with the powers given by the special acts of parliament under which these acts are done, they furnish no authority. To suppose that the acquiescence of railway shareholders for the last fifteen years, in any transaction conducted by a railway company, is any evidence whatever of their having a lawful right to enter into it, is, I think, wholly to forget the sort of frenzy which, during that period, the country has been in. . . . I must, in the absence of any legal decision, say that I consider that the acquiescence of the shareholders in such transactions affords no ground whatever for the presumption of their legality."

§ 40. *East Anglian Ry. Co. v. Eastern Counties Ry. Co., 11 C. B. 775 (1852).*—The question arose in this case on an action of covenant wherein the defendant, by an indenture under their common seal between themselves and the plaintiff, agreed to take a lease of their railways upon certain terms mentioned in the indenture, and to find the capital necessary for the construction of the extensions, branches and works authorized to be constructed by the bills then pending in parliament, and to pay the costs of preparing and promoting such bills, whether the same should pass into a law or not. The declaration further stated that the bills were proceeded with, and two were passed, and that the cost of the bills, amounting to a large sum, had not been paid by the defendants to the plaintiffs. It was held that it was not competent for the directors to enter into a contract with another railway company to take a lease of their line, and to pay the costs incurred by them in the soliciting and promoting of bills in parliament for the enterprise and improvement of such other line of railway, even though such extension and improvement would benefit their own company; and that such a contract, if entered into, was illegal and void, and could not be enforced in a court of law. Chief Justice Jervis, in delivering judgment, said:

"This act (6 and 7 W. 4, ch. cvi) is a public act, accessible to all, and supposed to be known to all, and the plaintiffs must therefore be presumed to have dealt with the defendants with a full knowledge of their respective rights, whatever those rights may be. . . . Every proprietor when he takes shares has a right to expect that the conditions upon which the act was obtained will be performed, and it is no sufficient answer to a shareholder, expecting his dividend, that the money has been expended upon an undertaking which, at some remote period, may prove highly beneficial to the line. . . . If the contract is illegal, as being contrary to the act of parliament, it is unnecessary to consider the effect of dissentiate shareholders; for if the company is a corporation only for a limited purpose, and a contract like that under discussion is not within their authority, the assent of all the shareholders to such a contract, though it may make them all personally liable to perform such contract, would not bind them in their corporate capacity or render liable their corporate funds. . . It is not within the scope authorized by the company as a corporation and is therefore void."

§ 41. *Ashbury Ry. Co. v. Riche, 7 H. L. 653 (1875).*—The case, however, most frequently quoted, and the one wherein the doctrine of *ultra vires* is most exhaustively considered and discussed and the question finally set at rest in England, came before the House of Lords on appeal from the Court of Exchequer in 1875. That was the celebrated case of *Ashbury Ry. Co. v. Riche.* The facts in that case were about these: A company was registered under the Joint-stock Companies Act of 1862. Its objects, as stated in the memorandum of association, were: "To make and sell, or lend on hire, railway carriages and wagons, and all kinds of railway plant, fittings, machinery and rolling-stock; to carry on the business of mechanical engineers and *general contractors;* to purchase, work, lease and sell mines, minerals, land and buildings; to purchase and sell, as merchants, timber, coal, metals or other materials, and to buy and sell any such materials on commission or as agents." The directors agreed to purchase a concession for making a railway in a foreign country, and afterwards (on account of difficulties existing by the law of that country) agreed to consign the concession to a *société anonyme* formed in that country, which *société* was to supply the materials for the construction of the railway, and to receive periodical payments from the English company. It was held that this contract, being of a nature not included in the memorandum of association, was *ultra vires* not only of the directors but of the whole company, so that even the subsequent assent of the whole body of shareholders would have no power to ratify it.

As this is the principal case and the leading decision upon which is founded the doctrine of *ultra vires* in England, it is considered of sufficient importance to take up some space in freely quoting from the opinions there delivered.

The Lord Chancellor (Lord Cairns), in the course of his elaborate opinion, said: "The provisions under which that system of limiting liability was inaugurated were provisions not merely, perhaps I might say not mainly, for the benefit of the shareholders for the time being in the company, but were enactments intended also to provide for the interests of two other very important bodies; in the first place, those who might become shareholders in succession to the persons who were shareholders for the time; and secondly, the outside public, and more particularly those who might be creditors of companies of this kind. And I will ask your lordships to observe, as I refer to some of the clauses, the marked and entire difference between the two documents which form the title deeds of companies of this description. I mean the memorandum of association on the one hand and the articles of association on the other hand. With regard to the memorandum of association, your lordships will find, as has often already been pointed out, although it appears somewhat to have been overlooked in the present case, that that is, as it were, the charter, and defines the limitations of the powers of a company to be established under the act. With regard to the articles of association, those articles play a part subsidiary to the memorandum of association. They accept the memorandum of association as the charter of incorporation of the company, and, so accepting it, the articles proceed to define the duties, the rights and the powers of the governing body as between themselves and the company at large, and the mode and form in which changes in the internal regulation of the company may from time to time be made. With regard, therefore, to the memorandum of association, if you find anything which goes beyond their memorandum, or is not warranted by it, the question will arise whether that which is so done is *ultra vires* not only of the directors of the company, but of the company itself.

With regard to the articles of association, if you find anything which, still keeping within the memorandum of association, is a violation of the articles of association, or in excess of them, the question will arise whether that is anything more than an act *extra vires* the directors, but *intra vires* the company. In a case such as that which your lordships have now to deal with, it is not a question whether the contract sued upon involves that which is *malum prohibitum* or *malum in se*, or is a contract contrary to public policy and illegal in itself. I assume the contract in itself to be perfectly legal, to have nothing in it obnoxious to the doctrine involved in the expressions which I have used. The question is not as to the legality of the contract; the question is as to the competency and power of the company to make the contract. Now I am clearly of opinion that this contract was entirely, as I have said, beyond the objects in the memorandum of association. If so, it was thereby placed beyond the powers of the company to make the contract. If so, my lords, it is not a question whether the contract ever was ratified or was not ratified. If it was a contract void at the beginning, it was void because the company could not make the contract. If every shareholder of the company had been in the room, and every shareholder of the company had said: 'That is a contract which we desire to make, which we authorize the directors to make, to which we sanction the placing the seal of the company,' the case would not have stood in any different position from that in which it stands now. The shareholders would thereby, by unanimous consent, have been attempting to do the very thing which, by the act of parliament, they were prohibited from doing."

And Lord Chelmsford, in the same case, in delivering his opinion, used the following language: "Now, the incorporation of a company with limited liability is entirely a creature of the statute. It was necessary not only for the protection of those who might join such companies, but also of persons who might enter into contracts with them, that the privilege of creating them should only be obtained upon certain conditions which should be made known to the public. The legislature, therefore, required that the objects for which the proposed company was to be established should be contained in the memorandum of association, which, when signed and registered, is to establish the incorporated company. . . .

"The real description of the contract entered into by the company is an engagement to supply the contractors for the construction of a foreign railway with the funds necessary to enable them to execute their contract. This is clearly not within any of the objects described in the memorandum of association, and the contract was *ultra vires*, and therefore not voidable merely, but absolutely void. The learned counsel for defendant in error, after arguing against the conclusion that the contract was *ultra vires*, contended that the contract having been in part performed, and the money of the company having been paid in respect of it, the shareholders, in order to have the benefit of their money so misapplied, had a right to abstain from objecting to the contract which might then be enforced against the directors. 'Because,' he said, 'the Companies Act, though it prohibits the contract being entered into, does not say, if the directors have made such a prohibited contract, what the stockholders may do with it.'

"This argument is really directed to the question whether the contract was capable of being ratified by the shareholders. . . . I have already observed that the contract entered into by the company with Messrs. Riche was not a voidable contract merely, but, being in violation of the prohibition contained in the Companies Act, was absolutely void.

"It is exactly in the same condition as if no contract at all had been made, and therefore a ratification of it is not possible. If there had been an actual ratification it could not have given life to a contract which had no existence in itself; but at the utmost it would have amounted to a sanction by the shareholders to the act of the directors, which, if given before the contract was entered into, would not have made it valid, as it does not relate to an object within the scope of the memorandum of association."

And says Lord O'Hagan in the same case: "Having, therefore, no doubt that the action of this company was *ultra vires*, I confess I have as little that there was no valid ratification of the impeached contract. Again, we must keep in mind the purpose of the legislation with which we are dealing. It was, as I have said, to give a privilege upon a condition; and the privilege was to be enjoyed upon the terms and with the limitations indicated in the memorandum of association. The memorandum, when put on record, was to be for contractors, for creditors, and for all the world, a reliable description of the exact character, purposes and powers of the company described in it. And the admission of an authority in shareholders to warrant anything inconsistent with that charter, antagonistic to those purposes and beyond those powers (and in this case it was so undoubtedly), would seem to encourage evasion of the statute to abrogate the condition whilst continuing the privilege, and so to give the benefit without the burden. By the memorandum the general community is to judge of the association; but how can that be so if shareholders, proposing to bind the corporation by resolution, perhaps effective between the shareholders themselves, altogether ignore that memorandum, and authorize dealings quite beyond the scope of its contemplation? It is plain that if the ratification for which the defendant in error contends could validly affirm the contract on which he relies, there is no amount of divergence from the original object of the company which might not have been approved, no extension of the limits prescribed by the memorandum which might not have been effected by a single resolution of all the stockholders. And if this be so, I cannot think that a conclusion pregnant with consequences so very serious can properly be sustained. It is not warranted by the statute, which equally condemns it by affirmative and negative provisions; and any such ratification, if relied on, being in clear contravention of the purpose and the letter of the law, should, in my opinion, be held void and illegal."

§ 42. *Attorney-General v. Great Eastern Ry. Co., 5 App. Cas. 473 (1880).*— Extracts from this and the following English cases are made for the purpose of showing that the rule of construction adopted in the *Riche Case, supra*, relative to the doctrine of *ultra vires*, has been strictly adhered to, and is the accepted application of the doctrine in that country. In this case the Lord Chancellor (Lord Selborne) says, among other things: "I assume that your lordships will not now recede from anything that was determined in *Ashbury Ry. Co. v. Riche:* it appears to me to be important that the doctrine of *ultra vires* as it was explained in that case should be maintained. But I agree with Lord Justice James that this doctrine ought to be reasonably and not unreasonably understood and applied, and that whatever may be fairly regarded as incidental to or consequential upon those things which the legislature has authorized ought not (unless expressly prohibited) be held by judicial construction to be *ultra vires*."

And Lord Blackburn, in the same case, said: "That case appears to me to decide at all events this: that where there is an act of parliament creating a corporation for a particular purpose, and giving it powers for that particular purpose, what it does not expressly or impliedly authorize is to be taken as prohibited. . . . Those things which are incident to and may reasonably and properly be done under the main purpose, though they may not be literally within it, would not be prohibited."

§ 43. *Small et al. v. Smith et al., 10 App. Cas. 119 (1884)*. In this case the Earl of Selborne, L. C., observed: "Now I entirely adhere to what was said in this House in the case of *Attorney-General v. Great Eastern Ry. Co.*, 5 App. Cas. 473, that when you have got a main purpose expressed and ample authority given to effect that main purpose, things which are incidental to it and which may reasonably and properly be done, and against which no express prohibition is found, may and ought *prima facie* to follow from the authority for effectuating the main purpose by proper and general means. I think it quite right to notify your lordships to apply that principle to the present case. In order to see how it applies we must ascertain first of all what the main purpose here is, then what are the general powers of the directors, then what are the special powers, and then, supposing that this is not within the natural meaning of these general powers or of these special powers, whether it can be brought in as incidental to the main purpose, and a thing reasonably to be done for effectuating it."

§ 44. *Baroness Wenlock, etc. v. The River Dee, 10 App. Cas. 354 (1885).*—Lord Watson, in this case, where the question was as to the power of borrowing money, used the following language: "Whenever a corporation is created by an act of parliament with reference to the purpose of the act and solely with a view for carrying those purposes into execution, I am of the opinion not only that the objects which the corporation may legitimately pursue must be ascertained from the act itself, but that the powers which a corporation may lawfully use in pursuance of these object must either be expressly conferred or derived by reasonable implication from its provisions. That appears to me to be the principal recognized by this House in *Ashbury Co. v. Riche* and in *Attorney-General v. Great Eastern Ry. Co.*"

§ 45. *Trevor et al. v. Whitworth et al., 12 App. Cas. 409 (1887).*— In passing upon the power of a corporation to purchase its own stock, Lord Herchell, in this case, said: "It cannot be questioned since the case of *Ashbury Co. v. Riche* that a company cannot employ its funds for the purpose of any transactions which do not come within the objects specified in the memorandum, and that a company cannot, by its articles of association, extend its powers in this respect. . . . But it is to be observed that at that time it was not so clearly settled as it has been since the judgment in *Ashbury Ry. v. Riche* that a transaction not within the scope of the memorandum is incapable of ratification."

CHAPTER III.

CONTRACTS OF CORPORATIONS.

THE DOCTRINE APPLIED TO CONTRACTS GENERALLY.

§ 46. Introductory.
47. Application of doctrine to contracts generally.
48. Province of court in applying doctrine.
49. Tendency of courts to disregard statutory enactments.
50. As to incidental contractual powers.
51. Irregularity no defense to liability on corporate contract.
52. When charter prescribes mode of contracting, it must be strictly pursued.
53. All persons bound to take notice of limits of corporate power.
54. Why corporations not liable on *ultra vires* contracts.
55. Distinction between *ultra vires* and illegal contracts.
56. Prohibited contracts regarded as illegal and void.
57. Unauthorized contracts none the less illegal because ignored by courts.

§ 46. *Introductory.*—While, as a general rule, the application of the doctrine of *ultra vires* to corporate contracts has been comparatively uniform in this country when the question has been squarely presented to the court, yet there has been a distinction made by some of the state courts in its application to executory contracts and to those that have been partially or wholly performed by one or the other of the parties. It is plainly apparent, however, that this lack of uniformity is not from any want of soundness in the doctrine itself, but rather from a lack of proper diligence and a more thorough investigation by the court called upon to decide the merits or demerits of the doctrine in its application to the particular case under consideration; on such occasions the defense being usually denied on the broad ground that it would be "unjust, inequitable and unconscionable." And it is a fact easy of verification by an earnest investigator, that the most soothing axioms relative to this doctrine — axioms whose rhythmic measures strike the ear of equity like unto the lascivious pleasings of the lute — have been evolved by a reminiscent court on occasions when the defense of *ultra vires* had not been earnestly urged, nor could it properly be applied in deciding the question submitted for the court's adjudication. It is a further fact worthy of mention, that these very musical maxims, conceived by a consenting court without legitimate connection, and brought forth at a period of convulsive irregularity before proper reflection had wrought maturity, are the very phrases most generally quoted by those of both bench and bar, whose equitable consciences are so supersensitive as to shrink from even the plainest rules of elementary law.

§ 47. *Application of doctrine to contracts generally.—* It is now the well-established rule that a corporation can make no contracts, either within or without the state which created it, except such as are authorized by its charter or law of creation.[1] The doctrine of *ultra vires*,

[1] Bank of Augusta v. Earle, 13 Pet. (U. S.) 588; Talmage v. North Amer. Coal Co., 3 Head (Tenn.). 337; Thomas v. Railroad Co., 101 U. S. 71; Pittsburg, etc. R. Co. v. Keokuk Bridge Co., 131 U. S. 385; Green Bay, etc. Co. v. Steamboat Co.. 107 U. S. 100; Davis v. Old Colony R. Co., 131 Mass. 258; Whitman Gold M. Co. v. Baker, 3 Nev. 386; Louisiana State Bank v. Orleans Nav. Co., 3 La. Ann. 294; Baltimore v. Baltimore, etc. R. Co., 21 Md. 50; Petersburgh v. Metzker, 21 Ill. 205; Jacksonville v. McConnel, 12 id. 138; Kinzie v. Chicago, 3 id. 187; Smith v. Eureka Flour Mills, 6 Cal. 1; McMasters v. Reed, 1 Grant Cas. (Pa.) 36; Straus v. Eagle Ins. Co., 5 Ohio St. 59; White's Bank v. Toledo Ins. Co., 12 id. 601; Downing v. Mt. Washington R.

however, in its relation to contracts of corporations, should be properly and reasonably applied; and whatever may be fairly regarded as incidental to and consequential upon those things which are authorized by the charter of the company, ought not, unless expressly prohibited, be held by judicial construction to be *ultra vires*.[1]

§ 48. *Province of court in applying doctrine.*— The court, however, in the exercise of a sound discretion in the application of this doctrine, should not seek to enlarge the domain of judicial speculation beyond the bounds of legitimate inquiry, and predicate its judgment upon what would seem, from lack of cited authority, a wise discretion alone, regardless of the provisions of the charter or the laws under which the corporation was organized, which are the sources of corporate powers. For it is not the province of the court, it is submitted, to indulge in hypothetical speculation concerning a given question, when it has been squarely settled by legislation. The doctrine of *ultra vires* was evolved for no other purpose than that of restricting corporations in their transactions to those acts and contracts with which their creator thought fit and proper to endow them. The defense of *ultra vires* is only the means used to arrive at the desired end. If a person make a contract which is contrary to law, it would seem but a simple matter to so declare it, and pronounce it void and of no effect. In an action on such a contract, the contract itself is the strongest possible evidence that the law has been violated; and why

Co., 40 N. H. 230; Beatty v. Insurance Co., 2 John. (N. Y.) 109; Beaty v. Knowler, 4 Pet. (U. S.) 152; State v. Stebbins, 1 Stew. (Ala.) 299; Head v. Providence Ins. Co., 2 Cranch (U. S.), 127.

[1] Attorney-General v. Great Eastern Ry., 5 App. Cas. 473; Ellerman v. Chicago, etc. Co., 49 N. J. Eq. 217, and cases cited in preceding note.

an inquiry into the relative conditions of the parties to it? Courts should take contracts as they find them, and not presume to attempt to make a new and different contract founded on the relative conditions and standing of the parties at the time of adjudication. Neither is it the province of the court, if a statute be clear and unambiguous, to say that it means something entirely different from that expressed. Corporations are very often prohibited, either directly or by necessary implication, from doing certain acts or making certain contracts, in which case the court should dismiss from its consideration any conjecture as to the reason or right of the legislature in enacting a particular statute, unless its constitutionality be directly attacked, and only lend its aid and guidance towards enforcing a compliance with the provisions of the law as they stand. It is the province and duty of the court, to be sure, to construe the meaning of doubtful and ambiguous terms, and to let the light of its judicial wisdom shine upon the dark and obscure passages in the laws, occasioned perhaps by legislative laxity or ill-advised haste; but when the provisions of a statute are certain and their meaning plain, to seek to evade or disregard their true import because they may be contrary to the preconceived notions of the court as to established principles of equity and justice is certainly stretching the "discretion" of the court beyond the pale of judicial dignity.

§ 49. *Tendency of courts to disregard statutory enactments.*—This tendency of the courts to seek to evade the plain provisions of a statute has been remarked and commented upon by a master mind. Mr. Sedgwick, in his admirable work on Construction of Statutes, says: "It seems to me difficult to deny that the practice of sanctioning the evasion or disregard of statutes, which we have had occasion to notice in the cases thus examined, has been carried beyond the line of sound discretion. This idea has been repeatedly expressed: 'I am not very well satisfied with the summary mode of getting rid of a statutory provision by calling it directory,' says Hubbard, J., in the supreme court of Vermont. 'If one positive requirement and provision of a statute may be avoided in that way, I see no reason why another may not.' (*Briggs v. Georgia*, 15 Vt. 61, 72.) It is equally obvious, however, that serious evils are sure to result from a latitude of construction so considerable as we find to exist; and I therefore attempt, with great deference for the able and learned magistrates who are practically engaged in the administration of justice, to frame the following rules as those which ought to govern in this department of our science:

"The intention of the legislature should control absolutely the action of the judiciary; where that intention is clearly ascertained, the courts have no other duty to perform than to execute the legislative will without any regard to their own views as to the wisdom or justice of the particular enactment. The means of ascertaining that intention are to be found in the statute itself, taken as a whole and with all its parts, in statutes on the same subject, antecedent jurisprudence and legislation, contemporaneous and more recent exposition, judicial construction and usage; and to the use of these means, and these alone, the judiciary is confined. No other extrinsic facts are in any way to be taken into consideration. It is not until these means fail, and until the attempt to ascertain the legislative intent is hopeless, that the judiciary can with propriety assume any power of construing a statute, strictly or liberally, with reference either to the particular character of the statute, or to their own ideas of policy or equity. Where the meaning of a statute as it stands is clear, they have no power to insert qualifications, engraft exceptions, or make modifications under the idea of providing for cases in regard to which the legislature has omitted any specific provisions.

"In cases where the intent of the legislature is ambiguous, and the effort to arrive at it is hopeless, and in these cases only, does the power of construing a statute strictly or liberally exist; and in regard to its exercise, as of discretionary power generally, no other rule can be laid down than that it must be exerted under the guidance of learning, fidelity and practical sagacity. . . .

"Every statute may be said to have two aspects: if it be severe in regard to an individual, it is beneficial to the community; if it punishes crime, it also prevents fraud; if it infringes on some venerable rule of the ancient law, it also introduces more simple, rapid and less expensive modes of procedure; so that every act is capable, if the doctrine be admitted, of being construed in two ways diametrically opposed to each other, *according to the temper of the magistrate to whom the task is confided.*

"The inconsistencies and discrepancies, as they now exist, in truth, *too often arise from a desire, often an unconscious one, to substitute the judicial for the legislative will; and they can only be corrected by adhering to the cardinal rule that the judicial functions are always best discharged by an honest and earnest desire to ascertain and effect the intention of the law-making body.*"[1]

§ 50. *As to incidental contractual powers.*—Every corporation, unless restrained by law, has the incidental power to make any contract which may be necessary to

[1] Sedgwick, Stat. & Const. Law (2d ed.), 325, 326, 327.

advance the objects of its creation.¹ In deciding whether a corporation can make a particular contract, it must be considered in the first place whether its charter, or some statute binding upon it, forbids or permits it to make such a contract; and if the charter and valid statutory law are silent upon the subject, in the second place, whether the power to make such a contract may not be implied on the part of the corporation as directly or incidentally necessary to enable it to fulfill the purposes of its existence; or whether the contract is entirely foreign to its purpose.² Whenever a corporation makes a contract, it is the contract of the legal entity — of the artificial being created by the charter — and not the contract of the individual members.³ If the foregoing distinctions be kept in mind, much doubt and needless confusion will be avoided.

§ 51. *Irregularity no defense to liability on corporate contract.*— A corporation is estopped to deny its liability under a contract on the ground that the officers were not technically authorized to make it, or that its own proceedings in the premises were irregular, when the contract was in the scope of its powers, was entered into by proper officers, and has been recognized by corporate acts.[4]

[1] Galena v. Corwith, 48 Ill. 423; Straus v. Eagle Ins. Co., 5 Ohio St. 59; Broughton v. Manchester Water Co., 3 B. & A. 1; Seibrecht v. New Orleans, 12 La. Ann. 496; Brooklyn Gravel Co. v. Sloughter, 33 Ind. 185; Weckler v. First Nat. Bank, 42 Md. 581; Goodrich v. Detroit, 12 Mich. 279; Bateman v. Ashton-under-Lynn, 3 H. & N. 323; Douglas v. Virginia City, 5 Nev. 147.

[2] Weckler v. First Nat. Bank, 42 Md. 581.

[3] Head v. Prov. Ins. Co., 2 Cranch (U. S.), 127; Dartmouth College v. Woodward, 4 Wheat. (U. S.) 636; Bank of U. S. v. Dandridge, 12 Wheat. (U. S.) 64; Petersborough R. R. Co. v. Nassau Co., 59 N. H. 385.

[4] Bakersfield Ass'n v. Chester, 55 Cal. 98; Dooly v. Cheshire Glass

§ 52. *But when charter prescribes mode of contracting, it must be strictly pursued.*— It is not necessary that the charter of a corporation should confer the power of contracting by an officer or agent in order to give him that right; but when the charter prescribes any mode in which the officers or agents of a corporation must act, that mode must be strictly pursued to render the contract obligatory upon the corporation.[1] Officers of a corporation are special and not general agents; consequently they have no power to bind the corporation by contract except within the limits prescribed by the charter and by-laws. Persons dealing with such officers are charged with notice of the authority conferred upon them and of the limitations and restrictions upon it contained in the charter.[2] Accordingly, an insurance company was held not liable on a contract, and was not estopped from setting up the defense of *ultra vires*, though its agent had led the other contracting party to believe, and he did believe, that the company had power to make it, and though no pretense

Co., 15 Gray (Mass.), 404; Merrick v. Reynolds Eng. Co., 101 Mass. 381; Salem Nat. Bank v. Almy, 117 Mass. 476; Chamberlin v. Huguenot Mfg. Co., 118 Mass. 532; Ewing v. Robeson, 15 Ind. 26; Hammond v. Straus, 53 Md. 1; Rush v. Steamboat Co., 84 N. C. 70; Whitney v. Wyman. 101 U. S. 392; Upton v. Hansborough, 3 Biss. (U. S.) 417.

[1] St. Andrew's Bay L. Co. v. Mitchell, 4 Fla. 192; Bank of Augusta v. Earle. 13 Pet. (U. S.) 588; Talmage v. Coal Co., 3 Head (Tenn.), 377; Norwich v. Norfolk P. Co., 4 El. & Bl. 397; s. c., 82 E. C. L. 396; Eastern Counties R. Co. v. Hawkes, 5 H. L. 331; Taylor v. Chichester, etc. R. Co., L. R. 2 Ex. 356; Canal, etc. R. Co. v. St. Charles R. Co., 44 La. Ann. 1069; Boyce v. Montauk Gas Co., 37 W. Va. 73; Ashbury Ry. Co. v. Riche, 7 H. L. 653; Hazlehurst v. Savannah R. Co., 43 Ga. 13; Cozart v. Georgia R. Co., 54 Ga. 379; Lucas v. White Line Trans. Co., 70 Iowa, 550.

[2] Adriance v. Roome, 52 Barb. (N. Y.) 399; Pittsburg R. Co. v. Keokuk Bridge Co., 131 U. S. 371; Pearce v. Madison R. Co., 21 How. (U. S.) 441; Thomas v. Railroad Co., 101 U. S. 71; Central Co. v. Pullman Co., 139 U. S. 24.

was set up by the company, or its agent, that the contract was *ultra vires*, until a loss thereunder was known by all parties to have occurred.[1]

§ 53. *All persons bound to take notice of limits of corporate powers.*— Every person who enters into a contract with a corporation is bound at his peril to take notice of the legal limits of its capacity.[2] A corporation is not held out by the government nor by the stockholders as authorized to make contracts which are beyond the purposes and scope of its charter; and if it exceeds its chartered pow-

[1] Webster v. Buffalo Ins. Co., 7 Fed. Rep. 399.

[2] Davis v. Old Colony Ry. Co., 131 Mass. 258; Whittenton Mills v. Upton, 10 Gray (Mass.), 582; Richardson v. Sibley, 11 Allen (Mass.), 65; Pearce v. Madison R. Co., 21 How. (U. S.) 441; East Anglian Ry. v. Eastern Counties Ry., 11 C. B. 775; Ashbury Co. v. Riche, 7 H. L. 653; Central Trans. Co. v. Pullman P. Car Co., 139 U. S. 24; Thomas v. Railroad Co., 101 U. S. 71; Mallory v. Hanauer Oil Works, 86 Tenn. 598; Zabriskie v. Cleveland, etc. R. Co., 23 How. (U. S.) 381; Pacific Postal Tel. Co. v. Western Union Tel. Co., 50 Fed. Rep. 493; Branch v. Jessup, 106 U. S. 468; Pennsylvania R. Co. v. St. Louis R. Co., 118 U. S. 290; Salt Lake City v. Hollister, 118 U. S. 256; Willamette Mfg. Co. v. Bank, 119 U. S. 191; Green Bay R. Co. v. Steamboat Co., 107 U. S. 98; Pittsburg, etc. R. Co. v. Keokuk Bridge Co., 131 U. S. 371; Oregon R. Co. v. Oregonian R. Co., 130 U. S. 1; Sutliff v. Lake County, 147 U. S. 230; Marcy v. Oswego, 92 U. S. 637; Humboldt v. Long, 92 U. S. 642; Dixon County v. Field, 111 U. S. 83; Lake County v. Graham, 130 U. S. 674; Chaffee County v. Potter, 142 U. S. 355; St. Louis Ry. Co. v. Terre Haute, etc. Co., 145 U. S. 393; Bailey v. M. E. Church, 71 Me. 472; Franklin County v. Lewiston, etc. Inst., 68 Me. 43; Hood v. N. Y. etc. R. Co., 22 Conn. 17; s. c., 23 Conn. 622; Naugatuck R. Co. v. Waterbury Button Co., 24 Conn. 482; Converse v. Norwich Trans. Co., 33 Conn. 179; In re Cork, etc. R. Co., L. R. 4 Ch. 748; Greeley v. Nashua Sav. Bank, 63 N. H. 145; Hall v. Paris, 59 N. H. 74; Simmons v. Troy Iron Works, 92 Ala. 427; Sherwood v. Alvis, 83 Ala. 115; Smith v. Alabama, etc. Co., 4 Ala. 558; Montgomery v. Montgomery, etc. Co., 31 Ala. 76; Waddill v. Alabama R. Co., 35 Ala. 323; Chambers v. Falkner, 65 Ala. 448; Wilkes v. Georgia, etc. R. Co., 79 Ala. 180; N. W. Packet Co. v. Shaw, 37 Wis. 655; Luthe v. Farmers' Ins. Co., 55 Wis. 543.

ers, not only may the government take away its charter,[1] but those who have subscribed to its stock may avoid any contract made by the corporation in clear excess of its powers, and a court of chancery, on the application of a stockholder, will restrain the corporation from carrying out the contract.[2]

§ 54. *Why corporations not liable on ultra vires contracts.*—The reasons why a corporation is not liable on a contract *ultra vires* are, first, the interest of the public that the corporation shall not transcend the limits of the

[1] Merchants' Nat. Bank v. Hanson, 33 Minn. 40; Hennesy v. St. Paul, 54 Minn. 219; National Bank v. Mathews, 98 U. S. 621; National Bank v. Whitney, 103 U. S. 99; Fortier v. N. O. Bank, 112 U. S. 439.

[2] Davis v. Old Colony R. Co., 131 Mass. 258; Pratt v. Pratt, 33 Conn. 446; Belmont v. Erie R. Co., 52 Barb. (N. Y.) 637; Black v. Delaware, etc. Canal Co., 22 N. J. Eq. 130; Tippecanoe Co. v. Lafayette R. Co., 50 Ind. 85; Teachout v. Des Moines, etc. R. Co., 75 Iowa, 722; Chicago v. Cameron, 120 Ill. 447; Bliss v. Anderson, 31 Ala. 612; Bergman v. St. Paul, etc. Ass'n, 29 Minn. 275; Cass v. Manchester, etc. Co., 9 Fed. Rep. 640; Zabriskie v. Hackensack, etc. Co., 18 N. J. Eq. 178; Zabriskie v. Cleveland, etc. R. Co., 23 How. (U. S.) 381; Memphis v. Dean, 8 Wall. (U. S.) 64; Bronson v. La Crosse R. Co., 2 Wall. (U. S.) 283; Dodge v. Woolsey, 18 How. (U. S.) 331; Heath v. Erie R. Co., 8 Blatch. (U. S.) 347; Rogers v. Oxford, etc. R. Co., 2 De G. & J. 662; Kernaghan v. Williams, L. R. 6 Eq. 228; Hodgson v. Powis, 1 De G., M. & G. 6; Cohen v. Wilkinson, 1 Macn. & G. 481; Ware v. Regents Canal Co., 3 De G. & J. 212; Pickering v. Stevenson, L. R. 14 Eq. 322; Mills v. Northern R. Co., L. R. 5 Ch. Div. 621; Aukland v. Westminster Board, L. R. 7 Ch. Div. 597; Bagshaw v. Eastern Counties Ry. Co., 7 Hare, 114; Ware v. Grand Junction Water-works Co., 2 Russ. & Mylne, 470; Cunliffe v. Manchester, etc. Canal Co., 2 id. 480, n.; Great Western R. Co. v. Rushout, 5 De G. & S. 290; Bird v. Bird's Pat. Co., L. R. 9 Ch. Div. 358; Solomons v. Lang, 12 Beav. 339; Lyde v. Eastern Bengal R. Co., 36 Beav. 13; Snell v. Minneapolis, etc. R. Co., 45 Minn. 264; Young v. Gaslight Co., 15 N. Y. Sup. 443; McCray v. Junction R. Co., 9 Ind. 358; Stewart v. Erie, etc. Trans. Co., 17 Minn. 348.

powers granted; second, the interest of the stockholders that the capital stock shall not be subjected to the risk of enterprises not contemplated by the charter, and therefore not authorized by the stockholders in subscribing for the stock; and third, the obligation of every one entering into a contract with a corporation to take notice of the legal limits of its powers.[1]

§ 55. *As to distinction between ultra vires and illegal contracts.* — It has been confidently asserted in a certain class of cases, and the position is restated and adopted by a very able author,[2] that when acts of corporations are spoken of as *ultra vires* it is not intended that they are unlawful, or even such as the corporation cannot perform, but merely those that are not within the powers conferred upon the corporation by the act of its creation, and are in violation of the trust reposed in the managing board by the shareholders that the affairs shall be managed, and the funds applied solely, for carrying out the objects for which the corporation was created; and that whether a contract *as originally made* was *ultra vires* is not a very important inquiry.[3] The learned judges and law writers who have adopted the views promulgated by Chief Justice Comstock in the *Bissell Case*, and to the same effect in the *Whitney Arms Company Case*, seem to have taken the position and involved the subject in more or less confusion by assuming that no act or contract can be unlawful or illegal unless it be infected with the taint of moral turpitude, or fruitful of fraud and felony. This is certainly an exaggerated idea of an illegal transaction

[1] Railway Co. v. Keokuk Bridge Co., 131 U. S. 384; Pearce v. Madison, etc. Ry. Co., 21 How. (U. S.) 441; Central Trans. Co. v. Pullman Co., 139 U. S. 24, and cases cited in preceding note.
[2] Beach on Priv. Corp., § 422.
[3] Whitney Arms Co. v. Barlow, 63 N. Y. 62.

when considered in connection with corporate undertakings. An act or contract may be illegal or unlawful because expressly or impliedly prohibited by law, and yet be for some benevolent and worthy purpose. Such transactions are made unlawful or illegal because prohibited by and contrary to law. The proposition that when acts of corporations are spoken of as *ultra vires* it is not intended that they are such as the corporation cannot perform is directly refuted by a long line of cases in the United States supreme court, and notably in the case of *Central Transportation Co. v. Pullman Car Co.*, 139 U. S. 24, where Mr. Justice Gray, delivering the opinion of the court, says: "A contract of a corporation which is *ultra vires* in the proper sense, that is to say, outside the objects of creation as defined in the law of its organization, and therefore beyond the powers conferred upon it by the legislature, is not voidable only, but wholly void and of no legal effect. *The objection to the contract is, not merely that the corporation ought not to have made it, but that it could not make it. . . . No performance on either side* can give the *unlawful contract* any validity or be the foundation of any right of action upon it."

So in *People v. Chicago Gas Trust Co.*, 130 Ill. 286, the court, in discussing this phase of the subject, say: "The word 'unlawful' as applied to corporations is not used exclusively in the sense of *malum in se* or *malum prohibitum*. It is also used to designate powers which they are not authorized to make, or acts which they are not authorized to do; or, in other words, *such acts, powers and contracts as are ultra vires.*"[1]

[1] And to the same effect are Pittsburg, etc. Ry. Co. v. Keokuk Bridge Co., 131 U. S. 371, 389; Mayor of Norwich v. Norfolk Ry., 4 El. & Bl. (Q. B.) 397; McGregor v. Railway Co., 18 Q. B. 457; Gunness v. Land Corp. of Ireland, 22 Ch. Div. 341; Taylor v. Chichester, etc.

§ 56. *Prohibited contracts regarded as illegal and void.*

It is the accepted doctrine of the courts of this country and England that a contract of a corporation which is prohibited by its charter or laws under which it is created, either expressly or by necessary implication, is considered as illegal and void, and that in passing upon such

Ry. Co., L. R. 2 Ex. 356; Wetherell v. Jones, 3 B. & A. 221; Bartlett v. Viner, Carth. 252; Smith v. Mawhood, 14 M. & W. 452; South Ry. etc. Co. v. Great Northern Ry., 9 Exch. 75, 84; Shrewsbury, etc. Ry. Co. v. Northwestern Ry. Co., 6 H. L. 113; Thomas v. Railroad Co., 101 U. S. 82; State v. Nebraska Distilling Co., 29 Neb. 700; Franklin Co. v. Lewiston Inst. etc., 68 Me. 43.

In State v. Nebraska Distilling Co., *supra*, the court say: "A corporation, therefore, can only be organized under our laws for a lawful purpose, and any acts done by such a corporation for the accomplishment of a purpose not lawful is unauthorized, in excess of its powers, and therefore illegal and void. The acts of a corporation to be unlawful need not necessarily be *mala prohibita* or *malum in se*, although such acts are illegal in all cases; but every act of a corporation which, by the terms of its charter, it is not authorized to do, is in excess of its charter, and therefore unlawful."

So in Franklin Co. v. Lewiston Inst., *supra*, the court say: "The agreement was that the Franklin Company should pay for the stock for which the trustee of the bank had subscribed, and take the stock and hold it as security. We thus see that by the very terms of the agreement the money was to be applied to a specific purpose, and that purpose an *illegal* one. We use the word 'illegal,' not in the sense of *malum in se* nor *malum prohibitum*, but in the sense in which it is used to describe the unauthorized acts of corporations — acts and contracts *ultra vires*."

And Selden, J., in Bissell v. Michigan, etc. Co., 22 N. Y. 258, says: "The contracts of corporations which are not authorized by their charters are *illegal* because they are made in contravention of public policy. . . . Although the unauthorized contract may be neither *malum in se* nor *malum prohibitum*, but, on the contrary, may be for some benevolent or worthy object — as to build an almshouse or a college, or to purchase and distribute tracts or books of instruction, — yet, if it is a violation of public policy for corporations to exercise powers which have never been granted to them, such contracts, notwithstanding their praiseworthy nature, are *illegal* and void."

contracts the courts have construed the meaning of the words "illegal" and "*ultra vires*" as identical.[1] In *Taylor v. Chichester & Midhurst Ry. Co., supra*, Mellor, J., said: "I think that the statutes by which the defendants were incorporated did constitute them a company created for particular purposes, with special powers, and that the application of the funds to be raised under them is limited to prescribed and definite objects; and that by reasonable inference from the provisions of the statute, the bargain now under consideration *is prohibited*, and that its performance by the defendants would amount, not merely to a breach of trust, the remedy for which would be in equity, *but that the contract itself, being ultra vires and illegal because prohibited*, the defense is properly raised in a court of law." So, in *Mayor of Norwich v. Norfolk Ry.*, above cited, the court say: "It remains to be considered whether this contract was *illegal, as not authorized by the act incorporating the defendant company, and therefore prohibited by that act.* . . . So a contract for a purpose unconnected with the purpose of incorporation is, or may result in, an application of the funds to a purpose unconnected with the purpose of incorporation, and is therefore *held to be prohibited and void.*"

§ 57. *Unauthorized contracts none the less illegal because statutes ignored by courts.*— It has been contended by a very learned author that a contract is not necessarily void and not to be enforced because it is prohibited by statute, by showing that courts have ignored such provisions in the statute as though they were not in exist-

[1] Taylor v. Chichester, etc. Ry. Co., L. R. 2 Ex. 356; Gunness v. Land Corp. of Ireland, 22 Ch. Div. 349; McGregor v. Railway Co., 18 Ad. & El. (Q. B.) 457; Mayor of Norwich v. Norfolk Ry., 4 El. & Bl. (Q. B.) 397; and see cases cited in preceding section.

ence.[1] This astonishing deduction is stated in the following language: "Statutes have frequently been passed expressly prohibiting corporations from exercising any powers except those conferred by their charters. Sometimes the prohibitions are enacted in the form of general laws applicable to all corporations, and sometimes they are incorporated in special charters applicable to particular corporations only.

"Prohibitions of this description are *merely declaratory of the general common-law prohibition against any exercise of corporate powers which have not been authorized by the legislature; and there is no reason for supposing that the legislature, in enacting such a prohibition, intends to give it any greater force or effect than the common-law rule.*

"There is probably no state or country in which a rule contrary to the views above expressed has been systematically enforced. In many instances these legislative prohibitions declaratory of the common law *have been tacitly ignored by the courts.* Thus, the Revised Statutes of New York declare that: 'In addition to the powers enumerated . . . and those expressly given in its charter, or in the act under which it shall be incorporated, *no corporation shall possess or exercise any* corporate powers except such as shall be necessary to the exercise of the powers so enumerated and given;' *but it has never been held that corporate acts and contracts in violation of this prohibition are necessarily null and unenforceable at law.* There are numerous cases in which prohibited acts and contracts falling within the prohibition have been recognized and given effect."[2] This is

[1] Morawetz on Corp., § 658.
[2] Mor. Priv. Corp., §§ 658, 659, the *numerous cases* resolving themselves into *three*—Moss v. Averhill, 10 N. Y. 460; Whitney Arms Co. v. Barlow, 63 id. 62; and Whitney v. Wyman, 101 U. S. 392,—the latter of which does not sustain any such propositions.

6

indeed a sad commentary on the courts of New York, and from some decisions which have been rendered by courts in that state the inference might be readily drawn that the learned author is speaking with some truth. While it is a matter of common knowledge in the profession that courts have frequently ignored certain statutes, judging from their decisions, yet it would seem to require a vast deal of hardihood to claim this as authority for a violation of the law. It is certainly one of the weakest arguments that could be adduced, and possesses not the slightest merit.

CHAPTER IV.

THE DOCTRINE APPLIED TO EXECUTED CONTRACTS.

§ 58. Estoppel — Defense of *ultra vires* to executed contracts.
  59. Same subject.
  60. Same subject — Corporation similar to one under legal disability.
  61. Performance by innocent party to contract *ultra vires* a corporation.
  62. Position of United States supreme court on alleged rule.
  63. San Antonio v. Mehaffy.
  64. Railway Co. v. McCarthey.
  65. Hitchcock v. Galveston.
  66. Jones v. Guaranty Co.
  67. National Bank v. Mathews.
  68. Central Transportation Co. v. Pullman Car Co.

§ 58. *Estoppel — Defense of ultra vires as to executed contracts.* — While a great majority of the courts of this country, both federal and state, agree, in the main, that a contract *ultra vires* a corporation must be deemed as illegal and void, and no suit can be maintained upon it,[1] yet if such a contract, though in contravention of law as originally made, be executed or partly performed by one or the other of the parties to it, in that case it has been held by some state courts that the defense of *ultra vires* should not be allowed.[2] The grounds upon which this denial is predicated are that the company is estopped from setting up its own unauthorized act and its own incapacity to evade performance on its part, after receiving the

[1] See §§ 9, 53, 54, and cases there cited.
[2] Whitney Arms Co. v. Barlow, 63 N. Y. 62; Bradley v. Ballard, 55 Ill. 413; Darst v. Gale, 83 Ill. 136; Beach on Priv. Corp., § 422.

fruits of the bargain; that the court refuses to entertain the defense which common honesty forbids the company to make; that a man may become bound by the act of an unauthorized agent and be held liable on the contract made for him, not on the ground that the agent in fact had any authority, but for some conduct on the part of the alleged principal which precludes him from raising the question of authority.[1]

§ 59. *Same subject.*—Let us see if the propositions contained in the next preceding section are not both fallacious and untenable. First, it is contended in the cases heretofore cited that the company is estopped from setting up its own unauthorized act and incapacity to evade performance on its part. It is asserted with much confidence, and it is submitted that the great weight of authority bears out the assertion, that the act set up as unauthorized is not, and by any possibility could not, under the charter of the corporation, have been *its own*, but is the *unauthorized act of its officer or agent*. It could not have been the corporate act, for in its creation the element of power for performing the particular act was left out of its organization—the power is wanting. As to the corporation, the legal entity, such act is null—as though it had never been performed. It is a creature resting under a legal disability. The law has said it may not and cannot perform such an act. It is created with specified powers only, and for those purposes enumerated in the act of its creation. It is not on the same footing as a person who may be bound by the act of an unauthorized agent by conduct of acquiescence or ratification, because it cannot ratify an act which it has no power in itself to perform.[2]

[1] See cases cited in preceding note.
[2] See § 78 *post*, and cases cited.

§ 60.] EXECUTED CONTRACTS.

§ 60. *Same subject — Corporation similar to person under legal disability.*— *Ultra vires* acts of corporations bear a striking similarity to those of persons resting under a legal disability, such as infants and married women; in fact a corporation and a married woman have many points in common. *Neither has any existence until created by law.* Individuals, by conforming to specified requirements of the law, acquire, in a corporate capacity, certain rights and powers, and are subject to certain liabilities, when acting in such legal capacity. Their individual identity is sunk and merged in the corporate entity, and in such capacity only are they recognized by the law when the acts of the corporation are involved. So, likewise, it may be said of a married woman. She becomes such only through methods prescribed by the law, and as such — the care and solicitude of the law — she is a creature of but slight volition. She rests under a legal disability which, when removed by the law, enables her to act and contract as a *feme sole*, free from legal restrictions. While such legal disability remains, a married woman is incapable of entering into any binding contract, and her agreements are not merely voidable, but absolutely void. She cannot ratify them during coverture so as to furnish a good consideration for a subsequent agreement made after she shall have become discovert. She cannot be estopped by anything in the nature of a contract. By the policy of the law she is prohibited from such acts and contracts, and "common honesty" has no place in the consideration of the question. The same is true of a corporation. The legislature may remove the legal disability by conferring upon it power to perform a given act or *any* act that an individual may do. Until such is done it cannot be held responsible for acts which the law says it may not and cannot do, though such acts be accomplished by its officers or agents. For absurd and contradictory would it be to hold that such a creature is absolutely disabled by legal incapacity from making certain contracts, and at the same time hold that an attempted contract, though void as a contract, still remains good by way of estoppel. If a corporation may give vitality to a contract expressly or impliedly prohibited, by mere representation of its power to enter into it, the statutory prohibition could be entirely evaded and abrogated. As was said by the court in *Keen v. Coleman*, 39 Pa. St. 299: " We do not see how there can be an estoppel involved in the very act to which the incapacity relates, that can take away that incapacity. If a legal incapacity can be removed by a fraudulent representation of capacity, then the legal incapacity would have only a moral bond or force, which is absurd." If estoppel arises against a corporation to plead *ultra vires* to an act beyond its powers to perform by the mere performance or part performance by the other party, who knows of the corporation's incapacity to enter into such a transaction, then there is no virtue in legislative enactments, and every person may safely become his own law-maker. This stand has been taken by some courts, but it is not the law.

§ 61. *Performance by innocent party of contract ultra vires a corporation.*— Great stress and no little polemical vaporing has been given to the argument respecting the *faithful performance* of a given *ultra vires* contract by an *innocent party.* This sort of sophistry has a pleasing sound to the ear of equity, but is delusive and without merit when urged in support of the enforcement of *ultra vires* contracts of corporations. In all transactions with corporations as now created, innocence may be said to be analogous to negligence, and no one can be allowed to plead his own laches as a defense. All persons who deal with a corporation are deemed by the law to know its powers and the limits imposed upon its acts and undertakings. The act by which a corporation obtains its powers is a public act open to all the world, and misrepresentations by officers or agents of a corporation regarding its powers or capacities can have no proper bearing in arriving at its liability. The charter is of record and open to inspection. There is no reason why a person should place greater trust and confidence in corporations than in individuals; and if he chooses to enter into agreements or business transactions with corporations without investigating as to its powers or liability, and involves himself in loss and hardship, he has no reasonable cause for complaint, because he is not deceived — it is his own fault. He in fact stands in the situation of a wrong-doer.[1] Even positive acts of encouragement that sometimes operate to estop one *sui juris* will not affect one under a legal disability.[2] No person who is considered as having any reasonable amount of business sagacity will blindly enter into an undertaking with another, and expend money and labor on such undertaking, without first investigating as to the responsibility of the person with whom such business venture is contemplated. Why, then, should he relax his vigilance, fling reason to the winds and tax his credulity when coming in contact with a legal creature which requires the combined watchfulness of the courts, the public and its creator to keep it within the legitimate confines of its prescribed powers and privileges? The charter or act of incorporation is supposed to be in his mind when he enters into the unauthorized agreement. He elects to go on and accept the conse-

[1] Carr v. Rogers, 7 Watts (Pa.), 394.
[2] Glidden v. Striplen, 52 Pa. St. 400.

quences and run the risk of being confronted with the defense of want of power in the corporation. When so confronted, and he brings suit for specific performance, can it be said that he comes into court with clean hands? Is it not more to the purpose and in the cause of truth to say: "You have gone on and performed this act in the light of a public statute. You knew the risks you were running and the probable consequences of your act. The court cannot help you in enforcing this contract. Your act was, in fact, a fraud upon the stockholders in attempting to subject the funds of the corporation, in which they all have an interest, to a purpose beyond the scope of the corporate business and to entail on them risks they never assumed or agreed to." Is there any room for a plea of "good faith" on the part of one who has performed his side of a contract which he knew the corporation, for want of power, was unable to carry out? Is there any room for a plea of fraud or deceit when, at the time the officer or agent of the corporation may have been misrepresenting the corporate powers, he knew or was bound to know that such representation was in fact false? Laws are not enacted for one person to obey and another to violate. Honesty of purpose is no excuse for one who contravenes the law. In plain "English," *ignorance*, ostensible or *bona fide*, cuts no figure when the provisions of a statute have been violated. He is presumed to know them; and if he do not, if allowed to suffer the consequences of disregarding them, it may so develop his discretion that future violation of such enactments will be avoided. It is indeed an anomalous procedure to ask the aid of the law to assist one in the violation of its very provisions. If the comforting arm of equity is to be extended, it may be done in a proper proceeding, and it should not support those who seek its aid to its own undoing.[1]

§ 62. *Position of United States supreme court on alleged rule.*— This alleged rule, that a corporation cannot evoke the defense of *ultra vires* when the other party has

[1] The doctrine alleged to be established by the Whitney Arms Company Case, the Bissell Case, and others, is so thoroughly exploded and the position there taken so learnedly combated by Mr. Taylor in his excellent work on Corporations, that it is deemed advisable and profitable to quote his views rather fully. The learned author says:

"The rules which this case (Bissell v. Michigan Southern & N. Ind. R. R. Co., 22 N. Y. 64) and sundry others in New York and elsewhere have tended to establish may be considered here. If the corporation has performed the contract on its side, the other contracting party cannot plead that the corporation was not authorized to make such a contract. This is held by Whitney Arms Co. v. Barlow, and even in the absence of all authority would seem clear. 'One who has received from a corporation the full consideration of his engagement to pay money . . . cannot avail himself of the objection that the contract thus fully performed by the corporation was *ultra vires* and not within its chartered privileges and powers.' (Whitney Arms Co. v. Barlow, 63 N. Y. 70.) Such a person having himself made the contract and received its benefit is clearly estopped from making any such allegation.

"The converse of this proposition is also said to be law. If the other contracting party has performed his side of the contract, the corporation cannot plead that its charter gave it no power to enter into the contract, at least if the corporate property has been benefited by the performance. It is submitted that this last proposition involves a fallacy. If the other contracting party had contracted through an agent whose instructions were contained in a written instrument which the corporation knew to contain all the authority which the agent possessed, and if the contract in question was unauthorized by this instrument, could any one maintain that the principal would be bound *because* the corporation had performed its side of the contract? Yet in reality it is in analogy with this to hold the corporation bound *because* the other contracting party has performed.

"To illustrate, let us imagine that B. is a land-owner, A. his agent

wholly or in part performed his side of the contract, is sought to be invested with added dignity by a citation of several cases in the federal supreme court where this position is asserted to have been vindicated and adopted.

and C. a manufacturer of fertilizers. If C., knowing that A. has no authority from B. to purchase fertilizers, sells a large amount of them to be applied on B.'s lands, and they are so applied, but without A.'s knowledge, C. has executed the contract on his side and B.'s lands have had the benefit. Yet it is clear that C. has no valid claim against B. Apply this to the case of a corporation. Let B. be the shareholders and creditors; let A. be the board of directors and C. the other contracting party. A. makes a contract with C. beyond the powers of the corporation — beyond A.'s power to represent the corporate interests. In legal intendment C. knows this contract to be beyond A.'s authority, but nevertheless performs his side of it, and the results of his performance are applied to the benefit of the corporate enterprise, but without the knowledge of the shareholders or creditors. Here the interests of the shareholders and creditors have been benefited, but through no voluntary action or acquiescence on their part, and through acts which C. knew they had not authorized. It is again clear that C. by his performance acquires no rights which can affect the interests of shareholders and creditors. And the same reasoning would apply even if the corporation, by a vote in corporate meeting, ratified the contract; the rights of absent or dissenting shareholders would not thereby be affected, provided they were guilty of no laches in asserting their rights. Undoubtedly, if the shareholders know that *ultra vires* contracts are being entered into and performed, and that the proceeds are being applied to the corporate enterprise, they cannot with honesty stand quietly by, but must do all in their power to prevent such application. Therefore, through acquiescence after they know, or, if they have been at all observant of corporate affairs, would have known, of the contracts, they would be estopped from objecting. And so, perhaps, might creditors estop themselves.

"The preceding argument leads to this unavoidable conclusion: The mere facts that the other contracting party has executed his side of the *ultra vires* contract, and that the corporate property has thereby been benefited, do not affect the rights of persons who have done nothing from which assent to the contract can in any way be inferred.

"If one examines with care the cases which are regarded as au-

These cases are, among others, *San Antonio v. Mehaffy*, 96 U. S. 312; *Railway Co. v. McCarthey*, 96 U. S. 258, and *Hitchcock v. Galveston*, 96 U. S. 341.

§ 63. *San Antonio v. Mehaffy, 96 U. S. 312.*—In this case the only reference to the doctrine of *ultra vires* was made in a casual observation, purely *dictum*, by Mr. Jus-

thority for this alleged general rule that sounds so just — if the other contracting party has performed, and by his performance benefited the property of the corporation, the latter cannot plead *ultra vires* — it will appear that the recovery of the other party really does not rest on the fact that he has performed, nor on the fact that his performance has benefited the corporate property, though undoubtedly he would not have had the same cause of action had he not performed; and that corporate interests were benefited may very likely have been a material point in establishing his case. It is submitted that in these cases the plaintiff's recovery rests on the circumstances that all the persons who would have been entitled to object to the contract allowed the plaintiff to go on and perform under the reasonable assumption on his part of general acquiescence in the contract. To be sure the shareholders are not supposed to be continually exercising an actual supervision over the affairs of the corporation. But they have a right to inspect the books, and, if they choose, may keep themselves acquainted with what is being done by the corporate management. At any rate, unless they keep a watch over the course of corporate affairs, they will not be entitled on a plea of their own ignorance to come forward at their pleasure and cause the repudiation of corporate obligations. Shareholders wishing to prevent illegal or *ultra vires* acts, or to absolve the corporation from responsibility for them, must be vigilant and swift.

"Darst v. Gale, 83 Ill. 186, is another case frequently cited in support of the alleged rule — which is indeed stated in so many words in the opinion of the court — 'that a private corporation cannot avail itself of the defense of *ultra vires* where the contract has in good faith been fully performed by the other party, and the corporation has had the benefit of the contract and the performance.' But in this case the defense was not set up by or on behalf of the corporation, nor on behalf of any person interested in it. A subsequent grantee of premises belonging to the corporation attempted to have a prior deed of trust covering the same property set aside, on the

tice Swayne, who used the following language: "The doctrine of *ultra vires*, whether invoked for or against a corporation, is not favored in the law. It should never be applied where it will defeat the ends of justice, if such result can be avoided." And citing only *Whitney Arms Co. v. Barlow*, 63 N. Y. 62. The doctrine of *ultra vires* was not "invoked" in this case, and the learned suggestion of the justice was wholly gratuitous, nor was its ap-

ground that such deed was *ultra vires* the corporation; he having bought with full notice of the prior deed. The *ultra vires* nature of the prior deed had injured no right of his; and, consequently, he had no standing in court to interpose the plea of *ultra vires*.

"The decision, if not the reasoning, in this case points to an important principle respecting the plea of *ultra vires*. As we have seen, the plea cannot be interposed by the party contracting with the corporation when the corporation has performed; and the reason for this lies not only in the estoppel in which, under the circumstances, such a person is affected, but in the following reasons as well: That the transaction was *ultra vires* infringes none of his rights; he cannot, therefore, interpose the defense. This is a plain principle which is not only law, but patent common sense. With a few special exceptions no one can represent another before the courts or elsewhere, without authority, express or implied, to do so. To an action brought against himself a man cannot ordinarily plead that the rights of another, whom he is not authorized to represent, will be affected by the prosecution of the suit. If the court consider that hardship and injustice will result unless the interests of each outside person are regarded, the court — at least a court of equity — may require him to be made a party to the suit, in order to afford him opportunity to protect his interests. Accordingly, when a contract *ultra vires* is entered into, it is not competent for persons whose rights are not infringed, any more than for those who by their actions have estopped themselves from complaining, would restrain the fulfillment of the contract on the ground that the interests of others, which they are not authorized to represent, will be injured. It may therefore be stated as a rule that a person whose rights are in no way infringed by the fact that a given act is *ultra vires* a corporation can found no action or defense on that fact." Taylor on Corp., §§ 275–281.

plication required in the decision of the case, and the case cited shows very clearly that the learned justice had given the subject little thought and less investigation.

§ 64. *Railway Co. v. McCarthey, 96 U. S. 258.*— In this case, which has been quite frequently cited as bearing out the alleged rule heretofore referred to, it was decided that, unless forbidden by its charter, a railroad company may contract for a shipment over connecting lines; and having done so is liable in all respects upon them as upon its own lines; also that where such a contract is not, on its face, necessarily beyond the scope of the powers of the corporation, it will, in the absence of proof to the contrary, be presumed to be valid. All of which propositions are universally conceded and are too clear to call for argument or authority. No reference is made to the defense of *ultra vires* by a person who has received the benefit of a contract executed by one party or the other; the same justice who delivered the opinion of the court in the San Antonio case also speaking for the court in this case. In the course of this opinion he says: "The doctrine of *ultra vires*, when invoked for or against a corporation, should not be allowed to prevail when it would defeat the ends of justice or work a legal wrong;" citing on *this* occasion, *Union Water Co. v. Murphy's Flat Flushing Co. et al.*, 22 Cal. 620; *Union Railroad Co. v. Railroad Co.*, 29 N. J. Eq. 542; and the old standby, *Whitney Arms Co. v. Barlow*, 63 N. Y. 62. From the cases here cited it would seem that the learned justice had widened the field of his investigation somewhat, but from the language used it is evident that he clung to the same opinion still. The latter part of the sentence last quoted has a lulling sound for those who prefer axioms to authority. Though often quoted, it has never been clearly explained what is meant by "working a legal wrong."

A legal wrong means, if it means anything at all, a wrong against the law, and it certainly cannot be considered as a legal wrong to see that the provisions of the law are vindicated and its terms complied with, in holding corporations strictly within their statutory powers and privileges. Whether it is "defeating the ends of justice" to allow corporations to repudiate the unauthorized and illegal acts of their officers and agents is also a proposition we will spend no time in vindicating.

§ 65. *Hitchcock v. Galveston, 96 U. S. 341.* — We now come to the bulwark behind which the adherents to the alleged rule under discussion confidently repose themselves — the case of *Hitchcock v. Galveston,* — which seems to call for a more extended examination to show its inapplicability. The facts in that case were, briefly stated, these: The city of Galveston, under an ordinance, had, through its mayor and chairman of the committee on streets and alleys, entered into a contract with Hitchcock and another for paving the sidewalks of said city, for which work the city agreed to pay, and the contractors agreed to accept, a specified sum per square yard, *payable in bonds of the city.* While the ordinance of the city empowered the mayor and the said chairman "to enter into and make contracts with proper and responsible parties to fill up, grade, curb and pave the said sidewalks," the city *had no power or authority to issue bonds in payment of such work.* Under this agreement Hitchcock made contracts for labor and materials, performed a large amount of work, completed the curbing and filling of some sidewalks, and was going on in earnest to finish the entire work, when, at the expiration of some forty-six days, he was compelled by force and by authority of the city to abandon the work without any fault of his own. Afterwards the city council declared the contract null and void, and directed the mayor to notify the contractors to that effect, which he did. Accordingly suit was brought *to recover damages for the breach of the contract.* Mr. Justice Stone, in delivering the opinion of the court, said:

"If it were conceded that the city had no lawful authority to issue the bonds described in the ordinance and mentioned in the contract, it does not follow that the contract was wholly illegal and void, or that the plaintiffs have no rights under it. *They are not suing upon the bonds,* and it is not necessary to their success that they should assert the validity of those instruments. It is enough for them that the city council *have power to enter into a contract* for the improvement of the sidewalks; that such a contract was made with them; that under it they have proceeded to furnish materials and do work as well as to assume liabilities; that the city has secured and now enjoys the benefit of what they have done and furnished; that for these things the city promised to pay, and that after having received the benefit of the contract the city has broken it. It matters not that the promise was to pay *in a manner* not authorized by law. If payments cannot be made in bonds because their issue is *ultra vires,* it would be sanctioning rank injustice to hold that payment need not be made at all. Such is not the law. The contract between the parties is in force so far as it is lawful. . . . *The promise to give bonds* to the plaintiffs in payment of what they undertook to do was, therefore, at farthest, only *ultra vires,* and in such a case, *though specific performance of an engagement to do a thing transgressive of its corporate powers may not be enforced,* the corporation can be held liable on its contract. Having received benefits at the expense of the other contracting party, it cannot object that it was not empowered to perform what it promised in return, *in the mode in which it promised to perform.*"

There was no question in this case as to the *power* of the city to *make the contract* for paving the sidewalks. How payment should be made was, at most, only incidental to the authority to make the contract. Had it been decided that the city was devoid of power to make the contract, it would have raised altogether a different phase of the question. When a corporation has the power to make certain contracts, it cannot plead its own irregularity in performing them. If it has power to make the contract at all, it is liable on it. "Though specific performance of an engagement to do a thing transgressive of its corporate powers *may not be enforced*, the corporation can be held liable on its contract." By this proposition is meant that the corporation may be held liable on its implied contract to pay for what it has received the benefit of, as on a *quantum meruit*. No other construction can be put upon it with any reason. To say that specific performance of an agreement may not be enforced, yet the corporation can be held liable under the specific terms of that agreement, is decidedly absurd. It is quite apparent that these statements were made by the learned justice having in mind the circumstances connected with this particular case. Does the decision in this case sustain the proposition laid down in the *Whitney Arms Company Case* that a corporation, having received benefits under a contract *which it had no power to make*, if executed by the other party, cannot avail itself of the defense of *ultra vires* in an *action on that contract?* It holds decidedly the reverse, and while admitting that *the contract cannot be enforced against the corporation* in the manner in which it agreed to perform it, yet it must be held liable for the *benefits received* by the performance of the other party to the contract. In other words, it is liable as for money had and received — a clear repudiation of the contract, and all that it is claimed a corporation has a right to do.

§ 66. *Jones v. Guaranty Co., 101 U. S. 622.*— Jones v. Guaranty Co., *supra*, is another case which has been cited in support of the rule alleged in the *Whitney Arms Company Case*. The nearest approach to the proposition in that case was made in the following language of Mr. Justice Swain, who delivered the opinion of the court: " Where money has been obtained by a corporation upon its securities which were irregular and *ultra vires*, but the money was applied for the benefit of the company with the knowledge and acquiescence of the stockholders, the company and the stockholders were estopped from denying the *liability of the company to repay it.* And the same result follows when such securities are issued with the knowledge of the shareholders, so far as the money thus raised is applied for the benefit of the company." If this case sustains the alleged rule it is difficult to understand the reasoning of its application.

§ 67. *National Bank v. Mathews, 98 U. S. 621.*— Another case which has been cited with some frequency in this connection is that of *National Bank v. Mathews.* The only question raised in that case was whether or not a bank which had parted with its money in good faith could be allowed to enforce a trust deed taken as security for the debt, when the other party who had received the bank's money set up the plea that such a transaction by the bank was *ultra vires* and illegal; and it was held that such a defense could not be allowed. This decision, like a great many others frequently cited, applies to the party contracting with the corporation and not to the corporation; the reasons why such a defense are not allowed in such cases being fully considered and explained by Mr. Taylor, quoted in note to section 61.

§ 68. *Central Transportation Co. v. Pullman Car Co.,
139 U. S. 24.*— The further consideration of this branch
of the subject will be dismissed with a quotation from the
recent case of *Central Transportation Co. v. Pullman Car
Co., supra,* wherein Mr. Justice Gray expressly repudiates
the alleged rule enunciated in the *Whitney Arms Case.*
In the course of his able opinion he says: "It was argued
in behalf of the plaintiff that, having been fully performed
on the part of the plaintiff, and the benefit of it received
by the defendant for the period covered by the declaration, the defendant was estopped to set up the invalidity
of the contract as a defense to this action to recover the
compensation agreed on for that period.

"But this argument, though sustained by the decisions
of some of the states, *finds no support in the judgments
of this court.* The passages cited by the plaintiff from
Railway Co. v. McCarthey, 96 U. S. 258, 267, and *San
Antonio v. Mehaffy,* 96 U. S. 315, *are no more than a
passing remark* that 'the doctrine of *ultra vires,* when invoked for or against a corporation, should not be allowed
to prevail when it would defeat the ends of justice or
work a legal wrong,' and a repetition in substance of the
same remark, adding, 'if such a result can be avoided.'"[1]

[1] Mr. Morawetz, in his admirable treatise on Corporations, at page
551, section 581, says:

"In some of the cases it has been said that, while the general rule
is that acts and contracts in excess of the charter of a corporation
are *ultra vires,* and therefore not binding on a company, yet, after
a corporation has enjoyed the benefit of an act or contract performed in its behalf, it will be estopped, when charged with responsibility on account of the act or contract, from setting up as a
defense that the transaction was *ultra vires.*

"This statement of the law is certainly inaccurate. It has never
been denied that the principles of the law of agency apply to corporations and to individuals alike, and it is certain that, according
to the elementary principles of the law of agency, a person does not
become responsible for acts performed in his name merely because

the acts have accrued to his benefit. A person may become responsible for an unauthorized act performed in his behalf by ratifying the act; but ratification would imply an intention to adopt the unauthorized act. Ratification by a corporation of an act in excess of its charter means ratification by the entire body of shareholders; no agent of a corporation has authority to ratify an act which he had not original authority to do. . . .

"Statements may be found in some of the authorities to the effect that 'a plea of *ultra vires*' should not prevail when it would 'accomplish a legal wrong.' These statements, however, refer merely to the effect of the legal prohibition against unauthorized corporate acts; they mean that the fact that a transaction is in excess of the charter of the corporation should not be a defense if there would be a liability according to the general principles of law applicable to unincorporated companies. It certainly cannot be maintained that the application of the established principles of the law of agency would 'accomplish a legal wrong.'"

The learned author then quotes the remarks made by Bramwell, B., in the case of Bateman v. Mayor of Ashton, 3 H. & N. 340, in the court of Exchequer Chamber, where the learned baron used the following language: "I cannot help adding an observation on the objection made to the *honesty* of a defense of this description. It is said that the company has contracted, and the company repudiates its contract. There cannot be a more perfect fallacy. 'Persons without authority have affected to contract for the company, and the company repudiates the act,' is the true expression. A., B. and C. are in partnership as hatters. A. buys boots in the name of the firm, and the seller sues A., B. and C., who say they did not contract. It may be wrong in A., but are B. and C. to blame? I do not say the corporation cases are cases of partnership, but the principle is the same."

So the observation made by Lord Wensleydale in Ernest v. Nicholls, 6 H. L. 400, would seem appropriate in this connection. He there says: "It is a captivating argument for a jury, and jurymen are very often misled by it in these cases of joint-stock companies, that the company has had the benefit of the plaintiff's goods, or service, or money, whereas, for the purposes of contract, the company exists only in the directors and officers, *acting by and according to the deed.*"

The learned lord might also truly have added that *courts* likewise are often captivated and misled by the same specious plea, losing sight altogether of the true issue involved and resting their decisions on the doubtful consideration of individual hardship.

CHAPTER V.

ACTIONS ON ULTRA VIRES CONTRACTS.

§ 69. General rule as to actions on illegal contracts.
70. *Ultra vires* as defense to action — General rule.
71. Court must be satisfied of legality of contract.
72. Actions on executed *ultra vires* contracts.
73. Actions on *ultra vires* contracts in courts of equity and at law.
74. *Quantum meruit* — Relief on *ultra vires* contracts.
75. Relief on contracts *ultra vires* and under statute of frauds.

§ 69. *General rule as to actions on illegal contracts.*—
It is a general rule of law that a contract made in violation of a statute is void; and that when a plaintiff cannot establish his cause of action without relying upon an illegal contract he cannot recover.[1] It is likewise well settled by the authorities that any promise, contract or undertaking, the performance of which would tend to promote, advance or carry into effect any object or purpose which is unlawful, is in itself void, and will not maintain an action. The law which prohibits the end will not lend its aid in promoting the means designed to carry it into effect, and in this respect the law gives no countenance to the old distinction between *malum in se* and *malum prohibitum*. That which the law prohibits either in terms, or by affixing a penalty to it, is unlawful; and it

[1] Pollock's Prin. of Cont., pp. 253-265; Penn v. Bornman, 102 Ill. 523; Alexander v. O'Donnell, 12 Kan. 608; Gunter v. Leckey, 30 Ala. 591; Kennedy v. Cochran, 65 Me. 594; Bank of U. S. v. Owens, 2 Pet. (U. S.) 527, 539; Pangborn v. Westlake, 36 Iowa, 546; Harris v. Runnells, 12 How. (U. S.) 79; Miller v. Ammon, 145 U. S. 426; American Pres. Trust Co. v. Taylor Mfg. Co., 46 Fed. Rep. 155.

will not promote in one form that which it declares wrong in another. So the rule is declared as general that all contracts or agreements which have for their objects anything which is repugnant to the general policy of the law, or contrary to the provisions of any statute, are void and not to be enforced.[1] It is a principle too salutary and well established to be in any measure infringed, and courts of justice ought not to assist an illegal transaction in any respect.[2] Though the objection that a contract is illegal or *ultra vires* may sound at all times very ill in the mouth of a defendant, it is not for his sake that the objection is ever allowed, but it is founded in general principles of policy; and whenever from the plaintiff's own stating, or otherwise, the cause of action appears to arise from the transgression of a positive law of the country, he has no right to be assisted.[3] Nor will courts, even with the consent of the parties, enforce a contract which is in violation of a statute, although not otherwise declared void.[4] "There is a great difference where a party comes to overturn an illegal contract and to be relieved against it. He shall not be relieved if he come to take the benefit of an illegal contract; there he never shall be relieved, because, to relieve him, the court must affirm the contract."[5] So

[1] White v. Bass, 3 Cush. (Mass.) 448; 1 Comyn, Cont. 30; Hunt v. Knickerbocker, 5 John. (N. Y.) 326; Guenther v. Dewein, 11 Iowa, 133; Craig v. Andreas, 7 Iowa, 17; Pittsburg v. Keokuk Bridge, 131 U. S. 371; Oregon Ry. v. Oregonian Ry., 130 U. S. 1; Thomas v. Railway Co., 101 U. S. 71; Central Trans. Co. v. Pullman Co., 139 U. S. 24; Spring Co. v. Knowlton, 103 U. S. 49.
[2] Belding v. Pitkin, 2 Caines (N. Y.), 149.
[3] Lord Mansfield in Holmes v. Johnson, Cowp. 343.
[4] Fowler v. Scully, 72 Pa. St. 456.
[5] Walker v. Chapman, Lofft, 342; Toppenden v. Randall, 2 Bos. & Pull. 467; Chitty. Cont. 533; White v. Franklin Bank, 22 Pick. (Mass.) 184; Aubert v. Walsh, 3 Taunt. 277; Busk v. Wash, 4 id. 290; Williams v. Hedley, 8 East, 380, n.; Hastelow v. Jackson, 8 B. & C. 224;

when a contract is tainted with illegality the law will not lend its aid to either party for the enforcement of such contract; and neither a court of law nor of equity will interpose to grant any relief to the parties, but will leave them where it finds them, if they have been equally cognizant of the illegality.[1] "The attempt to contravene the policy of a public statute is illegal. Nor is it necessary to render it so that *the statute should contain an express prohibition of such attempt.* It always contains an implied prohibition; and to such attempts the principles of the common law are invariably and deadly hostile, not always by an interference between the parties themselves, or by enabling the one to recall to the other, where *in pari delicto*, what may have been obtained; but by at all times refusing the aid of the law to carry into effect or *enforce any contract* which may be the result of such intended contravention."[2]

§ 70. *Ultra vires as defense to action — General rule.* — It is upon the principles stated in the next preceding section that it has been so frequently held that a contract made by the officers or agents of a corporation which is outside the pale of the corporate power confers no rights; and the making of such contract does not estop the corporation, *in an action on it*, from invoking the defense of *ultra vires*.[3] Accordingly the rule may be declared as

Utica Ins. Co. v. Kip, 8 Cow. (N. Y.) 20; Fowler v. Scully, 72 Pa. St. 456.

[1] 7 Wait, Act. & Def. 64; Smith v. Bromley, 2 Doug. 696; Birmington v. Wallis, 4 B. & Ald. 650; Cowan v. Milburn, 2 Exch. 230; Lowell v. Boston, etc. R. Co., 23 Pick. (Mass.) 32; Barker v. Hoff, 7 Hun (N. Y.), 284; Blasdell v. Fowler, 120 Mass. 447.

[2] Sharpe v. Teese, 9 N. J. L. 352.

[3] Sherwood v. Alvis, 83 Ala. 115; Smith v. Insurance Co., 4 Ala. 558; City Council v. Plank Road Co., 31 Ala. 76; Chewacla Lime Works v. Dismukes, 87 Ala. 347; Abbott v. Packet Co., 1 Md. Ch.

general, that any contract made by a corporation not necessary and proper, directly or indirectly, to enable it to answer the purpose of its creation, is void, and neither a court of law or of equity can enforce it.[1] No performance by the corporation of such a contract can give it any validity, or be the foundation of any right of action upon it.[2] So, where a third party makes with the officers of a corporation an illegal contract — beyond the powers of the corporation as shown by its charter, — such third party cannot recover *on the contract*, because he acts with knowledge that the officers have exceeded their powers and the powers of the corporation, and between him and the corporation or its stockholders no amount of ratification by those unauthorized to make the contract will make it valid.[3]

542; Brady v. Mayor, 20 N. Y. 312; Taft v. Pittsford, 28 Vt. 286; Franklin Co. v. Lewiston Inst., 68 Me. 43; Root v. Goddard, 3 McLean (U. S.), 102; Ex parte Williamson, 5 Ch. Div. 309; South Yorkshire Ry. v. Great Northern Ry. Co., 9 Exch. 55; Bateman v. Ashton-under-Lynn, 3 H. & N. 323; Norwich v. Norfolk Ry., 4 El. & Bl. 397; Taylor v. Chichester, etc. Ry., L. R. 2 Exch. 356; East Anglian Ry. v. Eastern Counties Ry., 11 C. B. 775; MacGregor v. Dover & D. Ry., 18 Q. B. 618; Bagshaw v. Eastern Union Ry., 2 Macn. & G. 389; Earl of Shrewsbury v. North Staf. Ry. Co., 1 Eq. Rep. 593; Chambers v. Manchester, etc. Ry. Co., 5 B. & S. 588; In re Building Society, 5 Ch. App. 309; Gregory v. Patchett, 33 Beav. 595; Shrewsbury, etc. Ry. v. Northwestern Ry., 6 H. L. Cas. 113; Gage v. Newmarket Ry., 18 Q. B. 457; Caledonia Ry. Co. v. Helensburgh, 2 Macq. 391; Pearce v. Madison Ry. Co., 21 How. (U. S.) 441; Thomas v. Railroad Co., 101 U. S. 71; Head v. Providence Ins. Co., 2 Cranch (U. S.), 127; Central Trans. Co. v. Pullman Co., 139 U. S. 24, and cases cited to §§ 9, 53.

[1] Alabama Ins. Co. v. Central Ass'n, 54 Ala. 73; Grand Lodge v. Waddell, 36 Ala. 313; Chambers v. Falkner, 65 Ala. 448; Sherwood v. Alvis, 83 Ala. 117; Simmons v. Troy Works, 92 Ala. 427, and cases cited in preceding note.

[2] Central Trans. Co. v. Pullman Co., 139 U. S. 24; Thomas v. Railway Co., 101 U. S. 71; Orr v. Lacey, 2 Doug. (Mich.) 230; Littlewort v. Davis, 50 Miss. 403.

[3] Allegheny City v. McClurkan, 14 Pa. St. 81; Holdsworth v. Evans,

§ 71. *Court must be satisfied of legality of contract.—* Before the court can act in the exercise of its peculiar jurisdiction to enforce specific performance of an agreement, it must be satisfied that there is not a reasonable ground for contending that the agreement is illegal or against the policy of the law;[1] and in the next place that the agreement is one ascribable to a class in which the court has been accustomed or has certainly jurisdiction to interfere.[2] In *Hunt v. Knickerbocker*, 5 Johns. 377, Mr. Justice Thompson, speaking for the court, said: "No case, I believe, can be found where an action can be sustained which goes in affirmance of an illegal contract, and when the object of it is to enforce the performance of an engagement prohibited by law. Wherever an action has been sustained against a party to prevent him from retaining the benefit derived from an unlawful act, the action proceeds in *disaffirmance of the contract*, and, instead of endeavoring to enforce it, presumes it to be void." So also, in *Union Pacific Ry. Co. v. Chicago*,

3 H. L. 263; Ex parte Grady, 9 Jur. (N. S.) 631; Lucas v. White Line Tr. Co., 70 Iowa, 541; National Trust Co. v. Miller, 33 N. J. Eq. 155; Black v. Del. & R. Canal Co., 24 N. J. Eq. 455; Thomas v. Railway Co., 101 U. S. 71; Mallory v. Hanauer Oil Co., 86 Tenn. 598.

[1] Johnson v. Shrewsbury, etc. Co., 3 De G., M. & G. 913; Hunt v. Knickerbocker, 5 Johns. (N. Y.) 326; Union Pac. Ry. Co. v. C., R. I. & P. Ry., 51 Fed. Rep. 309; Laughton v. Hughes, 1 Mau. & Selw. 593; Holmes v. Johnson, Cowp. 343; Morch v. Abel, 3 B. & P. 35; Russell v. De Grand, 15 Mass. 39; Shiffner v. Gordon, 12 East, 304; Cincinnati Co. v. Rosenthal, 55 Ill. 85; Thomas v. Railway Co., 101 U. S. 71.

[2] Johnson v. Shrewsbury, etc. Ry. Co., 3 De G., M. & G. 913.

In Laughton v. Hughes, *supra*, Lord Ellenborough said: "It may be taken as a general rule that what is done in contravention of the provisions of an act of parliament cannot be made the subject-matter of an action."

And Le Blanc, J., in same case, said: "It is an established principle that the court will not lend its aid in order to enforce a contract entered into with a view of carrying into effect anything which is prohibited by law."

Rock Island & Pacific Ry. Co., 51 Fed. Rep. 309, which was a suit to compel specific performance of a contract for joint use and occupancy of a bridge across the Missouri river, and which was held not be *ultra vires* and that such joint use would not interfere with the present or prospective use thereof by the lessor, or with the discharge of the duties it owed to the government under the provisions of its charter, Sanborn, C. J., delivering the opinion of the court, said: "Corporations created under statutory authority are the creatures of the statute. By it their powers are measured. Beyond the limit of the powers there granted, and those fairly incidental thereto, they may not act; they may not *agree* to act. Their contracts for the just exercise of these powers are binding and enforceable; but their contracts beyond the scope of these granted powers are null — as though they had not been. They are void as against the state, because they are unlawful usurpations of power reserved by the state. They are void as against other parties to the contract, because they are bound to take notice of the law of the limits of corporate powers there found; and no formal assent of corporations or officers, no alleged estoppel, can give validity to such contracts, or *induce the courts to enforce them* against the objection of the citizen or the state."

§ 72. *Actions on executed ultra vires contracts.*— It is the generally accepted doctrine of the courts of England and a large majority of the courts of this country, where the subject has been well considered, that a contract beyond the scope of the powers conferred on the corporation cannot, by any partial performance, become the foundation of any right of action.[1] The reason for this

[1] Thomas v. Railway Co., 101 U. S. 71; Oregon Ry. v. Oregonian Ry., 130 U. S. 1; Central Trans. Co. v. Pullman Co., 139 U. S. 24;

rule is forcibly stated by Mr. Justice Miller in *Thomas v. Railroad Co.*, a leading case: "It remains to consider the suggestion that the contract, having been executed, the doctrine of *ultra vires* is inapplicable to the case. There can be no question that, in many instances, where an invalid contract, which the party to it might have avoided or refused to perform, has been fully performed *on both sides*, whereby money has been paid or property has changed hands, the courts have refused to sustain an action for the recovery of the property or the money so transferred. . . . Having entered into the agreement, it was the duty of the company to rescind or abandon it at the earliest moment. . . . Though they delayed for several years, it was nevertheless a rightful act when it was done. Can this performance of a legal duty, a duty both to stockholders and the company and to the public, give to plaintiffs a right of action? Can they found such a right on an agreement void for want of corporate authority and forbidden by the policy of the law? To hold that they can is, in our opinion, *to hold that an act performed in executing a void contract makes all its parts valid, and that the more that is done under a contract forbidden by law the stronger is the claim to its enforcement by the courts.*" [1]

Pennsylvania Co. v. St. Louis Ry. Co., 118 U. S. 310; Greenville Compress v. Planters' Press, 70 Miss. 669; Ashbury Ry. Co. v. Riche, 7 H. L. 653; East Anglian Ry. v. Eastern Counties Ry. Co., 11 C. B. 775; National Trust Co. v. Miller, 33 N. J. Eq. 155; Black v. Delaware, etc. Co., 24 N. J. Eq. 455; Buckeye Marble Co. v. Harvey, 92 Tenn. 115.

[1] So Cooper, J., in Greenville Compress v. Planters' Press, 70 Miss. 669, says: "The agreement between the directors of the respective companies was clearly beyond the corporate powers of either company to make, and it had not been fully executed when the appellant withdrew from it. There are some decisions which proceed on the apparent postulate that an *ultra vires* agreement, executed

§ 73.]   ACTIONS ON CONTRACTS.   107

§ 73. *Actions on ultra vires contracts in courts of equity and at law.*— The general rule, in equity as at law, is *in pari delicto potior est conditio defendentis;* and therefore neither party to an illegal contract will be aided by the fully by one of the corporations, or so far executed that the *status quo* cannot be restored, may be made the basis of an action. But in many of these cases it will be found that the measure of recovery would be the same, whether the injury done to the plaintiff by the failure of the defendant to perform, or the benefit received by the defendant under the agreement, is taken as the standard. Cases of this sort may therefore be well assigned to that other and far more numerous class, in which the right of recovery is not rested upon the invalid agreement, but is recognized to exist notwithstanding the agreement, upon the principle that the defendant may not repudiate the contract and yet retain the benefit which has been derived under it.

"The decided weight of authority in England and America is that no action lies upon the void contract; that no decree can be made by a court of equity for its specific performance, nor a recovery had at law for its breach; but that, by proceeding in the proper court, the plaintiff may recover to the extent of the benefit received by the defendant from the execution of the agreement by the plaintiff." And see Union Pac. Ry. Co. v. C., R. I. & P. Ry. Co., 51 Fed. Rep. 309; Laughton v. Hughes, 1 Mau. & Sel. 593; Holman v. Johnson, Cowp. 343; Morck v. Abel, 3 B. & P. 35; Russell v. De Grand, 15 Mass. 39; Sheffner v. Gordon, 12 East, 304; Selwyn, Nisi Prius, 69; Mayor v. Norfolk Ry., 4 El. & Bl. 397; Cincinnati Co. v. Rosenthal, 55 Ill. 85; Greenville Compress v. Planters' Press, 70 Miss. 669; Buckeye Marble Co. v. Harvey, 92 Tenn. 115.

In Buckeye Marble Co. v. Harvey, *supra*, in the supreme court of Tennessee, 1892, Lurton, J., in speaking of the defense of *ultra vires* where the contract had been executed, said:

"But it has been insisted very earnestly by the able and learned counsel for complainant, that, when the contract had been fully executed by the plaintiff, the defendants should not be permitted to invoke such defense in a suit brought to compel performance; that to permit such a defense would work injustice, and enable defendant to repudiate his liability while holding on to the price he has received. There are cases where, the contract being fully executed on both sides, the court, in the interest of justice, has refused to aid either in obtaining a rescission. Arms Co. v. Barlow, 63

108   ACTIONS ON CONTRACTS.   [§ 73.

court, whether to enforce it or to set it aside. If the contract is illegal, affirmative relief against it will not be granted, at law or in equity, unless the contract remains executory, or unless the parties are not considered in

N. Y. 62, is one of this class. So there are cases where the defense of *ultra vires* has not been entertained when the defect was in the mode of executing the contract or in the power of the agent. So there are many cases holding the party relying upon the defense of *ultra vires* to an accountability for the benefit received. Green's Brice's Ultra Vires, 717, and note at end of chapter. Again there are cases when the courts have refused to entertain suits to recover property from corporations which is held in excess of charter capacity. In such cases the courts have held that the defect in the power could not be set up in a collateral way, and that the state could only complain of such violation. To this effect were our own cases of Barrow v. Turnpike Co., 9 Humph. 303, and Heiskell v. Lodge, 87 Tenn. 668. The question here is not like any of these. The complainant *sues upon its contract*, and in affirmance of it seeks to have the defendant perform an agreement which sprung from and was collateral to it. It has received the shares it purchased and holds onto them. It simply asks that the defendant be further compelled to perform its contract by contributing, in accordance with his agreement, his proportion of the liability paid off by complainant in protection of the property of the McMillan Marble Company. The suit is clearly in furtherance of the original unlawful and void contract. That the contract has been executed by the plaintiff does not make it lawful or entitle it to an enforcement of it. This proposition was very plainly put in Pittsburg, C. & St. L. Ry. Co. v. Keokuk & H. Bridge Co., where it was stated as a result of all the previous discussions of that court upon this subject, that 'a contract made by a corporation, which is unlawful and void because beyond the scope of its corporate powers, does not, by being carried into effect, become lawful and valid; but the proper remedy for the party aggrieved is by disaffirming the contract and suing to recover as on a *quantum meruit* the value of what the defendant has actually received.' 131 U. S. 389. The case of Central Transportation Co. v. Pullman Car Co. is an exceedingly interesting case, as it involves a consideration of the circumstances under which a defendant may interpose the defense of *ultra vires*, notwithstanding full performance by the plaintiff. In that case the Central Transportation Company had leased and transferred all its property of every kind to

equal fault, or where the law violated is intended for the coercion of the one party and the protection of the other, or where there has been fraud or oppression on the part of the defendant.[1] The difference, however, between

the defendant company, which was engaged in a similar and competitive business. The lessee company undertook to pay all the debts of the lessor company, and to pay it annually the sum of $264,000 for a term of ninety-nine years. Possession was taken, and the instalments paid for a number of years. The suit was for a part of the instalment for the last year before suit. The defense of *ultra vires* was interposed and sustained. The court held that the sale was unauthorized and in excess of the powers of the selling company. It was urged for the plaintiffs, as in this case, that even if the contract was void because *ultra vires* and against public policy, yet that having been fully executed on the part of the plaintiff, and the benefits of it received by the defendant for the period covered by its duration, the defendant was estopped to set up the invalidity of the contract as a defense to an action to recover the compensation agreed on for that period. After reviewing its own decisions on this branch of the case the court said: 'The view which the court has taken of the question presented by this branch of the case, and the only view which appears to us consistent with legal principles, is as follows: A contract of a corporation which is *ultra vires* in the proper sense, that is to say, outside the objects of its creation as defined in the law of its organization, and therefore beyond the powers conferred upon it by the legislature, is not voidable only, but wholly void, and of no legal effect. The objection to the contract is not merely that the corporation ought not to have made it, but that it could not make it. The contract cannot be ratified by either party because it could not have been authorized by either. No performance on either side can give the unlawful contract any validity, or be the foundation of any right of action upon it. When a corporation is acting within the general scope of the powers conferred upon it by the legislature, the corporation, as well as persons contracting with it, may be estopped to deny that it has complied with the legal formalities which are prerequisite to its existence or to its action, because such requisites might in fact have been complied with. But when the contract is beyond the power conferred upon it by the existing

---

[1] St. Louis Ry. v. T. H. R. R., 145 U. S. 407; Thomas v. Richmond, 12 Wall. (U. S.) 349; Spring Co. v. Knowlton, 103 U. S. 49.

courts of law and those of equity in respect of such contracts is mainly one of forms and remedies, rather than in the matter of absolute rights and obligations. If a contract be pronounced absolutely void in a court of law,

law, neither the corporation nor the other party to the contract can be estopped by assenting to it, or by acting upon it, to show that it was prohibited by those laws. . . . A contract *ultra vires* being unlawful and void, not because it is in itself immoral, but because the corporation, by the law of its creation, is incapable of making it, the courts, while refusing to maintain any action upon the unlawful contract, have always striven to do justice between the parties, so far as could be done consistently with adherence to law, by permitting money or property parted with on the faith of the unlawful contract to be recovered back or compensation to be made for it. In such case, however, the action is not maintained upon the unlawful contract, nor according to its terms, but on an implied contract of the defendant to return, or, failing to do that, to make compensation for property or money which it has no right to retain. To maintain such an action is not to affirm but to disaffirm the unlawful contract.' 139 U. S. 60. This seems to us to fully and clearly state the rule. The passage cited by counsel from Railway Co. v. McCarthey, 96 U. S. 267, 'that the doctrine of *ultra vires*, when invoked for or against a corporation, should not be allowed to prevail when it would defeat the ends of justice or work a legal wrong,' is misleading, and, if literally construed, would result in an erroneous practical extension of the powers of corporations. We do not understand that a result required by adherence to the law would be either unjust or a legal wrong. The learned judge doubtless intended to be understood that the defense should be a legal wrong only when the law did not require its consideration by the court.

"This passage, and one of similar character in San Antonio v. Mehaffy, 96 U. S. 312, was uncalled for in the case in which it was used, and in Central Transportation Co. v. Pullman Car Co., *supra*, characterized as a mere passing remark. To sustain the suit as now presented would be in affirmance and furtherance of an unlawful and void contract. It is in no sense a suit in disaffirmance. Whether complainant could tender back the shares recovered, and maintain a suit to recover the money paid for the shares upon an implied agreement to return money which the defendant had no right to retain, is a question not presented upon this record."

To the same effect is Mayor of Norwich v. Norfolk Ry., *supra*,

it must expect and should receive the same denunciation in a court of equity. Courts of equity, like those of law, must accept contracts as they are made, and have no power to make contracts for parties. If the contracts

where the court say: "Where a corporation has been created for the purpose of carrying on a particular trade, or making a railway from one place to another, and it attempts to substitute another trade, or to make the railway to another place, the objection is to its entire want of power for the new purpose; its life and functions are the creation of the legislature, and they do not exist for any other than the specified purpose; for any other, the members are merely unincorporated individuals. . . . A transgression of the law cannot be the foundation of an action. The covenant being illegal, the covenantee can as little maintain an action for breach of it as he can file a bill in equity for a specific performance of it."

In Cincinnati Co. v. Rosenthal, 55 Ill. 85, the court say: "When the legislature prohibits an act, or declares that it shall be unlawful to perform it, every rule of interpretation must say that the legislature intended to interpose its power to prevent the act, and, as one of the means of its prevention, that the courts shall hold it void. This is as manifest as if the statute had declared that it should be void. To hold otherwise would give the person, or corporation, or individual, the same rights in enforcing prohibited contracts as the good citizen who respects and conforms to the law. To permit such a contract to be enforced, if not offering a premium to violate a law, it certainly withdraws a large portion of the fear that deters men from defying the law. To do so, places the person who violates the law on an equal footing with those who strictly observe its requirements."

Van Vlete, V. C., in National Trust Co. v. Miller, 6 Stew. (N. J.) 155, says: "Nor can the powers of a corporation be in the slightest degree enlarged or extended by the assent of its stockholders, or by any action they may take. . . . And the supreme court of the United States has recently declared, following a judgment of the House of Lords, in which the present Lord Chancellor (Selborne) and the late Lord Chancellor (Cairns) and Lords Chelmsford, Hatherly and O'Hagan concurred, that the broad doctrine is now established that a contract not within the scope of the powers conferred on a corporation cannot be made valid by the consent of every one of the stockholders, nor can it, by any partial performance, become the foundation of any right of action. (Thomas v.

which parties attempt to make are void because in defiance of some statute, they are void alike in either court, and neither court can change a void into a valid contract.[1] As Mr. Justice Brewer, in *Hedges v. Dixon County, supra*, said: "This court can make no contract for the parties. It must take the contract which they make. That contract was one which the county was not authorized to

West Jersey R. R. Co., 101 U. S. 71.) While it must be admitted that this doctrine has not received the sanction of every eminent judge who has been called to enforce it, yet I think it is now vouched for by such august authority, and is so manifestly supported by sound reason and the highest considerations of policy, that it must hereafter be accepted universally as expressing the true rule of judgment in such cases."

In the light of the foregoing decisions and extracts, the following suggestion of Mr. Wood in his work on Railroads (ed. 1894, p. 570) is almost nonsensical: "It has never been contended that a contract *ultra vires* could be set up by the corporation which made it, and whose want of power is the ground of the invalidity of the contract. *A corporation is bound to know the extent of its own powers, and if it makes a contract in excess of them and is worsted* it cannot be held to complain. It is the other contracting party that is protected. . . . The doctrine that a corporation when sued upon a contract by it cannot plead the defense of *ultra vires*, but is estopped, except where the contract is void as opposed to public policy or for other reasons — that is to say, that the mere fact that the contract was beyond the powers of the corporation renders it invalid only — has been long recognized and acquiesced in *by courts of every jurisdiction*." This is almost as radical a position (but in the opposite direction) as that taken by a wise justice of the peace at Buffalo. It is reported that some years ago a farmer sued an orphan asylum at that place for injury to his sheep by a dog kept at the asylum. The case was tried in the justice's court, and the judge held as follows: "I have carefully looked over the defendant's charter, and I find it is not authorized to keep anything but orphans — keeping a dog was therefore *ultra vires*, and it is not liable in this action."— Green Bag.

---

[1] Hedges v. Dixon County, 37 Fed. Rep. 304; In re Cork & Youghal Ry., 4 Ch. 748; s. c., 9 Ex. 262.

make. The bonds were void as adjudged in a court of law, void in whole and in part, and they must be so adjudged in a court of equity."

§ 74. *Quantum meruit — Relief on ultra vires contract.* Though courts acting under proper construction of the law will sustain no action on contracts made by corporations which are beyond the scope of their powers, and therefore unlawful and void, yet relief may be had by the party aggrieved by disaffirming the contract and suing to recover as on a *quantum meruit* the value of what the defendant has actually received the benefit of.[1]

[1] Railway Co. v. Keokuk Bridge Co., 131 U. S. 387; Parkersburg v. Brown, 106 U. S. 487; Central Trans. Co. v. Pullman Car Co., 139 U. S. 24; Chapman v. Douglas Co., 107 U. S. 348; Salt Lake City v. Hollister, 118 U. S. 256; Pennsylvania R. Co. v. St. Louis, etc. Co., 118 U. S. 290; Mayor v. Ray, 19 Wall. (U. S.) 468; Allegheny City v. McClurkin, 14 Pa. St. 81; In re Cork, etc., 4 Ch. Div. 748; Atlas Bank v. Nahant Bank, 4 Met. (Mass.) 581; Curtis v. Leavitt, 15 N. Y. 297; Leavitt v. Palmer, 3 Comst. (N. Y.) 19; Pratt v. Short, 79 N. Y. 437; Norton v. Bank, 61 N. H. 589; Greenville Compress v. Planters' Press, 70 Miss. 669; Ohio Life Ins. Co. v. Trust Co., 11 Humph. (Tenn.) 1; Williams v. Bank, 71 Miss. 858; Marble Co. v. Harvey, 92 Tenn. 115; Powder River Live Stock Co. v. Lamb, 38 Neb. 353; Eyser v. Weissgerber, 2 Iowa, 463; Freher v. Geiseka, 5 Iowa, 472; Formholz v. Taylor, 13 Iowa, 500; Imhoff v. House, 36 Neb. 28; Ossippee Mfg. Co. v. Canney, 54 N. H. 295; White v. Franklin Bank, 22 Pick. (Mass.) 181; Howson v. Hancock, 8 T. R. 577; Utica Ins. Co. v. Scott, 19 John. (N. Y.) 1; Little v. O'Brien, 9 Mass. 423; Rich v. Errol, 51 N. H. 361; National Bank v. Globe Works, 101 Mass. 57; Gas Light Co. v. United Gas Co., 85 Me. 541; Twiss v. Life Association, 87 Iowa, 733; Day v. Spiral Spring Co., 57 Mich. 146; Union Hardware Co. v. Plume Co., 58 Conn. 219; Miller v. American Ins. Co., 21 S. W. Rep. 39 (Tenn., 1893); Farmers' L. & T. Co. v. St. Joseph R. Co., 1 McCrary (U. S.), 247; Carey v. East Saginaw, 79 Mich. 73; Paul v. Kenosha, 22 Wis. 266; Hull v. Swansea, 5 Q. B. 526; Athenæum, etc. Co. v. Pooley, 3 De G. & J. 294; In re Phœnix Co., 2 J. & H. 441; In re Sea Foam, etc. Ins. Co., 5 De G., M. & G. 465; Logan Co. Bank v. Townsend, 139 U. S. 67; Northwestern Pack. Co. v. Shaw, 37 Wis. 655; Oneida Bank v.

As was said by the court in *Pratt v. Short, supra:* "It is no doubt the general rule that no right of action can spring out of an illegal contract. And the rule that an illegal contract cannot be enforced applies as well to contracts *malum prohibitum* as to contracts *malum in se.* But it does not necessarily follow that all the consequences attending a contract which is contrary to public morals, or founded on an immoral consideration, attend and affect a contract *malum prohibitum* merely. The law in the former case will not undertake to relieve parties from the position in which they have placed themselves, or to adjust the equities between them. But in the latter case, while the law will not enforce the prohibited contract, it will take notice of the circumstances, and if justice and equity require a restoration of money or property secured by either party thereunder, it will, and in many cases has, given relief. So also a prohibitory statute may itself point out the consequences of its violation, and if, on a consideration of the whole statute, it appears that the legislature intended to define such consequences, and to exclude every other penalty or forfeiture than such as is declared in the statute itself, no other will be enforced, and if an action can be maintained on the transaction of which the prohibited transaction was a part without sanctioning the illegality, such action will be entertained." Accordingly, in *Day v. Spiral Spring Co., supra,* plaintiff contracted to sell to defendant corporation one hundred and seventy-four tons of excelsior, not to be used by defendant in its business, but to be resold by it on speculation, as plaintiff was fully advised. After de-

Ontario Bank, 21 N. Y. 490; Southern Ins. Co. v. Lanier, 5 Fla. 110; Hall v. Paris, 59 N. H. 71; Whitney v. Peay, 24 Ark. 22; Roberts v. Deming Co., 111 N. C. 432; Curtis v. Piedmont Co., 109 N. C. 401; Maher v. Chicago, 38 Ill. 266; Thomas v. Port Huron, 27 Mich. 323.

livering a considerable quantity plaintiff refused to deliver more, and defendant refused to pay for what had been delivered unless the whole amount was delivered as agreed; whereupon plaintiff sued for the value of the excelsior delivered, and defendant set up as a counter-claim damages resulting from a failure by plaintiff to fully perform the contract. It was held, Chief Justice Cooley delivering the opinion of the court, that plaintiff was entitled to recover for the excelsior actually delivered, although the contract was *ultra vires*, and that defendant was not entitled to recoup the damages arising from the breach thereof. So a corporation agreed with plaintiff to sell goods of their manufacture on commission at a price to be fixed by plaintiff, and to account for all sales. The goods were received and sold by the corporation for less than the price fixed, and the money received for them accounted for to the plaintiff. It was held, on suit brought to recover the balance, that the corporation could not set up in defense that the undertaking was *ultra vires*, and that plaintiffs were entitled to recover the balance of the price agreed on, deducting the defendant's commission on the same.[1]

[1] Union Hardware Co. v. Plume, etc. Co., 58 Conn. 269.

In Ohio Life Ins. Co. v. Merchants' Ins. & Trust Co., 11 Humph. (Tenn.) 1, the defendant, a corporation created under the laws of the state of Tennessee, had entered into a contract beyond its corporate powers, and had received benefits therefrom. Being sued *in equity*, it defended upon the ground that it had no power to make the contract. The court held that while the *defendant was not liable on the contract*, relief should be afforded to the complainant outside of it, saying: "We are of opinion, therefore, that the complainant is not repelled by reason of the illegality relied upon in defense, but is entitled to relief, and that in granting it the court will promote both the claims of private justice and the ends of public policy. It is to be observed, however, *that the relief is against the contract and not upon the contract;* for we have seen that, in the nature of things,

§ 75. *Relief on contract ultra vires and under statute of frauds.*— It will be noticed that there is a striking similarity in the principles controlling relief granted on *ultra vires* contracts, and recovery had when a contract the law *cannot enforce an illegal contract*, although the parties be not *in pari delicto*. But it is consistent with itself that the law shall annul such contracts, and place the parties in all respects in *statu quo*."

So in Gas Light Co. v. United Gas Co., 85 Me. 511, the court say: "But it is claimed that, inasmuch as the defendant company took and held possession of the plaintiff company's works by virtue of the lease, *ultra vires* is no defense to an action to recover the agreed rent. We do not doubt that the plaintiff company is entitled to recover a reasonable rent for the time the defendant company actually occupied the works; but *do not think the amount can be measured by the ultra vires agreement*. We think that in such a case the recovery must be had *upon an implied agreement to pay a reasonable rent;* and that while the *ultra vires* agreement may be used in evidence in the nature of an admission of what is a reasonable rent, it cannot be allowed to govern or control the amount. It seems to us that it would be absurd to hold *that the ultra vires lease is void and at the same time hold that it governs the rights of the parties* with respect of the amount of rent to be recovered. A void instrument governs nothing. We think the correct rule is the one stated by Mr. Justice Gray in a recent case in the United States supreme court. He said that a contract made by a corporation which is unlawful and void because beyond the scope of its corporate powers does not, by being carried into execution, become lawful and valid; and that the proper remedy of the aggrieved party is to disaffirm the contract and sue to recover as on a *quantum meruit* the value of what the defendant has actually received the benefit of. Pittsburgh, etc. Co. v. Keokuk, etc. Co., 131 U. S. 371. We think this is the correct rule."

Another leading case, which might be noticed in this connection, is that of Miller v. Insurance Co., 21 S. W. Rep. 39, where this branch of the subject is pretty thoroughly discussed. The court there said: "We recognize a diversity of opinion in the courts of America as to the right of either party to rely upon the defense of *ultra vires*, when the contract is not expressly prohibited, and is not immoral, and has been fully executed upon *one* side. The theory upon which the cases rest which hold that the defense is not to be entertained

§ 75.] ACTIONS ON CONTRACTS. 117

is void under the statute of frauds. Thus, where a contract for the sale of personal property is void under the statute of frauds, and there has been a delivery of the thing sold to the purchaser and an acceptance thereof by

when the act is one merely in excess of express authority seems to be that such a contract should be regarded as a mere breach of duty by the agents of the corporation, and that the state has ample remedy for such abuse, or for a usurpation of power, in a proceeding to annul the charter; that to permit such a defense is of no service to the state in preventing corporate usurpation or in promoting the public interests, and only operates to encourage dishonesty and promote injustice. Resting upon one or more of these arguments many cases might be cited. There are, then, a class of cases, which make a distinction between acts merely in excess of authority and those which, in addition, are affirmatively forbidden, or immoral, or in contravention of some principle of public policy. It seems to us that the true foundation of the doctrine of *ultra vires* lies in the proposition that *every act of a corporation in excess of its powers is an act in contravention of public policy*, and, for that reason, to be held null and void. The ground upon which corporate privileges are conferred is that the public interests may be thereby subserved. If this is not so, then all such concessions are mere acts of legislative favoritism, and contravene the foundation upon which government is supposed to rest,— that all are to be protected in the enjoyment of equal rights and privileges. Charters must be supposed to be, therefore, granted upon the supposition that some public interest is thereby advanced. 'The legislature is therefore presumed,' says Judge Selden in Bissell v. Railroad Co., 22 N. Y. 285, 'to have granted just so much power, and so many peculiar privileges, as those interests are supposed to require.' It must be, therefore, that any act in excess of these granted powers is an act contrary to public policy, and, upon that ground, illegal and void. Any other view by which such acts are to be supported because executed would operate as an enormous practical extension of the power of corporations. The view this court has taken has therefore been that 'all acts outside the objects of its creation, as defined in the law of organization, and therefore beyond the powers conferred upon it,' are acts not voidable only but wholly void. Marble Co. v. Harvey, 92 Tenn. 115; Elevator Co. v. Memphis & C. R. Co., 85 Tenn. 705; Mallory v. Oil Works, 86 Tenn. 598. The rule and the foundation upon which it rests, as held by the English courts, are identical

him, the plaintiff may recover the reasonable value of the property, if his petition is so framed; but a party cannot recover on a *quantum meruit* where he pleads and relies solely upon a special contract.[1]

with our own. . . . The Tennessee rule is in accord with the holding of many of the American courts. Pittsburg, etc. R. Co. v. Keokuk & Hamilton Bridge Co., 131 U. S. 389; Central Trans. Co. v. Pullman's Car Co., 139 U. S. 60; Davis v. Railroad Co., 131 Mass. 258; Chambers v. Falkner, 65 Ala. 448; Bank v. Dunkin, 54 Ala. 471. The remedy in case one of the parties has received a benefit under such a contract, which *ex æquo et bono,* it ought not to retain, is a suit in disaffirmance and for an accounting. Marble Co. v. Harvey, *supra.* The plaintiff's suit is upon the contract, and in affirmance of it, and, if there be nothing else in the case, could not be maintained."

[1] Powder River Live Stock Co. v. Lamb, 38 Neb. 353; Eyser v. Weissgerber, 2 Iowa, 463; Freher v. Geiseka, 5 Iowa, 472; Formholz v. Taylor, 13 id. 500; Imhoff v. House, 36 Neb. 28; Rich v. Errol, 51 N. H. 361; Little v. O'Brien, 9 Mass. 423; White v. Franklin Bank, 22 Pick. (Mass.) 181; Howson v. Hancock, 8 T. R. 577; Robinson v. Bland, 2 Burr. 1077; Utica Ins. Co. v. Scott, 19 Johns. (N. Y.) 1; Same v. Cadwell, 3 Wend. (N. Y.) 296; Same v. Bloodgood, 4 Wend. (N. Y.) 652; Ossipee Mfg. Co. v. Canney, 54 N. H. 295.

CHAPTER VI.

ADOPTION AND RATIFICATION OF CONTRACTS.

§ 76. General doctrine of ratification stated.
77. Nature and effect of ratification.
78. *Ultra vires* contracts of corporations cannot be ratified.
79. Ratification by corporation of acts of promoters.

§ 76. *General doctrine of ratification stated.*—It is the general rule that when a contract is made or an act performed by any officer or agent of a corporation in its behalf and for a purpose authorized by its charter, and the corporation receives the benefit of the act or contract without objection, it may be presumed to have authorized and adopted or ratified the act of such agent.[1] In such case the maxim *omnis ratihabitio retro trahitur et mandato priori æquiparatur* applies. This proposition is but an application of the doctrine of the law of agency, that when a person ratifies the unauthorized act of another who has purported to act on his behalf, the legal effect of the act will be the same as if it had been authorized before it was done. The ratification, to be binding on a corporation, however, must be the act or acquiescence of some corporate agency which itself would have the power to do or authorize the act committed; for a ratification cannot arise from the action either of the officers who did

[1] Pittsburg, etc. R. Co. v. Keokuk, etc. Bridge Co., 131 U. S. 371; Pneumatic Gas Co. v. Berry, 113 U. S. 322; Gold Mining Co. v. National Bank, 96 U. S. 640; Zabrieskie v. Cleveland, etc. R. Co., 23 How. (U. S.) 381; Bank of U. S. v. Dandridge, 12 Wheat. (U. S.) 64; Bank of Columbia v. Patterson, 7 Cranch (U. S.), 279.

the unauthorized acts or of those who would have had no authority to do them.[1]

§ 77. *Nature and effect of ratification.*— The general nature and effect of ratification is stated by Mr. Justice Field as follows: "The general rule as to the effect of a ratification by one of the unauthorized act of another respecting the property of the former is well settled. The ratification operates upon the act ratified precisely as though authority to do the act had been previously given, except where the rights of third parties have intervened between the act and the ratification. In other words, it is essential that the party ratifying should be able not merely to do the act ratified at the time the act was done, but also at the time the ratification was made."[2] Although this reasoning was adduced in discussing the law of agency, yet the same principle is involved in applying the doctrine of ratification by corporations to unauthorized acts of their officers or agents, such ratification being equivalent to antecedent authority.[3] Accordingly, if a person assuming to act as agent of a corporation, but without legal authority, or an agent in excess of his proper authority, make a contract, and the corporation knowingly receive and retain the benefit of it, this will be ratification of the contract, and render the corporation liable as a party to it; provided, of course, such contract be within the scope of the corporate powers.[4]

[1] Taylor, Priv. Corp., § 211; Tracy v. Guthrie County Agl. Soc., 47 Iowa, 127; Crunis' Appeal, 66 Pa. St. 474; Beach on Priv. Corp., § 196.
[2] Cook v. Tullis, 18 Wall. 332.
[3] Taylor, Priv. Corp., § 211; First National Bank v. Fricke, 75 Mo. 178; Planters' Bank v. Sharp, 12 Miss. 75; Fleckner v. Bank of United States, 8 Wheat. 338, 363.
[4] Bank of Kentucky v. Schuylkill Bank, 1 Par. Sel. Cas. (N. Y.) 180; Merchants' Bank v. Central Bank, 1 Ga. 418; Proprietors, etc.

§ 78. *Ultra vires contracts of corporation cannot be ratified.*— The foregoing rule must not be confounded, however, with the well-settled doctrine that a corporation cannot ratify an act or contract beyond the scope of its chartered powers; for it is a well-established principle in the law of corporations that an act or contract *ultra vires* a corporation is void, and cannot be made valid by

v. Gordon, 1 Pick. (Mass.) 297; Randall v. Van Vechten, 19 John. (N. Y.) 60; Moss v. Rossie Lead Min. Co., 5 Hill (N. Y.), 137; Episcopal Soc. v. Episcopal Church, 1 Pick. (Mass.) 372; Haywood v. Pilgrim Soc., 21 Pick. (Mass.) 270; Ohio, etc. R. Co. v. Middleton, 20 Ill. 629; Corn Exch. Bank v. Cumberland Coal Co., 1 Bosw. (N. Y.) 436; Keyser v. School Dist., 35 N. H. 477; McCullough v. Talladega Ins. Co., 46 Ala. 376; Durar v. Hudson County Ins. Co., 22 N. J. L. 171; Hooker v. Eagle Bank, 30 N. Y. 83; Whiting v. Union Trust Co., 65 N. Y. 576; Conant v. Canal Co., 29 Vt. 263; Shaver v. Bear River Min. Co., 10 Cal. 396; Dispatch Line v. Bellamy Man. Co., 12 N. H. 205; Bank of Lyons v. Demon, Lalor, 398; Germantown Ins. Co. v. Dhein, 43 Wis. 420; State v. Smith, 48 Vt. 266; Stark Bank v. United States Pottery Co., 34 Vt. 144; Whitwell v. Warner, 20 Vt. 424; Aurora Agl. Soc. v. Paddock, 80 Ill. 263; Ottowa R. Co. v. Murray, 15 Ill. 336; Houghton v. Dodge, 5 Bosw. (N. Y.) 326; Farmers', etc. Bank v. Sherman, 6 Bosw. (N. Y.) 181; Woodbridge v. Addison, 6 Vt. 204; Bank of Columbia v. Patterson's Adm'rs, 7 Cranch (U. S.), 299; Peterson v. New York, 17 N. Y. 449; Davidson v. Bridgeport, 8 Conn. 472; Church v. Sterling, 16 Conn. 389; Medomak Bank v. Curtis, 24 Me. 36; Emmet v. Reed, 8 N. Y. 312; Alexander v. Brown, 9 Hun (N. Y.), 641; City Bank v. Baltimore, 7 Har. & J. (Md.) 104; Weeden v. Mad River R. Co., 14 Ohio, 563; Perry v. Waterproof Co., 37 Conn. 520; Union Gold Min. Co. v. Rocky Mountain Nat. Bank, 1 Colo. 531; s. c., 2 Colo. 248; s. c., 96 U. S. 640; Rich v. State Nat. Bank, 7 Neb. 201; Peninsular Bank v. Hanmer, 14 Mich. 208; Humphrey v. Patrons' Merc. Ass'n, 50 Iowa, 607; Fishkill Sav. Inst. v. Bostwick, 19 Hun (N. Y.), 354; International, etc. Co. v. United States, 13 Ct. of Cl. 209; Delaware Canal Co. v. Pennsylvania Coal Co., 21 Pa. St. 131; Ridley v. Plymouth Grinding Co., 2 Exch. 711; Stuart v. London, etc. R. Co., 15 Beav. 513; Smith v. Hull Gas Co., 11 C. B. 897; Ex parte Scholbred, 28 Week. Rep. 339; Troup's Case, 29 Beav. 353; Edwards v. Grand Junc. R. Co., 1 Myl. & Cr. 650; Preston v. Railroad Co., 1 Sim. (N. S.) 586; s. c., 7 Eng. L. & Eq. 124.

any subsequent act of the corporation purporting to ratify the same, because there is no residuary power to confirm it. What they could not make they cannot ratify. Nor can a void act or contract become valid, merely because it remains unquestioned. A ratification is in law treated as equivalent to a previous authority, and it follows that, as a general rule, a person or body of persons, or a corporation, not competent to authorize an act, cannot give it validity by ratifying it.[1] This rule is stated by a learned author thus: "An act which is in excess of the charter of a corporation involves an unauthorized exercise of corporate power on the part of the company; and this objection cannot be obviated by any subsequent ratification, either by the agents or by the shareholders of the corporation. So it is clear that, if an act performed by an agent on behalf of a corporation is prohibited by statute or by the charter of the company, or by some general rule of the common law, no ratification by either agents or the shareholders of the corporation can cure the illegality of the act. Ratification of an act has no greater effect than a previous grant of authority to do the act; it merely obviates the objection that the principal did not authorize the act to be done."[2]

[1] Tippecanoe Co. v. Lafayette, etc. R. Co., 50 Ind. 86, 112; Irvine v. Union Bank, 2 App. Cas. 366; Dimpfel v. Ohio Ry. Co., 110 U. S. 209; Green's Brice's Ultra Vires, ch. VI; Dillon, Munic. Corp., §§ 385, 386 (3d ed.); Christian University v. Jordon, 29 Mo. 68; Ang. & Ames, § 304; McCullough v. Moss, 5 Denio (N. Y.), 567; Ashbury Ry. Co. v. Riche, 7 H. L. 653, 673; s. c. (below), 9 Exch. 224, 262; Bird v. Bird's Patent Co., 9 Ch. 358; National Trust Co. v. Miller, 33 N. J. Eq. 155; Thomas v. Railway Co., 101 U. S. 73; Oregon Ry. v. Oregonian Ry., 130 U. S. 22; Central Transp. Co. v. Pullman's Car Co., 139 U. S. 24.

[2] Mor. Priv. Corp., § 619.

In Ashbury Ry. Co. v. Riche, *supra*, the Lord Chancellor said: "Now, I am clearly of opinion that this contract was entirely, as I have said, beyond the objects of the memorandum of association.

§ 79.] ADOPTION AND RATIFICATION OF CONTRACTS. 123

§ 79. *Ratification by corporation of acts of promoters.* The promoters, or individuals organizing a corporation, are not, of course, the corporation. The legal body, as has been shown, is distinct from the individuals composing it. The statutes confer no authority upon the promoters of a corporation, as a general rule, to enter into preliminary contracts binding the corporation when it shall come into existence. Such contracts may, however, bind the individuals who make them. If ratified and adopted by the corporation, and they are within the cor-

If so, it was thereby placed beyond the powers of the company to make the contract. If so, my lords, it is not a question whether the contract ever was ratified or was not ratified. If it was a contract void at its beginning, it was void because the company could not make the contract. If every shareholder of the company had said: 'That is the contract which we desire to make, to which we sanction the placing the seal of the company,' the case would not have stood in any different position from that in which it stands now. The shareholders would thereby, by unanimous consent, have attempted to do the very thing which, by the act of parliament, they were prohibited from doing. But, my lords, if the shareholders of the company could not *ab ante* have authorized a contract of this kind to be made, how could they subsequently sanction the contract after it had, in point of fact, been made? I endeavored to follow, as accurately as I could, the very able argument of Mr. Benjamin at your lordships' bar, on this point; but it appeared to me that this was a difficulty with which he was entirely unable to grapple. He endeavored to contend that when the shareholders had found that something had been done by the directors which ought not to have been done they might be authorized to make the best they could of a difficulty into which they had thus been thrown, and therefore might be deemed to possess power to sanction the contract being proceeded with. My lords, I am unable to adopt that suggestion. It appears to me that it would be perfectly fatal to the whole scheme of legislation to which I have referred if you were to hold that, in the first place, directors might do that which even the whole company could not do, and that then, the shareholders finding out what had been done, could sanction, subsequently, what they could not antecedently have authorized."

porate powers, and are not otherwise subject to objection, they may become the contracts of the corporation and enforceable as such.[1] In respect of contracts of promoters, Judge Redfield says: "The promoters are in no sense identical with the corporation, nor do they represent it in any relation of agency, and their contracts could, of course, only bind the company so far as they should be subsequently adopted by it, as their successors."[2] Such a contract must derive its vitality from the meeting of minds when both parties are in existence; until then, it can be nothing more than an offer by one party.[3] And

[1] Munson v. Railroad Co., 103 N. Y. 58; Rockford R. Co. v. Sage, 65 Ill. 328; Safety Dep. Life Co. v. Smith, id. 309; Western Screw Co. v. Cousley, 72 Ill. 531; Franklin Ins. Co. v. Hart, 31 Md. 59; N. Y. R. Co. v. Ketchum, 27 Conn. 170; Marchand v. Loan Co., 26 La. Ann. 389; Frost v. Belmont, 6 Allen (Mass.), 152; White v. Manufacturing Co., 1 Pick. (Mass.) 215; Earl of Shrewsbury v. North Staf. Ry. Co., 1 Eq. 593; Bell's Gap Ry. Co. v. Christy, 79 Pa. St. 54; Frankfort Co. v. Churchill, 6 T. B. Mon. (Ky.) 427; Caledonian Ry. Co. v. Helensburgh, 2 Macq. 391; Payne v. New South Wales Coal Co., 10 Ex. 283; Pennsylvania Match Co. v. Hapgood, 141 Mass. 145; Touche v. Warehousing Co., 6 Ch. App. 671; Spiller v. Paris Rink Co., 7 Ch. Div. 368; Whitney v. Wyman, 101 U. S. 392; McDonough v. Bank, 34 Tex. 309; Morrison v. Gold Mountain Co., 52 Cal. 307.

[2] 1 Redf. on Rys., § 9.

In Bell's Gap Railroad Co. v. Christy, *supra*, an action was brought against a railroad company to recover the value of services performed before the incorporation, in procuring the charter, making surveys, etc. It was held that the plaintiff could not recover in the absence of proof that a majority of the incorporators or promoters of the corporation authorized the service.

In Morrison v. Gold Mountain Co., *supra*, an agreement was made among parties owning a mine, and who expected to incorporate themselves but did not then do so, that a person was entitled to two thousand five hundred shares of the stock of the company. It was held not to be the agreement of the corporation; that the mere acceptance of the benefit of a contract does not imply a promise on the part of the company to adopt and perform it.

[3] Pennsylvania Match Co. v. Hapgood, 141 Mass. 145.

a contract made by the promoters, to become binding on the corporation, should be adopted in the same way that its own contracts are made. Formal action by the board of directors is necessary in the former case only if it would be so in the latter.[1]

As contracts of promoters are peculiarly adapted to companies formed under the acts of parliament and the Companies Act of England, the subject is not deemed of sufficient importance in this country to require further consideration here.

[1] Batelle v. Northwestern Cement Co., 37 Minn. 89.

CHAPTER VII.

THE DOCTRINE APPLIED TO INCIDENTAL POWERS OF CORPORATIONS.

§ 80. Introductory.
81. Power to acquire real property.
82. Devises to corporations.
83. *Jus disponendi* in corporations.
84. Power to sell implies power to mortgage.
85. Power of bank to hold real estate.
86. Power to acquire by eminent domain.
87. Alienation by deed.
88. Conveyances by agent.
89. Acknowledgment to corporate deeds.
90. Affixing seal to deeds.
91. Assignment for benefit of creditors.
92. Power to act as trustee.
93. Trust must be within scope of corporate purposes.
94. Cannot be compelled to execute repugnant trust.
95. Power to take by bequest.
96. Power to borrow money.
97. Test to determine if transaction is borrowing.
98. Instances of implied power to borrow.
99. Power to loan money.
100. Power as to negotiable notes.
101. Power as indorsee.
102. Power of savings bank to make negotiable paper.
103. Power as to discount and purchase.
104. Liability on accommodation paper.
105. Power to pledge securities.

§ 80. *Introductory.*—In addition to the powers usually granted to a corporation by its charter or the laws under which it is organized and created, there are certain other powers, which a long line of adjudications have established, that are now generally regarded as incidental to

§ 81.] INCIDENTAL POWERS OF CORPORATIONS. 127

those specially conferred; and it has usually been in the application of the doctrine of *ultra vires* to these incidental powers that so much conflict in judicial opinion has occurred. In the succeeding sections of this chapter will be set forth such powers as have been declared by the great weight of authority as incidental to those specially enumerated.

§ 81. *Power to acquire real property.*— At common law, unless in a case where a corporation purchases and undertakes to hold real property for purposes wholly outside and foreign to the objects of its creation, or unless restricted by its charter or by statute, a corporation generally had the legal capacity to take title in fee to real property.[1] And even under modern statutes, if the objects for which the corporation is formed cannot be accomplished without acquiring and holding title to real estate, then such power may be implied.[2] In modern times, however, and more especially in this country, the

[1] 1 Bl. Com. 478; 2 Kent, Com. 281; 1 Wash. Real Prop. (4th ed.) 75; Beach, Priv. Corp., § 377; Boone, Corp., § 40; Natoma, etc. Co. v. Clarkin, 14 Cal. 544; Hayward v. Davidson, 41 Ind. 212; Lathrop v. Commercial Bank, 8 Dana (Ky.), 114: Inhabitants of Sutton Parish v. Cole, 3 Pick. (Mass.) 232; Thompson v. Waters, 25 Mich. 214; Calloway M. Co. v. Clark, 32 Mo. 305; McCartee v. Orphan Asylum, 9 Cow. (N. Y.) 437; Champlain R. Co. v. Valentine, 19 Barb. (N. Y.) 484; Robie v. Sedgwick, 35 Barb. (N. Y.) 319; Reynolds v. Stark Co., 5 Ohio, 204; Leazure v. Hillegas, 7 Serg. & Rawle (Pa.), 313; The Banks v. Poitiaux, 3 Rand. (Va.) 136; Rivanna Nav. Co. v. Dawson, 3 Grat. (Va.) 19; Page v. Heineberg, 40 Vt. 81; Auerbach v. Le Sueur Mill. Co., 28 Minn. 291; Ossipee, etc. Co. v. Canney, 54 N. H. 295; Ashville Division, etc. v. Aston, 92 N. C. 578; State v. Madison, 7 Wis. 688; Blanchard's Factory v. Warner, 1 Blatch. (U. S.) 258; Dry Dock Co. v. Hicks, 3 McL. 115.

[2] Crawford v. Longstreet, 43 N. J. L. 326; State v. Mansfield, 23 N. J. L. 510; State v. Newark, 1 Dutch. (N. J.) 315; 2 Kent, Com. 282; Blackburn v. Selma, etc. R. Co., 2 Flip. (U. S.) 525.

legislature generally prescribes some limits to the powers of corporations to purchase and hold real property, the charter and law under which it is organized and created being the source to which we must go to ascertain whether a corporation possesses such power.[1] But corporations created for a specific object have no power to take and hold real estate for purposes wholly foreign to that object.[2] So where the charter of a corporation prescribed that "the lands, tenements and hereditaments which it shall be lawful for the said corporation to hold shall be only such as shall be required for its accommodation in relation to the convenient transacting of its business, or such as shall have been *bona fide* mortgaged to it by way of security, or conveyed to it in satisfaction of debts previously contracted in the course of its dealings, or purchased at sales upon judgments which shall have been obtained for such debts," it was held that the corporation was prohibited from buying or selling or becoming a speculator in real estate.[3] But it has been held in many cases that where a corporation has purchased or is holding more land than it is authorized to acquire or hold, it still has the right to hold it against all others except the state.[4] In *Natoma W. & M. Co. v. Clarkin*, 14

[1] Russell v. Topping, 5 McL. (U. S.) 194; Perrine v. Canal Co., 9 How. (U. S.) 172; Moor's Heirs v. Moor's Devisees, 4 Dana, 354; Lathrop v. Commercial Bank, 8 Dana (N. Y.), 114; Chambers v. St. Louis, 29 Mo. 543; Revanna Nav. Co. v. Dawson, 3 Grat. (Va.) 19; Case v. Kelly, 133 U. S. 21; Fritts v. Palmer, 132 U. S. 293.
[2] Inhabitants of Sutton Parish v. Cole, 3 Pick. (Mass.) 232.
[3] Bank of Michigan v. Niles, 1 Doug. (Mich.) 401.
[4] Natoma, etc. Co. v. Clarkin, 14 Cal. 543; Hough v. Cook County, etc. Co., 73 Ill. 23; Hayward v. Davidson, 41 Ind. 212; Land v. Coffman, 50 Mo. 243; Whitman M. Co. v. Baker, 3 Nev. 386; De Camp v. Dobbins, 29 N. J. Eq. 36; Bogardus v. Trinity Church, 4 Sand. Ch. (N. Y.) 633; Farmers' T. & T. Co. v. Curtis, 7 N. Y. 466; Mallett v. Simpson, 94 N. C. 37; Leazure v. Hillegas, 7 S. & R. (Pa.) 313; Baird

Cal. 552, Mr. Justice Field, in discussing this subject, said: "Whether or not the premises in controversy are necessary for these purposes it is not material to inquire; that is a matter between the government and the corporation, and is no concern of the defendants. It would lead to infinite inconvenience and embarrassments if, in the suits by corporations to recover the possession of their property, inquiries were permitted as to the necessity of such property for the purposes of their incorporation, and the title made to rest upon the existence of that necessity." And in *Mallett v. Simpson*, 94 N. C. 37, Ashe, J., in delivering the opinion of the court, used language to the same effect, namely: "The authorities go to the extent that even when the right to acquire real property is limited by the charter, and the corporation transcends its power in that respect, and for that reason is incompetent to take title to real estate, a conveyance to it is not void, but only the sovereign (here the state) can object. It is valid until assailed in a direct proceeding instituted by the sovereign for that purpose." So in *Southern Pacific R. Co. v. Orton, supra*, it was held that where a corporation authorized to receive grants of land for the purpose of the corporation brings an action against a trespasser to recover possession of lands granted to it, such trespasser will not be heard to question the title of the corporation on the ground that it had no authority to take them; that that was a question between the state and the corporation. And where a corporation is authorized

---

v. Bank, 11 id. 411; Goundie v. Water Co., 7 Pa. St. 233; Blunt v. Walker, 11 Wis. 334; Southern Pac. R. Co. v. Orton, 6 Saw. (C. C. U. S.) 157; Runyan v. Lessee, etc., 13 Pet. (U. S.) 122; Cornell v. Colorado Springs, 100 U. S. 55; Jones v. Habersham, 107 U. S. 174; Oil Co. v. Railway Co., 32 Fed. Rep. 22; Alexander v. Tolleston Club, 110 Ill. 65.

to receive conveyances of and hold title to real estate, but is prohibited from so doing for any but specified purposes, the question as to the validity of the title to the real estate conveyed to it cannot be made to depend upon proof as to whether the land is held for such specified purpose or not. The title will vest in the corporation, and the question as to whether the corporation has exceeded its powers can be raised only by the state or by a stockholder.[1] And corporations chartered in one state, and not forbidden by the laws of its creation, may acquire and hold lands in another state, unless prohibited from so doing either by direct enactments of the latter

[1] Hough v. Cook County L. Co., 73 Ill. 23.

In Case v. Kelly, *supra*, the court say: "A corporation, in order to be entitled to buy and sell, to receive and hold, the title to real estate, must have some statutory authority of the state in which such lands lie, to enable it to do so, and the absence of such provision in the law of its incorporation does not create any general statute which authorizes any such right. The enumeration of the purposes for which the corporation could acquire title to real estate must necessarily be held exclusive of all other purposes."

And in Fritts v. Palmer, 132 U. S. 293, Mr. Justice Miller, speaking of the general powers of corporations to acquire and transfer real estate, in his masterly dissenting opinion says: "It has been the recognized doctrine of this court for a great many years, perhaps a century, that the transfer of title to real estate, whether by inheritance, by purchase and sale, or by any other mode by which title to property is acquired, is rightfully governed by the laws of the state in which the land is situated. The policy of permitting corporations to hold real estate has always been a restricted one. Corporate bodies, whether for public use or private purposes, have always been subjects of limitation on this right to hold real estate. It may be prohibited altogether. It may be allowed with distinct limitations as to amount either in quantity or in value. I can conceive of cases where corporations have been authorized to acquire a limited amount of real estate such as the legislature may conceive to be useful and necessary to the purpose for which they are organized, or to take property for specific uses, in which the question as to whether they have exceeded that amount or perverted the use may be one for the state alone, and not of any private person."

state or by its public policy, to be deduced from settled adjudications of its courts.[1]

§ 82. *Devises to corporations.* — Generally, corporations may not take lands by devise unless specially authorized so to do, this manner of acquiring real estate being regulated by statute or by the provisions of its charter. In New York corporations have been held incapable of taking lands by devise unless so authorized by statute or by charter,[2] whilst in Massachusetts[3] and Kentucky[4] no such limitations as to devises to corporations existed. And where the provisions in the charter of a corporation permitted it to acquire land " by direct purchase or otherwise," it was held to have the power to acquire by devise.[5]

§ 83. *Jus disponendi in corporations.* — The power to acquire real or personal property in a corporation as in an individual implies absolute *jus disponendi*, unless such power be restrained by statute or by considerations of public policy.[6] It is a necessary incident to ownership,

[1] American, etc. Union v. Yount, 101 U. S. 352; Thompson v. Waters, 25 Mich. 214; Whitman Min. Co. v. Baker, 3 Nev. 386; Lumbard v. Aldrich, 8 N. H. 31; State v. Boston, etc. R. Co., 25 Vt. 433; Props. Claremont Bridge v. Royce, 42 id. 730; Northern T. Co. v. Chicago, 7 Biss. (C. C.) 45; s. c., 99 U. S. 635; Carroll v. East St. Louis, 67 Ill. 568; Santa Clara Academy v. Sullivan, 116 Ill. 375.

[2] McCartee v. Orphan Asylum, 9 Cow. (N. Y.) 437; Downing v. Marshall, 23 N. Y. 366; White v. Howard, 46 N. Y. 144; Holmes v. Mead, 52 N. Y. 332.

[3] Dickson v. United States, 125 Mass. 311.

[4] Moor's Heirs v. Moor's Devisees, 4 Dana (N. Y.), 354.

[5] Downing v. Marshall, 23 N. Y. 366.

[6] 2 Kent, Com. 281; Burton's Appeal, 57 Pa. St. 213; Reichwald v. Commercial Hotel, 106 Ill. 439; Binney's Case, 2 Bland (Mo.), 97; Ardesco Oil Co. v. N. A. Min. etc. Co., 66 Pa. St. 375, 382; State v. College, 38 Cal. 161; Miners' Ditch Co. v. Zellerbach, 37 Cal. 543; Canal Co. v. Vallette, 21 How. (U. S.) 424; Partridge v. Badger, 25 Barb.

and has the power without any express grant. A corporation may therefore, in the absence of any such restraint, sell whatever it has the right to own. So it may sell all its corporate property for a corporate or lawful purpose.[1] Thus, where a corporation, organized for the purpose of creating a water-power, finds that it can no longer profitably use its privileges, and its water-power has been extinguished by contract with the state, it may sell its lands and receive payment therefor in its own stock.[2] So, a corporation organized for the purpose of owning ditches for the conveyance and sale of water has power to sell and convey all its corporate property, provided the sale is made for corporate purposes, and strangers taking a conveyance are entitled to assume, as against the corporation, that the sale was for a lawful purpose.[3] The foregoing rules apply more particularly to strictly private corporations, established solely for trading or manufacturing purposes, and in the management of which neither the public nor the state has any direct concern.[4]

(N. Y.) 146; Barry v. Merchants' Exchange, 1 Sandf. Ch. (N. Y.) 280; Burr v. Glass Co., 14 Barb. (N. Y.) 358; Dater v. Bank, 5 Watts & S. (Pa.) 223; Frazier v. Wilcox, 4 Rob. 517; United States Bank v. Huth, 4 B. Mon. (Ky.) 423; State v. Bank, 6 Gill & J. (Md.) 323; Pierce v. Emery, 32 N. H. 484; Reynolds v. Commissioners, 5 Ohio, 205; De Ruyter v. St. Peter's Ch., 3 N. Y. 238; Clark v. Titcomb, 42 Barb. (N. Y.) 122; Central Gold M. Co. v. Platt, 3 Daly (N. Y.), 263; Banks v. Poitiaux, 3 Rand. (Va.) 136.

[1] Miners' Ditch Co. v. Zellerbach, 37 Cal. 543; Sargent v. Webster, 13 Met. (Mass.) 498; Treadwell v. Salisbury Mfg. Co., 7 Gray (Mass.), 393; Hodges v. Screw Co., 1 R. I. 322, 3 R. I. 9; Dupee v. Boston Water-power Co., 114 Mass. 37.

[2] Dupee v. Boston Water-power Co., 114 Mass. 37.

[3] Miners' Ditch Co. v. Zellerbach, 37 Cal. 543.

[4] State v. College, 38 Cal. 166; Commonwealth v. Smith, 10 Allen (Mass.), 448; Webster v. Turner, 12 Hun (N. Y.). 264; Hancock v. Holbrook, 4 Woods (U. S. C. C.), 52; Sheldon Hat Co. v. Eickemeyer, etc. Co., 90 N. Y. 613; Dupee v. Boston Water-power Co., 114 Mass. 37; Buford v. Keokuk Packet Co., 3 Mo. App. 159.

§ 84. *Power to sell and convey implies power to mortgage.*— Power in a corporation to alienate its real property absolutely, clearly carries with it the implied power to mortgage for corporate purposes. It may therefore, in the absence of any prohibition in its charter or the law of its organization, borrow money for the purpose of carrying out the legitimate objects of its incorporation, and mortgage its realty to secure the same.[1] And it has lately been held that a corporation, acting in good faith and without any purpose of defrauding its creditors, but with the sole object of continuing a business which promises to be successful, may give a mortgage to directors who have lent their credit to it, in order to induce a continuance of that credit, and to obtain renewals of maturing paper at a time when the corporation, although it may not be then in fact possessed of assets equal at cash prices to its indebtedness, is in fact a going concern, and is intending and expecting to continue in business.[2] And it has been held that a corporation, authorized by its charter to purchase, hold and convey such real estate as was requisite and necessary for the transaction of the business for which it was created, or such as had been mortgaged or conveyed to it for the security or payment of debts due it, might mortgage such realty to secure a debt owing by it.[3] So an agricultural society may mortgage its fair grounds to raise money to advance the ob-

[1] Aurora Agl. Soc. v. Paddock, 80 Ill. 263; Thompson v. Lambert, 44 Iowa, 239; Beardstown, etc. R. Co. v. Metcalf, 4 Met. (Mass.) 199; Susquehanna Bridge Co. v. Insurance Co., 3 Md. 305; Richards v. Railroad Co., 44 N. H. 135; Jackson ex dem. People v. Brown, 5 Wend. (N. Y.) 590; Barry v. Merchants' Exch., 1 Sandf. Ch. (N. Y.) 280; Burt v. Rattle, 31 Ohio St. 116; Gordon v. Preston, 1 Watts (Pa.), 385; Watts' Appeal, 78 Pa. St. 370; Leggett v. Banking Co., 1 Sax. Ch. (N. J.) 541; s. c., 23 Am. Dec. 728.
[2] Sanford Tool Co. v. Howe, Brown & Co., 157 U. S. 312.
[3] Jackson ex dem. People v. Brown, 5 Wend. (N. Y.) 590.

jects of its creation.¹ And a corporation created for the purpose of building a public exchange building may mortgage its realty to carry out that object.²

§ 85. *Power of bank to hold and sell real estate.*— A bank is usually authorized by its charter to acquire, hold and sell real estate that may be necessary for its banking purposes, or conveyed to it in satisfaction of a debt contracted in the course of its dealings, or purchased by it at a sale under a mortgage held by the bank.³ But holding, acquiring and selling to any greater extent or for any other purpose than is set forth in its charter is illegal.⁴ So the power to convey real estate includes the power to mortgage it; and power to purchase includes power to sell.⁵

¹ Thompson v. Lambert, 45 Iowa, 239.
² Barry v. Merchants' Exchange, 1 Sandf. Ch. (N. Y.) 280.
³ Thomaston Bank v. Stimpson, 21 Me. 195; Jackson v. Brown, 5 Wend. (N. Y.) 590.
⁴ Metropolitan Bank v. Godfrey, 23 Ill. 579; Bank of Michigan v. Niles, 1 Doug. (Mich.) 401; Pacific R. Co. v. Seeley, 45 Mo. 211; Chapman v. Colby, 47 Mich. 51; Case v. Kelly, 133 U. S. 21; Russell v. Topping, 5 McLean (U. S.), 194.
⁵ Jackson v. Brown, *supra*.

In Russell v. Topping, *supra*, the lines are rather finely drawn. In that case a bank under its charter had power to purchase, hold and convey real estate as follows: "First, such as shall be required for its immediate accommodation in the transaction of its business, or such as shall have been mortgaged to it in good faith by way of security for loans previously contracted for money due; or second, such as shall have been conveyed to it in satisfaction of debts previously contracted in the course of its dealings; or third, such as shall have been purchased at sales upon judgments, decrees or mortgages obtained or made for such debts; and said bank shall not purchase, hold or convey real estate in any other case, or for any other purpose," etc. The facts are stated by the court as follows: It appears that a man by the name of Howard, being indebted to the plantiff, gave him a mortgage on some real property to secure the debt,

§ 86. *Power to acquire real property by right of eminent domain.* — Corporations of a *quasi*-public character have been authorized to take private property for the purpose of making public highways, turnpike roads and canals, of erecting wharves and basins, of establishing ferries, of draining swamps and marshes, and of bringing water to cities and villages.[1] But statutes delegating the right of

which included the tract in question. The plaintiff foreclosed his mortgage by a proceeding on the equity side of this court. The State Bank of Illinois was made a party defendant, and filed an answer to the bill, alleging that Howard was largely indebted to the bank, for which indebtedness a mortgage had been given by Howard, but subsequent to that of the plaintiff, and which included several parcels of land conveyed by the plaintiff's prior mortgage, but not the lot in controversy. At this time Howard was insolvent, and the bank asked that the lands not included in this mortgage should first be sold to pay the plaintiff's debt, and that the lands included in the mortgage of the bank (and which were also in the plaintiff's mortgage) should be sold only in the event of the other lands not being sufficient to pay the plaintiff's debt. The court decreed accordingly, and ordered that, unless the plaintiff's debt be paid within twenty days, the land should be sold by a commission. It was sold in pursuance of the decree. At the sale the bank purchased the tract in controversy, and a deed was made to the bank by the commissioners. The defendants claim through the bank. The plaintiff received the purchase money paid by the bank. Howard being liable to the plaintiff for other indebtedness, suit was brought against him by the plaintiff, judgment recovered, execution issued, and the tract in question levied on and sold. At that sale the plaintiff was the purchaser, and he now holds a deed for the premises. Both parties claiming through Howard, his title is not questioned. After a thorough examination of the subject it was held by the court that such purchase by the bank was *ultra vires;* that the receipt of the purchase price of such property from the bank did not estop the persons receiving it from disputing the power of the bank to purchase the property, and that its grantee in possession of such property could be ejected.

[1] Beekman v. Saratoga R. Co., 3 Paige (N. Y.), 44; Johnson v. Utica Water-works, 67 Barb. (N. Y.) 415; Inhabitants of Wayland v. Commissioners, 4 Gray (Mass.), 500; In re Mt. Washington R. Co., 35

eminent domain to corporations are not to be extended by implication and must be strictly complied with.[1] The real estate acquired by a public corporation in the exercise of a delegated right of eminent domain and necessary for uses in which the public is concerned cannot be sold under execution apart from the franchise and its incidents so as to give the purchaser a title to the property divested of all the duties and obligations assumed by the company.[2]

§ 87. *Alienation by deed.*— The right of alienation is, as we have seen,[3] an incident of ownership, and belongs to a corporation as well as to an individual, when no restraint is imposed in the charter.[4] As a general rule, deeds of conveyance by a corporation must be executed in the corporate name and under the corporate seal.[5] It is also a general principle that a conveyance of property by a corporation may be executed like a conveyance by an individual through any agent having authority to represent the company for that purpose.[6]

N. H. 134; Hildreth v. Lowell, 11 Gray (Mass.), 345; Reeves v. Wood Co., 8 Ohio St. 333; Barrington v. Neuse River, 69 N. C. 165; Curry v. Mt. Sterling, 15 Ill. 320; East St. Louis v. St. John, 47 Ill. 463; Patterson v. Boom Co., 3 Dill. (U. S.) 465; Re Corporation of Haddersfield, 10 Ch. App. 92.
[1] Trumpler v. Bernerly, 39 Cal. 490; N. Y. etc. R. Co. v. Kip, 46 N. Y. 546; Iron R. R. Co. v. Ironton, 19 Ohio St. 299; People v. Brighton, 10 Mich. 57; Leslie v. St. Louis, 47 Mo. 474.
[2] Gooch v. McGee, 83 N. C. 59.
[3] § 83.
[4] Burton's Appeal, 57 Pa. St. 213; Dana v. Bank, 5 W. & S. (Pa.) 243; Walker v. Vincent, 19 Pa. St. 369.
[5] Boone, Corp., § 54; Hatch v. Barr, 1 Ohio, 390; Miners' Ditch Co. v. Zellerbach, 37 Cal. 543; Hutchins v. Byrnes, 9 Gray (Mass.), 367; Flint v. Clinton Co., 12 N. H. 430; Tenney v. E. Warren L. Co., 43 id. 343.
[6] Musser v. Johnson, 42 Mo. 74; Morris v. Kiel, 20 Minn. 531; Nason

§ 88. *Conveyance of corporate lands by agent.*— A corporation cannot appoint an agent to convey lands except by vote of its directors or other managing board, in whom the power to sell is reposed by charter or by the general laws; and without legal proof of such corporate act a deed purporting to be executed in its name by an agent is not evidence of title, though it may operate as color of title.[1] If the corporation be held to have ratified the acts of one assuming to act as its agent in selling and conveying lands, by its knowledge of the fact that he was so acting, such a ratification would only operate as an equitable estoppel, of which courts of law cannot take cognizance in an action involving the legal title.[2] The authority of the agent need not be under seal.[3]

§ 89. *Acknowledgment of corporate deeds.*— The certificate to the deed of a corporation should state the ministerial position of the officer who affixes the corporate seal, the authority under which he acts, that he knows the corporate seal, and that the same is affixed to the conveyance by the order of the board of directors or other trustees of the corporation, and that he subscribes his name thereto as a witness to the execution thereof.[4]

---

v. King Mountain M. Co., 90 N. C. 417; Hutchins v. Byrnes, 9 Gray (Mass.), 367; Blackshire v. Homestead Co., 39 Iowa, 624; Hamilton v. McLaughlin, 12 N. E. Rep. (Mass., 1887) 424; Haven v. Adams, 4 Allen (Mass.), 80.

[1] Standifer v. Swann, 78 Ala. 88; Tenney v. Lumber Co., 43 N. H. 343; Burr v. McDonald, 3 Grat. (Va.) 215; Hopkins v. Gallatin Turnpike Co., 4 Humph. (Tenn.) 403.

[2] Standifer v. Swann, 78 Ala. 80.

[3] Hopkins v. Gallatin Turnpike Co., 4 Humph. (Tenn.) 403, 4 Am. & Eng. Ency. Law, 240; Beckwith v. Windsor Mfg. Co., 14 Conn. 594.

[4] 4 Am. & Eng. Ency. Law, 242; Lovett v. Sawmill Ass'n, 6 Paige (N. Y.), 54.

If no particular mode of acknowledgment of deeds of corporations is directed by statute, and a deed is acknowledged by the officer who affixes the seal thereto, it is a sufficient compliance with general laws requiring a deed to be acknowledged by the "grantor."[1]

§ 90. *Affixing corporate seal to deeds.*—The corporate name should be used and the corporate seal must be affixed, though a seal adopted for the occasion has been permitted.[2] A deed of trust executed by officers of a corporation in their own names by mistake, but intended as the deed of the corporation, was held capable of being reformed in equity.[3] Where the president or other officer of the corporation executes a deed in his own name and under his own seal, it is invalid, because not the deed of the company.[4] The deed of the corporation can be proved only by proving that the seal affixed is the seal of the corporation, or that it was affixed as the corporate seal by an officer of the corporation or other person thereto duly authorized.[5]

§ 91. *Assignment of property for benefit of creditors.*— Another mode of alienation by a corporation of its property is by assignment for benefit of creditors; and, unless there be some provision in the statute under which the incorporation takes place prohibiting it, a corporation may make an assignment of its property for the benefit of creditors.[6] So an insolvent corporation, it has been held,

---

[1] Boone on Corp., § 54; Kelly v. Calhoun, 95 U. S. 710.
[2] Hutchins v. Byrnes, 9 Gray (Mass.), 367.
[3] West v. Madison Co. Ag. Board, 82 Ill. 205.
[4] Wheelock v. Moulton, 15 Vt. 519; Isham v. Bennington Iron Co., 19 Vt. 230; Hatch v. Barr, 1 Ohio, 390.
[5] Osborne v. Tunis, 25 N. J. L. 633.
[6] Lamb v. Cecil, 25 W. Va. 288; Planters' Bank v. Whittle, 78 Va. 737; Whitwell v. Warner, 20 Vt. 425; Dabney v. Bank, 3 S. C. 124;

may sell and transfer its property, and may prefer its creditors, unless prohibited by law.[1] But corporations and their officers may not divert the corporate property from the payment of debts.[2] An assignment which purports on its face to be the contract of the company, and is signed by the president for the company, is the company's contract.[3] And it has been held that shares of stock of a corporation owned by it may be assigned to a creditor in satisfaction of a debt, though the creditor may have been a trustee, and took part in the proceedings authorizing the assignment, if the proceedings were afterward ratified by the corporation.[4]

§ 92. *Power to act as trustee.*— It is now well established, and may be laid down as a general rule, that a corporation with legal capacity to hold property may take and hold it in trust, in the same manner and to the same extent as a private individual may do.[5] As the court

Ardesco Oil Co. v. North Am. Co., 66 Pa. St. 375; Coates v. Donnell, 94 N. Y. 168; Arthur v. Bank, 17 Miss. 394; Pierce v. Emery, 32 N. H. 484; Lionberger v. Broadway Bank, 10 Mo. App. 499; Shockley v. Fisher, 75 Mo. 498; Covert v. Rogers, 38 Mich. 363; Merrick v. Bank, 8 Gill (Mo.), 59; Union Bank v. Elliott, 6 Gill & J. (Md.) 363; Sargent v. Webster, 13 Met. (Mass.) 497; Reichwald v. Hotel Co., 106 Ill. 439; De Camp v. Alward, 52 Ind. 468; Savings Bank v. Bates, 8 Conn. 23; Ringo v. Biscoe, 13 Ark. 563; Canal Co. v. Vallette, 21 How. (U. S.) 414.

[1] Bergen v. Fishing Co., 42 N. J. Eq. 397, 41 N. J. Eq. 238; Wilkinson v. Bauerle, 41 N. J. Eq. 635.

[2] Wilkinson v. Bauerle, *supra*.

[3] Gottfried v. Miller, 104 U. S. 521.

[4] Reed v. Hoyt, 51 N. Y. Sup. Ct. 121.

[5] Vidal v. Girard, 2 How. (U. S.) 127; First Cong. Soc. v. Atwater, 23 Conn. 34; Phillips Acad. v. King, 12 Mass. 546; First Parish, etc. v. Cole, 3 Pick. (Mass.) 232; Wade v. American, etc. Soc., 7 Sm. & M. (Miss.) 663; Robertson v. Bullions, 11 N. Y. 243; Farmers,' etc. Co. v. Insurance Co., 51 Barb. (N. Y.) 33; Lincoln Sav. Bank v. Ewing, 12 Lea (Tenn.), 518; Montpelier v. East Montpelier, 29 Vt. 12.

say in *Vidal v. Girard, supra:* "Although it was in early times held that a corporation could not take and hold real or personal estate in trust, upon the ground that there was a defect of one of the requisites to create a good trustee, namely, the want of confidence in the person, yet that doctrine has long since been exploded as too artificial; and it is now held that where a corporation has a legal capacity to take real and personal estate, it may take and hold it upon trust in the same manner and to the same extent as a private individual may do."

§ 93. *Trust must be within scope of corporate purposes.* But a corporation cannot be a trustee unless the objects and purposes which the trust is intended to accomplish are within the general scope of the purposes of the corporation, and the trust relates to matters which will promote and aid its general purposes.[1] So a corporation may hold and execute a trust for charitable objects in accord with or tending to promote the purposes of its creation, although such as it might not, by its charter or by general laws, have authority itself to establish or to spend its corporate funds for.[2] But where property is devised to a corporation, partly for its own use and partly in trust for others, the power to take the property for its own use carries with it the power to execute the trust in favor of others.[3]

§ 94. *Cannot be compelled to execute repugnant trust.*— If the trust be repugnant or inconsistent with the proper

[1] Trustees v. Peaslee, 15 N. H. 317; Mason v. Methodist Episcopal Church, 27 N. J. Eq. 47.

[2] Jones v. Habersham, 107 U. S. 174; Vidal v. Girard, 2 How. (U. S.) 27; McDonough v. Murdock, 15 How. 367; Perin v. Carey, 24 How. 465.

[3] In re Howe, 1 Paige (N. Y.), 214; Wetmore v. Parker, 52 N. Y. 450.

§ 95.] INCIDENTAL POWERS OF CORPORATIONS. 141

purposes for which the corporation was created, it cannot be compelled to execute the trust;[1] but in proper cases, the performance of the trusts confided to corporations may be enforced.[2] And a corporation which expressly accepts a donation upon the trusts and for the purposes for which it was given cannot afterwards renounce it, but may be compelled to apply it to those purposes.[3]

§ 95. *Power to take by bequest.* — In the absence of any statutory restriction, corporations may take bequests of personal property the same as individuals.[4] So it has been held that a bequest to a corporation of its own stock is valid.[5] The following bequests have been sustained: of money to a church to be laid out in bread, annually, for ten years for the poor of the congregation, and of another sum for the education of students for the ministry;[6] a bequest to a city of money to purchase a lot and erect thereon a hospital for the indigent blind and lame;[7] of money for the relief of such indigent residents as the town trustees should select;[8] of money to a town to buy land and erect a town hall thereon.[9]

[1] Vidal v. Girard, *supra*.
[2] Chambers v. Baptist Soc., 1 B. Mon. (Ky.) 215; Hadden v. Chorn, 8 id. 70; Van Houten v. Dutch Church, 17 N. J. Eq. 126; Congregational Church v. Trustees, 19 Pick. (Mass.) 492; University v. Yarrow, 23 Beas. (N. J.) 150; Thornton v. Howe, 31 Beas. (N. J.) 14; Shore v. Wilson, 9 Cl. & F. 355.
[3] Amer. Acad. v. Howard Co., 12 Gray (Mass.), 582; Drury v. Inhabitants, 10 Allen (Mass.), 169.
[4] Boone, Corp., § 52; McCartee v. Orphan Asylum, 9 Cow. (N. Y.) 437; Trustees v. King, 12 Mass. 546; Dutch Church v. Brandow, 52 Barb. (N. Y.) 228; New York Inst. v. Howe, 10 N. Y. 84.
[5] Revanna Nav. Co. v. Dawson, 3 Grat. (Va.) 19.
[6] Whitman v. Lex, 17 S. & R. (Pa.) 88.
[7] Mayor v. Elliott, 3 Rawle (Pa.) 170.
[8] Shotwell v. Mott, 2 Sand. Ch. (N. Y.) 46.
[9] Coggeshell v. Pelton, 7 John. Ch. (N. Y.) 292.

§ 96. *Power to borrow money.*— At the present time it seems to be generally conceded that private corporations organized for the purpose of pecuniary profit have, unless specially restricted in this particular, the implied power to borrow money.[1] This power would seem nec-

[1] Memphis, etc. Ry. Co. v. Dow, 120 U. S. 287; Mahoney Min. Co. v. Anglo-Cal. Bank, 104 U. S. 192; Gorrell v. Life Ins. Co., 63 Fed. Rep. 371; Chicago, etc. R. Co. v. Howard, 7 Wall. (U. S.) 392; Canal Co. v. Vallette, 21 How. 414; Partridge v. Badger, 25 Barb. (N. Y.) 146; Barry v. Merchants' Exchange, 1 Sandf. Ch. (N. Y.) 280; Farnum v. Blackstone Canal, 1 Sumn. (U. S.) 46; Lucas v. Pitney, 27 N. J. L. 221; Munn v. The Commission, 15 John. (N. Y.) 44; Mott v. Hicks, 1 Cow. (N. Y.) 513; Kelly v. Mayor, etc., 4 Hill (N. Y.), 263; Hackettstown v. Swackhamer, 8 Vroom (N. J.), 191; Beers v. Phœnix Glass Co., 14 Barb. (N. Y.) 358; Clark v. Titcomb, 42 Barb. (N. Y.) 122; Commissioners v. Railway, 77 N. C. 289; Tucker v. City of Raleigh, 75 N. C. 267; Barnes v. Ontario Bank, 19 N. Y. 152; Smith v. Law, 21 N. Y. 296; Nelson v. Eaton, 26 N. Y. 410; Bradley v. Ballard, 55 Ill. 413; Mobile, etc. Ry. v. Talman, 15 Ala. 474; Moss v. Academy, 7 Heisk. (Tenn.) 283; Oxford Ins. Co. v. Spradley, 46 Ala. 98; Alabama, etc. Co. v. Central Association, 54 Ala. 73; Bank v. Chillicothe, 7 Ohio, 415; Ridgway v. Bank, 12 S. & R. (Pa.) 256; Magee v. Mokelumne, etc. Co., 5 Cal. 258; Hamilton v. New Castle Ry., 9 Ind. 359; Rockwell v. Elkhorn Bank, 13 Wis. 653; Fay v. Noble, 12 Cush. (Mass.) 188; Commercial Bank v. Newport Mfg. Co., 1 B. Mon. (Ky.) 13; Holbrook v. Bassett, 5 Bosw. (N. Y.) 147; Furniss v. Gilchrist, 1 Sandf. Sup. Ct. (N. Y.) 53; Forbes v. Marshall, L. R. 11 Ex. 166; Re International Ins. Co., 10 Eq. 312; Australian, etc. Co. v. Mounsey, 4 K. & J. 733; In re German M. Co., 4 De G., M. & G. 19; Taylor v. Agl. Ass'n, 68 Ala. 229; Savanna, etc. R. Co. v. Lancaster, 62 Ala. 555; Smith v. Eureka F. Mills, 6 Cal. 1; Union Min. Co. v. Bank, 2 Colo. 248; Ward v. Johnson, 95 Ill. 215; Smead v. Indianapolis, etc. R. Co., 11 Ind. 104; Thompson v. Lambert, 44 Iowa, 239; Booth v. Robinson, 55 Md. 419; England v. Dearborn, 141 Mass. 590; Donnell v. Lewis Co. Bank, 80 Mo. 165; Connecticut R. Sav. Bank v. Fiske, 60 N. H. 363; Kent v. Quicksilver M. Co., 78 N. Y. 159; Curtis v. Leavitt, 15 N. Y. 9; Larwell v. Hanover Sav. Soc., 40 Ohio St. 274; Union Bank v. Jacobs, 6 Humph. (Tenn.) 515; Burr v. McDonald, 3 Grat. (Va.) 215; Gibbs' Case, L. R. 10 Eq. 312; Bank of Australasia v. Breilat, 6 Moore, P. C. 152; 4 Am. & Eng. Enc. Law, 222.

In Hackettstown v. Swackhamer, *supra*, the court say: "This

essarily incident to every corporation whose business involved the expenditure of large sums of money, and often upon sudden and unforeseen contingencies. But when there is an express prohibition against borrowing, it must be obeyed, and in a case of a company or society constituted for special purposes, no borrowing can be permitted without express authority, unless it be properly incident to the course and conduct of the business for its proper purposes.[1]

result is the appropriate product of the principle that corporate powers which are the necessary accompaniments of powers conferred will be implied. In these instances the ability to borrow money is so essential that without it the business authorized could not be conducted with reasonable efficiency; and, as it cannot be supposed that it was the legislative intent to leave the company in so imperfect a condition, the inference is properly drawn that the power to raise money in this mode is inherent in the very constitution of such corporate bodies. Such a deduction is simply, in effect, a conclusion that the law-maker designed to authorize the use of the means fitted to accomplish the purpose in view. It has been often said that the means which can thus be raised up by implication must be necessary to the successful prosecution of the enterprise, and that the circumstance that they are convenient will not legalize their introduction. But the necessity here spoken of does not denote absolute indispensableness, but that the power in question is so essential that its non-existence would render the privileges granted practically inoperative or incomplete. It is, consequently, obvious that a presumption resting on such a basis as this must spring up in favor of almost the entire mass of commercial and manufacturing corporations, for, without the franchise to effect loans, the chartered business could be but imperfectly transacted. And yet, even in such instances, the usual inference that such an implied power exists may be repelled by the language of the particular charter or the peculiar circumstances of the case. In a word, the rule of law in question is nothing but the discovery, by the courts, of the legislative intent, such intent having been ascertained by a construction of charters, as applied to the subject-matter."

[1] Blackburne Bldg. Soc. v. Cunliffe, Brooks & Co., 29 Ch. Div. 902; Record & G. R. Co., 4 Ch. Div. 748; Davis' Case, L. R. 12 Eq. 516.

§ 97. *Test to determine if transaction is borrowing.—* In *Blackburne Building Society v. Cunliffe, Brooks & Co., supra*, the test as to whether a given transaction was a borrowing or not was said to be this: "Has the transaction really added to the liabilities of the company? If the amount of the company's liabilities remain in substance unchanged, but there is, merely for the convenience of payment, a change of the creditor, there is no substantial borrowing in the result, so far as relates to the position of the company. Regarded in that light it is consistent with the general principles of equity that those who pay legitimate demands, which they are bound in some way or other to meet, and have had the benefit of other people's money advanced to them for that purpose, shall not retain that benefit so as, in substance, to make those other people pay their debts. I take that to be a principle sufficiently sound in equity; and if the result is that by the transaction, which assumes the shape of an advance or loan, nothing is really added to the liabilities of the company, there has been no real transgression of the principle on which they are prohibited from borrowing."

§ 98. *Instances as to implied power to borrow.—* Banks have implied power to borrow money, when necessary in the prosecution of their business, and may issue the usual evidences of debt therefor.[1] A railroad company, under an authority to borrow money, has no right to raise money by the issue of irredeemable bonds entitling the holder merely to a share of the earnings after the payment of a certain dividend to the stockholders.[2] But a benefit society has no power to borrow money unless

[1] Curtis v. Leavitt, 15 N. Y. 9; Barnes v. Ontario Bank, 19 N. Y. 152; Bank of Australasia v. Breilat, 6 Moore's P. C. 152, 194; Magee v. Mokelumne, etc. Co., 5 Cal. 258.

[2] Taylor v. Philadelphia, etc. R. Co., 7 Fed. Rep. 386.

its rules specifically authorize it to do so. The directors of a benefit building society, the rules of which gave no power to borrow money, borrowed a sum of money for the purpose of advancing it to their members on the security of their shares. The lender of the money afterwards presented a petition for an order to wind up the company. It was held by the court that the transaction was *ultra vires* and that the petitioner had no legal or equitable debt against the company, and the petition was dismissed.[1] Where a mining company, among others, had the power to "enter into any obligation or contract essential to the transaction of its ordinary affairs, or for the purposes for which it was created," it was held that the board had authority not only to designate the banking institution in which the money of the company should be deposited, but to prescribe the mode in which, and the officers by whom, it should be withdrawn, from time to time, for the use of the company; that it was equally clear that the board had, as incident to the general powers conferred by law upon the company, power to borrow money for the purposes of the corporation, and to invest certain officers with authority to negotiate loans, to execute notes, and to sign checks against its bank account.[2] So a corporation created for the purpose of constructing a road has the power to borrow money as one of the implied means necessary to carry into effect the specified powers; and this is so though the charter directs that the funds shall be raised by subscription.[3] Though there be no express power given to a corporation in its charter to borrow money on mortgage, but

---

[1] Ex parte Williamson, L. R. 5 Ch. 309; Laing v. Reed, L. R. 5 Ch. 4.
[2] Mining Co. v. Anglo-California Bank, 104 U. S. 192.
[3] Union Bank v. Jacobs, 6 Humph. (Tenn.) 515.

power is conferred on the directors to make all necessary contracts, and to sell or otherwise dispose of any portion of its property, whenever in their judgment it shall be found to the interest of the company, the exercise of the power to borrow, and to secure the loan by mortgage from the company, has been held valid.[1] So the raising money by debentures in the case of a trading company simply established for the conveyance of passengers and luggage by omnibuses was held within the powers of the company, although there was no express authority conferred either by the memorandum or articles of association for borrowing.[2] And a shipping company without any express powers in the memorandum or articles of association has power to borrow money for the purposes of the company.[3]

§ 99. *Power to loan money.*— A corporation has no power to loan money unless there is a special clause to that effect in its charter. The rule is declared to be that if the means employed are necessarily adapted to the ends for which the corporation was created, they come within the implied or incidental powers, though they may not be specifically designated by the act of incorporation.[4] So where a corporation had no express grant of power to lend money, no such power could be implied from the declared purposes and objects for which the charter was granted; on the contrary, such power was held to be excluded by the declaration that the corporation was not created for pecuniary profit.[5] So, also, it has been held

[1] Booth v. Robinson, 55 Md. 419.
[2] Byron v. Metropolitan Co., 3 De G. & J. 123.
[3] Australian Steam Clipper Co. v. Mounsey, 4 K. & J. 733.
[4] Madison Plank Road Co. v. Watertown R. Co., 5 Wis. 173; Chambers v. Falkner, 65 Ala. 448; Workingmen's Banking Co. v. Routenberg, 103 Ill. 460; s. c., 42 Am. Rep. 26.
[5] Chambers v. Falkner, *supra.*

that where a director, while indebted to his bank for an amount greater than seventy-five per cent. of the stock held by him, obtained a loan for a further amount, giving his note therefor, guarantied by A., when the charter of the bank prohibited its lending to a director more than seventy-five per cent. of the amount of his stock, the note was void, and could be enforced neither against the director nor against the guarantor.[1]

§ 100. *Powers as to negotiable instruments.*— It is now the well-established rule that corporations authorized generally to engage in a particular business have, as an incident to such authority, the power to contract debts in the legitimate transactions of such business, unless they are restrained by their charters from so doing.[2] It is likewise an equally acknowledged rule, that the right to contract debts carries with it the power to give negotiable notes or bills in payment or security for such debts, unless the corporations are in like manner prohibited. It may therefore be laid down as a general rule, that a corporation not prohibited by law from so doing, and without any express power in its charter for that purpose, may make a negotiable promissory note, payable either at a future day or on demand, when such note is given for any of the legitimate purposes for which the company was incorporated.[3] And it has been repeatedly

[1] Workingmen's Banking Co. v. Routenberg, *supra.*
[2] See cases cited to § 96.
[3] Moss v. Averell, 10 N. Y. 449; Rockwell v. Elkhorn Bank, 13 Wis. 653; Barker v. Mechanics' Ins. Co., 3 Wend. (N. Y.) 94; Moss v. Oakley, 2 Hill (N. Y.), 265; Safford v. Wyckoff, 4 Hill (N. Y.), 442; Whitewater Valley Co. v. Vallette, 21 How. (N. Y.) 414; Partridge v. Badger, 25 Barb. (N. Y.) 146; Barry v. Merchants' Exchange, 1 Sandf. Ch. (N. Y.) 280; Burr v. Glass Co., 14 Barb. (N. Y.) 358; United States Bank v. Hoth, 4 B. Mon. (Ky.) 423; State v. Bank of Maryland, 6 G. & J. (Md.) 205; Pierce v. Emery, 32 N. H. 484; Conn. Mut. Ins. Co. v.

held that a law forbidding certain corporations from issuing commercial paper as a circulating medium, or from dealing in commercial paper, will not be construed as prohibiting such corporations from issuing and receiving such commercial paper in the course of their ordinary business.[1]

Cleveland R. Co., 41 Barb. (N. Y.) 9; Monument Nat. Bank v. Globe Works, 101 Mass. 57; Fay v. Noble, 12 Cush. (Mass.) 1; Narragansett Bank v. Silk Co., 3 Met. (Mass.) 282; Smith v. Flour Co., 6 Cal. 1; Union Bank v. Jacobs, 6 Humph. (Tenn.) 515; Richmond, etc. R. Co. v. Snead, 19 Grat. (Va.) 354; Oxford Iron Co. v. Spradley, 46 Ala. 98; Caine v. Brigham, 39 Me. 35; Lucas v. Pitney, 27 N. J. L. 221; Clarke v. School District, 3 R. I. 199; Ward v. Johnson, 95 Ill. 215; Olcott v. Tioga R. Co., 40 Barb. (N. Y.) 179; s. c., 27 N. Y. 546; Clark v. Farmers' Mfg. Co., 15 Wend. (N. Y.) 256; Mead v. Keeler, 24 Barb. (N. Y.) 20; Mechanics' Ass'n v. Lead Co., 35 N. Y. 505; Munn v. Commission Co., 15 Johns. (N. Y.) 44; Auerbach v. Mill Co., 28 Minn. 291; Hamilton v. Railroad Co., 9 Ind. 359; McMasters v. Reed, 1 Grant Cas. (Pa.) 36; Hardy v. Merriweather, 14 Ind. 203; Buckley v. Briggs, 30 Mo. 452; Commercial Bank v. Newport Mfg. Co., 1 B. Mon. (Ky.) 13; Ridgway v. Farmers' Bank, 12 S. & R. (Pa.) 256; Butts v. Cuthberson, 6 Ga. 166; Richards v. Merrimac, etc. R. Co., 44 N. H. 127; Harvey v. Chase, 38 N. H. 278; Montague v. School District, 34 N. J. L. 218; Curtis v. Leavitt, 15 N. Y. 9; McCullough v. Moss, 5 Denio (N. Y.), 567; Donnelly v. Church, 26 La. Ann. 738; Brode v. Firemen's Ins. Co., 8 Rob. (La.) 244; Magee v. Mokelumne, etc. Co., 5 Cal. 258; Ketchum v. Buffalo, 14 N. Y. 356; Savage v. Ball, 17 N. J. Eq. 142; Milliard v. St. Francis, etc. Academy, 8 Ill. App. 341; Hascall v. Life Ass'n, 5 Hun (N. Y.), 151; Louisville, etc. R. Co. v. Caldwell, 98 Ind. 245; Talladega Ins. Co. v. Peacock, 67 Ala. 253; Sullivan v. Murphy, 23 Minn. 6; Attorney-General v. Insurance Co., 9 Paige (N. Y.), 470; Mott v. Hicks, 1 Cow. (N. Y.),513; Kelley v. Brooklyn, 4 Hill (N. Y.), 263; Police Jury v. Britton, 15 Wall. (U. S.) 566; Watts' Appeal, 78 Pa. St. 370; Comm. v. Pittsburg, 41 Pa. St. 278.

[1] Blair v. Insurance Co., 10 Mo. 561; Buckley v. Briggs, 30 Mo. 452; Western Cottage Co. v. Reddish, 51 Iowa, 55; Smith v. Eureka Flour Mills, 6 Cal. 1; Attorney-General v. Insurance Co., 9 Paige (N. Y.), 470; Partridge v. Badger, 25 Barb. (N. Y.) 146; White's Bank v. Toledo Ins. Co., 12 Ohio St. 601; Mumford v. Insurance Co., 4 N. Y. 463; Potter v. Bank, 28 N. Y. 641.

§ 101. *Power of corporation as indorsee.*— Whenever a corporation exceeds its powers in taking commercial paper as payee or indorsee, the parties liable on the paper cannot take advantage of that fact as a defense to the action on the paper by the corporation; for, having made the paper payable to the corporation, and received its funds as a consideration therefor, the maker, drawer, acceptor or indorser, as the case might be, is estopped from denying the capacity of the corporation to take the paper.[1]

§ 102. *Power of savings bank to make negotiable paper.* A savings bank incorporated by special charter has the implied power, inherent in corporations created for business purposes, of borrowing money required in the course of its business, and of making negotiable paper or a pledge of its securities as a means of borrowing; and a purchaser of such paper before maturity from a third person, in whose hands it is apparently as business paper, has a right to act on the assumption that it was made for a purpose which gives validity to the paper and to the pledge of securities therewith.[2]

§ 103. *Power to discount does not include power to purchase.*— A bank empowered to discount negotiable notes, it has been held, has no power to purchase such notes.[3] In

[1] Tied. Com. Paper, § 118; Farmers,' etc. Co. v. Needles, 53 Mo. 17; National Ins. Co. v. Bowman, 60 Mo. 252; St. Louis v. Shields, 62 Mo. 247; Stoutimore v. Clark, 70 Mo. 471; John v. Farmers' Bank, 2 Blackf. (Ind.) 367; Snyder v. Studebaker, 19 Ind. 462; Ray v. Indianapolis Ins. Co., 39 Ind. 290; Greiner v. Ulery, 20 Iowa, 266; Massey v. Building Ass'n, 22 Kan. 624.

[2] Fifth Ward Sav. Bank v. First Nat. Bank, 48 N. J. L. 513, and cases cited.

[3] Bank of Augusta v. Earle, 13 Pet. (U. S.) 519; Farmers' & Merchants' Bank v. Baldwin, 23 Minn. 198; First Nat. Bank v. Pierson, 24 Minn. 140; s. c., 16 Alb. Law Jour. 319; Niagara County Bank v. Baker, 15 Ohio St. 68.

Farmers' & Merchants' Bank v. Baldwin, supra, the bank was authorized "to carry on the business of banking by discounting bills, notes and other evidences of debt, by receiving deposits, by buying and selling gold and silver bullion, foreign coin and foreign and inland bills of exchange, by loaning money on real and personal security, and by exercising such incidental powers as may be necessary to carry on such business." In a suit by the bank upon a promissory note, the defense was that the bank had no title to the note, since it had purchased it outright instead of discounting it. It was held by the court that the bank had no capacity to purchase promissory notes, and the attempted act of purchase was *ultra vires* and conferred no right whatever. The court distinguish between purchasing and discounting and say: "The power to carry on the business of banking, by discounting notes, bills and other evidences of debt, is only an authority to loan money thereon, with the right to deduct the legal rate of interest in advance. This right can be fully enjoyed with the possession of the unrestricted power of buying and dealing in such securities as choses in action and personal property. Though, as is urged by the plaintiff, the bank acquires a title to discounted paper, and hence may, in a certain sense, be said to have purchased it, yet it is a purchase by discount — which is permitted, — and does not involve the exercise of a power of purchase in any other way than by discount." The term "discounting" has, however, in other cases, been held to include purchase as well as loan, and the purchase of negotiable paper by a bank empowered to discount notes has been sustained.[1]

---

[1] Pope v. Capitol Bank of Topeka, 20 Kan. 440; Smith v. Exchange Bank, 26 Ohio St. 141; Fleckner v. Bank of United States, 8 Wheat. (U. S.) 338.

§ 104. *Liability on accommodation paper.*— The note of a corporation in the hands of a holder in good faith, for value, who took it before maturity and without knowledge that the maker had not received full consideration, can be enforced against the corporation, although it was made as an accommodation note.[1] Notice which would put a prudent man on inquiry, and lead to discovery of fraud, will not vitiate the corporation's negotiable paper.[2]

§ 105. *Power to pledge securities.*— Where a corporation has power to contract a debt, it may lawfully pledge its securities for its payment.[3] Accordingly, a corporation may pledge its bonds and stock issued by itself for its own debts.[4] In *Leo v. Union Pacific R. Co., supra,* the court say: " The purpose to raise money to meet debts or for other corporate uses, by pledge of these securities, seems to be clearly within the scope of the corporate powers, and lawful and proper. The corporation has these securities not yet due. . . . It owes debts, and was created with the expectation that it would owe them, and has implied power to raise money to pay them. It is not disputed that it could sell these securities to raise money to pay its debts, and the power to pledge them is included fairly in the power to sell for the same purpose."

[1] Monument National Bank v. Globe Works, 101 Mass. 57; Webster v. Howe Machine Co., 54 Conn. 394; National Bank of Republic v. Young, 41 N. J. Eq. 531.

[2] National Bank v. Young, 7 Atl. Rep. 488; Webster v. Howe Machine Co., 8 Atl. Rep. 482; 54 Conn. 394.

[3] Leo v. Union Pac. R. Co., 17 Fed. Rep. 273; Platt v. Union Pac. R. Co., 99 U. S. 48.

[4] Combination Trust Co. v. Weed, 2 Fed. Rep. 24; Mor. Corp., § 349; Lehman v. Tallasse Mfg. Co., 64 Ala. 567; Androscoggin R. Co. v. Auburn Bank, 48 Me. 335; Duncomb v. N. Y. etc. R. Co., 84 N. Y. 190; Chouteau v. Allen, 70 Mo. 290.

CHAPTER VIII.

POWERS AND LIABILITIES AS TO CAPITAL STOCK.

§ 106. Introductory — Nature and purpose of capital stock.
107. Capital stock as a trust fund.
108. Limitation on doctrine that capital stock a trust fund.
109. Power to increase capital stock.
110. Consent of stockholders necessary to increase capital stock.
111. Power of national bank to increase capital stock.
112. Irregularity in exercising power as affecting stockholders.
113. Power to reduce capital stock.
114. Reduction of capital stock in England.
115. Power to issue new stock.
116. Powers as to special stock.
117. Power to issue shares at discount.
118. Power to issue preferred stock.
119. Liability on *ultra vires* issue of preferred stock.
120. Power to deal in own stock.
121. Power to purchase stock of other corporations.
122. Instances where power denied.
123. Power of foreign corporation to purchase stock of domestic company.
124. Power to declare dividends.
125. Power to pledge future calls.
126. Liability on dividends declared.
127. Liability on illegal issue of stock.

§ 106. *Introductory — Nature and purpose of capital stock.*— The capital stock of a corporation has been defined to be the aggregate amount of the funds of a corporation, which are combined together under a charter, for the attainment of some common object of public convenience or private utility.[1] This amount is usually fixed in

[1] Barry v. Merchants Exch., 1 Sandf. Ch. 305; Hightower v. Thornton, 8 Ga. 486; Webster v. Upton, 91 U. S. 65; Chubb v. Upton, 5

the charter or articles of incorporation, and a limit placed on its increase by statutory enactment. This limit is fixed in deference to the convenience, information and security of the public at large, as well as to the convenience of the intended corporation. To the corporators it prescribes the amount and subdivisions of their respective contributions to the common fund, the voice which each shall have in its control and management, and the apportionment of the profits of the enterprise. To the community it announces the extent of the means contributed and forming the basis of the dealings of the corporate body, and enables every man to judge of its ability to meet its engagements and perform what it undertakes. And when the statute requires the stock to be paid in before the corporation can transact business, security to those contracting with it is thereby superadded to the information of its resources.[1]

§ 107. *Capital stock as a trust fund.*—The capital stock of an incorporated company is also said to be a trust fund set apart for the payment of its debts; that it is a substitute for the personal liability which subsists in private copartnerships; that when debts are incurred, a contract arises with the creditors that it shall not be withdrawn or applied otherwise than upon their demands, until such demands are satisfied; that the creditors have a lien upon it in equity, and, if diverted, they may follow it as far as it can be traced and subject it to the payment of their claims, except as against holders who have taken it *bona fide* for a valuable consideration and without notice; and that it is publicly pledged to those who deal

Otto (U. S.), 665; Eaton v. Aspinwall, 19 N. Y. 119; Aspinwall v. Sacchi, 57 N. Y. 331; Kent v. Quicksilver, etc. Co., 78 N. Y. 159; Sheldon Co. v. Eickemeyer Co., 90 N. Y. 613.

[1] See cases cited in preceding section.

with the corporation for their security.¹ "Unpaid stock is as much a part of this pledge and as much a part of the assets of the company as the cash which has been paid in upon it. Creditors have the same right to insist upon its payment as upon the payment of any other debt due to the company. And, as regards creditors, there is no distinction between such a demand and any other asset which may form a part of the property and effects of the corporation."² These objects for the public benefit are sometimes defeated by fraud and deception, but they are such as the legislature have in view in limiting the amount of capital stock and requiring a specified sum or proportion to be paid in. As was said in *Handley v. Stutz, supra:* "The stock of a corporation is supposed to stand in the place of actual property of substantial value, and as being a convenient method of representing the interest of each stockholder in such property, and to the extent to which it fails to represent such value it is either a deception and fraud upon the public or an evidence that the original value of the corporate property has become depreciated. The market value of such shares rises with an increase in the value of the corporate assets, and falls in the case of loss or misfortune, whereby the value of such assets is impaired. And the increase of value of such stock is taken to represent either an appreciation in value of the company's property beyond the par value of original shares, or so much money paid to the corporation as is represented by such shares. The law implies a

[1] Sanger v. Upton, 91 U. S. 60; Curran v. Arkansas, 15 How. (U. S.) 304; Wood v. Dummer, 3 Mason (U. S.), 308; Slee v. Bloom, 19 Johns. (N. Y.) 456; Briggs v. Penniman, 8 Cow. (N. Y.) 387; Society, etc. v. Abbott, 2 Beav. 559; Walworth v. Holt, 4 Myl. & C. 789; Ward v. Griswoldville Co., 16 Conn. 593; Fowler v. Robinson, 31 Me. 189; Handley v. Stutz, 139 U. S. 417.
[2] Sanger v. Upton, *supra.*

promise by the original subscribers of stock who did not pay for it in money or other property to pay for the same when called upon by creditors, and a contract between themselves and the corporation that the stock shall be treated as fully paid and non-assessable, or otherwise limiting their liability therefor, is void as against creditors."

§ 108. *Limitation on doctrine that capital stock is trust fund.*— The general proposition that the capital stock of a corporation is a trust fund for the benefit of creditors cannot with reason be controverted or denied, but this theory applies only to corporations after they have become insolvent. Prior to its insolvency, and while the corporation is still a going concern, it holds its property as absolutely and with as great a power of dominion and control as any other person exercises over his individual possessions.[1] "But when a corporation becomes insolvent, then, according to the holding of courts of equity, its property becomes a trust fund for the payment of creditors. The trust embraces all the property of a corporation; embraces its real estate and choses in action. If debts are due to the corporation they are part of that fund, and may be collected by the proper representatives of the corporation, whether a trustee appointed by a court of equity, an assignee in bankruptcy, or other agent, for the parties interested. But it is only those claims or assets which a company has that belong to the trust fund. Unpaid instalments on stock in the ordinary case are assets; they are claims which a company could enforce, and therefore they are claims which the creditors can compel the en-

[1] Coit v. North Carolina Gold Co., 14 Fed. Rep. 12; Sawyer v. Hoag, 17 Wall. (U. S.) 610; Tuckerman v. Brown, 33 N. Y. 297; Ogilvie v. Knox Ins. Co., 22 How. (U. S.) 380; Osgood v. Laytin, 3 Keyes (N. Y.), 521; 37 How. Prac. 63, affirming 48 Barb. 463.

forcement of through the instrumentality of a court of equity."[1]

§ 109. *Power to increase capital stock.*— As a general rule, corporations are not invested with the power or authority to increase or diminish their capital stock. But this power is sometimes conferred, with express limitations, by some of the states in the general law under which they are organized and created; otherwise application must be made to the legislature for such authority, and every application for such an increase or diminution of their capital stock is regarded as equivalent to a request for an amendment of their charter powers in that respect, and all attempts on their part to effect such increase without the sanction or approval of the sovereign are destitute of authority and wholly wanting in legal validity.[2] The implied or incidental powers corporations may rightfully exercise never have been extended to changes of the purpose for which a corporation was created. And it has been held changes of the capital stock of corporations involve changes in organization, and a displacement of the power and influence of the original stockholders, or their legitimate successors, who are of right entitled to exercise the privilege of electing officers and have general management of the corporate affairs and business.[3] The general power to perform all corporate acts refers to the ordinary business transactions of the corporation, and does not extend to a reconstruction of the body itself or to an

[1] Mr. Justice Bradley in Coit v. North Carolina Gold Co., 14 Fed. Rep. 12.

[2] Grangers', etc. Ins. Co. v. Kamper, 73 Ala. 325; Green's Brice's Ultra Vires, § 112; Thompson, Liab. Stock, § 115; Lathrop v. Kneeland, 46 Barb. (N. Y.) 432; Mutual Life Ins. Co. v. McElway, 12 N. J. Eq. 133; New York, etc. R. Co. v. Schuyler, 34 N. Y. 30; Railway Co. v. Allerton, 18 Wall. (U. S.) 233; Scovill v. Thayer, 105 U. S. 143.

[3] Cases cited in preceding note.

enlargement of its capital stock. A corporation, like a partnership, it has been stated, is an association of natural persons who contribute a joint capital for a common purpose, and, although the shares may be assigned to new individuals in perpetual succession, yet the number of shares and the amount of capital stock cannot be increased except in the manner authorized by the charter or the general law regulating such procedure.[1] So where a corporation, formed under a general law, of its own act, without legislative consent, attempted to increase its capital stock, it was held that such attempt to increase the capital stock of the company beyond the limit fixed by the charter was *ultra vires*, and the stock itself therefore void, and conferred on the holders no rights and subjected them to no liabilities.[2]

§ 110. *Consent of stockholders necessary to increase capital stock.*— Authority to increase the capital stock of a corporation may be conferred by a law passed subsequent to the grant of a charter; but such a law should regularly be accepted by the stockholders, and such assent may be inferred by subsequent acquiescence; but in some form or other it must be given to render the increase valid and binding on them.[3] And it has been held that an increase

[1] Railway Co. v. Allerton, *supra*.
[2] Railway Co. v. Allerton, 18 Wall. (U. S.) 233. And see generally, Scovill v. Thayer, 105 U. S. 143; Knowlton v. Congress, etc. Co., 14 Blatch. (U. S.) 364; Grangers', etc. Ins. Co. v. Kamper, 73 Ala. 325; Moses v. Ocoee Bank, 1 Lea (Tenn.), 398; Ferris v. Ludlow, 7 Ind. 517; In re Ebbw. Vale, etc. Co., 4 Ch. Div. 827; Droitwich, etc. Co. v. Curzon, L. R. 3 Exch. 35, 42; Stace & Worth's Case, L. R. 4 Ch. 682; Salem Mill Dam Co. v. Ropes, 6 Pick. 23; New York, etc. R. Co. v. Schuyler, 34 N. Y. 30; Sutherland v. Olcott, 95 N. Y. 93, 100; Mechanics' Bank v. New York, etc. R. Co., 13 N. Y. 599; Lathrop v. Kneeland, 46 Barb. (N. Y.) 432; Handley v. Stutz, 139 U. S. 417; Winters v. Armstrong, 37 Fed. Rep. 508.
[3] Railway Co. v. Allerton, *supra*; Eidman v. Bowman, 58 Ill. 444;

in the capital stock of a corporation, if made with consent of all the stockholders, is binding, although not made with all the statutory formalities.[1]

§ 111. *Power of national banks to increase capital stock.* In *Winters v. Armstrong*, 37 Fed. Rep. 508, Mr. Justice Jackson, speaking of the power of national banking associations to increase their capital stock, said: "National banking associations have no authority of law by their own action to increase their capital stock to any amount whatever. They can make no increase to any extent without the approval of the comptroller, as the representative of the government. His approval confers the right to make and fixes the limit or amount of such increase. Within its own powers and by its own action a

Payson v. Stoever, 2 Dill. (U. S.) 428; Sewell's Case, L. R. 3 Ch. 131; Lane's Case, 1 De G., J. & S. 504.

[1] Poole v. West Point, etc. Ass'n, 30 Fed. Rep. 513.

In Scovill v. Thayer, *supra*, an action was brought by the assignee in bankruptcy of a mining company against a stockholder to recover unpaid assessments upon stock. The statutes of Kansas provided that any corporation might increase its capital stock to any amount not exceeding double the amount of its authorized capital. The corporation in question had increased its capital stock, as it was authorized to do, by doubling it, thus quadrupling the original amount, the defendant in the case having attended by proxy the meeting at which such illegal increase was voted, and received a quantity of the stock thus issued. It was held that such increase was *ultra vires* and void, and that the defendant was not estopped from denying the validity of the overissue, or his obligation to pay for it.

There has been some criticism made relative to the decision in this case as compared with that of Handley v. Stutz, 139 U. S. 417, but there is a distinct difference between these two cases; as in the Scovill Case the corporation had no power, by statute or otherwise, to so increase its capital stock; while in the Handley Case the power was conferred by the General Statutes of Kentucky, and the legality of the stock was attacked on the ground of irregularity in its issue — a wide difference in affecting the legality of the issue.

national bank can make no increase of its capital stock. It might and doubtless would be true that with or after the comptroller's approval of an increase, which involves the exercise of discretion, supervisory on his part, and wholly beyond the control and independent of the action or wish of the association or of its stockholders, the steps taken or mode of procedure adopted by the bank might not strictly conform to the requirements of the law; that for want of such conformity the action on the part of the association might be illegal; and that the stockholders or subscribers for such stock who had accepted an allotment of shares thereunder, and acquiesced in the steps taken and the proceedings had by the association in the preliminaries to be performed on its part, would be bound. In effecting an increase of its capital stock the association may, as far as relates to its own action, proceed in an irregular and informal manner, which a stockholder who has acquiesced therein may not, as against either the corporation or its creditors, take advantage of or insist upon as invalidating his subscription, or the stock issued to him thereunder. But in regard to the sovereign's consent to such increase, to be expressed in and by the approval of its comptroller of the currency, that is an essential prerequisite or condition precedent, like a special enabling act, in conferring the power and authority to make the proposed increase valid. Such approval involves the grant of power to complete and perfect the proceedings commenced by the association looking to an increase of its capital stock. It is something lying beyond the action or control of the association and its stockholders seeking to effect an organic and fundamental change in the constitution of the bank; and in respect to this essential thing, in nowise involved in the action or steps taken by the association, the question of irregularity or informality in its own mode of procedure, and the consequences then resulting, do not apply."

§ 112. *Irregularity in exercising power as affecting stockholder.*— Where the power to increase its capital stock exists, and is exercised, the corporation's failure to perform some act devolving upon itself in connection therewith, such as recording and publishing its action, constitutes an irregularity or neglect of duty of which the state only can complain or take advantage in a direct proceeding against the corporation; but stockholders who have accepted portions of such increased stock are estopped from denying the validity of the increase upon any such irregularity or neglect.[1]

§ 113. *Power to reduce capital stock.*— As a general rule, power conferred on a corporation to increase its capital stock gives it no power to diminish the same.[2] And where the constitution and laws provide for an increase and are silent as to decrease of stock, the power to decrease has been held intentionally denied.[3] So if a corporation is created with a fund limited by the act, it cannot enlarge or diminish that fund but by license from the legislature, and if the capital stock is parceled out into a fixed number of shares, this cannot be changed by the corporation.[4] A decrease of capital stock affects injuri-

---

[1] Upton v. Tribilcock, 91 U. S. 47; Stutz v. Handley, 41 Fed. Rep. 531; s. c., 139 U. S. 417; Sanger v. Upton, 91 U. S. 56; Webster v. Upton, 91 U. S. 65; Chubb v. Upton, 95 U. S. 665; Pullman v. Upton, 96 U. S. 328; Casey v. Galli, 94 U. S. 673.

[2] Salem Mill Dam Co. v. Ropes, 6 Pick. (Mass.) 23; Droitwich Patent Salt Co. v. Curzon, L. R. 3 Exch. 42; In re Financial Corporation, L. R. 2 Ch. App. 714; Smith v. Goldworthy, 4 Ad. & El. (N. S.) 430; Sutherland v. Olcott, 95 N. Y. 93; In re Ebbw. etc. Co., 4 Ch. Div. 827.

[3] Seignouret v. Home Ins. Co., 24 Fed. Rep. 332; Sutherland v. Olcott, 95 N. Y. 93.

[4] See cases cited in note 2.

ously more parties and interests than would an increase. Creditors and customers have a claim to the preservation of the capital stock in its original integrity, and a reduction of the capital stock is practically the dissolution of the company and the organization of a new one.[1]

§ 114. *As to reduction of capital stock in England.*— There seems to be a lack of uniformity in the English courts as to the reduction of the capital stock of a corporation, the diversity of opinion arising, however, in exercising this power relative to common and preferential shares; some cases holding that it is not essential that the reduction should be made equally, or ratably, on all the shares,[2] while others hold that the court has power to sanction a special resolution for the reduction of some only of the shares of a company.[3] The controversy which has been going on between Mr. Justice North and Mr. Justice Kay relative to this question had not, up to a late date, been settled by the court of appeals.

§ 115. *Power to issue new stock.*— The question as to whether an active corporation — a "going concern"— may not, for the purpose of recuperating itself and providing new conditions for the successful prosecution of its business, issue new stock, put it upon the market and sell it for the best price that can be obtained, is comparatively a new one in this country, first coming before the United States supreme court in *Handley v. Stutz*, 139 U. S. 417, in 1890. It was held in that case that a corporation had such power, Mr. Justice Brown, in delivering

---

[1] Seignouret v. Home Ins. Co., *supra*.

[2] Re Union Plate Glass Co., 42 Ch. Div. 513; In re Quebrada Ry., 40 Ch. Div. 363.

[3] In re Barrow, etc. Co., 39 Ch. Div. 582; In re Gatling Gun, Lim., 43 Ch. Div. 628.

the opinion of the court, saying: "To say that a corporation may not, under the circumstances above indicated, put its stock upon the market and sell it to the highest bidder, is practically to declare that a corporation can never increase its capital by a sale of shares, if the original stock has fallen below par. The wholesome doctrine, so many times enforced by this court, that the capital stock of an insolvent corporation is a trust fund for the payment of its debts, rests upon the idea that the creditors have a right to rely upon the fact that the subscribers to such stock have put into the treasury of the corporation, in some form, the amount represented by it; but it does not follow that every creditor has the right to trace every share of stock issued by such corporation, and inquire whether its holder, or the person from whom he purchased, has paid its par value for it. It frequently happens that corporations, as well as individuals, find it necessary to increase their capital in order to raise money to prosecute their business successfully, and one of the most frequent methods resorted to is that of issuing new shares of stock and putting them upon the market for the best price that can be obtained; and so long as the transaction is *bona fide*, and not a mere covering for 'watering' the stock, and the consideration obtained represents the actual value of such stock, the courts have shown no disposition to disturb it."[1]

§ 116. *Powers as to special stock.*— In Massachusetts they have what is termed "special stock," the character-

[1] See New Albany v. Burke, 11 Wall. (U. S.) 96; Coit v. Gold Co., 119 U. S. 345; Clark v. Bever, 139 U. S. 96; Fogg v. Blair, id. 118; Morrow v. Nashville, etc. Co., 87 Tenn. 262, which hold that the general rule that holders of stock in favor of creditors must respond for its par value is subject to exceptions where the transaction is not a mere cover for an illegal increase. See, also, Stein v. Howard, 65 Cal. 616.

istics of which are that it is limited in amount to two-fifths of the actual capital; it is subject to redemption by the corporation at par after a fixed time, to be expressed in the certificates; the corporation is bound to pay a fixed half-yearly sum or dividend upon it as a debt; the holders of it are in no extent liable for the debts of the corporation beyond their stock, and the issue of special stock makes all the special stockholders liable for all debts and contracts of the corporation until the special stock is fully redeemed.[1]

§ 117. *Power to issue shares at a discount.*— As a general rule, a company limited by shares under the act of its creation has no power to issue shares at a discount so as to render the shareholder liable for a smaller sum than that fixed for the value of the shares by the charter or memorandum of association.[2] Such an act would be

[1] Mass. Stat. 1855, ch. 290; 1870, ch. 224, §§ 25, 39, cl. 4; Pub. Stat., ch. 106. §§ 42, 61, cl. 3; Williams v. Parker, 136 Mass. 204; American Tube Works v. Boston Machine Co., 139 Mass. 5.

[2] In re Almada & Tirito Co., 38 Ch. Div. 415; Trevor v. Whitworth, 12 App. Cas. 409; In re Addlestone Co., 37 Ch. Div. 191; In re Weymouth Packet Co., 1 Ch. Div. 66; The Ooregum G. Min. Co. v. Roper, 61 L. J. (N. S.) 337, 66 L. J. (N. S.) 427 (1892).

The decision in Handley v. Stutz, *supra*, has called forth from the legal profession, generally, a vast deal of adverse criticism. A position directly opposite has been taken by the House of Lords in the case of Ooregum Gold Mining Co. v. Roper, *supra*. The question in that case was whether it was or was not competent for a company limited by shares to issue shares at a discount so as to relieve persons taking shares so issued from liability to pay up their amount in full. The House of Lords expressly held that where a corporation puts its new stock on the market and sells it for the best price it can get,— in that case for double what the old stock was selling for,— the purchasers are liable for the difference between what they paid and the par value of the stock, not only to the creditors of the corporation, but also to the corporation itself.

It must be admitted that both the logic and the law would seem

ultra vires, and such issue would be invalid, although the contract with the shareholders under which the shares were issued had been registered under the act regulating such transactions. There is no practical distinction, it has been held, between issuing shares at a discount and returning to the shareholder a portion of the capital to which the creditors have a right to look as that out of which they are to be paid.[1]

§ 118. *Power to issue preferred stock.*— The question as to whether a corporation has or has not power to issue shares of stock to which a preferential dividend shall be attached has been the subject of much legal controversy. When such power is expressly granted in the charter by which the company is incorporated, then, of course, there is no question as to the legality of the issue.[2] It seems pretty well settled by the weight of authority, however, that a corporation has no implied power, either at the time of its organization or at any subsequent time, to issue preferred stock. The power can exist only when expressly conferred by the charter or by statute.[3] In

to be with the House of Lords on this particular question, and it is doubtful whether the Handley v. Stutz case will be generally accepted as a final disposition of this important question.

[1] In re Almada, etc. Co., 38 Ch. Div. 415; Trevor v. Whitworth, 12 App. Cas. 409; In re Addlestone Co., 37 Ch. Div. 191; In re Weymouth Packet Co., 1 Ch. Div. 66 (1890); Ex parte Maude, L. R. 6 Ch. 51; Birch v. Cropper, 14 App. Cas. 525; Ooregum Gold M. Co. v. Roper, 61 L. J. (N. S.) 337, 66 L. J. (N. S.) 427 (1892); s. c., 28 Am. L. Rev. 861.

[2] Cook, Stock & Stockholders, § 268; Everhardt v. West Chester Ry. Co., 28 Pa. St. 339; Rutland, etc. Ry. v. Thrall, 35 Vt. 536; Taylor, Corp., §§ 571, 572.

[3] Hutton v. Scarborough Co., 4 De G., J. & S. 672; Sturge v. Eastern, etc. Ry. Co., 7 De G., M. & G. 158; Guiness v. Corporation of Ireland, 22 Ch. Div. 349; Hoole v. Great Western Ry. Co., L. R. 3 Ch. App. 262.

American Tube Works v. Boston Machine Co., supra, the court say: "Corporations have sometimes, no doubt, at the outset of their organization, assumed the authority to divide their capital stock into two classes, preferred and common; and when such stockholder subscribes for and takes his shares of common stock with full knowledge and consent, there is perhaps no legal objection to this course. The question is a different one whether a corporation, with an existing capital stock all subscribed for and taken, can increase its capital by the issue of further shares which shall be preferred, and if so, under what circumstances this may be done, and whether by a mere majority or only by a unanimous vote of the existing stockholders." A company may, however, when it is authorized to issue preferred stock, contract with the preferred stockholders that they shall be entitled to a preference not only in the payment of dividends, but also in the distribution of the company's assets.[1]

§ 119. *Liability on ultra vires issue of preferred stock.* In the light of what has heretofore been shown in preceding sections as to the power of corporations to issue preferred stock, the general rule may be declared to be that, if a corporation issue preference shares of stock without authority so to do either in its charter or the law under which it is organized, such issue is *ultra vires* and void, and no liability attaches to the company *on such stock;* but an action may be maintained against the company to recover the money paid for such illegal issue.[2]

[1] In re Bangor & Slate Co., L. R. 20 Eq. 59.
[2] Anthony v. Household Machine Co., 16 R. I. 571. And see 2 Mor. Corp., §§ 721, 722; Dill v. Wareham, 7 Met. (Mass.) 438; Congress, etc. Co. v. Knowlton, 103 U. S. 49; Mayor, etc. v. Ray, 19 Wall. (U. S.) 468; Oneida Bank v. Ontario Bank, 21 N. Y. 490; Thomas v. Railway, 101 U. S. 71; New Castle Ry. v. Simpson, 21 Fed. Rep. 533; White v. Franklin Bank, 22 Pick. (Mass.) 181; 2 Pars. Cont. 746; Gordon's Ex'rs

But it has been held that although a corporation issues preferred stock without express authority, yet a purchaser, who voluntarily subscribes and pays for it, for the purpose of promoting the scheme under which it was issued, cannot hold it for over two years after the condition upon which it was issued has been fulfilled, and then, on the insolvency of the company, assert the invalidity of the stock, and recover back the money paid for it.[1] Nor is one's right to recover money paid on an *ultra vires* issue of such stock impaired by reason of a subsequent enactment of a statute authorizing the corporation to issue preferred stock.[2]

v. Richmond. etc. Co., 78 Va. 501, 81 Va. 621; Warren v. King, 108 U. S. 389; Burt v. Rattle, 31 Ohio St. 116.

[1] Bard v. Banigan, 39 Fed. Rep. 13.

In Anthony v. Household Sewing Machine Co., *supra*, the plaintiff was one of several persons who lent a large amount of money to the defendant corporation, under agreement with the corporation that they were to be repaid in preferred stock, to be subsequently issued by it. It was supposed when the money was lent that the corporation had power to issue such stock in discharge of the agreement, but it was afterwards discovered that as a matter of law it did not have power, and therefore the plaintiff demanded a return of the money which he had lent, and, upon failure of the company to return it, brought an action to recover it. Chief Justice Durfee, in delivering the opinion of the court, said:

"The agreement was not an agreement to repay the loan in preferred stock, but an agreement absolutely to repay it in that form. It was an agreement by the corporation to do something which it had no power to do. It was therefore void, and the plaintiff was entitled to treat it as void and to reclaim the money. Where money has been advanced under such a contract, it can be recovered back by the party advancing it so long as the contract remains wholly unperformed by the other party, the recovery being had, not under the contract but in disaffirmance of it, on a promise implied independent of it."

[2] In re Bridgewater Nav. Co., 39 Ch. Div. 1; Congress Spring Co. v. Knowlton, 103 U. S. 49; Anthony v. Household Sewing Machine Co., 16 R. I. 571.

§ 120.] CAPITAL STOCK. 167

§ 120. *Power of corporation to deal in its own stock.*—
It has been held in some of the states of the Union that
the shares of capital stock of a corporation are the lawful
subjects of purchase and sale, may be bought and sold in
the market, and, in the absence of statutory provisions
to the contrary, a corporation, if it acts in good faith,
may buy such shares for its own benefit from owners of
them upon such terms as may be agreed on, subject to the
rights of its creditors in proper cases to resort to its capital stock, paid and unpaid, as a trust fund out of which
they may be entitled to have these debts paid.[1] In many
of the states, however, this power is regulated by direct
statutory enactment, but in those states where no such
statutory provisions exist, such power is left to the determination of the courts. The true rule is perhaps laid
down by the court in *Clapp v. Peterson, supra*, where it
is said: " Corporations may purchase their own stock in
exchange for money or other property, and hold, reissue
or retire the same, provided such act is had in entire good
faith, in an exchange of equal value, and is free from all
fraud, actual or constructive; this implying that the corporation is neither insolvent nor in process of dissolution,
and that the rights of creditors are not thereby injuri-

[1] Cook, Stockholders, §§ 311, 312; Blalock v. Kernesville Mfg. Co.,
110 N. C. 99; First Nat. Bank v. Salem Mills, 39 Fed. Rep. 89; Bank,
etc. v. Bruce, 17 N. Y. 510; Taylor v. Export Co., 6 Ohio, 176; In re
Ins. Co., 3 Biss. (U. S.) 452; Bank v. Transportation Co., 18 Vt. 138;
Clapp v. Peterson, 104 Ill. 26; Dupee v. Water Power Co., 114 Mass.
37; Republic Ins. Co. v. Swigert, 135 Ill. 150; Chicago, etc. R. Co. v.
Marseilles, 84 Ill. 145; Chetlain v. Insurance Co., 86 Ill. 220; Fraser
v. Ritchie, 8 Ill. App. 554; Eggeman v. Blanke, 46 Mo. App. 318; Leland v. Hayden, 102 Mass. 542; Eby v. Guest, 94 Pa. St. 160; Early's
Appeal, 89 Pa. St. 160; Coleman v. Columbus Oil Co., 51 Pa. St. 74;
Iowa Lumber Co. v. Foster, 49 Iowa, 25; State Bank v. Fox, 3 Blatch.
(U. S.) 431; Hartridge v. Rockwell, R. M. Charlt. (Ga.) 260; Robinson
v. Beale, 26 Ga. 17; Hagie v. People's Ass'n, 107 N. C. 581.

ously affected." In Ohio no corporation can buy or sell its own shares unless permitted so to do by its charter or law of incorporation.[1] So in Kansas, banks organized under the laws of that state are held to have no power to purchase their own stock, except in some cases for the purpose of securing a previously existing debt.[2] In Ontario, Canada, it is the rule that a corporation cannot cancel or accept the surrender of shares of stock in compromising a claim against it by a shareholder, where the validity of the shares or his right to them is not in dispute.[3] In England the question has been settled by a long line of decisions that no such power exists unless it has been specifically granted, and that such a purchase is beyond the corporate powers, illegal and void.[4] So it has been held that insolvent corporations can neither purchase, nor receive in payment of debts owing it, shares of its own stock.[5] Nor can business corporations exchange their goods for their capital stock so as to reduce or retire the latter.[6] And if the statutes which govern a company only allow the company to make advances on the security of landed property, a company cannot advance money to its members on the security of their shares.[7]

[1] Chapin v. Greenlees, 38 Ohio St. 275.

[2] German Sav. Bank v. Wulfekuhlen, 19 Kan. 60.

[3] Livingstone v. Temperance Society, 17 Ont. App. 379.

[4] In re London, etc. R. Co., 5 De G. & S. 402; Evans v. Coventry, 5 De G., M. & G. 911, 8 De G., M. & G. 835; In re Northern Coal Min. Co., 13 Beav. 472; Zulueta's Case, L. R. 5 Ch. 444; Ernest v. Nichols, 6 H. L. Cas. 401; In re United States Co., 5 Ch. 707, L. R. 7 Eq. 76; In re Marseilles, etc. Co., 7 Ch. 161; Hope v. International Co., 4 Ch. Div. 327; Trevor v. Whitworth, 12 App. Cas. (H. L.) 409.

[5] Currier v. Lebanon Co., 56 N. H. 262; Savings Bank v. Wulfekuhlen, 19 Kan. 60; Taylor, Corp, § 135.

[6] St. Louis Carriage Mfg. Co. v. Hilbert, 24 Mo. App. 338.

[7] Collerne v. London Bldg. Soc., 25 Q. B. Div. 485.

§ 121. *Power to purchase stock of another corporation.*— It is now well settled that a corporation cannot purchase or deal in the stock of other corporations unless expressly authorized by law so to do.[1] But a corporation may take stock in another company in payment of a debt.[2] Though a corporation may take the stock of another corporation by way of security for a debt, it has no right to invest its corporate funds in the purchase of such stock.[3] So it is beyond the scope of the powers of a corporation, having the right to mine, to organize another corporation for mining purposes or to deal in the stock of such corporation.[4]

§ 122. *Instances where power denied.*— A corporation formed for the purpose of manufacturing and selling gas has no power to purchase and hold or sell shares of stock in other gas companies as an incident to the purpose of its formation, even though such power is specified in its articles of incorporation.[5] Nor has an insurance company the power or legal right to subscribe for stock in a savings bank and building association;[6] nor to purchase

---

[1] Talmage v. Pell, 7 N. Y. 348; Berry v. Yates, 24 Barb. (N. Y.) 200; Milbank v. New York, etc. R. Co., 64 How. Pr. (N. Y.) 20; Mechanics' Sav. Bank v. Meriden, etc. Co., 24 Conn. 159; Central R. Co. v. Penn. R. Co., 31 N. J. Eq. 475; Hazlehurst v. Savannah, etc. R. Co., 43 Ga. 13; Valley R. Co. v. Lake Erie Ins. Co., 46 Ohio St. 44; People v. Chicago Gas Trust Co., 130 Ill. 268, 284; Franklin Co. v. Lewiston, etc., 68 Me. 43; Hill v. Nisbet, 100 Ind. 341; Compagnie Francaise v. Western Union Co., 11 Fed. Rep. 862; Solomans v. Laing, 12 Beav. 339; Franklin Bank v. Commercial Bank, 36 Ohio St. 350; Buford v. Keokuk Co., 3 Mo. App. 159.

[2] Holmes, etc. Mfg. Co. v. Holmes, etc. Co., 127 N. Y. 252; Howe v. Boston Carpet Co., 16 Gray (Mass.), 493.

[3] Milbank v. N. Y. etc. R. Co., 64 How. Pr. (N. Y.) 20.

[4] McMillan v. Carson Min. Co., 12 Phila. (Pa.) 404.

[5] People v. Chicago Gas Co., 130 Ill. 268.

[6] Mutual, etc. Ass'n v. Meriden Agency Co., 24 Conn. 159.

stock in another insurance company.¹ So it has been held that neither a note-selling company,² nor a lumber company,³ has power to invest in the shares of a bank; nor a steamship company to subscribe for stock in a dry-dock company.⁴ On the other hand, it has been held that a steamboat company may purchase stock in another rival line, even though the evident purpose be to injure it.⁵ And it is clearly legal for a manufacturing company to take the stock of another in payment of a debt.⁶ So religious and charitable, and other like corporations, not for profit, have, it seems, implied power to invest their funds in stock of other corporations.⁷ There has been some controversy, however, whether one corporation could sell all its property to another corporation, taking pay in stock of the latter, and dividing such stock among the shareholders of the selling corporation. The weight of authority holds that such a transaction is *ultra vires*, and may be prevented by any stockholder of the former corporation.⁸ So a contract by a corporation created under the laws of Ohio, while solvent and engaged in a profitable business, to sell its plant and assets for a consideration, the greater part of which is stock and bonds of another corporation to be organized to carry on the business, no exigency making such a sale necessary for the protection of the stockholders, is *ultra vires*, as, under

[1] Re British Life Ins. Ass'n, 8 Ch. Div. 679; Berry v. Yates, 24 Barb. (N. Y.) 199.
[2] Joint Stock Co. v. Brown, L. R. 8 Eq. 381.
[3] Sumner v. Marcy, 3 W. & M. (U. S.) 105.
[4] New Orleans Co. v. Ocean Dry-Dock Co., 28 La. Ann. 173.
[5] Booth v. Robinson, 55 Md. 419; Parker v. Bernal, 66 Cal. 112.
[6] Howe v. Boston Carpet Co., 82 Mass. 493.
[7] Pearson v. Concord R. R. Co., 62 N. H. 537; Hodges v. Screw Co., 1 R. I. 322, 3 R. I. 9.
[8] Taylor v. Earle, 8 Hun (N. Y.), 1; Frothingham v. Barney, 6 Hun (N. Y.), 366.

the laws of that state, one corporation cannot become the owner of stock in another, unless such power is clearly conferred by statute.[1]

§ 123. *Power of foreign corporation to purchase stock of domestic company.*— So it has been held that the purchase by a foreign corporation of the stock of a domestic corporation for the purpose of controlling it is *ultra vires* and void, though they are engaged in a similar business; and in an action by the foreign company to recover half of a debt of the domestic company, which the plaintiff was obliged to pay to protect the property of such company, brought against the president of the domestic company, who had agreed, in consideration of the price paid for the stock, to discharge one-half of the debts of the domestic company, defendant is not estopped to set up the invalidity of the contract, though he received the benefits of it.[2]

§ 124. *Power to declare dividends.*— A dividend is a fund which a corporation sets apart from its profits to be divided among its members.[3] It is ordinarily a matter of discretion resting with the managers or directors of a corporation whether a dividend shall be made, how much it shall be, and when and where payable.[4] While, as a general rule, the officers of a corporation are the sole

[1] Easum v. Buckeye Brew. Co., 51 Fed. Rep. 156; Buckeye Marble, etc. Co. v. Harvey, 92 Tenn. 115.
[2] Buckeye Marble Co. v. Harvey, 92 Tenn. 115.
[3] Lockhart v. Van Alstyne, 31 Mich. 76; Pennsylvania Co. v. Erie R. R., 108 Pa. St. 621; Williston v. Michigan R. Co., 13 Allen (Mass.), 404.
[4] Williams v. Western Union Tel. Co., 93 N. Y. 162; Chaffee v. Rutland R. Co., 55 Vt. 110; Barry v. Merchants' Exch., 1 Sandf. Ch. (N. Y.) 280; New York, etc. R. Co. v. Nickals, 119 U. S. 296; Jackson v. Plank Road Co., 31 N. J. L. 277.

judges as to the propriety of declaring dividends, and the courts will not interfere with the proper exercise of their discretion, where the right to a dividend is clear and fixed by contract, and requires the directors to take action before the right can be asserted by an action at law, a court of equity will interfere to compel such action, and, when necessary, to restrain by injunction any action adverse to such right.[1] While it is usually left to the directors' discretion as to the amount of the dividend to be declared, yet the directors have no power to discriminate between its stockholders, where no such power of discrimination is conferred by the charter of the corporation.[2]

§ 125. *Power to pledge or mortgage future calls.*— Under the power to pledge, mortgage or charge the works, hereditaments, plant, property and effects of a company, in order to secure the payment of moneys borrowed, the proceeds of a call already made, but not yet paid, may be charged, but not the proceeds of a future call.[3] But where power to mortgage a future or unpaid-up capital is given by the memorandum or articles of association, a mortgage by the company of its future or uncalled capital is valid, even as against creditors in a winding up, the calls in a winding up being part of the assets or capital of the company.[4]

[1] Boardman v. Lake Shore, etc. Co., 84 N. Y. 167, and cases cited.
[2] Jones v. Terre Haute R. Co., 57 N. Y. 196; Phelps v. Farmers' Bank, 26 Conn. 269; Stoddard v. Foundry Co., 34 Conn. 542; Goodwin v. Hardy, 57 Me. 143; March v. Eastern, etc. R. Co., 43 N. H. 515; Coles v. Bank of England, 10 Ad. & Ell. 437; Festial v. King's College, 10 Beav. 491; City of Ohio v. N. Y. etc. R. Co., 5 Abb. Pr. (N. Y.) 277; King v. Paterson R. R. Co., 29 N. J. L. 82; Brown v. Lehigh Canal Co., 49 Pa. St. 270; Granger v. Bassett, 98 Mass. 462; Kent v. Quicksilver Min. Co., 78 N. Y. 159; Reese v. Bank, 81 Pa. St. 78.
[3] In re Sankey Brook Coal Co., L. R. 10 Eq. 381, 9 Eq. 721; Ex parte Stanley, 33 L. J. (Ch.) 535.
[4] In re Pyle Works, 44 Ch. Div. 534.

§ 126. *Liability of corporation on dividend declared.—* When a dividend upon its stock has been declared by a corporation, it belongs to the holders of the stock at the time of the declaration, without regard to the source from which, or the time during which, the funds derived were acquired by the corporation.[1] Accordingly, when such dividend is declared, it thereupon becomes the individual property of the stockholder, and he is entitled to receive the same on demand of the proper agent, and if not paid on demand he may maintain an action therefor.[2] Although directors have the right to fix the time and place of payment of such dividend, the time should not be remote, or the place so far distant as to prejudice the rights of the stockholders; and if directors select a banking house of good credit and deposit the money there to pay dividends, and give notice to each stockholder of such deposit, and the stockholder, after receiving such notice, neglects to draw the money within a reasonable time and a loss is incurred by a failure of the bank, it will fall upon the stockholder, and he cannot call upon the company to reimburse him.[3] But if a dividend is declared payable elsewhere than at the office of the corporation, the party through whom it is paid becomes the agent of the company; and if such agent fail to pay it over to the stockholder, the loss falls upon the corporation.[4]

[1] Jermain v. Lake Shore Ry. Co., 91 N. Y. 483; Brisbane v. Delaware, etc. R. Co., 94 N. Y. 204, 25 Hun (N. Y.), 438; Cleveland R. Co. v. Robbins, 35 Ohio St. 483.
[2] Granger v. Bassett, 98 Mass. 462; King v. Paterson, etc. R. Co., 29 N. J. L. 82; Stoddard v. Shetucket Co., 34 Conn. 542; City of Chicago v. Cleveland, 6 Ohio St. 489; Harris v. San Francisco R. Co., 41 Cal. 393.
[3] King v. Paterson, *supra.*
[4] King v. Paterson, *supra.*

§ 127. Liability on illegal issue of stock.—When the issue of shares by a corporation is illegal, and no sufficient steps have been taken to authorize the creation of the capital stock, where a person has acted and been treated as a stockholder in respect of shares which the company had no power to issue, the person taking them cannot, by estoppel or otherwise, become a member of the company in respect to them, nor is the corporation liable on such illegal issue.[1] But where a clerk of the corporation fraudulently filled out a certificate of shares of its stock in the name of a fictitious person, procured the signatures of the officers and negotiated it, signing the name of the fictitious person to the assignment and power of attorney, and the transferee bought in good faith, and obtained a transfer on the books and a new certificate to himself, the corporation was held estopped from denying its validity and consequent liability.[2]

---

[1] Lindley on Part. 134; Allen v. Herrick, 81 Mass. 274; Turnbul v. Payson, 95 U. S. 418; American Tube Works v. Boston Mach. Co., 139 Mass. 5; Bank of Hindustan v. Alison, L. R. 6 C. P. 54.

[2] Manhattan Beach Co. v. Harned, 23 Blatch. (U. S.) 494; s. c., 27 Fed. Rep. 484. And see Kent v. Quicksilver M. Co., 78 N. Y. 159; Eaton v. Pacific National Bank, 144 Mass. 260.

CHAPTER IX.

THE DOCTRINE APPLIED TO RAILROAD CORPORATIONS.

§ 128. General power to make contracts.
129. Contracts to carry beyond own line.
130. Traffic agreements between railroads.
131. Pooling contracts.
132. Railroad bonds — Definition.
133. Power to issue bonds.
134. Formalities prescribed must be strictly pursued.
135. Negotiability of railroad bonds.
136. Power to guaranty bonds of another company.
137. Power to lease road and franchises.
138. Ultra vires lease will not be set aside at suit of lessor.
139. Instances where power denied.
140. Power to mortgage property.
141. Power to mortgage franchises.
142. Consolidation and amalgamation — Definition.
143. Power of corporations to consolidate.
144. Effect of consolidation.
145. Effect of interstate consolidation.
146. Rights and liabilities of consolidated company.
147. Consolidation as affecting stockholders.
148. Consolidation as affecting taxation.
149. Trusts and illegal combinations.

§ 128. *General power to make contracts.*— A railroad company, like other corporations, has the implied power to enter into contracts which are necessary to its business, and incidental to the proper construction, maintenance and operation of its road.[1] But a railroad corporation,

---
[1] Pierce on Railroads, § 499; South Wales R. Co. v. Redmond, 10 C. B. N. S. 675, 100 E. C. L. 674; Mayor, etc. v. Baltimore, etc. R. Co., 6 Gill (Md.) 297, 21 Md. 50; Hamilton v. Newcastle R. Co., 9 Ind. 859;

being in its nature of a *quasi*-public character, may not enter into any contract or obligation whereby it releases itself from any of its duties or obligations to the public.[1]

§ 129. *Contract to carry beyond own line.*— It is now well settled that a railroad company may make contracts with passengers or shippers for carriage beyond its own lines; and in order to fulfill such contracts may make suitable arrangements with connecting lines of railway or steamship. Such contracts have been held not to be *ultra vires* in numerous cases.[2] And where such contract is entered into, the company so contracting is liable not only for the loss of the goods upon their own line, but also for loss of any goods upon connecting lines.[3] And it has been

Frye v. Tucker, 24 Ill. 180; Joy v. St. Louis, 138 U. S. 1; Shrewsbury, etc. R. Co. v. Northwestern R. Co., 6 H. L. 113; Smith v. Nashua, etc. R. Co., 27 N. H. 86; Buffit v. Troy, etc. R. Co., 40 N. Y. 168; Church v. Sterling, 16 Conn. 388; Rorer on Railroads, 228; Western Bank v. Tallman, 17 Wis. 530.

[1] Thomas v. Railroad Co., 101 U. S. 71; York, etc. R. Co. v. Winans, 17 How. (U. S.) 39. And see cases cited in § 137, *post.*

[2] Beach, Priv. Corp., § 407; Thompson, Com. Corp., § 5871; Taylor, Priv. Corp., § 308; Weed v. Saratoga, etc. R. Co., 19 Wend. (N. Y.) 534; Wylde v. North River, etc. Co., 53 N. Y. 156; Root v. Great Western R. Co., 55 N. Y. 524; East Tenn. etc. R. Co. v. Nelson, 1 Coldw. (Tenn.) 276; Newell v. Smith, 49 Vt. 255; Roberts v. Van Buskirk, 31 N. Y. 661; Steamboat Co. v. Brown, 54 Pa. St. 77; Noyes v. Railroad Co., 27 Vt. 110; Peet v. Railway Co., 19 Wis. 118; St. Louis, etc. R. Co. v. Pipes, 13 Kan. 505; Wahl v. Holt, 26 Wis. 703; Illinois Cent. R. Co. v. Johnson, 34 Ill. 389; Pennsylvania R. Co. v. Berry, 68 Pa. St. 272; Southern Ex. Co. v. Shea, 38 Ga. 519; Bryan v. M. & P. R. Co., 11 Bush (Ky.), 597; Bennett v. Peninsular S. Co., 6 C. B. 775.

[3] Great Western Ry. Co. v. Blake, 7 H. & N. 986; Stewart v. Erie, etc. Ry. Co., 17 Minn. 372; Wiggins Ferry Co. v. Chicago R. Co., 73 Mo. 389; Green Bay. etc. R. Co. v. Union S. Co., 107 U. S. 98; Arnot v. Erie R. Co., 5 Hun (N. Y.), 608; Parish v. Wheeler, 22 N. Y. 494; Wheeler v. San Francisco R. Co., 31 Cal. 46; Rutland, etc. R. Co. v. Proctor, 29 Vt. 93; Shawmut's Bank v. Plattsburg Ry., 31 Vt. 491;

held in many cases that even the acceptance of goods for shipment whose destination is beyond the company's own lines implies a contract to deliver at destination.[1] However, the general rule in the United States seems to be that the acceptance of goods for shipment beyond the company's own lines, in the absence of any contract, obligates the carrier only to transportation to end of own line and a delivery there to the next connecting carrier.[2]

§ 130. *Traffic agreements between railroad companies.* A railroad company may, if not restrained by its charter, enter into contracts with connecting carriers for the purpose of providing for through transportation over its road and over the line of such carrier, if made with a *bona fide* purpose of regulating traffic in a reasonable and

---

Feital v. Middlesex R. Co., 109 Mass. 398; Morse v. Brainerd, 41 Vt. 550; Railroad Co. v. Transportation Co., 16 Wall. (U. S.) 324; Evansville Ry. Co. v. Androscoggin, etc., 22 Wall. (U. S.) 594; Phillips v. Railroad Co., 78 N. C. 294; Pratt v. Railroad Co., 22 Wall. (U. S.) 132; Hill Mfg. Co. v. Railroad Co., 104 Mass. 122; Gray v. Jackson, 51 N. H. 9; Woodward v. Railroad Co., 1 Biss. (U. S.) 403.

[1] Illinois Cent. R. Co. v. Frankenberg, 54 Ill. 88; Chicago, etc. R. Co. v. People, 56 Ill. 365; Adams Ex. Co. v. Wilson, 81 Ill. 339; Southern Ex. Co. v. Shea, 38 Ga. 519; Kyle v. Railroad Co., 10 Rich. (S. C.) 382; Carter v. Peck, 4 Sneed (Ky.), 201; Bennet v. Filyaw, 1 Fla. 403; Mulligan v. Railway Co., 36 Iowa, 181; East Tenn. etc. Co. v. Rogers, 6 Heisk. (Tenn.) 143; Lock Co. v. Railroad Co., 48 N. H. 339.

[2] Nutting v. Railroad Co., 1 Gray (Mass.), 502; Darling v. Railroad Co., 11 Allen (Mass.), 295; Hood v. Railroad Co., 22 Conn. 502; Perkins v. Railroad Co., 47 Me. 573; Skinner v. Hall, 60 Mo. 477; Railroad Co. v. Manufacturing Co., 16 Wall. (U. S.) 318; Santwood v. St. John, 6 Hill (N. Y.), 158; Railroad Co. v. Pratt, 22 Wall. (U. S.) 123; Brintnall v. Railroad Co., 32 Vt. 665; Farmers,' etc. Bank v. Transportation Co., 23 Vt. 186; McMillan v. Railroad Co., 16 Mich. 79; Crawford v. Railroad Ass'n, 51 Miss. 222; Burroughs v. Railroad Co., 100 Mass. 26; Camden, etc. R. Co. v. Forsyth, 61 Pa. St. 81; Baltimore, etc. R. Co. v. Schumaker, 29 Md. 170; Irish v. Railroad Co., 54 N. Y. 502.

just manner.[1] All contracts between rival railroad companies which prevent competition are not necessarily contrary to public policy, illegal and detrimental to the public welfare, the vehement declarations of demagogic politicians to the contrary notwithstanding. When such contracts prevent an unhealthy competition, and furnish the public with adequate facilities at fixed and reasonable rates, they are beneficial and in accordance with sound principles of public policy.[2] So where two groups of railway companies, being respectively the owners of independent coterminous routes, agreed to divide the profits of the whole traffic in certain fixed proportions, calculated on the experience of the past course of traffic, it was held that such agreement was not *ultra vires*.[3]

§ 131. *Pooling contracts.*— "Pools" have been defined by a very able writer to be contracts between rival railway companies whereby, in order to prevent competition, their business is united in one common total, from which the business or the money received therefor is divided among the combining companies in fixed percentages.[4] The same author has further declared them to be of two kinds — traffic pools and money pools. A traffic pool is an agreement allotting a certain percentage of the total traffic to each road, and providing that, if any road exceeds its share of the business, freight shall be diverted

[1] Stewart v. The Erie, etc. Transp. Co., 17 Minn. 372; South Wales Ry. v. Redmond, 100 E. C. L. 674; Sussex, etc. Ry. v. Morris, etc. R. Co., 19 N. J. Eq. 13; Simpson v. Denison, 10 Hare, 51; Midland Ry. Co. v. Great Western Ry. Co., L. R. 8 Ch. 841, 7 Moak's Rep. 408; Llanelly Ry. v. London, etc. Ry., L. R. 7 H. L. 550, 13 Moak's Rep. 73.

[2] Hare v. London, etc. Ry. Co., 2 Johns. & H. 80, 7 Jur. (N. S.) 1145, 30 L. J. Ch. 817; Manchester, etc. Ry. Co. v. Concord R. R., 20 Atl. Rep. (N. H.) 383; 1 Redf. Rys., § 146; Mor. Priv. Corp., § 1131.

[3] Hare v. London, etc. Ry. Co., *supra*.

[4] The Railways of the Republic, Hudson, 196.

from it to the other roads until the agreed proportion is restored. A money pool is an agreement whereby the money received by all the combining roads for transportation is brought together into one total and divided among the roads in certain fixed percentages, which do not necessarily correspond to the proportion of the freight actually carried by each road.[1] Whether or not pooling contracts are illegal and void would seem to depend upon the laws of the state under which the company was organized. For instance, in New Jersey, such contracts have been recognized by the courts as valid;[2] while in Louisiana it has been quite recently held that pools are not enforceable, as contrary to public policy.[3] But in New York it has been decided that a pooling combination for dividing certain territory between parallel railroads is not contrary to public policy.[4] The railroad commission of that state, however, has declared pooling contracts invalid.[5] And in Pennsylvania a pool formed for the division of a coal district, whereby the committee were to fix prices of coal, rates of freight, etc., was held to be both against the statute of New York — where the contract was made — and also against the public policy of the state, wherein the coal district was situated.[6] So in Indiana combinations between common carriers to prevent competition are regarded as *prima facie* illegal, and in order to establish the legality of any pool the burden is on the carrier to show that the pool was formed to prevent ruinous competition, and that it does not establish

[1] The Railways of the Republic, Hudson, 197.
[2] Sussex R. Co. v. Morris, etc. Co., 19 N. J. Eq. 13, 20 N. J. Eq. 542; Elkins v. Camden, etc. R. Co., 36 N. J. Eq. 241.
[3] Tex. & Pac. R. Co. v. Southern Pac. R. Co., 41 La. Ann. 970.
[4] Ives v. Smith, 3 N. Y. Supp. 645; affirmed, 55 Hun (N. Y.), 606.
[5] 1 N. Y. Railroad Com. Rep. (1885), 77.
[6] Morris Run Coal Co. v. Barclay Coal Co., 68 Pa. St. 186.

unreasonable rates, unjust discrimination or oppressive regulations.[1] The regulation of rates and freight charges between railroad corporations is now, in many of the states, intrusted to the wise discretion of a railroad commission, these officers usually being men with little or no railroad experience, and whose resplendent abilities toward confusing seemingly plain business transactions is strikingly exemplified in the number of suits brought in the United States courts praying relief from the heavy hand of these political blunderers. It must be added, in concluding this branch of the subject, that interstate commerce pooling has been forbidden by act of congress.[2]

§ 132. *Railroad bonds — Definition.*— Railroad bonds are instruments under seal containing an acknowledgment of certain debts and an agreement to pay the same upon the terms stated. They are a kind of public funds put on the market and dealt in as such. Coupons, or interest certificates for each instalment of interest accruing during the time the bonds have to run, are attached to them and form a part of the original bonds.[3] The mortgage provides for the security of the particular bonds it describes, and the company puts the bonds out from time to time as occasion requires. When thus put upon the market they are treated as current until past due or actually retired. The security is considered a continuing one, and the bonds negotiable by the company so as to carry the mortgage security until they have become com-

[1] Cleveland, etc. R. Co. v. Closser, 126 Ind. 348. And see Denver, etc. Co. v. Atchison, etc. R. Co., 110 U. S. 667.
[2] Interstate Commerce Act, 24 Stat. at L. 380.
[3] 19 Am. & Eng. Ency. Law, 719; Cooper v. Corbin, 105 Ill. 224; Peoria, etc. R. Co. v. Thompson, 103 Ill. 187; Harmock v. Farmers' L. & T. Co., 105 U. S. 77; Farmers' L. & T. Co. v. St. Joseph, etc. R. Co., 3 Dill. 412, 2 Fed. Rep. 117; Titus v. Mabee, 25 Ill. 257.

mercially dishonored, or something else has been done to deprive the company of its power of floating them.[1]

§ 133. *Power to issue bonds.*—The power of a railroad corporation to issue bonds for the purpose of raising money for its extension, maintenance and operation is now so well established that it would almost seem a work of supererogation to cite authorities to support the proposition. This is one of the incidental powers necessary for its very existence. A bond is merely an obligation under seal; and such corporation having the right to make contracts under which it may incur debts, and the right to make and use a common seal, a contract under seal is not only within the scope of its powers, but was originally the usual and peculiarly appropriate form of corporate agreement.[2] This power, however, is usually given by charter or by general statute.

§ 134. *Formalities prescribed must be strictly pursued.* When the statute under which the corporation was organized prescribes certain formalities to be followed in the issuance of bonds, they must be strictly complied with by the officers of the company, or they will be void as against the corporation, even though such bonds be in the hands of *bona fide* holders.[3] So where the statutes prescribed that such bonds should be certified across their face, and further required them to be registered, bonds

[1] Claflin v. South Carolina, etc. R. Co., 8 Fed. Rep. 118, 4 Hughes, 12, 4 Am. & Eng. Ry. Cases, 231, 19 Am. & Eng. Ency. Law, 719.

[2] Comm. v. Smith, 10 Allen (Mass.), 448; Treadwell v. Salisbury Mfg. Co., 7 Gray (Mass.), 393.

[3] Hackensack Water Co. v. De Kay, 36 N. J. Eq. 548; Singer v. St. Louis R. Co., 6 Mo. App. 427; Webb v. Herne Bay, L. R. 5 Q. B. 642; Chambers v. Manchester, etc. R. Co., 5 Best & S. 588; Comm. v. Smith, 10 Allen (Mass.), 448; Rockwell v. Elkhorn Bank, 13 Wis. 653; Morrison v. Inhabitants, etc., 7 Vroom (N. J.), 219.

that were issued without these formalities were held to be void.¹ As was said by the court in *Hackensack Water Co. v. De Kay, supra:* "Persons taking securities of this character are chargeable with knowledge of the power to make them as conferred by the charter. If the power granted by the charter is subject to a condition, relating either to the form in which the security shall be made in order to be valid, or to some preliminary proceeding extraneous to the acts of the corporation or its officers, securities issued not in the prescribed form, or without the preliminary proceedings had, are subject to defenses in consequence thereof even in the hands of *bona fide* holders."

§ 135. *Negotiability of railroad bonds.*— Coupon bonds of a railroad company, issued under special legislative authority and designed for the purpose of raising money on a credit, if they contain words of negotiability, are negotiable instruments the same as ordinary commercial paper, and the same immunity from defenses in the hands of *bona fide* holders applies to mortgages securing such bonds as to the bonds themselves.² Railroad bonds are usually made payable to the trustee named in the mortgage or the bearer, and pass by delivery from hand to hand with all the ordinary properties of negotiable instruments.³ Under the law merchant such bonds are not

[1] Morrison v. Inhabitants of Bernards, 7 Vroom (N. J.), 219.

[2] Hackensack Water Co. v. De Kay, 36 N. J. Eq. 548, and cases cited.

[3] White v. Vermont, etc. R. Co., 21 How. (U. S.) 575; Clark v. Iowa City, 20 Wall. (U. S.) 583; Gelpcke v. Dubuque, 1 Wall. (U. S.) 175; Aurora City v. West, 7 Wall. (U. S.) 82; Haven v. Grand Junction, etc. Co., 109 Mass. 88; Connecticut Life Ins. Co. v. Cleveland R. Co., 41 Barb. (N. Y.) 9; Reed v. Mobile Bank, 70 Ala. 199; Lehman v. Tallahassee Mfg. Co., 64 Ala. 567; Morris Canal Co. v. Fisher, 9 N. J. Eq.

regarded so strictly negotiable as are promissory notes or bills of exchange; but being expressly designated to pass from hand to hand, they are by common usage actually transferred and capable of passing by delivery so as to enable the holder to maintain an action on them in his own name.[1]

§ 136. *Power to guaranty bonds of another company.*— Unless express authority be given by charter or by statute, a railroad company has no power or authority to guaranty the bonds of or lend its credit to another corporation.[2] But it has been held that on sufficient consideration such corporation may guaranty the payment of the bonds of another company, even if there is no authority conferred upon them by charter or by statute.[3] So it has been held that a railroad corporation which has power by its charter to issue its bonds has power to guaranty the bonds of another, which it receives in payment of a debt

667; Carr v. Le Fevre, 27 Pa. St. 413; Chapin v. Vermont, etc. R. Co., 8 Gray (Mass.), 575; Langstone v. Southern Carolina R. Co., 2 S. C. 248; Ex parte Williams, 18 S. C. 299; Bonner v. New Orleans, 2 Woods (U. S.), 135; Zabrieskie v. Cleveland, etc. R. Co., 23 How. (U. S.) 381; Knox County v. Aspinwall, 21 How. (U. S.) 539; Beaver County v. Armstrong, 44 Pa. St. 63; Craig v. Vicksburg, 31 Miss. 216; Rice v. Southern Pac. R. Co., 9 Phila. 294; Brainerd v. Railroad Co., 25 N. Y. 496; Welch v. Sage, 47 N. Y. 143; Junction R. Co. v. Cleneay, 13 Ind. 161.

[1] Carr v. Le Fevre, *supra*; Junction R. Co. v. Cleneay, *supra*.

[2] Humboldt Min. Co. v. American Com. Co., 62 Fed. Rep. 361; Mor. Priv. Corp., § 423; McLennan v. File Works, 56 Mich. 579; Ætna Nat. Bank v. Insurance Co., 50 Conn. 167; National Park Bank v. German Am. etc. Co., 116 N. Y. 281; Madison, etc. Plank Road Co. v. Watertown, etc. Co., 7 Wis. 59; Davis v. Railroad Co., 131 Mass. 258; Coleman v. Railway Co., 10 Beav. 1; Pennsylvania R. Co. v. St. Louis, etc. Co., 118 U. S. 290; Marble Co. v. Harvey, 92 Tenn. 115; Green Bay, etc. Co. v. Steamboat Co., 107 U. S. 98.

[3] Low v. Cent. Pac. R. Co., 52 Cal. 53; Chicago, etc. Co. v. Howard, 7 Wall. (U. S.) 392; Arnot v. Erie R. Co., 67 N. Y. 315.

due to it, and which it sells for value or transfers in payment of its own debt, the guaranty being given as the means of strengthening and increasing the credit of the bonds, or to enable it to obtain an adequate price for them.[1] And it has been held that where a corporation guaranties the bonds of another company, its stockholders may be estopped from repudiating the guaranty, though the indorsement of guaranty be *ultra vires*.[2]

§ 137. *Power to lease its road and franchises.*— It is a general rule that, unless specially authorized by its charter or aided by some other legislative action, a railroad company cannot, by lease or by any other contract, turn over to another company for a long period of time its road and all its appurtenances, the use of its franchises and the exercise of its powers, such contract not being among the ordinary powers of a railroad company, and is not to be presumed from the usual grant of powers in a railroad charter.[3] This rule is based on the theory that public or

[1] Rogers Locomotive Works v. Southern R. Ass'n, 34 Fed. Rep. 278.

[2] Cozart v. Georgia, etc. R. Co., 54 Ga. 379; Atchison, etc. R. Co. v. Fletcher, 35 Kan. 236.

[3] Thomas v. Railroad Co., 101 U. S. 71; Green Bay, etc. R. Co. v. Steamboat Co., 107 U. S. 98; Davis v. Railroad Co., 131 Mass. 258; Eastern Counties R. Co. v. Hawkes, 5 H. L. 331; Ashbury Ry. v. Riche, 7 H. L. 653; Pennsylvania R. Co. v. St. L. etc. R. Co., 118 U. S. 290; Oregon Ry. Co. v. Oregonian Ry. Co., 130 U. S. 1; Central Trans. Co. v. Pullman Co., 139 U. S. 24; Beman v. Rufford, 1 Sim. (N. S.) 550; Johnson v. Shrewsbury, etc. R. Co., 3 De G., McN. & G. 914; Shrewsbury, etc. R. Co. v. Northwestern, etc. Co., 6 H. L. 113; South Yorkshire R. Co. v. Great Nor. Ry. Co., 3 De G., M. & G. 576; Winch v. Birkenhead Ry. Co., 5 De G. & Sm. 562; Great Nor. R. Co. v. Railway Co., 9 Hare, 306; Troy, etc. R. Co. v. Kerr, 17 Barb. (N. Y.) 601; Ohio, etc. R. Co. v. Indianapolis, etc. Co., 5 Am. L. Reg. (N. S.) 733; York, etc. R. Co. v. Winans, 17 How. (U. S.) 39; Comm. v. Smith, 10 Allen (Mass.), 448; Richardson v. Sibley, 11 Allen (Mass.), 66; Georg v. Nevada Cent. Ry. Co., 38 Pac. Rep. (Nev.) 441; Visalia Gas,

§ 137.] RAILROAD CORPORATIONS. 185

quasi-public corporations, which possess and exercise the right of eminent domain or its equivalent, owe duties to the public as well as to their stockholders; and they cannot sell or lease their corporate powers and privileges, and

etc. Co. v. Sims, 104 Cal. 326; Rabe v. Dunlap, 51 N. J. Eq. 40; Stockton v. Central Ry., 50 N. J. Eq. 52; National Trust Co. v. Miller, 33 N. J Eq. 155; Brunswick Gas L. Co. v. United Gas Co., 85 Me. 532; Keokuk v. Fort Wayne Elec. Co., 57 Mo. 689; Wasmer v. Delaware, etc. R. Co., 80 N. Y. 312; Abbott v. Johnstown, etc. R. Co., 80 id. 27; Dinsmore v. Atlantic, etc. R. Co., 46 How. Pr. (N. Y.) 193; Peters v. Lincoln, etc. R. Co., 2 McCrary (U. S.), 275; Ohio, etc. R. Co. v. Indianapolis, etc. R. Co., 5 Am. L. Rep. 733; Freeman v. Minnesota, etc. R. Co., 28 Minn. 443; Middlesex R. Co. v. Boston, etc. R. Co., 115 Mass. 347; Camden, etc. R. Co. v. May's Landing R. Co., 48 N. J. L. 530; Kean v. Johnson, 9 N. J. Eq. 407; Black v. Delaware, etc. R. Co., 22 N. J. Eq. 130, 24 N. J. Eq. 455; Clarke v. Omaha R. Co., 4 Neb. 458; McMillan v. Mich. So. R. Co., 16 Mich. 79; Occum Co. v. Sprague Co., 34 Conn. 529; Campbell v. Marietta R. Co., 23 Ohio St. 138; Lauman v. Lebanon Valley R. Co., 30 Pa. St. 42; Pinto Co. Case, 8 Ch. Div. 273; Boston, etc. R. Co. v. New York, etc. Co., 13 R. I. 260; Campbell's Case, 9 Ch. App. 1; Simpson v. Westminster Co., 8 H. L. 712; Smith v. St. Louis Ins. Co., 2 Tenn. Ch. 727; Price v. St. Louis Ins. Co., 3 Mo. App. 262; Cozart v. Georgia R. Co., 54 Ga. 379; New Orleans R. Co. v. Harris, 27 Miss. 517; In re Albert Ass. Co., 6 Ch. App. 381; Eakin v. St. Louis R. Co., 3 Cent. L. Jour. 655.

In Stockton v. Central R. R. Co., *supra*, Chancellor McGill says: " Corporate bodies that engage in a public or *quasi*-public occupation are created by the state upon the hypothesis that they will be a public benefit. They enjoy privileges that individuals cannot have. Perpetual or certain life is accorded to them. Usually the authority of the right of eminent domain is delegated to them, often to be exercised in whatever locality they may be pleased to locate. . . . The use of the common highways is frequently subordinated to their operations, and, indeed, the individual is compelled even in his own home to submit without redress to discomforts incident to their lawful operation which he would not be required to tolerate from other sources. . . . Thus they are given special privileges because of the benefits they are presumed to confer upon the communities. Railways afford speedy and comfortable passage to and from divers parts of the country, carry produce of

thereby disable themselves from performing their public duties, without legislative authority.[1] Accordingly, where a railroad corporation, under a provision of its charter declaring it to "be lawful for the said company, at any time during the continuance of its charter, to make contracts and engagements with any other corporation, or with individuals, for the transporting or carrying any kind of goods, merchandise, freight or passengers, and to enforce the fulfillment of such contract," leased its road, franchises and property for a period of twenty years, yielding complete control of it to the lessees, and receiving as rent one-half the gross sum collected by the lessee from the operation of the road; the agreement containing

mines, farms and factories to markets, distribute the industries throughout the land, feed the multitudes in populous cities, and accomplish many other beneficent ends. Water, gas, telegraph and similar corporations also render to the public benefits which readily suggest themselves to the mind as it contemplates their work. While the state confers special privileges upon these favorites, it at the same time exacts from them duties which also tend to the public welfare. The whole scheme of the laws of their organization is to equip and control them as instruments for the public good. Such corporations hold their powers not merely in trust for the pecuniary profit of their stockholders, but also in trust for the public weal. The impress for the public good is stamped upon their very being, and it becomes a duty which, though not prescribed in express language of the law, is to be implied from the nature of every power conferred. When, therefore, it appears that such a corporation, unmindful of this plain duty, acts prejudicially to the public in order to make undue gains and profits for the stockholders, it uses its powers in a manner not contemplated by the law which confers them. The use becomes abuse, and is tantamount to excess of power."

[1] Fietsam v. Hay, 122 Ill. 293; People v. Chicago Gas Trust Co., 130 Ill. 268; People v. Sugar Ref. Co., 121 N. Y. 582; Brunswick Gaslight Co. v. United Gas, etc. Co., 85 Me. 532; City of Keokuk v. Fort Wayne Elec. Co., 57 Mo. 689; Visalia Gas & E. Co. v. Sims, 104 Cal. 326; Mor. Corp., §§ 658, 1114, 1116, 1129.

a condition that the railroad company might at any time terminate the contract and take possession of the property, and, under said agreement, did so take possession, and suit was brought to recover the value of the lease for the remaining period of twenty years to which the lease extended,— it was held that the charter did not grant permission to the railroad company to sell, lease or transfer to others the entire railroad and the rights and franchises of the corporation, and that such lease of its road and corporate franchises was *ultra vires* and void.[1] So it was held that a lease for ninety-nine years of a railroad in Illinois and Indiana from a railroad corporation of Indiana, whose road connected with the road leased, though within the authority conferred on the lessor by the statute of Illinois, yet was unlawful and void because beyond the authority conferred upon the lessee by the statute of Indiana.[2] And again, where under a general law authorizing companies to organize themselves by written articles of association filed with the secretary of state for "any lawful enterprise, business, pursuit or occupation" designated in the articles, including "making or constructing any railroad, and to purchase, possess and dispose of such real or personal property as may be necessary and convenient to carry into effect the object of the incorporation," it was held that such provisions did not authorize a railroad company to be incorporated either for leasing its railroad to another corporation, or for taking leases from other corporations of their roads, although these objects were included in their articles of association.[3] But where

[1] Thomas v. Railroad Co., 101 U. S. 71.
[2] Pennsylvania, etc. R. Co. v. St. Louis, etc. R. Co., 118 U. S. 290.
[3] Oregon Ry. v. Oregonian Ry., 130 U. S. 1.

In Oregon Ry. v. Oregonian Ry., *supra*, Mr. Justice Miller, delivering the opinion of the court, says: "One of the most important powers with which a corporation can be invested is the right to

a railroad company by its charter had power "to have, purchase, possess, enjoy and retain lands, rents, hereditaments, tenements, goods, chattels and effects of whatsoever kind, nature or quality the same may be, and the same to sell, grant, demise, alien or dispose of," which power was transferred to another company, which company by its charter might at any time incorporate its stock with the stock of any other company, it was held that the latter company had express power to incorporate its stock with the stock of any other company, and that the sale of its road, equipment and franchises was not *ultra vires*, but lawful and void.[1] So also, on the same

sell out its whole property together with the franchises under which it is operated, or the authority to lease its property for a long term of years. In the case of a railroad company these privileges . . . would be the most important which could be given it, and this idea would impress itself upon the legislature. Naturally we would look for the power to do these things in some express provision of law. We would suppose that if the legislature saw fit to confer such rights, it would do so in terms which could not be misunderstood. To infer, on the contrary, that it either intended to confer them or to recognize that they already existed by the simple use of the word 'assigns,' a very loose and indefinite term, is a stretch of the power of the court in making implications which we do not feel to be justified."

[1] Branch v. Jessup, 16 Otto (U. S.), 468.

In Branch v. Jessup, *supra*, Mr. Justice Bradley says: "Generally the power to sell and dispose has reference only to the transactions in the ordinary course of business incident to a railroad company, and does not extend to a sale of the railroad itself, or of the franchise connected therewith. Outlying lands not needed for railroad uses may be sold. Machinery and other personal property may be sold. But the road and franchises are generally inalienable; and they are so not only because they are acquired by legislative grant, or in the exercise of special authority given for the specific purposes of the incorporating act, but because they are essential for the fulfillment of those purposes; and it would be a dereliction of the duty owed by the corporation to the state and to the public to part with them."

principle, where an electric light and gas company has a franchise granted by a municipal corporation to operate its gas and electric works and to supply the inhabitants of the city with gas and electricity, it is bound to operate its gas and electric works, and a lease thereof to a third party for a period of years is *ultra vires* and void as against public policy.[1]

§ 138. *Ultra vires lease will not be set aside at suit of lessor.*— A lease, however, by one railroad corporation of its road and franchises to another railroad corporation which is *ultra vires* of one or of both will not be set aside by a court of equity at the suit of the lessor, where the lessee has been in possession, paying the stipulated rent for a number of years, and has taken no steps to repudiate or rescind the contract.[2] This relief is denied under the general rule that *in pari delicto potior est conditio defendentis;* and therefore neither party to an illegal contract will be aided by the court, whether to enforce it or to set it aside. If the contract is illegal, affirmative relief against it will not be granted, at law or in equity, unless it remains executory, or unless the parties are considered not in equal fault, or where there has been fraud or oppression on the part of the defendant.[3]

§ 139. *Instances where power to lease denied.*— Where the charter of a corporation only empowers it to sell the

[1] Visalia Gas & E. L. Co. v. Sims, 104 Cal. 326.
[2] St. Louis R. Co. v. Terre Haute R. Co., 145 U. S. 393; Thomas v. Railroad Co., 101 U. S. 71; Pennsylvania, etc. R. Co. v. St. Louis, etc. R. Co., 118 U. S. 290, 630; Oregon Ry. v. Oregonian Ry., 130 U. S. 1; Central Trans. Co. v. Pullman Co., 139 U. S. 24.
[3] St. Louis R. Co. v. Terre Haute R. Co., 145 U. S. 393; Thomas v. Richmond, 12 Wall. (U. S.) 349, 355; Spring Co. v. Knowlton, 103 U. S. 49; Story, Eq. Jur., § 298; Penn. R. Co. v. St. Louis R. Co., 118 U. S. 290; Union Trust Co. v. Illinois, etc. Co., 117 U. S. 434.

real estate necessary for the transaction of its business when not required for the uses of the corporation, it cannot lease such real estate nor maintain an action for rent under the lease, such leasing not being necessary to the exercise of the purposes for which the charter was given.[1] An unauthorized lease made by the officers of a corporation is void, and the acquiescence of the corporation is not to be inferred from silence merely.[2] So directors of one company, who are also directors of another which owns two-fifths of the stock of the former, cannot properly vote to lease the former company to the latter.[3] The holders of a majority of the capital stock of a corporation, by their votes in a stockholders' meeting, cannot lawfully authorize the officers to lease its property to themselves, or to another corporation formed for the purpose, and exclusively owned by them, unless such lease is made in good faith and is supported by an adequate consideration.[4]

§ 140. *Power to mortgage its road and property.*—The broad rule that the power of a corporation to mortgage its property is dependent upon the general right of disposal[5] cannot be applied to railroad or other *quasi*-public corporations, as by this means they could abandon the duties they owe to the public and disable themselves from such performance. The power to mortgage, like a power to lease the property and franchises of a railroad corporation, must be given by charter or by statute.[6]

[1] Metropolitan Concert Co. v. Abbey, 52 N. Y. Sup. Ct. 97.
[2] Kersey Oil Co. v. Oil Creek R. Co., 12 Phila. (Pa.) 374.
[3] Bill v. Western U. Tel. Co., 16 Fed. Rep. 143.
[4] Meeker v. Winthrop Iron Co., 17 Fed. Rep. 48.
[5] §§ 83, 84 *ab ante.*
[6] See § 137 and cases cited.

§ 141. *Power to mortgage or transfer its franchises.*— It is now well settled that a railroad corporation cannot mortgage, sell or transfer its franchises unless express authority is given so to do.[1] This power is denied on the hypothesis that a corporation is an artificial being which only the law can create, and when created it cannot transfer its own existence into another body, nor can it enable natural persons to act in its name, save as its agents or as members of the corporation acting in conformity with the modes required or allowed by its charter.[2] As a consequence of this principle, the franchise of a corporation cannot be levied upon by execution, although the property of the corporation may be taken.[3] Where authority to mortgage its franchises by a corporation is given, such authority necessarily implies the power to bring the franchises so mortgaged to sale, and to transfer them with the corporeal property of the company to the purchaser.[4] Where a mortgage or transfer of franchises is made, however, without legislative authority, it may be ratified by subsequent enactment, and such ratification in reality constitutes a grant of franchises.[5] There has been a distinction declared, however, between a franchise *to be a corporation and a franchise as a corporation to maintain and*

[1] Thomp. Corp., §§ 6137-6144; Beach, Priv. Corp., § 389; Home v. Freeman, 14 Gray (Mass.), 566; Shaw v. Norfolk Ry., 5 Gray (Mass.), 162; Staten v. Morgan, 28 La. Ann. 482. And see cases cited in § 137.

[2] See cases in preceding note.

[3] Gue v. Canal Co., 24 How. (U. S.) 257; Randolph v. Larned, 27 N. J. Eq. 557; Stewart v. Jones, 40 Mo. 140; Susquehanna Canal Co. v. Bonham, 9 W. & S. (Pa.) 27.

[4] New Orleans, etc. Co. v. Delamore, 114 U. S. 501; Memphis R. Co. v. Commissioners, 112 U. S. 609, 623; Galveston v. Cowdrey, 11 Wall. (U. S.) 459.

[5] 8 Am. & Eng. Ency. Law, 634d; Richards v. Merrimack R. Co., 44 N. H. 127; Shaw v. Norfolk Co., 5 Gray (Mass.), 162; Pollard v. Maddox, 28 Ala. 321.

operate a railway; the latter may be mortgaged without the former, and may pass to a purchaser at a foreclosure sale. But such mortgage confers no right upon purchasers at foreclosure sale to exist as the same corporation; if it confers any right of corporate existence upon them, it is only a right to reorganize as a corporation, subject to laws existing at the time of reorganization.[1]

§ 142. *Consolidation and amalgamation — Definition.* — The "consolidation" of a corporation has been defined to be "a surrender of the old charters by the companies, the acceptance thereof by the legislature, and the formation of a new corporation out of such portions of the old as enter into the new."[2] The more modern understanding of a consolidation, however, might be better stated by saying that when the rights, franchises and effects of

---

[1] Memphis R. Co. v. Commissioners, 112 U. S. 609; Railroad Co. v. Georgia, 98 U. S. 359; Eldridge v. Smith, 34 Vt. 484.

In Eldridge v. Smith, *supra*, the court say: "When a railroad company mortgages its road and appurtenances as a security for debt, and also its franchise, it is not to be understood as conveying its corporate existence or its general corporate powers, but only the franchise necessary to make the conveyance productive and beneficial to the grantees, to maintain and support, manage and operate the railroad, and receive the tolls and profits therefor for their own benefit. If it were held that all the corporate franchises, including the power of corporate existence, were conveyed by the mortgage, the conclusion would seem to be logical that, on breach and foreclosure, the mortgagees would step into the shoes of the company and merely succeed to their rights in the property, and also to their corporate liabilities — a result by no means favorable to their interests. Or, if it were held that the mortgagees did not succeed to the corporate existence and functions of the railroad company, and that they did not remain in the company, then it must operate as a dissolution of the company, and lands taken compulsorily for their road would revert to the owners in fee."

[2] State v. Bailey, 16 Ind. 46; Lauman v. Lebanon Valley R. Co., 30 Pa. St. 42.

two or more corporations are by legal authority and agreement of the parties combined and united into one whole, and committed to a single corporation, the stockholders of which are composed of those of the companies thus agreeing, this is in law a consolidation, whether the consolidated company be a new one then created, or one of the original companies continuing in existence with only larger rights, capacities and property.[1] "Amalgamation" has been declared to be when the existing companies agree to abandon their respective articles of association and regulation, and to register themselves under new articles as one body. This would be a new company formed by the coalition or amalgamation of the companies previously existing.[2] The expression "amalgamation," however, is of English origin, has never appealed to the judicial sense of this country, and is seldom used to designate the union of two or more corporations, the word "consolidation" being the term in common use.[3]

[1] Meyer v. Johnston, 64 Ala. 603; Houston & Tex. Cent. R. R. v. Shirley, 54 Tex. 125, 4 Am. & Eng. Ency. of Law, 272.

[2] In re Bank of Hindustan, 2 Hen. & M. 66, L. R. 5 Ch. 400; Clinch v. Financial Corp., 4 Ch. App. 117; In re Empire Assurance Corp., L. R. 4 Eq. 341.

[3] In Meyer v. Johnston, *supra*, Manning, J., in discussing the adoption of the word "amalgamate," says: "In its origin and use it is peculiarly technical. It pertains especially to the arts, and belongs to the language of physical science; and inasmuch as by amalgamation, as ordinarily understood, a material product results which, by transfusion into it of the properties and qualities of the two or more material things from whose union it proceeds, partakes of the nature of each, and is yet unlike either, it is not surprising that English judges have had trouble in perceiving the appropriateness of the word to not a few of the cases of united corporations that have come before them. When parties and parliament, in providing for the union of two or more corporations, passed by familiar words that were not inapplicable, and have a broader meaning — such as combination, conjunction, association, union, coalition, consolida-

§ 143. *Power of companies to consolidate.*— It is well settled that corporations can only consolidate with the consent and authority of the legislature.[1] Such authority to consolidate may be conferred in the original charter,[2] or by the provisions of a general or special act of the legislature,[3] or, it has been held, even by the express sanction of an unauthorized agreement.[4] But such consolidation to be valid must obtain the assent of the legislature either by express grant or necessary implication.[5] Accordingly, it was held in a leading American case that where two separate corporations were created to build railroads, they had no right, without express authority, to unite and conduct their business under one management, nor to establish a steamboat line to run in connection with railroads.[6] So, in the absence of authority conferred by the charter, an agreement between directors of corporations to consolidate and merge the two into a new corporation is *ultra vires*, although such invalid agreement has been partly performed.[7]

tion — and selected, as expressive of their purpose, so technical a term as 'amalgamation,' judges felt constrained to preserve, as far as possible, its original and peculiar signification, in their new application of it to legal subjects."

[1] International R. Co. v. Bremond, 53 Tex. 96; Charlton v. New Castle R. Co., 5 Jur. (N. S.) 1096; State v. Bailey, 16 Ind. 46; Central Ry. Co. v. Georgia, 40 Ga. 582; s. c., 92 U. S. 665; State v. Green Co., 54 Mo. 540; Denike v. Lime Co., 80 N. Y. 599; s. c., 5 Fed. Rep. 19; Shields v. Ohio, 95 U. S. 319; Sharon Coal Co. v. Fulton Bank, 7 Wend. 412; Pearce v. Madison R. Co., 21 How. (U. S.) 441.

[2] Nugent v. Supervisors, 19 Wall. (U. S.) 241.

[3] Bishop v. Brainerd, 28 Conn. 289; Black v. Canal Co., 22 N. J. Eq. 130; Southall v. Insurance Co., L. R. 11 Eq. 65.

[4] McAuley v. Columbus R. Co., 83 Ill. 348; Mead v. N. Y. etc. R. Co., 45 Conn. 199.

[5] Fisher v. Evansville R. Co., 7 Ind. 407.

[6] Pearce v. Madison, etc. R. Co., 21 How. (U. S.) 441.

[7] Greenville Compress v. Planters' Press, 70 Miss. 669.

§ 144.] RAILROAD CORPORATIONS. 195

§ 144. *Effect of consolidation.*— The effect of consolidating two or more corporations has been variously stated by different courts. Declaring that one of the companies loses its actual identity, abandons its name, and therefore its legal identity and its corporate existence, and can no longer claim any legal recognition; that such a merger is a dissolution destroying the actual identity of both, while the legal identity of one of them is preserved.[1] That such consolidation or amalgamation works a dissolution of the corporations previously existing, and at the same instant creates a new corporation, with property, liabilities and stockholders derived from those passing out of existence.[2]

[1] Lauman v. Lebanon Valley R. Co., 30 Pa. St. 42.
[2] Miller & Mississippi, etc. R. Co. v. Lancaster, 5 Coldw. (Tenn.) 514; Clearwater v. Meredith, 1 Wall. (U. S.) 40; Mowrey v. Indiana, etc. R. Co., 4 Biss. (U. S.) 85: State v. Railroad Co., 66 Me. 488; Shields v. Ohio, 95 U. S. 324; Railroad Co. v. Georgia, 98 U. S. 359; Central R. Co. v. Georgia, 92 U. S. 665; State v. Sherman, 22 Ohio St. 411; State ex rel. Wine v. Keokuk, etc. R. Co., 99 Mo. 30; Maine Cent. R. Co. v. Maine, 96 U. S. 499; Atlantic, etc. R. Co. v. State, 55 Ga. 312; Railway Co. v. Berry, 113 U. S. 465; Memphis, etc. R. Co. v. Railroad Comm., 112 U. S. 609; Railroad Co. v. Palmes, 109 U. S. 244; Keokuk, etc. R. Co. v. State, 152 U. S. 301; Edison E. L. Co. v. New Haven E. L. Co., 35 Fed. Rep. 233; Bank v. Colby, 21 Wall. (U. S.) 609; Pomeroy v. Bank, 1 Wall. (U. S.) 23; Racine R. Co. v. Farmers' L. & T. Co., 49 Ill. 331; Houston R. Co. v. Shirley, 54 Tex. 125; Ferguson v. Meredith, 1 Wall. (U. S.) 25; Fee v. Gas Co., 35 La. Ann. 413; Gas Co. v. Manufacturing Co., 115 U. S. 697.

In Railroad Co. v. Georgia, 98 U. S. 359, Mr. Justice Strong, in referring to the act under which the respective companies were empowered to consolidate their stocks, and discussing the effect of such consolidation, said:

"It is conceded that under this act a consolidation took place. It is therefore a vital question, What was its effect? Did the consolidated companies become a new corporation, holding its powers and privileges as such under the act of 1863? Or was the consolidation a mere alliance between two pre-existing corporations, in which each preserved its identity and distinctive existence? Or, still fur-

That the effect of consolidation upon former companies, except so far as the contrary may be provided by statute, is to dissolve all the old corporations and to create a new one, assuming the liabilities and succeeding to the rights

ther, was it an absorption of one by another, whereby the former was dissolved, while the latter continued to exist? The answer to these inquiries must be found in the intention of the legislature as expressed in the consolidating act. We think that intention was the creation of a new corporation out of the stockholders of the two previously existing companies. The consolidation provided for was clearly not a merger of one into the other, as was the case of Central Railroad & Banking Co. v. Georgia, 92 U. S. 665. Nor was it a mere alliance or confederation of the two. If it had been, each would have preserved its separate existence as well as its corporate name. But the act authorized the consolidation of the stocks of the two companies, thus making one capital in place of two. It contemplated, therefore, that the separate capital of each company should go out of existence as the capital of that company; and, if so, how could either have a construed separate being? True, the proviso to the first section declared that nothing therein contained should relieve or discharge either of the companies from any contract theretofore entered into by either, adding: 'But this company (that is, the company created by the act) shall be liable on the same.'

"It is thus distinguished between the two original companies and the one contemplated to be formed by this consolidation. And the proviso would have been quite unnecessary had it not been thought by the legislature that the consolidation would work a dissolution of the amalgamated companies. Hence it was considered necessary to preserve the rights of parties who might have contracted with them. Only their contracts were mentioned in the proviso, and that in order to authorize a novation. . . . Looking thus at the legislative intent appearing in the consolidation act, we are constrained to the conclusion that a new corporation was created by the consolidation effected thereunder in the place and in lieu of the two companies previously existing, and that whatever franchises, immunities or privileges it possesses it holds them solely by virtue of the grant that act made. That generally the effect of consolidation, as distinguished from a union by merger of one company into another, is to work a dissolution of the companies consolidating, of the old companies.¹ That the consolidation of two companies does not necessarily work a dissolution of both, and the creation of a new corporation. Whether such be its effect is dependent upon the legislative intent manifested in the statute under which the consolidation takes place.² That consolidation is not a sale, and when two companies are authorized to consolidate their roads it is to be presumed that the franchises and privileges of each continue to exist in respect to the several roads so consolidated.³ And that upon such consolidation the business of the old corporations is not wound up, nor their property sequestered or disturbed; but the very object of the consolidation, and of the statutes which permit it, is to continue the business of the old corporation. Whether

and to create a new corporation out of the elements of the former, is asserted in many cases, and it seems to be a necessary result. . . . When as in this case the stock of two companies is consolidated, the stockholders become partners, or *quasi*-partners, in a new concern. Each set of stockholders is shorn of the power which, as a body, it had before. Its action is controlled by a power outside of itself. To illustrate: The stockholders of the Savannah & Albany Railroad Company could not, after consolidation, have exercised any of the powers or franchises they had prior to their consolidation with the stockholders of the Atlantic & Gulf Railroad Company. They could not have built their road or controlled its management. They could not, therefore, have performed the duties which by their original charter were imposed upon them. . . . Their powers, their franchises and their privileges were therefore gone, no longer capable of exercise or enjoyment. Gone where? Into the new organization, the consolidated company, which exists alone by virtue of the legislative grant, and which has all its powers, facilities and privileges by virtue of the consolidation act."

[1] McMahan v. Morrison, 16 Ind. 172; Paine v. Lake Erie, etc. Co., 31 Ind. 283; Zimmer v. State, 30 Ark. 677; Robertson v. Rockford, 21 Ill. 451; Railroad Co. v. Maine, 96 U. S. 499; Thompson v. Abbott, 61 Mo. 176; Chicago, etc. Co. v. Moffitt, 75 Ill. 524.
[2] Central R. Co. v. Georgia, 92 U. S. 665.
[3] Green Co. v. Conness, 109 U. S. 104.

the old corporations are dissolved in the new corporation, or are continued in existence under a new name and with new powers, and whether in either case the consolidated company takes the property of each of the old corporations charged with a lien for the payment of the debts of that corporation, depends upon the terms of the agreement of consolidation and the statutes under whose authority the consolidation is effected.[1]

§ 145. *Effect of interstate consolidation.* — In general, the *status* of a consolidated company, formed by the union or consolidation of two or more companies of different states, is an association incorporated in and by each of the states, and where acting as a corporation in either of the states, it acts under the authority of the charter of the state in which it is then acting, and that only, the legislation of the other states having no operation beyond its territorial limits.[2] Nor does the consolidation of the stock of two companies of different states constitute the corporations thus consolidated one corporation of both states, or of either, but the corporation of each state continues a corporation of the state of its creation, although the same persons, as officers and directors, manage and control both corporations as one body. Such a consolidation does not convert the respective corporations into one company in the same way and to the same degree that might follow a consolidation of two companies within the same state.[3] So, where two corporations of different

[1] Wabash, St. Louis, etc. Co. v. Ham, 114 U. S. 587.

[2] Quincy Bridge Co. v. Adams Co., 88 Ill. 615; Attorney-General v. Boston, etc. R. Co., 109 Mass. 99; Bridge Co. v. Metz, 32 N. J. L. 199; McGregor v. Erie, etc. R. Co., 35 N. J. L. 115, Id. 89; Chicago, etc. Co. v. Chicago, etc. R. Co., 6 Biss. 219; Sprague v. Hartford, etc. Co., 5 R. I. 233.

[3] Racine, etc. R. Co. v. Farmers,' etc. Co., 49 Ill. 331; Ohio, etc. R.

states are consolidated by virtue of acts of assembly of the two states, the consolidated company is subject to the control of each state as far as concerns its property and business therein,[1] and is to be treated in each state as a domestic corporation.[2] And where two corporations of different states are consolidated under lawful authority, one of which was subject in one state to a mortgage prior to such consolidation, the courts of the other state do not thereby acquire jurisdiction so as to enforce a foreclosure of the mortgage.[3]

§ 146. *Rights and liabilities of consolidated company.*— As a general rule a consolidated company has all the rights and powers and is subject to all the liabilities of the various corporations of which it may be composed.[4] Accordingly, it may take advantage of all contracts and

Co. v. Wheeler, 1 Blackf. (U. S.) 297; Farnum v. Canal Co., 1 Sumn. (U. S.) 46; Delaware Tax Cases, 18 Wall. (U. S.) 206.

[1] Peck v. Chicago & N. W. R. Co., 94 U. S. 164.

[2] Sage v. Lake Shore, etc. R. Co., 70 N. Y. 220.

[3] Eaton, etc. Co. v. Hunt, 20 Ind. 457.

[4] Philadelphia v. Ridge Ave. etc. R. Co., 143 Pa. St. 444, 102 Pa. St. 190; Root v. Oil Creek, etc. Co., 31 Phila. Leg. 140; Lake Shore, etc. Co. v. Hutchins, 37 Ohio St. 282; Coyley v. Coburg, etc. Co., 14 Grant's Cas. (Pa.) 571; Cashman v. Brownlee, 128 Ind. 266; Ridge Ave. etc. Co. v. Philadelphia, 124 Pa. St. 219; McAlpine v. Union Pac. Co., 23 Fed. Rep. 168, 129 U. S. 305; Warren v. Mobile, etc. Co., 49 Ala. 582; New Bedford, etc. Co. v. Old Colony Co., 120 Mass. 397; Marsh v. New York, etc. Co., 45 Conn. 199; Paine v. Lake Erie, etc. Co., 31 Ind. 283; Chicago, etc. Coal Co. v. Hall, 34 N. E. Rep. 704; Western, etc. Co. v. Smith, 75 Ill. 497; Joy v. St. Louis, 138 U. S. 1; Whipple v. Union Pac. R. Co., 28 Kan. 474; Louisville, etc. Co. v. Boney, 117 Ind. 501; Cleveland, etc. Co. v. Prewitt, 33 N. E. Rep. 367; Indianapolis, etc. Co. v. Jones, 29 Ind. 465; Columbus, etc. Co. v. Powell, 40 Ind. 37; Chicago, etc. Co. v. Moffitt, 75 Ill. 524; Coggin v. Central R. Co., 62 Ga. 685; State v. Baltimore, etc. R. Co., 77 Md. 489; Northern Cent. R. Co. v. Drew, 3 Woods (U. S.), 391; Smith v. Los Angeles, etc. Co., 78 Cal. 289.

enforce all debts of the old companies.¹ So a consolidated company is liable for all torts committed by the companies of which it is composed, prior to consolidation.² The presumption is, however, that where two companies are consolidated, each of them will be respectively held with the privileges and burdens originally attaching thereto, unless the contrary is expressed.³ But where one corporation goes entirely out of existence by being consolidated or merged into another, and no arrangements are made respecting the property and liabilities of the extinguished corporation, the newly-created one will be entitled to all the property.⁴ And where the indebtedness of an old company has not ripened into a lien, the effect of consolidation with another is to release the former of all indebtedness where the latter becomes the proprietor of the property and franchises of the former.⁵

§ 147. *Consolidation as affecting stockholders.*— As a general rule stockholders are not bound by an act of consolidation without their consent.⁶ The relation between

¹ Atchison, etc. R. Co. v. Commissioners, 25 Kan. 261; Niantic Sav. Bank v. Douglas, 5 Ill. App. 579; Powell v. North. Mo. R. R. Co., 42 Mo. 63.

² Chicago, etc. Co. v. Moffitt, 75 Ill. 524; Coggin v. Central R. Co., 62 Ga. 685; New Bedford R. Co. v. Old Colony R. Co., 120 Mass. 397.

³ Tomlinson v. Branch, 15 Wall. (U. S.) 460; New Jersey, etc. Ry. Co. v. Straight, 35 N. J. L. 322; Fisher v. New York, etc. Co., 46 N. Y. 644; Rome, etc. R. Co. v. Ontario, etc. Co., 16 Hun (N. Y.), 445; Railroad Co. v. Maine, 96 U. S. 497; Philadelphia, etc. R. Co. v. Maryland, 10 How. (U. S.) 376.

⁴ Thompson v. Abbott, 61 Mo. 176; Lightner v. Boston, etc. R. Co., 1 Low. (U. S.) 338; County of Scotland v. Thomas, 94 U. S. 682; State v. Green Co., 54 Mo. 540; Nugent v. Supervisors, 19 Wall. (U. S.) 241.

⁵ Bruffett v. Great Western R. Co., 25 Ill. 353.

⁶ McCray v. Junction, etc. R. Co., 9 Ind. 358; Campbell's Case, 8 Eng. Rep. 678; Clearwater v. Meredith, 1 Wall. (U. S.) 25; State v.

a stockholder and a corporation is one of contract, and any legislative enactment authorizing a material change in the powers or purposes of a corporation not in aid of the original object, if acted upon by the corporation, is not binding upon the stockholder without his consent.[1] Accordingly, stockholders of the old corporations who do not enter into the new are entitled to withdraw their shares and may enjoin until they are secured.[2] The reasons why non-consenting shareholders are not bound by such act of consolidation are forcibly and clearly stated by Mr. Justice Lowrie in *Lauman v. Lebanon R. Co., supra.* He there said: "The dissentiate shareholder may object that his co-corporators have no power to make a new contract for him and thereby constitute him a member of a new and different corporation; for it is of the very nature of a contract relation that it can be instituted only by real parties to it, unless it be a mere constructive contract, which is only a convenient form or fiction of law, invented to enforce a corresponding legal duty. He may object that even the legislature cannot authorize this, for by so doing they would authorize the destruction of one private contract and the compulsory creation of another in its stead, and would take away the remedy by due course of law which the dissenting shareholder is entitled to because of the departure or the diversion of the association from its agreed purposes; and would, besides this, change the essential nature of contracts, which even legislative power cannot do, and much less legislative authority."

Bailey, 16 Ind. 46; Spering's Appeal, 71 Pa. St. 11; Lauman v. Lebanon R. Co., 30 Pa. St. 42.

[1] McCray v. Junction Ry., 9 Ind. 358.
[2] State v. Bailey, 16 Ind. 46; Spering's Appeal, 71 Pa. St. 11; Clearwater v. Meredith, 1 Wall. (U. S.) 25.

§ 148. *Consolidation as affecting taxation.*— When two corporations are consolidated into one by act of the legislature, an exemption from taxation contained in the charter of one of such corporations will not, by such consolidation, be extended to the property of the other, whose charter contained no such exemption, which by the consolidation became joint property; and in the absence of a clear expression of intent to the contrary, the property of each of the united corporations will be held, after such consolidation, with the same privileges and burdens as ordinarily attached thereto.[1] So where two or more corporations, subjected to a special tax upon the net income of their roads, with immunity from other taxation, the amount of such special tax being dependent upon reports to be made and information to be communicated by their directors and other officers, are consolidated into a new corporation with different directors and other officers, who are neither bound nor able to make reports and give the information required of the original companies, the new corporation thus created is not entitled to the immunity of the original corporations from general taxation.[2] But where two railroad corporations whose shares are, by a state statute, exempt from taxation in the state, consolidate themselves into a new company under a state law, which makes no provision to the contrary, and issues shares in the new company in exchange for shares in the old company, the right of exemption from taxation in the state passes into the new shares, and into each of them.[3] The same is true where three rail-

---

[1] State v. Commissioners, 37 N. J. L. 228; Philadelphia, etc. Co. v. Maryland, 10 How. (U. S.) 376; Tomlinson v. Branch, 15 Wall. (U. S.) 460; Delaware Tax Cases, 18 Wall. (U. S.) 206; Central Railroad v. Georgia, 92 U. S. 665; Branch v. Charleston, 92 U. S. 677.

[2] Railroad Co. v. Maine, 96 U. S. 499.

[3] Tennessee v. Whitworth, 117 U. S. 129.

roads consolidate, one of which is a corporation of another state, unless the law of that state makes provision to the contrary.[1]

§ 149. *"Trusts" or illegal combinations.*— A "trust" may be defined to be a voluntary association by and between the stockholders of two or more corporations, engaged in a like business, to contribute their stock shares and agree to share the profits of such business on all the shares when placed in a common fund, agreeing indirectly also to share the losses naturally falling upon stockholders in other companies in which no profits are made.[2] Such a trust or combination is usually consummated by an agreement where all or a majority of the stockholders of a corporation transfer their stock to certain trustees, in consideration of the agreement of the stockholders of other companies and of the members of limited partnerships engaged in the same business to do likewise; by which agreement all are to receive, in lieu of their stocks and interests so transferred, trust certificates, to be issued by the trustees, equal at par to the par value of their stock and interests; and by which the trustees are empowered, as apparent owners of the stock, to elect directors of the several companies, and thereby control their affairs in the interests of the trust so created; and are to receive all dividends made by the several companies and limited partnerships, from which, as a common fund, dividends are to be made by the trustees to the holders of the trust certificates. Such a trust or combination entered into by corporations has been held as tending to create a monopoly, to control production as well as prices, and is against public policy, illegal and void.[3]

[1] Pearce v. Madison, etc. R. Co., 21 How. (U. S.) 441; Balfour v. Ernest, 5 C. B. (N. S.) 691, 28 L. J. (C. P.) 170.
[2] The Legality of Trusts, p. 621, by Theodore W. Dwight.
[3] State v. Standard Oil Co., 49 Ohio St. 137; American Preserves

Trust v. Taylor Mfg. Co., 46 Fed. Rep. 152; People v. Chicago Gas Trust, 130 Ill. 268; Emery et al. v. Ohio Candle Co., 24 N. E. Rep. 660; Richardson v. Buhl, 77 Mich. 632; People v. North River Sugar Refining Co., 121 N. Y. 582; Mallory v. Hannauer Oil Works, 86 Tenn. 598; New York, etc. Canal Co. v. Fulton Bank, 7 Wend. (N. Y.) 412; Clearwater v. Meredith, 1 Wall. 29; Whittenton Mills v. Upton, 10 Gray (Mass.), 582.

In People v. The North River Sugar Refining Co., *supra*, in a general discussion of this subject, the court say:

"It remains to determine whether the conduct of the defendant in participating in the creation of the trust, and becoming an element of it, was illegal, and tended to the public injury; and we may consider the two questions together, and without formal separation. It is quite clear that the effect of the defendant's action was to divest itself of the essential and vital elements of its franchise by placing them in trust; to accept from the state the gift of corporate life, only to disregard the conditions on which it was given; to receive its powers and privileges merely to put them in pawn; and to give away to an irresponsible board its entire independence and self-control. When it had passed into the hands of the trust, only the shell of a corporation was left standing as a seeming obedience to the law, but with its internal structure destroyed or removed. Its stockholders, retaining their beneficial interests, have separated from it their voting powers, and so parted with the control which the charter gave them and the state required them to exercise. It has a board of directors nominally and formally in office, but qualified by shares which they do not own, and owning their official life to the board which can end their power at any moment of disobedience. It can make no dividends, whatever may be its net earnings, and must incumber its property at the command of its master, and for purposes wholly foreign to its own corporate interests and duties. At the command of that master it has ceased to refine sugar, and, without any doubt, for the purpose of so far lessening the market supply as to prevent what is termed 'overproduction.' In all these respects it has wasted and prevented the privileges conferred by the charter, abused its powers, and proved unfaithful to its duties. But graver still is the illegal action substituted for the conduct which the state has a right to expect and require. It has helped to create an anomalous trust, which is, in substance and effect, a partnership of twenty separate corporations. The state permits in many ways an aggregation of capital, but, mindful of the possible dangers to the people, overbalancing the benefits, keeps upon it a restraining hand.

and maintains over it a prudent supervision, where such aggregation depends upon the permission and grows out of corporate grants. It is a violation of law for corporations to enter into partnerships. . . . That the combination of the refineries partakes of the nature of a partnership is not denied. Indeed, in one of the papers added to the appellant's brief, it is not only admitted, but asserted and defended. This paper shows quite clearly that by force of the arrangement there was a community of interest in the fund created by the corporate earnings before division, and that each member of the trust shared in the profit and loss of all. It is said, however, that a consolidation of manufacturing corporations is permitted by the law, and that the trust or combination or partnership, however it may be described, amounts only to a practical consolidation, which public policy does not forbid, because the state permits it. . . . The refineries did not avail themselves of the statute. They chose to disregard it, and to reach its practical results without subjecting them to the prudential restraints with which the state accompanied its permission. If there had been a consolidation under the statute, one single corporation would have taken the place of the others dissolved. They would have disappeared utterly, and not, as under the trust, remained in apparent existence to threaten and menace other organizations, and occupy the ground which otherwise would be left free. Under the statute, the resultant combination would itself be a corporation deriving its existence from the state, owing duties and obligations to the state, and subject to the control and supervision of the state; and not, as here, an unincorporated board, a colossal and gigantic partnership having no corporate functions and owing no corporate allegiance. Under the statute, the consolidated, taking the place of the separate, corporations, could have capital stock only in an amount equal to the fair aggregate value of the rights and franchises of the companies absorbed; and not, as here, a capital stock double that value at the outset, and capable of an elastic and irresponsible increase. The difference is very great, and serves further to indicate the inherent illegality of the trust combination.

"And here I think we gain a definite view of the injurious tendencies developed by its organization and operation, and of the public interests which are menaced by its action. As corporate grants are always assumed to have been made for the public benefit, any conduct which destroys their nominal functions, and maims and cripples their separate activity and takes away their free and independent action, must so far disappoint the purpose of their creation as to affect unfavorably the public interests; and that to a much greater extent when, beyond their own several aggregations of capital, they compact them all into one combination which stands outside the ward of the state, which dominates the range of an entire industry and puts upon the market a capital stock proudly defiant of actual value and capable of an unlimited expansion. It is not a sufficient answer to say that similar results may be lawfully accomplished, that an individual having the necessary wealth might have bought all their refineries, manned them with his own chosen agents and managed them as a group at his sovereign will; for it is one thing for the state to respect the rights of ownership and protect them out of regard to the business freedom of the citizen, and quite another thing to add to that possibility of further extension of those consequences by creating artificial persons to aid in producing such aggregations. The individuals are few who hold in possession such enormous wealth, and fewer still who peril it all in a manufacturing enterprise; but if corporations can combine and mass their fortunes in a solid trust or partnership, with little added risk to the capital already embarked, without limit to the magnitude of the aggregation, a tempting and early road is opened to enormous combinations vastly exceeding in number and in strength and in their power over industry any possibilities of individual ownership; and the state, by the creation of the artificial persons constituting the elements of the combination, and failing to limit and restrain their power, becomes itself the responsible creator, the voluntary cause, of an aggregation of capital which it simply endures in the individual as the product of its free agency. What it may bear is one thing; what it should cause and create is quite another."

CHAPTER X.

THE DOCTRINE IN ITS RELATION TO DIRECTORS AND OTHER OFFICERS AND AGENTS OF CORPORATIONS.

§ 150. Introductory.
151. Distinction between corporate acts and unauthorized acts of directors.
152. Test to distinguish acts of directors from corporate acts.
153. Directors as trustees.
154. General powers of directors.
155. Instances of directors' powers.
156. General liability of directors.
157. Power of bank directors.
158. Liability of bank directors.
159. Powers and liabilities of bank president.
160. Powers and duties of bank cashier.
161. Instances of cashier's powers.

§ 150. *Introductory.*— In the adjudications by the courts of the various questions arising out of the dealings and business transactions of corporations in this country, the unauthorized acts and contracts of the directors and other agents of the corporation have been so frequently confounded and regarded as the acts and contracts of the corporation itself, thereby involving the doctrine of *ultra vires* in a maze of uncertainty and confusion, that it is deemed proper to give some attention and devote some space to the examination of the office and powers of this very numerous class of corporate representatives.

§ 151. *Distinction between corporate acts and unauthorized acts of directors.*— Much of the unintelligible confusion which has arisen in many of the state courts in the application of the doctrine of *ultra vires* is the result of confounding the distinction between a corporation and its directors or other representatives. To properly apply this doctrine and arrive at its legitimate construction, such distinction should be carefully observed and kept steadily in mind, to avoid confusion. Ordinarily, the managing officers or directors of a corporation and the corporation itself are regarded as identical; and as the acts of such officers or directors, when within the scope of the corporate powers, are held to be the acts of the corporation itself, the former is often meant when the latter is mentioned, and the acts of the one confounded with the acts of the other. As was remarked in one of the opening paragraphs of this work, a corporation is an ideal person, intangible, invisible, and, to a certain extent, is invested with the elements of immutability.[1] The directors are simply the agents of the corporation, and when their acts are confined within the limits of the agency they are a perfect representative. Beyond that — acts committed *ultra vires* the corporation — their actions may be regarded as unlawful usurpations. The charter of the corporation may properly be said to be its constitution, and the powers therein recited the limit of its authority. Whatever may be attempted, therefore, outside the scope of its prescribed powers, is not the act of the corporation — the ideal person — but is the unauthorized act of the agent. As the corporation can act only by law, the logical deduction would be that whatever it does must be lawful. *A priori*, that which is unlawful, because made so by the law of its creation, is not the act or deed of the corporation, but is a wrong or usurpation of those who falsely act in its name.[2]

---

[1] See § 2, *ante.*

[2] In Bank of United States v. Dandridge, 12 Wheat. 64, the court say: "It is most manifest that the corporation is altogether a distinct body from the directors, possessing all the general powers and

§ 152. *Test to distinguish acts of directors from corporate acts.*— To distinguish the acts of a corporation from the unauthorized acts of the directors, a test has been very clearly laid down by Vice-chancellor Wickens in the case of *Pickering v. Stephenson*, L. R. 14 Eq. 340. The learned vice-chancellor, in discussing the powers which directors may exercise, said: "To distinguish unauthorized acts of directors from those of the corporation, the test is whether the acts performed or the contracts entered into are for purposes which are reasonably incidental to the carrying on of the business of the company. To arrive at this determination, the charter, which is the constitution of the corporation, and the law under which it is organized, must be consulted. *Bona fides* cannot be the sole test; otherwise, it is truly said, you might have a lunatic conducting the affairs of the company, and paying away its money with both hands in a manner perfectly *bona fide*, yet perfectly irrational. The test must be what is reasonably incidental and within the reasonable scope of carrying on the business of the company."

attributes of an aggregate corporation, and entitled to direct and superintend the management of its own property and the government of the institution, and to enact by-laws for this purpose. So far as the act delegates authority to the directors, the latter possess it, and may exercise it, not as constituting the corporation itself, but as its express statutory agents to act in the ordinary business of the institution. The directors are created a board, and not a corporate body. If the authority delegated to them can only be expressed by them when assembled as a board, with a proper quorum, and not by the separate assent of a majority of the whole body, still it is clear that their meeting and acts are but the meetings and acts of a board of agents acting *ex officio*, and not the meetings and acts of the corporation itself. The whole structure of the charter, and the whole proceedings under it, as well as the by-laws and regulations which have come under our review, demonstrate that this has been the uniform construction of the corporation itself and of the directors."

§ 153. *Directors as trustees.*—The relation of a director to the stockholders of the corporation is generally regarded as analogous to the position of a trustee towards his *cestui que trust*.¹ This statement of his relation, however, must be taken with some modification, as, technically, there is an essential distinction between a director and a trustee, which has been stated as follows: "A trustee is a man who is the owner of property and deals with it as a principal, as owner, and as master, subject only to an equitable obligation to account to some persons to whom he stands in the relation of trustee, and who are his *cestui que trust*. The same individual may fill the office of director and also be a trustee having property, but that is rare, exceptional, and a casual circumstance. The office of director is that of a paid-servant of the company. A director never enters into a contract himself, but he enters into contracts for his principal, that is, for the company of whom he is a director, and for whom he is acting. He cannot sue on such contracts, nor be sued on them unless he exceeds his authority. That seems to be the broad distinction between trustees and directors."²

¹ Cumberland, etc. Co. v. Parish, 42 Md. 598; Aberdeen R. Co. v. Blaikie, 1 Macq. (H. L.) 461; Great Luxembourg R. Co. v. Magnay, 25 Beav. 586; Hoffman, etc. Co. v. Cumberland, etc. Co., 16 Md. 456; s. c., 20 Md. 117; Attorney-General v. Wilson, 1 Craig & P. 1; Benson v. Heathorn, 1 Younge & C. 326; York, etc. R. Co. v. Hudson, 16 Beav. 495; Hoyle v. Plattsburg, etc. R. Co., 54 N. Y. 314; European, etc. R. Co. v. Poor, 59 Me. 277; Ency. Law, vol. 17, p. 91, and cases cited; Spering's Appeal, 71 Pa. St. 11.

² Smith v. Anderson, 15 Ch. Div. 275.

In Spering's Appeal, *supra*, Sharswood, J., speaking for the court, says: "It is by no means a well-settled point what is the precise relation which directors sustain to stockholders. They are undoubtedly said in many authorities to be trustees, but that, as I apprehend, is only in a general sense, as we term an agent or any bailee intrusted with the care and management of the property of another. It is certain that they are not technical trustees. They can

§§ 154, 155.]   DIRECTORS AND AGENTS.   211

§ 154. *General powers of directors.*— It is a well established rule that the directors of a corporation are merely its agents for limited purposes, and they have no power to bind it by any acts or contracts outside the general scope of the powers conferred by the charter and by-laws of the corporation.[1] Being but agents, it can never be presumed that they have authority to transact business which the corporation itself is not authorized to engage in.[2] The power of directors of private corporations to bind them by contracts depends exclusively upon the charters and by-laws of such corporations. So the declarations and acts of directors will not bind or affect in any manner the corporation, unless they are within the scope of their ordinary powers.[3]

§ 155. *Instances of directors' powers.*— Directors of an insolvent corporation cannot, as creditors of such corpo-

only be regarded as mandataries — persons who have gratuitously undertaken to perform certain duties, and they are therefore bound to apply ordinary skill and diligence, but no more. Indeed, as the directors are themselves stockholders, interested as well as all others that the affairs and business of the corporation should be successful, when we ascertain and determine that they have not sought to make any profit not common to all the stockholders, we raise a strong presumption that they have brought to the administration their best judgment and skill. Ought they to be held responsible for mistakes of judgment or want of skill and knowledge? . . . I do not mean to say, by any means, that their responsibility is limited to these cases, and that there might not exist such a case of negligence, or of acts clearly *ultra vires*, as would make perfectly honest directors personally liable."

[1] Bank of U. S. v. Dandridge, 12 Wheat. 64; Pickering v. Stephenson, L. R. 14 Eq. 340; In re Faure Electric Co., 40 Ch. Div. 141; Spering's Appeal, 71 Pa. St. 111; Overend & Gurney Co. v. Gibbs, 5 H. L. 480; Hodges v. Screw Co., 1 R. I. 322; Briggs v. Spaulding, 141 U. S. 132.

[2] Alexander v. Cauldwell, 83 N. Y. 480.

[3] Soper v. Buffalo R. R. Co., 19 Barb. (N. Y.) 310; East River Bank v. Hoyt, 41 id. 441.

ration, secure to themselves a preference.¹ They may make a valid assignment of the property of the corporation for the benefit of its creditors, even against the will of the stockholders.² Where directors declare a dividend with knowledge that there are no profits, such action is illegal.³ Where an agreement has been made by the president of a railroad company, subject to the approval of the directors and stockholders, to do something which is *ultra vires*, and the directors have approved it, the court will interfere by injunction upon application of a single stockholder.⁴ A director of a corporation cannot enforce a contract made with his co-director under which he is to have one-third of the profit for selling a railroad property, such contract being beyond the powers of the director to make.⁵ So, also, resolutions passed by directors, without any authority either by statute or charter, to assume the debts and to buy a majority of the stock and bonds and the equipments of a rival company, are *ultra vires*, and the proposed purchase could not be executed even if ratified by the stockholders.⁶

§ 156. *General liability of directors.*— As a general rule the directors of a corporation are only required in the management of its affairs to keep within the limits of its powers and to exercise good faith and honesty.⁷ They only undertake by virtue of the assumption of the

[1] Smith v. Putnam, 61 N. H. 632.
[2] Hutchinson v. Green, 91 Mo. 367.
[3] Slayden v. Seip, 25 Mo. App. 439.
[4] Elkins v. Camden, etc. R. Co., 36 N. J. Eq. 5; Hubbard v. Investment Co., 14 Fed. Rep. 675.
[5] Hubbard v. Investment Co., 14 Fed. Rep. 675.
[6] Elkins v. Camden, etc. R. Co., 36 N. J. Eq. 5.
[7] Bank v. St. John, 25 Ala. 611; Smith v. Manufacturing Co., 29 Ala. 503; Ryan v. Railroad Co., 21 Kan. 365; Shea v. Mabry, 1 Lea (Tenn.), 319; Vance v. Insurance Co., 4 Lea (Tenn.), 385

duties incumbent on them to perform those duties according to their best judgment and with reasonable diligence, and a mere error of judgment will not subject them to personal liability for its consequences.[1] And unless there has been some violation of the charter of the company, or unless there is shown to be a want of good faith, or a wilful abuse of discretion, or negligence, there will be no personal liability.[2] The degree of care and prudence which directors must exercise depends upon the subject to which it is applied, and each case must be determined in view of all the circumstances.[3] Directors are personally liable if they suffer the corporate funds or property to be wasted by gross negligence and inattention to the duties of their trust.[4] But a director will not incur personal liability if the other party knew, or had equal means with the officer of knowing, that the act was beyond his powers.[5]

§ 157. *Powers of bank directors.*— However broad and general the powers of the directors may be for the government of a bank by the general language of the charter and by-laws, those powers are not unlimited. The bank, being a body corporate under the law, is a person, although

[1] Godbold v. Bank, 11 Ala. 191; Van Dyke v. McQuade, 86 N. Y. 38; Spering's Appeal, 71 Pa. St. 11; Hodges v. Screw Co., 1 R. I. 322; Citizens' Bldg. Ass'n v. Coriell, 34 N. J. Eq. 383; Briggs v. Spaulding, 141 U. S. 132.
[2] Overend v. Gibb, 5 H. L. 480; Hedges v. Pacquett, 3 Oreg. 77; Excelsior Co. v. Lacey, 63 N. Y. 422; Vance v. Insurance Co., 4 Lea (Tenn.), 385; Godbold v. Bank, 11 Ala. 191.
[3] Briggs v. Spaulding, 141 U. S. 132; Mor. Priv. Corp., §§ 551 et seq.; Citizens' Ass'n v. Coriell, 34 N. J. Eq. 383; Hodges v. Screw Co., 1 R. I. 322.
[4] Robinson v. Smith, 3 Paige (N. Y.), 222; Citizens' Ass'n v. Coriell, 36 N. J. Eq. 383; Brinckerhoff v. Bostwick, 88 N. Y. 52.
[5] Bank of Augusta v. Earle, 13 Pet. (U. S.) 519.

artificial, with legal identity, and capable of owning and holding its own property.¹ They must exercise ordinary care and prudence in the administration of the affairs of a bank, and this includes something more than officiating as mere figure-heads; they are entitled under the law to commit the banking business, as defined, to their duly authorized officers, but this does not shield them from liability because of want of knowledge of wrongdoing, if that ignorance is the result of gross inattention.² Directors of a bank have no ownership in or title to the assets, and cannot act otherwise than as officers and agents of the bank.³

§ 158. *Liability of bank directors.*—If the directors of a bank knowingly issue spurious stock and obtain a loan on it, they are personally liable.⁴ Bank directors are not chargeable with the assets of the bank as for property to which they have taken title or possession for some use or purpose, and unless they actually misappropriate them they cannot be held to account.⁵ So a director of a bank is not liable to make good a loss occasioned by the fraud or misconduct of a co-director in which he had no part and which was perpetrated without his connivance or knowledge.⁶ As a general proposition the liability of bank directors is subject to the same rules as apply to directors of any other corporation, and the subject needs no separate consideration.

¹ Morris v. Lee, 30 Fed. Rep. 298; Briggs v. Spaulding, 141 U. S. 132.
² Briggs v. Spaulding, 141 U. S. 132; Morris v. Lee, 30 Fed. Rep. 298.
³ Morris v. Lee, *supra;* Exchange Bank v. Sibley, 71 Ga. 726; Bank of Augusta v. Earle, 13 Pet. 519; Bank of U. S. v. Dandridge, 12 Wheat. (U. S.) 64.
⁴ Exchange Bank v. Sibley, 71 Ga. 726.
⁵ Morris v. Lee, *supra.*
⁶ Morris v. Lee, *supra;* Corgill v. Bower, 10 Ch. Div. 502; Perry's Case, 34 L. T. 716; Joint-stock Co. v. Brown, L. R. 8 Eq. 381; Weir v.

§ 159.] DIRECTORS AND AGENTS. 215

§ 159. *Powers and liabilities of bank president.*— In the absence of anything in the act of incorporation bestowing special power upon the president of a bank, he has, from his mere official station, no more control over the corporate property and funds than any other director; and, unless his acts are shown to pertain to his official duties, or to be within the scope of his legitimate employment, they cannot be regarded as the acts of the corporation, and are not binding upon it.[1] So, in the absence of authority, the president cannot dispose of the cash and credits of the bank for the purpose of settling the demands of its creditors.[2] Nor by virtue of his office can he surrender or release any claims of the bank against any one.[3] It has been held, however, that when the president has been permitted by the directors to do acts not within the sphere of his official duties, and is thus held out to the public as having authority to do such acts, the bank will be bound on the ground of implied authority.[4] But

Bell, 3 Exch. Div. 238; Turquand v. Marshall, L. R. 4 Ch. 376; Land Credit Co. v. Lord Fermoy, 8 Eq. 7; Wakeman v. Dalley, 51 N. Y. 27; Arthur v. Griswold, 55 N. Y. 400; Robinson v. Smith, 3 Paige (N. Y.), 222. And see, as to general liability, Briggs v. Spaulding, 141 U. S. 132; Spering's Appeal, 71 Pa. St. 11, 20; Citizens' Bldg. Ass'n v. Coriell, 34 N. J. Eq. 383; Wakeman v. Dalley, *supra;* Brinkerhoff v. Bostwick, 88 N. Y. 52; Ackerman v. Halsey, 37 N. J. Eq. 356, 38 id. 501; White v. Skinner, 13 Johns. (N. Y.) 307; Randall v. Van Vechten, 19 Johns. (N. Y.) 60; Tippets v. Walker, 4 Mass. 595; Clark v. Edgar, 84 Mo. 106; Widrig v. Newport Co., 82 Ky. 512; Ward v. Davidson, 89 Mo. 445.

[1] Titus v. Railroad Co., 37 N. J. L. 98; Gibson v. Goldthwaite, 7 Ala. 282; Hoyt v. Thompson, 5 N. Y. 320; s. c., 19 N. Y. 207; Olney v. Chadsey, 7 R. I. 224; Parker v. Donnally, 4 W. Va. 648; Dougherty v. Hunter, 54 Pa. St. 380; Hallowell Bank v. Hamlin, 14 Mass. 178; Holt v. Winfield Bank, 25 Fed. Rep. 812.

[2] Gibson v. Goldthwaite, 7 Ala. 282; Hoyt v. Thompson, *supra.*

[3] Olney v. Chadsey, *supra.*

[4] Hoyt v. Thompson, *supra;* Parker v. Donnally, 4 W. Va. 648; Dougherty v. Hunter, 54 Pa. St. 380.

a president may, by the acts of the directors or managers, be invested with capacity to bind the company by his acts beyond those powers which are inherent in his office; as where, in the general course of the company's business, the directors or managers have permitted such officer to assume the control and direction of its affairs, and have held him out to the public as its general agent, his authority to act for the company in a particular transaction may be implied from the manner in which he has been permitted by the directors or managers to transact its business.[1] If the president of a corporation has, however, the power to contract on its behalf, he has power to release a contract.[2] But where the charter provides that the bank shall not at any time be indebted in excess of its paid-up capital, the president is personally liable for the amount of a bill which he indorses when the bank is indebted in excess of that amount.[3] So the president of a bank has been held personally liable for overdrafts which he has directed or allowed,[4] and for loss caused by his permitting a customer to take away for inspection securities of the bank deposited as collateral.[5]

§ 160. *General powers and duties of bank cashier.*— Ordinarily, the cashier of a bank, being the ostensible executive officer, is presumed to have all the power necessary for such an officer in the transaction of the legitimate business of banking.[6] Evidence of powers habitually exercised by a cashier of a bank with its knowledge and

---

[1] Fifth Ward Sav. Bank v. First Nat. Bank, 48 N. J. Eq. 513.
[2] Ind. Roll. Mill v. Railway Co., 120 U. S. 256.
[3] Brannen v. Loving, 6 Ky. 328.
[4] Oakland Bank v. Wilcox, 60 Cal. 126.
[5] Citizens' Bank v. Wiegand, 12 Phila. (Pa.) 496.
[6] West St. Louis Bank v. Shawnee Bank, 95 U. S. 557; Martin v. Webb, 110 U. S. 7; Merchants' Bank v. State Bank, 10 Wall. (U. S.) 604; Bank of United States v. Dandridge, 12 Wheat. 64; Minor v.

acquiescence defines and establishes, as to the public, those powers, provided that they be such as the directors of the bank may, without violation of its charter, confer on such cashier. So where, during a series of years, or in numerous business transactions, the cashier of a bank has been permitted, in his official capacity and without objection, to pursue a particular course of conduct, it may be presumed, as between the bank and those who in good faith deal with it, that he has acted in conformity with instructions received from those who have the right to control its operations.[1] So far as the public are concerned, it is immaterial whether the powers thus exercised are in disregard of the by-laws or not, provided they are within the corporate powers conferred by the charter.[2] So a bank cashier is generally understood to have authority to indorse the commercial paper of his bank,[3] receive all the funds which come to the bank and give certificates of deposit for the same, and do all those things usually exercised by a cashier in the performance of his daily duties.[4]

§ 161. *Instances of cashier's powers.*— The cashier of a bank has been held to have the following powers: To

Bank, 1 Pet. (U. S.) 46; Wild v. Bank, 3 Mason (U. S.), 505; Nichol v. Insurance Co., 3 W. & M. 530; Smith v. Van Co., 8 C. B. 668; Agar v. Insurance Co., 3 C. B. (N. S.) 725; Royal Bank v. Turquand, 6 E. & B. 327.

[1] Martin v. Webb, 110 U. S. 7.
[2] Merchants' Bank v. State Bank, 10 Wall. (U. S.) 604, and cases *supra.*
[3] St. Louis Sav. Bank v. Shawnee Bank, 95 U. S. 557.
[4] Burnham v. Webster, 19 Me. 234; Elliott v. Abbott, 12 N. H. 549; Bank of Virgennes v. Warren, 7 Hill (N. Y.), 91; Lloyd v. Bank, 15 Pa. St. 172; Badger v. Bank, 26 Me. 428; Bank of Kentucky v. Schuylkill Bank, 1 Park. S. Cas. (N. Y.) 182; Fleckner v. Bank of United States, 8 Wheat. (U. S.) 338; Commercial Bank v. Norton, 1 Hill (N. Y.), 501; Beers v. Glass Co., 14 Barb. (N. Y.) 358; Farmers'. etc. Bank v. Bank, 14 N. Y. 624; Barnes v. Ontario Bank, 19 N. Y. 152.

take such measures for the security and eventual collection of debts owing to the bank as he may deem proper.[1] He may release a debt secured by a mortgage.[2] He may borrow money in the ordinary course of the daily business of the bank, and may bind the bank by a promissory note executed therefor.[3] He may draw checks or drafts upon the funds of the bank deposited elsewhere.[4] He has authority to indorse its negotiable paper and securities[5] and transfer its shares of stock.[6] He may deliver notes to an attorney for collection and bind the bank for costs of suit.[7] But he has no general power to compromise claims due the bank,[8] nor transfer non-negotiable paper,[9] nor bind the bank to indemnify an officer for levying upon property on execution in favor of the bank,[10] nor power to discharge the surety on a note.[11]

[1] Bridenbecker v. Lowell, 32 Barb. (N. Y.) 9; Badger v. Bank, 26 Me. 428; Corser v. Paul, 41 N. H. 24; Bank of Pennsylvania v. Reed, 1 W. & S. (Pa.) 101.

[2] Ryan v. Dunlap, 17 Ill. 40.

[3] Ballston Bank v. Marine Bank, 16 Wis. 120; Sturges v. Bank, 11 Ohio St. 153; Barnes v. Ontario Bank, 19 N. Y. 152.

[4] Mechanics' Bank v. Bank of Colorado, 5 Wheat. (U. S.) 326; Chemical Bank v. Kohner, 8 Daly (N. Y.), 530; Northern Bank v. Johnson, 5 Coldw. (Tenn.) 88; State Bank v. Wheeler, 21 Ind. 90; City Bank v. Perkins, 29 N. Y. 554; Elliott v. Abbott, 12 N. H. 549; Cooper v. Curtis, 30 Me. 488; Pratt v. Topeka Bank, 12 Kan. 570.

[5] State Bank v. Wheeler, 21 Ind. 90; City Bank v. Perkins, 29 N. Y. 554; Elliott v. Abbott, 12 N. H. 549; Cooper v. Curtis, 30 Me. 488; Pratt v. Topeka Bank, 12 Kan. 570.

[6] Smith v. Bank, 4 Cush. (Mass.) 1; Commercial Bank v. Kortright, 22 Wend. (N. Y.) 348.

[7] Eastman v. Coos Bank, 1 N. H. 23.

[8] Chemical Nat. Bank v. Kohner, 8 Daly (N. Y.), 530.

[9] Holt v. Bacon, 25 Miss. 567; Berrick v. Austin, 21 Barb. 196.

[10] Watson v. Bennett, 12 Barb. (N. Y.) 196.

[11] Savings Ass'n v. Sailor, 63 Mo. 24; Merchants' Bank v. Rudolf, 5 Neb. 527; Bank v. Haskell, 51 N. H. 116.

CHAPTER XI.

THE DEFENSE OF ULTRA VIRES AS TO TORTIOUS ACTS OF OFFICERS AND AGENTS.

§ 162. General rule as to corporation's liability for torts.
163. Liability for tortious acts of agent.
164. Authority of agent in fixing liability.

§ 162. *General rule as to liability for torts.*—As a general proposition, corporations are liable for every wrong of which they are guilty, and in such a case the doctrine of *ultra vires* has no application.[1] The rule is stated by an eminent author in the following language: "The rule is now well settled that, while keeping within the apparent scope of corporate powers, corporations have a general capacity to render themselves liable for torts, except for those where the tort consists in the breach of some duty which, from its nature, could not be imposed upon or discharged by a corporation. The rule of liability embraces not only the negligence and omission of its officers and agents who are put in charge of or employed in the corporate business, but also all tortious acts which have been authorized by the corporation, or which are

[1] Nims v. Mount Hermon School, 160 Mass. 177; Moore v. Fitchburg R. Co., 4 Gray (Mass.), 465; Reed v. Savings Bank, 130 Mass. 443; Fogg v. Railroad Co., 148 Mass. 513; Philadelphia, etc. R. Co. v. Quigley, 21 How. (U. S.) 202; Merchants' Bank v. State Bank, 10 Wall. (U. S.) 209; National Bank v. Graham, 100 U. S. 699; Gruber v. Washington, etc. R. Co., 92 N. C. 1; Hussey v. Norfolk R. Co., 98 N. C. 34; Green v. London Omnibus Co., 7 C. B. (N. S.) 290; Life & Fire Ins. Co. v. Insurance Co., 7 Wend. (N. Y.) 31; Green's Brice's Ultra Vires, 364.

done in pursuance of any general or special authority to act in its behalf on the subject to which they relate, or which the corporation has subsequently ratified."[1] It was formerly argued that such torts as implied malice, as batteries, libels, and the like, could not be committed by corporations, because the state, in granting rights and privileges, had conferred no power to commit unlawful acts, and such torts, if committed by corporate agents, must consequently be *ultra vires* and the individual wrongs of the agents themselves.[2] This idea, however, has long since been exploded, and the great weight of modern authority holds a corporation liable for such tortious acts of officers and agents. Accordingly, corporations are now held liable for malicious prosecution,[3] or a libel,[4] or false imprisonment,[5] or the false representation of its agent.[6] So a corporation may be liable even where

[1] Cooley on Torts, 120, citing Mayor v. Herley, 1 Bing. N. C. 222, 240; Smith v. Birmingham Gas Co., 1 Ad. & El. 526; Maund v. Monmouthshire Co., 4 M. & G. 452; Eastern R. R. Co. v. Brown, 6 Exch. 314; Goff v. Great Nor. R. Co., 3 El. & El. 672; Phila. & Balt. R. Co. v. Quigley, 21 How. 202; Thayer v. Boston, 19 Pick. 511; Monument Nat. Bank v. Globe Works, 101 Mass. 57; Shelden v. Kalamazoo, 24 Mich. 383; Brokaw v. New Jersey R. Co., 32 N. J. L. 328.

[2] Cooley on Torts, 119.

[3] Vance v. Erie Ry., 32 N. J. L. 334; Copley v. Grover & Baker Co., 2 Woods (U. S.), 494; Goodspeed v. East Haddam Bank, 22 Conn. 530; Carter v. Howe Mach. Co., 51 Md. 290; Wheless v. Bank, 1 Baxter (Tenn.), 469; Williams v. Insurance Co., 57 Miss. 759; Iowa Mountain Bank v. Mercantile Bank, 4 Mo. App. 505; Walker v. Railway Co., L. R. 5 C. P. 640; Edwards v. Midland Ry., 6 Q. B. Div. 287; Boogher v. Life Ass'n, 75 Mo. 319.

[4] Phila. etc. R. Co. v. Quigley, 21 How. (U. S.) 202; Whitfield v. Railway Co., 1 E. B. & E. 115; Maynard v. Insurance Co., 34 Cal. 48; s. c., 47 Cal. 207; Johnson v. Dispatch Co., 2 Mo. App. 565; Evening Journal Ass'n v. McDermott, 44 N. J. L. 430; Tench v. Railway Co., 32 Up. Can. (Q. B.) 452.

[5] Denver, etc. R. Co. v. Harris, 122 U. S. 597.

[6] Barwick v. English, etc. Bank, L. R. 2 Exch. 259; Mackay v.

a fraudulent or malicious intent is necessary to be proved, the fraud or malice of its authorized agents being imputable to the corporation.[1] There is some doubt, however, as to whether a corporation can be held liable for slander uttered by its officer or agent. Mr. Odgers is of the opinion that they cannot be so held, "unless it can be proved that the corporation expressly ordered and directed that officer to say those very words, for a slander is the voluntary and tortious act of the speaker."[2] So an action may be maintained against a corporation to recover damages caused by conspiracy.[3]

§ 163. *Liability for tortious acts of agent.*— It is also generally admitted that corporations are liable for the acts of their agents and servants, while engaged in the business of their employment, in the same manner and to the same extent that individuals are liable.[4] Corporations are likewise responsible for acts not strictly within the corporate powers, but done in their corporate name and by corporate officers, who were competent to exercise all the corporate powers.[5] Accordingly, a corporation when sued for tort cannot defend on the ground

Bank, L. R. Priv. Coun. App. 394; Ranger v. Railway Co., 5 H. L. 72; Erie City Iron Works v. Barber, 102 Pa. St. 156; Peebles v. Patapsco Guano Co., 77 N. C. 233; Cragie v. Hadley, 99 N. Y. 131; Caudy v. Knitting Co., 37 N. J. Eq. 175.

[1] National Exch. Co. v. Drew, 2 Macq. 103; New Brunswick Ry. Co. v. Conybeare, 9 H. L. 711; Barwick v. English, etc. Bank, 2 Exch. 259.

[2] Odgers, Lib. & Slan., § 368.

[3] Buffalo Oil Co. v. Oil Co., 106 N. Y. 669; Reed v. Bank, 130 Mass. 443; Krulevitz v. Railway, 140 Mass. 573; Western News Co. v. Wilmarth, 33 Kan. 510; Jordon v. Alabama R. Co., 74 Ala. 85.

[4] Wheeler, etc. Mfg. Co. v. Boyce, 36 Kan. 350; Lake Erie Ry. Co. v. Acres, 108 Ind. 548; First Nat. Bank v. Graham, 100 U. S. 699; Gruber v. Washington, etc. R. Co., 92 N. C. 1.

[5] Salt Lake City v. Hollister, 118 U. S. 256.

that the act from which the tort resulted was *ultra vires*.¹ For example, a corporation cannot defeat liability for an injury caused by the negligence of an officer on a steamboat with the plea that the running of the steamboat was *ultra vires*, it being chartered only as a railroad and banking company.² So a corporation was held liable in damages for its conductor's forcible osculation of a lady passenger, for it was the duty of the conductor, however great the temptation might have been, to smother and subdue his amatory emotions, and protect passengers from wanton insult.³ And where there has been acquiescence and ratification by the corporation, such as accepting the benefits of an *ultra vires* tort, it will be estopped from pleading *ultra vires*.⁴

¹ Gruber v. Washington, etc. R. Co., 92 N. C. 1; First Nat. Bank v. Graham, *supra*.

² Central R. Co. v. Smith, 76 Ala. 572; s. c., 52 Am. Rep. 353.

³ Craker v. Chicago. etc. R. Co., 36 Wis. 657. See, also, generally, Stewart v. Brooklyn R. Co., 90 N. Y. 588; Louisville, etc. R. Co. v. Kelley, 13 Am. & Eng. R. Cas. 1; Gilliam v. South, etc. R. Co., 15 id. 138; Bryan v. Chicago, etc. R. Co., 16 id. 335; International, etc. R. Co. v. Kentle, id. 337; Louisville, etc. R. Co. v. Flemming, 18 id. 347; Heenrich v. Pullman Co., id. 379; Miller v. Burlington, etc. R. Co., 8 Neb. 219; Alexander v. Relfe, 74 Mo. 495.

⁴ Alexander v. Relfe, *supra*. Mr. Taylor, in his excellent work on Private Corporations, § 336, in discussing the general doctrine as to the liability of corporations for the torts of their agents, says: "If the corporation, acting within the scope of its corporate authority, employs agents or servants in such a manner as to put it within their power to cause a violation of a duty owed by the corporation, the corporation will not be sustained in the defense that the violation complained of was not authorized by it. And thus it is if the tort was committed in the course of an employment, or in connection with transactions which the corporation had completely authorized or acquiesced in, and the duty owed by the corporation is violated by the tort, it will be no valid defense to the corporation that the tort itself was not only unauthorized, but was even *ultra vires* the corporation. To the tort itself, under such circumstances, the doc-

§ 164. *Authority of agent in fixing liability.*— To fix the liability of the corporation for the tortious act of one of its agents or employees, done in obedience to commands of its officers, the act must be connected with the transaction of the business for which the company was incorporated. For the acts of the servant, within the general scope of his employment, while engaged in his master's business and the master's interest, the master will be responsible, whether the act be done negligently, wantonly, or even wilfully.[1] In *Brokaw v. Railroad Co.*, 32 N. J. L. 328, Depue, J., discussing this point, said: "In considering the question whether the agent has the authority of the corporation, so as to make it answerable for his act, the purpose for which the company was incorporated must not be overlooked. An authority given even by the board of directors in express terms will not, in all cases, be the authority of the corporation. The directors are only agents themselves, and their powers are necessarily limited within the scope of the purposes for which the corporation was created, beyond which they are not authorized to bind the corporation. . . . If the directors should order an agent to take a person out of his house and beat him, the corporation could not be held for an assault and battery; or if the directors of a banking company should purchase a steamboat and en-

---

trine of *ultra vires* has no application; but it does apply where the employment in the course of which, or the transaction in connection with which, the tort was committed was *ultra vires* the corporation."

[1] Mott v. Ice Co., 73 N. Y. 543; Miller v. Burlington R. Co., 8 Neb. 219; Goodspeed v. Bank, 22 Conn. 530; Gillette v. Missouri, etc. R. Co., 55 Mo. 315; Brokaw v. New Jersey, etc. R. Co., 32 N. J. 328, 332; Helfrich v. Williams, 84 Ind. 553; Illinois Cent. R. Co. v. Downey, 18 Ill. 260; Hussey v. King, 98 N. C. 34; Hood v. Railroad Co., 22 Conn. 502; Taylor, Priv. Corp., § 341.

gage in transporting passengers, the corporation would be liable for the misfeasance or non-feasance of agents employed in that business. But if the directors of a corporation, having power to hold lands, order an agent to enter on lands and take possession of them for the legitimate uses of the company, his entry, if unlawful, will be the trespass of the corporation. So if the directors, acting in their official capacity, adopt rules and regulations for the transaction of the corporate business of the company, and provide for the enforcement of those rules and regulations, and authorize its agents or servants to carry them into effect, the corporation will be liable for the acts of such agents or servants in the course of such employment."

CHAPTER XII.

POWERS AND LIABILITIES OF FOREIGN AND DE FACTO CORPORATIONS.

§ 165. General powers of foreign corporations.
166. The absence of prohibitory legislation presumes a tacit adoption of foreign laws.
167. Contractual powers similar to domestic corporation.
168. *De facto* corporation — Estopped to deny corporate existence.

§ 165. *General powers of foreign corporations.*— It is a general rule so universally accepted as to need no citation of authorities, that a corporation created by a state can exercise none of the functions or privileges conferred by its charter in any other state, except by the comity and consent of the latter. By the law of comity among nations, a corporation created by one sovereignty is permitted to make contracts in another and to sue in its courts; and the same law of comity prevails among the several sovereignties of this Union. The comity of suit brings with it the comity of contract; and where one is adopted the other must be presumed.[1] Every power which a corporation exercises in another state depends for its validity upon the laws of the sovereignty in which it is exercised; and a corporation can make no valid contract without their sanction, express or implied. Courts of justice have always expounded and executed contracts made by corporations in a foreign country according to the laws of the place in which they are made; provided that law was

[1] Bank of Augusta v. Earle, 13 Pet. (U. S.) 519; Tombigbie, etc. Co. v. Kneeland, 4 How. (U. S.) 16.

not repugnant to the laws or policy of their own country. The comity thus extended to other nations, it has been said, is no impeachment of sovereignty. It is the voluntary act of the nation by which it is offered, and is inadmissible when contrary to its policy or prejudicial to its interests.[1]

§ 166. *The absence of prohibitory legislation presumes a tacit adoption of foreign laws.*— In the silence of any positive rule affirming or denying or restraining the operation of foreign laws, courts of justice presume the tacit adoption of them by their own government, unless they are repugnant to its policy or prejudicial to its interests.[2] Accordingly it is held that where there is no prohibitory legislation or action by a state excluding foreign corporations, individual citizens cannot complain because a foreign corporation is doing business in the state.[3] Agreeably to the foregoing principles, a corporation of one state, not forbidden by the laws of its being, may exercise within any other state the general powers conferred by its own charter, unless it is prohibited from so doing either by the direct enactments of the latter state, or by its public policy to be deduced from the general course of its legislation, or from the settled adjudications of its highest court.[4]

[1] Bank of Augusta v. Earle, *supra.*
[2] Story, Conf. Laws, pp. 36, 37.
[3] Pensacola Tel. Co. v. Western Union Tel. Co., 96 U. S. 1.
[4] Christian Union v. Yount, 101 U. S. 352; Tombigbie, etc. Co. v. Kneeland, 4 How. (U. S.) 16; Cowell v. Springs Co., 100 U. S. 55; Williams v. Creswell, 51 Miss. 817; Silver Lake Bank v. North, 4 John. Ch. 370; Bard v. Poole, 12 N. Y. 495; Merrick v. Van Santford, 34 N. Y. 208; British Am. Land Co. v. Ames, 9 Metc. (Mass.) 391; Martin v. Mobile, etc. R. Co., 7 Bush (Ky.), 116; Guaga Iron Co. v. Dawson, 4 Blackf. (Ind.) 202; Leasure v. Life Ins. Co., 91 Pa. St. 491; Dodge v. City of Council Bluffs, 57 Iowa, 560; Frazier v. Wilcox, 4 Rob. (La.)

§ 167. *Contractual powers similar to domestic corporation.*— Any foreign corporation doing business in a state under permission of the legislature of such state must be deemed as to its contracts made in the course of such business to possess the powers and be subject to all the liabilities of similar domestic corporations as adjudicated by the courts of that state.[1] It must be borne in mind, then, that two questions should be considered in determining the contractual powers of a foreign corporation: first, whether it has been endowed with the power in the state of its creation; and second, conceding the original existence of the power, whether the state in which it proposes to exercise the power will permit such exercise. These questions being resolved, such corporations, generally speaking, are governed by the same principles and rules of law as are applicable to domestic corporations.

§ 168. *De facto corporations — Estopped to deny corporate existence.*— Where a corporation is proceeding in the performance of corporate functions, and the public are dealing with it on the supposition that it is what it professes to be, and the questions suggested are only whether there has been exact regularity and strict com-

517; Life Association v. Levy, 33 La. Ann. 1203; Kennebec Co. v. Insurance Co., 6 Gray (Mass.), 204; Flash v. Conn, 16 Fla. 428; Newburg Petroleum Co v. Weare, 27 Ohio St. 343; Western Union Tel. Co. v. Mayer, 28 Ohio St. 521; Santa Clara F. Acad. v. Sullivan, 116 Ill. 375; Baltimore, etc. R. Co. v. Glenn, 28 Md. 287; Wood Hydraulic Co. v. King, 45 Ga. 34; Home Ins. Co. v. Davis, 29 Mich. 238; Kerchner v. Gettys, 18 S. C. 521; Taylor, Priv. Corp., § 384; 8 Am. & Eng. Ency. Law, 331, 332, and cases cited.

[1] Milnor v. New York, etc. R. Co., 53 N. Y. 363; Bard v. Poole, 12 N. Y. 495; Silver Lake Bank v. North, 4 John. Ch. 370; McGregor v. Erie R. Co., 35 N. J. L. 115; Bank of Augusta v. Earle, 13 Pet. (U. S.) 539; Lewis v. Bank of Ky., 12 Ohio, 132; Pierce v. Crompton, 13 R. I. 312.

pliance with the provisions of the law relating to incorporation, in controversies between such *de facto* corporation and those who have entered into contract relations with it, it will be estopped from denying the legality of its corporate organization and existence.[1] So one who deals with a corporation as existing in fact will also be estopped to deny as against the corporation its legal incorporation when sued on his contract.[2] So, also, it is the general rule of law that the regularity and validity of the organization of a corporation, effected under color of its charter, cannot be impeached in any collateral proceeding, and the acts of its officers *de facto* under color of an election are valid and binding upon the corporation.[3] And where a corporation assumed to act before

---

[1] McCullough v. Insurance Co., 46 Ala. 376; Empire Mfg. Co. v. Stewart, 46 Mich. 482; Dooley v. Chesire Glass Co., 15 Gray (Mass.), 494; Merrick v. Reynolds Engine Co., 101 Mass. 381; Humphrey v. Patrons' Merc. Ass'n, 50 Iowa, 607; Close v. Glenwood Cemetery, 107 U. S. 466; Swartout v. Michigan, etc. R. Co., 24 Mich. 389; Bakersfield, etc. Ass'n v. Chester, 55 Cal. 98; Ewing v. Robeson, 15 Ind. 26; Hammond v. Straus, 53 Md. 1; Priest v. Hat Co., 115 Mass. 380; Salem Nat. Bank v. Almy, 117 Mass. 476; Chamberlin v. Huguenot Mfg. Co., 118 Mass. 532; Rush v. Steamboat Co., 84 N. C. 70; Whitney v. Wyman, 101 U. S. 392; Upton v. Hansborough, 3 Biss. (U. S.) 417; Taylor, Priv. Corp., § 146.

[2] Taylor, Priv. Corp., § 146; Frost v. Frostburg Coal Co., 24 How. (U. S.) 278; French v. Donohue, 29 Minn. 111; Johnston Harvester Co. v. Clark, 30 Minn. 308; Franz v. Building Ass'n, 24 Md. 259; Keene v. Van Reuth, 48 Md. 184; Ramsey v. Insurance Co., 55 Ill. 311; Stoutimore v. Clark, 70 Mo. 471; Studebaker Co. v. Montgomery, 74 Mo. 101; Beatty v. Bartholomew, etc., 76 Ind. 91; Smelser v. Turnpike Co., 82 Ind. 417; Butchers' Bank v. McDonald, 130 Mass. 264; Spahr v. Bank, 94 Pa. St. 429; Jones v. Bank, 8 B. Mon. (Ky.) 122.

[3] Attorney-General v. Stevens, 1 N. J. Eq. 369; National Docks v. Railway Co., 5 Stew. (N. J.) 755; Knight v. Corporation, Lutw. 508; In re Assurance Co., 5 Ch. App. 288; Mahoney v. Mining Co., 7 H. L. 869; Hackensack Water Co. v. Dekay, 36 N. J. Eq. 548.

the amount of its capital stock had been taken and ten per cent. of that amount had been paid in, and without a compliance with this condition, it was held that it had exceeded its powers in thus commencing and prosecuting its business; that such action was *ultra vires* and void, and any promise or undertaking which induced it to pursue such a course was in contravention of the law and could not be invoked an an estoppel in a suit to recover the amount of stock subscribed.[1] So where a corporation continued to prosecute its business in its corporate name just as it had done before its charter expired, after the expiration of its legal right to exist, it was held to have become a corporation *de facto*, and that the acts and dealings had by and with it were not necessarily legally ineffective and of no binding force.[2]

[1] Academy of Music v. Flanders Brothers, 75 Ga. 14; Hackensack Water Co. v. Dekay, 36 N. J. E. 548.

[2] Miller v. Newberg Coal Co., 31 W. Va. 836; Mor. Priv. Corp., §§ 1002, 1003; St. Louis Gas Light Co. v. St. Louis, 11 Mo. App. 55; Briggs v. Cape Cod Canal Co., 137 Mass. 71.

In Miller v. Coal Co., *supra*, the court say: "The principle, it seems to me, to be deduced from our statute and these authorities is that a private business corporation, acting and carrying on its corporate business in its corporate name after its legal existence has ended by the expiration of its charter, must be held to be a corporation *de facto;* and that as such, so long as it in fact carries its business and contracts and incurs liabilities with or to third persons dealing with it as such *de facto* corporation, it may sue and be sued at law, either in actions *ex contractu* or *ex delicto*, and it cannot defeat such action by alleging that its charter had expired before the cause of action arose."

Hackensack Water Co. v. Dekay, *supra*, was a case where a water company was incorporated in 1869 with a capital of $50,000. The charter provided for an organization as soon as $20,000 of the capital stock should be subscribed and paid in. In 1873 the corporation was organized and directors elected. Very little of the stock had been subscribed, and less of it had been paid in. The directors were not qualified for the office and were irregularly chosen. Under this organization the company bought and took title for lands in its own name, constructed its works, acquired property to a considerable amount and contracted debts to a larger amount. The charter authorized the company to increase its capital stock to $100,000. The charter also empowered the company to borrow money not exceeding two-thirds of the capital paid in, and to secure the same by bonds and mortgage upon the property and franchises. In August, 1873, a resolution was passed to increase the capital to $100,000. In September, 1873, the directors adopted a resolution that one hundred and thirty-three bonds of $500 each be issued, payable to a trustee or bearer, with coupons for the semi-annual interest. The bonds authorized by this resolution, and in fact issued, amounted to $66,500, nearly two-thirds of the capital authorized when increased. At that time not over $2,000 of capital had been paid in. In a suit to foreclose a mortgage made in pursuance of this resolution by the company, duly executed under the corporate seal, it was held that the corporation was a corporation *de facto* and its directors officers *de facto*, and that the acts of the latter were binding on the corporation. Further, that the mortgage being within the powers granted by the charter, and on its face having the appearance of being within the company's power to mortgage, was a valid security in favor of *bona fide* holders of the bonds, notwithstanding the directors acted illegally in making the mortgage and the bonds, and putting the bonds in circulation without first obtaining subscriptions to the capital to be made and paid in sufficient amount to justify them in making the mortgage.

CHAPTER XIII.

THE DOCTRINE OF ULTRA VIRES APPLIED TO MUNICIPAL CORPORATIONS.

GENERAL MUNICIPAL POWERS.

§ 169. Introductory — Nature of municipal corporation.
170. Exercise of municipal powers.
171. Ordinances — Power to enact.
172. Nature and effect of ordinances.
173. Ministerial and judicial ordinances distinguished.
174. Effect of *ultra vires* ordinances.
175. Instances of *ultra vires* ordinances.
176. Ordinances must be reasonable.
177. Courts cannot interfere with discretion of municipality.
178. Courts may restrain passage of *ultra vires* ordinances.
179. Powers as to taxation.
180. Power to tax may be revoked.
181. Power can be exercised only for public purposes.
182. Taxation and power to license distinguished.
183. Power to exercise right of eminent domain.
184. Eminent domain and taxation distinguished.
185. Powers as to property.
186. Powers of divided municipality.
187. As to extinguished municipality.

§ 169. *Introductory — Nature of municipal corporations.* — The underlying principle of municipal government is that the management of local affairs shall be intrusted to local authorities, while general affairs are left to the state legislature. Under the power given by constitutions to general assemblies to provide for the organization of cities and incorporated villages, these corporations are made the depositaries of certain limited governmental powers, to be exercised on behalf of the state for the public welfare.¹ They are agencies or instrumentalities to which the general assembly, vested with the legislative power of the state, delegates a portion of its governmental power in order to meet those local wants of the people in cities and villages for which state laws make only general provisions, leaving a more particular provision to local councils.²

§ 170. *Exercise of general municipal powers.*— The manner and extent to which governmental powers delegated to municipal corporations for the public good are to be exercised must rest in a large measure in their judgment and discretion; but, acting as state instrumentalities, they cannot be held liable to individuals for a defect in the execution of such powers, unless a right of action is given by statute.³ Municipal corporations can exercise only such powers as are expressly granted to them, or such as are necessary to carry into effect those that are granted.⁴

[1] City of Toledo v. Cone, 41 Ohio St. 149.
[2] City of Toledo v. Cone, *supra.*
[3] City of Toledo v. Cone, 5 Am. & Eng. Corp. Cas. 623; Wheeler v. Cincinnati, 19 Ohio, 19; Western College v. Cleveland, 12 Ohio St. 375.
[4] Richards v. Clarksburg, 30 W. Va. 491; Parkersburg Gas Co. v. Parkersburg, etc. Co., 30 W. Va. 435; Grand Rapids, etc. Co. v. Grand Rapids, etc. Co., 35 Mich. 265; Petersburg v. Metzker, 21 Ill. 205; People v. Weber, 89 Ill. 347; Mather v. Ottawa, 114 Ill. 659; New London v. Brainerd, 32 Conn. 552; Bridgeport v. Railway Co., 15 Conn. 475; Somerville v. Dickerman, 127 Mass. 272; Roylston Market v. Boston Association, 113 Mass. 528; Clark v. Davenport, 14 Iowa, 494; Keokuk v. Scroggs, 39 Iowa, 447; Hauger v. Des Moines, 52 Iowa, 193; Green v. Cape May, 41 N. J. L. 45; State v. Passaic, 41 N. J. L. 90; Fulton v. Lincoln, 9 Neb. 358; Hurford v. Omaha, 4 Neb. 350; Brenham v. Water Co., 67 Tex. 542; Williams v. Davidson, 43 Tex. 33; Allen v. Galveston, 51 Tex. 302; People v. Bank, 1 Doug. (Mich.) 282; Smith v. Newburgh, 77 N. Y. 130; Francis v. Troy, 74 N. Y. 338; Paine v. Spratley, 5 Kan. 525; State v. Marion Co., 21

No powers can be implied except such as are essential to the objects and purposes of the corporation as created and established. To the extent of their authority they can bind the people and the property subject to their regulation and governmental control by what they do, but beyond their corporate powers their acts are of no effect.[1]

§ 171. *Ordinances — Power to enact.* — Municipal ordinances are laws passed by the governing body of a municipal corporation for the regulation of the affairs of the corporation. They are not merely rules or regulations in the ordinary sense of those terms, but they are in the nature of laws, being decreed by a body vested with definite legislative authority, coupled with power to enforce obedience to its enactments.[2] The legislature may delegate to a municipal corporation the power to enact ordi-

Kan. 419; Hayes v. Appleton, 24 Wis. 544; Lord v. Oconto, 47 Wis. 386; Kansas City v. Flanagan, 69 Mo. 22; Kelly v. Meeks, 87 Mo. 396; St. Louis v. Bell Tel. Co., 96 Mo. 623; St. Paul v. Traeger, 25 Minn. 248; Bentley v. County Com'rs, 25 Minn. 259; Mayor, etc. v. Moag, 53 Ala. 561; Selma v. Mullen, 46 Ala. 411; McCracken v. San Francisco, 16 Cal. 591; McCoy v. Briant, 53 Cal. 247; Glass v. Ashbury, 49 Cal. 571; Vance v. Little Rock, 30 Ark. 435; De Russey v. Davis, 13 La. Ann. 468; Louisiana State Bank v. Navigation Co., 3 La. Ann. 294; Walker v. Cincinnati, 21 Ohio St. 14; Bloom v. Xenia, 32 Ohio St. 461; Indianapolis v. Ind. etc. Co., 66 Ind. 396; Cullen v. Carthage, 103 Ind. 196; Nichol v. Mayor, etc., 9 Humph. (Tenn.) 252; Head v. Prov. Ins. Co., 2 Cranch (U. S.), 128; Minturn v. Larue, 23 How. 435; Kirkham v. Russell, 76 Va. 956; Peters v. Lynchburg, 76 Va. 927; Logan City v. Buck, 3 Utah, 301; Blake v. Mayor, 53 Ga. 177; Sherman v. Carr, 8 R. I. 431; Henderson v. Covington, 14 Bush (Ky.), 312; Alley v. Inhabitants, etc., 53 Me. 446; Weith v. Wilmington, 68 N. C. 24; Treadway v. Schrauber, 1 Dak. 236; Leonard v. Canton, 36 Miss. 189.

[1] Ottawa v. Carey, 108 U. S. 110; 1 Dill. Mun. Corp., § 89, and cases cited.

[2] Horr & Bemis, Munic. Ord., §§ 1, 2.

nances for the government of the municipality, and, if the organic law contains nothing restricting the exercise of the power to any particular part of the municipal body, it may be conferred upon any department thereof, as may appear to be most just and expedient in the judgment of the legislature.[1]

§ 172. *Nature and effect of ordinances.*— Ordinances are to be made in subordination and not contrary to the general laws of the state. Still, they go far beyond the general laws in prescribing the civil conduct of persons in relation to their conduct and property. In order to make these additional regulations binding, the charter of the city must be put in operation by an organization, or by the action of officers under it.[2] Public policy demands the delegation of various powers of local legislation to the municipal body, and ordinances enacted in the execution of these powers have, within the limits of the corporation, the force of laws. They are just as binding as the laws of the state and general government; they are enforced in a similar manner and under like rules of construction.[3] A grant of power to pass ordinances is under-

[1] Boone, Corp., § 202; St. Paul v. Coulter, 12 Minn. 41; State v. Clark, 8 Fost. 176; Trigally v. Memphis, 6 Coldw. (Tenn.) 382; Hill v. Decatur, 22 Ga. 203; Brieswick v. Mayor, etc., 51 Ind. 639; Horn v. People, 26 Mich. 221; Blanchard v. Bissell, 11 Ohio St. 96; St. Louis v. Bank, 49 Mo. 574; Ileland v. Lowell, 3 Allen (Mass.), 407; Gas Co. v. San Francisco, 6 Cal. 190; Kepner v. Comm., 40 Pa. St. 124; Sower v. Philadelphia, 35 Pa. St. 231; Blazier v. Miller, 10 Hun (N. Y.), 435; People v. Special Sessions, 10 Hun (N. Y.), 214.

[2] Williams v. Davidson, 43 Tex. 1.

[3] Horr & Bemis, § 2; Dill. Mun. Corp., § 308; Sedgw. Stat. Law, 462; Bish. Stat. Cr., § 11; Cooley, Const. Lim. 211; Jones v. Insurance Co., 2 Daly (N. Y.), 307; McDermott v. Board, 5 Abb. Pr. (N. Y.) 422; Milne v. Davidson, 5 Martin (La.), 409; State v. Williams, 11 S. C. 288; Gabel v. Houston, 29 Tex. 336; Bearden v. Madison, 73 Ga. 184; Ileland v. Lowell, 3 Allen (Mass.), 407; State v. Tryon, 39 Conn. 183;

stood to be subject to the implied limitation that they shall not be contrary to the general laws of the state.[1] And a power to pass ordinances and appoint officers to enforce them includes all necessary power to make such ordinances effectual.[2]

§ 173. *Ministerial and judicial ordinances distinguished.*— The true principle seems to be that ordinances directing the mere repairing or repaving of streets, or the reconstruction of sewers or bridges, which are enjoined upon municipal corporations as matters of duty, are purely ministerial; while ordinances directing new streets to be opened or altered, new sewers to be constructed, or other similar public improvements to be made, by which the property of individuals is taken or affected, are in their nature judicial.[3] So when a municipal corporation is authorized by ordinance to require the paving of streets, not as a matter of ordinary repair, but upon specified conditions only, and to impose the burden not upon the city treasury, but upon a specified class of individuals, the ordinance is in its nature judicial.[4] Municipal powers requiring the exercise of discretion cannot be delegated, yet such corporations may appoint agents and committees to discharge duties of an administrative or ministerial character.[5]

Hopkins v. Swanson, 4 M. & W. 621; Burmeister v. Howard, 1 Wash. Ty. 207; Wright v. Railroad Co., 7 Ill. App. 438; Church v. City, 5 Cow. (N. Y.) 538; Mason v. Shawnee, 77 Ill. 533; Bott v. Pratt, 33 Minn. 323; Gas Co. v. Des Moines, 44 Iowa. 508; Starr v. Burlington, 45 Iowa. 87; Indianapolis v. Gas Co., 66 Ind. 396.

[1] St. Louis v. Kaime, 2 Mo. App. 66; Canton v. Nist, 9 Ohio St. 439; Thomas v. Richmond, 12 Wall. (U. S.) 349.

[2] Boone, Corp. § 292; Reinhard v. New York, 2 Daly (N. Y.), 243; State v. Cleveland, 3 R. I. 117; Roddy v. Finnegan, 40 Md. 490.

[3] Camden v. Mulford, 26 N. J. L. 49.

[4] Camden v. Mulford, *supra.*

[5] State v. Trenton, 42 N. J. L. 72; Parker v. New Brunswick, 1

§ 174. *Effect of ultra vires ordinances.*— An ordinance passed by a municipal corporation which it has no power to pass, as levying a tax for a purpose not authorized by its charter, is an act of usurpation, and all proceedings under it are void; but where the corporation has the power to pass an ordinance for a certain purpose, but exercises that power in an unauthorized manner, the ordinance is valid and binding until set aside by legal proceedings brought for that purpose, and its validity cannot be brought in question collaterally as a matter of defense to an action under it.[1]

§ 175. *Instances of ultra vires ordinances.*— An ordinance making an appropriation of the funds of a city, derived from taxation, for purposes wholly beyond the purview of municipal government, is a wrongful appropriation of the funds held in trust for the tax-payers and people to pay the legitimate expenses of the city, and is illegal, *ultra vires*, null and void.[2] An ordinance passed

---

Vroom (N. J.), 395; State v. Paterson, 5 Vroom (N. J.), 163; Dill. Mun. Corp., § 60; Meuser v. Risdon, 36 Cal. 239; Mathews v. Alexandria, 68 Mo. 115; Gale v. Kalamazoo, 23 Mich. 344; Lord v. Oconto, 47 Wis. 386; State v. Hauser, 63 Ind. 158; Bradsall v. Clark, 73 N. Y. 73; East St. Louis v. Wehrung, 50 Ill. 28; Kinmundy v. Mayham, 72 Ill. 462; State v. Fiske, 9 R. I. 94; Hydes v. Joyes, 4 Bush (Ky.), 464; State v. Jersey City, 25 N. J. L. 209; State v. Newark, 47 N. J. L. 117; State v. Trenton, 51 N. J. L. 498; Schenley v. Commissioners, 36 Pa. St. 62; State v. Bell, 34 Ohio St. 194; Darling v. St. Paul, 19 Minn. 389.

[1] City of Camden v. Mulford, 26 N. J. L. 49; Bergen v. Clarkson, 1 Halst. (N. J.) 352; State v. Jersey City, 5 Dutch. (N. J.) 175.

[2] The Liberty Bell, 23 Fed. Rep. 843; Dill. Mun. Corp.. § 52; Hood v. Lynn, 1 Allen (Mass.), 103; Tash v. Adams, 10 Cush. (Mass.) 252; Claflin v. Hopkinton, 4 Gray (Mass.), 502; Murphy v. Jacksonville, 18 Fla. 318; Grant Co. v. Bradford, 72 Ind. 455; Henderson v. Covington, 14 Bush (Ky.), 312; Cornell v. Guilford, 1 Denio (N. Y.), 510; Halstead v. Mayor, etc., 3 N. Y. 433; New London v. Brainerd, 22 Conn. 552.

by the city council of New Orleans appropriating $5,000 to pay the expenses incurred in transporting from Philadelphia to said city and return the "Liberty Bell" obtained for exhibition at the "World's Industrial and Cotton Centennial Exposition," and also for paying the expenses of a "junketing expedition" to go to Philadelphia, ostensibly in charge of said bell, though patriotic and praiseworthy, was held illegal and void.[1] So an ordinance of a city that declares it unlawful for any person, society, association or organization, under whatsoever name, to parade any public street, avenue or alley of the city, shouting, singing or beating drums or tamborines, or playing upon any other musical instrument, etc., without first having obtained in writing the consent of persons named in the ordinance, is illegal and void.[2]

§ 176. *Ordinances must be reasonable.*— Ordinances to be valid must be reasonable.[3] An unreasonable ordinance is void.[4] And where a charter expressly grants a power,

[1] The Liberty Bell, *supra*.

[2] Anderson v. City, 10 Pac. Rep. 719; Frazee's Case, 30 N. W. Rep. 72; Sweet v. Wabash, 41 Ind. 7; McConvill v. Jersey City, 39 N. J. L. 38; Bronson v. Oberlin, 41 Ohio St. 476; Austin v. Mundy, 16 Pick. (Mass.) 121; Duckwall v. New Albany, 25 Ind. 283; Shallcross v. Jeffersonville, 26 Ind. 193; State v. White (N. H.), 5 Atl. Rep. 828.

[3] State v. Clark, 54 Mo. 17; Coal Float v. Jeffersonville, 112 Ind. 19; Chamberlain v. Evansville, 79 Ind. 542; Corrigan v. Gage, 68 Mo. 541; Kirkham v. Russell, 76 Va. 956; Baltimore v. Radecke, 49 Md. 217; Boston v. Shaw, 1 Met. (Mass.) 130; Comm. v. Worcester, 3 Pick. (Mass.) 462; Delaware, etc. R. Co. v. East Orange, 41 N. J. L. 127; Kipp v. Mayor, etc., 2 Dutch. (N. J.) 298; Dayton v. Quigley, 29 N. J. Eq. 77; People v. Troop, 12 Wend. (N. Y.) 183; Ex parte Frank, 52 Cal. 606; Mayor, etc. v. Winfield, 8 Humph. (Tenn.) 707; Walters v. Leech, 3 Ark. 110; Fisher v. Harrisburg, 2 Grant's Cas. (Pa.) 291; Mayor, etc. v. Beasley, 1 Humph. (Tenn.) 232; Pedrick v. Bailey, 12 Gray (Mass.), 161; State v. Freeman, 38 N. H. 426; Tugman v. Chicago, 78 Ill. 405; Clason v. Milwaukee, 30 Wis. 316.

[4] Cooley, Const. Lim. 243; Chicago v. Trotter, 26 N. E. Rep. (Ill.) 359.

but prescribes neither the time nor the mode of its exercise, it must be exercised in a mode and at a time deemed reasonable by the court.[1] An ordinance cannot be held to be unreasonable, however, if expressly authorized by the legislature.[2] But the courts will, in certain cases, declare a municipal ordinance void, simply on the ground that the unreasonableness of the ordinance amounts to an abuse of authority.[3] Thus, an ordinance was held to be unreasonable and so void, which required druggists to furnish quarterly statements of the kind and quantity of intoxicating liquors sold and to whom the sales were made.[4] Also requiring the building of a sidewalk in an uninhabited portion of the city.[5] So an ordinance requiring all persons who sell hay or other produce, who deliver the same within the limits of the city, to pay a fee of five cents, was held unreasonable, unauthorized by the charter and illegal: not because the fee was regarded as exorbitant and would have a tendency to restrain trade and hence against public policy, but because, under the general power vested in the council of passing such ordinances as they may deem expedient for regulating the general police and the peace and good order of the city, there was no power to impose a tax on persons occupying market stands in the streets, or huckstering or selling produce, by way of raising a revenue.[6]

[1] Commissioners v. Gas Co., 12 Pa. St. 318; Comm. v. Robinson, 5 Cush. (Mass.) 438; Davis v. Anita, 73 Iowa, 325; Comm. v. Steffee, 7 Bush (Ky.), 161; Ex parte Chin Yan, 60 Cal. 78; Gilham v. Wells, 64 Ga. 192.
[2] Coal Float v. Jeffersonville, 112 Ind. 10; Chamberlain v. Evansville, 79 Ind. 542; State v. Clark, 54 Mo. 17.
[3] Baltimore v. Radecke, 49 Md. 217.
[4] Clinton v. Phillips, 58 Ill. 102.
[5] Corrigan v. Gage, 68 Mo. 541.
[6] Kip v. Paterson, 2 Dutch. (N. J.) 298; State v. Mayor, 4 Vroom (N. J.), 283; State v. Jersey City, 5 Vroom (N. J.), 431.

§ 177. *Courts cannot interfere with discretion of municipality.*— Power to do an act is often conferred upon municipal corporations in general terms without being accompanied with any prescribed mode of exercising it. In such a case the council necessarily have, to a certain extent, a discretion as to the manner in which the power shall be used. This discretion, where it exists, cannot be judicially interfered with or questioned, except where the power is exceeded, or fraud is imputed or shown, or there is a manifest invasion of private rights.[1] So if a city has power to grade streets, the courts will not inquire into the necessity of the exercise of it, or the refusal to exercise it; nor whether a particular grade adopted, or the particular mode of exercising the power, is judicious.[2] The discretion of municipal corporations within the sphere of their powers is as wide as that possessed by the government of the state.[3] The law-making power of municipal corporations, within its prescribed limits, is as much a co-ordinate branch of the state government as the general assembly, and it is no more competent for the judiciary to interfere with the legislative acts of one than the other.[4] A tax-payer cannot set the courts in motion to

[1] City of Topeka v. Huntoon (Kan.), 33 Am. & Eng. C. C. 67; Evansville R. Co. v. Evansville, 15 Ind. 395; Kelly v. Milwaukee, 18 Wis. 83; Stack v. Maysville, 13 B. Mon. (Ky.) 1; Bridgeport v. Housatonic R. Co., 15 Conn. 475; Page v. St. Louis, 20 Mo. 136; Mayor v. Gill, 31 Md. 375; Union Pacific R. Co. v. Cheyenne, 113 U. S. 516.

[2] Teegarden v. Racine, 56 Wis. 545; Sheridan v. Colvin, 78 Ill. 237; Hovey v. Mayo, 43 Me. 722; Richmond v. McGirr, 78 Ind. 192.

[3] St. Louis v. Boffinger, 19 Mo. 15; Des Moines Gas Co. v. Des Moines, 44 Iowa, 505.

[4] State v. Swearingen, 12 Ga. 23; Danilly v. Cabanness, 52 Ga. 111; Mayor v. Comak, 75 Ga. 429; Satterthwaite v. Beaufort Co., 76 N. C. 153; Wilson v. Charlotte, 74 N. C. 748; Inhabitants v. New Orleans, 14 La. Ann. 455; New Orleans, etc. v. Dunn, 51 Ala. 128; Lockwood v. St. Louis, 24 Mo. 20; Sheidley v. Lynch, 95 Mo. 487; Dean v.

interfere with the exercise of municipal powers upon the ground that the act done is unwise or oppressive; to sustain such interference it must appear either that the act was *ultra vires*, fraudulent or corrupt.[1] So where the city has power to contract for a water supply, the price, kind of water, and amount, are matters of legislative discretion vested in the city council; and when the city confines herself within the limits of her power to contract, its legal discretion exercised by the council will not be inquired into by the courts, in the absence of fraud and corrupt and extravagant legislation, which are beyond the objects and purposes of municipal government.[2]

§ 178. *Courts may restrain passage of ultra vires ordinances.*— The courts have jurisdiction to grant an injunction to restrain the passage of a municipal ordinance when the same would be beyond the power of the municipal officers and where the passage of such ordinance would work an irreparable injury.[3] Equity cannot, however, stand between the public and their regularly elected authorities, unless the latter exceed their power, and, so long as they do not, the people must bear the consequences of their folly or choose wiser representatives.

§ 179. *Power of municipality as to taxation.*— While the general proposition that the exclusive power of taxation belongs to the legislative branch of government can-

---

Todd, 22 Mo. 90; Schanck v. Mayor, 69 N. Y. 444; Wiggins v. New York, 9 Paige, 16; Kelly v. Milwaukee, 18 Wis. 83.

[1] Wells v. Atlanta, 43 Ga. 67.

[2] Conery v. New Orleans Water Works, 39 La. Ann. 770.

[3] Poyer v. Des Plaines, 20 Ill. App. 30; Moore v. Hoffman, 2 Cin. (Ohio), 453; Whitney v. Mayor, 28 Barb. (N. Y.) 232; Baltimore v. Radecke, 49 Md. 217; Gartside v. East St. Louis, 43 Ill. 47; West v. Mayor, 10 Paige (N. Y.), 539; Banking Co. v. Jersey City, 12 N. J. Eq. 258.

not be denied, yet under our system of government such power may be delegated to municipal corporations, which are merely the instrumentalities of the state for the better administration of the government in matters of local concern. Where such a corporation is created, the power of taxation is vested in it as an essential attribute for all the purposes of its existence, unless its exercise be in express terms prohibited.[1]

§ 180. *Power to tax may be revoked.*— The power of taxation on the part of a municipal corporation is not private property or a vested right of property in its hands; but the conferring of such power is an exercise by the legislature of a public and governmental power which cannot be imparted in perpetuity, and is always subject to revocation, modification and control.[2]

---

[1] United States v. New Orleans, 98 U. S. 392, 393; Loan Ass'n v. Topeka, 20 Wall. (U. S.) 660; Comm. v. Commissioners, etc., 37 Pa. St. 277; Lowell v. Boston, 111 Mass. 460.

In United States v. New Orleans, *supra*, the court, by Mr. Justice Field, says: "For the accomplishment of those purposes, its authorities, however limited the corporation, must have the power to raise money and control its expenditure. In a city even of small extent they have to provide for the preservation of peace, good order and health, and the execution of such measures as conduce to the general good of its citizens; such as the opening and repairing of streets, the construction of sidewalks, sewers and drains, the introduction of water, and the establishment of a fire and police department. All of them require for their execution considerable expenditures of money. Their authorization without providing the means for such expenditures would be an idle and futile proceeding. Their authorization, therefore, implies and carries with it the power to adopt the ordinary means employed by such bodies to raise funds for their execution, unless such funds are otherwise provided. And the ordinary means in such cases is taxation."

[2] Williamson v. New Jersey, 130 U. S. 190, and cases cited; New Orleans v. Water Works, 142 U. S. 79.

§ 181. *Power can be exercised only for public purposes.* It is well settled by the courts of this country that no taxation is valid unless imposed for public purposes; and municipalities cannot, therefore, impose taxation for other than such purposes, nor can the legislature sanction the imposition of taxation which is intended for private ends.[1] Accordingly a municipality has no power to levy a tax the purpose of which is to assist or encourage private or corporate enterprises for manufacturing or mining.[2] As the court say in *Lowell v. Boston, supra:* "The power to levy taxes is founded on the right, duty and responsibility to maintain and administer all the governmental functions of the state, and to provide for the public welfare. To justify any exercise of the power requires that the expenditures which it is intended to meet shall be for some public service, or some object which concerns the public welfare. The promotion of the interests of individuals, either in respect of property or business, although it may result incidentally in the advancement of the public welfare, is, in its essential character, a private and not a public object. However certain and great the result-

[1] Dill. Mun. Corp., § 736; Hanson v. Vernon, 27 Iowa, 28; People v. McCreery, 34 Cal. 432; Doyle v. Austin, 47 Cal. 360; Weismer v. Douglas, 64 N. Y. 91; Hilbish v. Catherman, 64 Pa. St. 154; Glasgow v. Rouse, 43 Mo. 489; Warren v. Henley, 31 Iowa, 31; Stockton, etc. Ry. Co. v. City Council, 41 Cal. 149; Opinion of Judges, 58 Me. 591; Allen v. Joy, 60 Me. 124; Feldman v. Charleston, 23 S. C. 57; Sharpless v. Philadelphia, 21 Pa. St. 147; Citizens' Sav. etc. v. Topeka, 20 Wall. 655; Parkersburg v. Brown, 106 U. S. 487; Cole v. La Grange, 113 U. S. 1; Lowell v. Boston, 111 Mass. 454; Brewer Brick Co. v. Brewer, 62 Me. 62; State v. Clark, 29 Wis. 664; In re Eureka Basin Co., 96 N. Y. 42; English v. People, 96 Ill. 566.

[2] Loan Ass'n v. Topeka, 20 Wall. (U. S.) 655; Weismer v. Douglas, 64 N. Y. 91; People v. Parks, 58 Cal. 624; Bissell v. Kankakee, 64 Ill. 249; McConnell v. Hamm, 16 Kan. 228; Tyler v. Beacher, 44 Vt. 648; Allen v. Joy, 60 Me. 124; Commercial Bank v. Iola, 2 Dill. (C. C.) 353.

ing good to the general public, it does not, by reason of its comparative importance, cease to be incidental. The incidental advantage to the public, or to the state, which results from the promotion of private interests, and the prosperity of private enterprises or business, does not justify their aid by the use of public money raised by taxation, or for which taxation may become necessary. It is the essential character of the direct object of the expenditure which must determine its validity, as justifying a tax, and not the magnitude of the interests to be affected nor the degree to which the general advantage of the community, and thus the public welfare, may be ultimately benefited by their promotion." So taxes cannot be imposed to aid persons suffering from a great fire or flood, either by providing them with money, food, seed, or otherwise.[1] Nor to pay the selectmen the costs and damages sustained by them in resisting criminal proceedings at the instance of the town.[2]

§ 182. *Taxation and power to license distinguished.—* The distinction between the power to license as a police regulation and the same power as a revenue measure is of the utmost importance. If granted with a view to revenue, the amount of tax, if not limited by the charter, is in the discretion and judgment of the municipal authorities; if given as a police power, it must be exercised as a means of regulation only and cannot be used as a source of revenue.[3] So a provision in its charter granting power to "license and regulate" does not authorize the

[1] Lowell v. Boston, 111 Mass. 460.
[2] Lowell v. Boston, *supra.*
[3] North Hudson Co. v. Hoboken, 41 N. J. L. 71; State v. Hoboken, 4 Vroom (N. J.), 280; Mayor v. Second Ave. R. Co., 32 N. Y. 261; Comm. v. Markham, 7 Bush (Ky.), 486; State v. Cassidy, 22 Minn. 312.

city to exact license fees for revenue purposes.[1] A power to license is a police power. The exaction of license fees for revenue purposes is the exercise of the power of taxation.

§ 183. *Power to exercise right of eminent domain.*—The right of eminent domain, that is to say, the right to take private property for public uses, may be exercised by municipal corporations under delegated legislative authority in the execution of works in which the public is interested.[2] This is a right which appertains to and is inherent in every independent government, and one that is without any legal limitations except such as may exist in the organic restraints upon legal action. It requires no constitutional recognition; it is an attribute of sovereignty. When the use is public, the necessity or expediency of appropriating any particular property is not subject to judicial interference.[3]

§ 184. *Distinction between eminent domain and taxation.*—The distinction between the right of eminent domain and that of taxation is very clearly explained by Mr. Justice Ruggles in *People v. The Mayor, etc.*, 4 N. Y. 421.[4] The learned justice says: "Private property may be

---

[1] North Hudson Co. v. Hoboken, *supra;* Cooley, Const. Lim. 201; Dill. Mun. Corp., § 357.

[2] Boom Co. v. Paterson, 98 U. S. 406; Dill. Mun. Corp., § 584 et seq.; Cavanagh v. Boston, 139 Mass. 426; People v. Smith, 21 N. Y. 595; Hyde Park v. Oakwoods Cemetery, 119 Ill. 141; West River, etc. Co. v. Dix, 6 How. (U. S.) 507; Mercer v. Pittsburg, etc. Co., 36 Pa. St. 99; Scudder v. Trenton, etc. Co., 1 Saxt. (N. J.) 694; Harbeck v. Toledo, 11 Ohio St. 219; Shaffner v. St. Louis, 31 Mo. 264; Cemetery Ass'n v. New Haven, 43 Conn. 234. And see cases cited in § 604, Dill. Mun. Corp.

[3] Boom Co. v. Paterson, *supra.*

[4] And see Dill. Mun. Corp., § 738, and cases cited.

constitutionally taken for public use in two modes; that is to say, by taxation and by eminent domain. These are rights which the people collectively retain over the property of individuals to resume such portions of it as may be necessary for public use. The right of taxation and the right of eminent domain rest substantially on the same foundation. Compensation is made when private property is taken in either way. Money is property. Taxation takes it for public use; and the tax-payer receives or is supposed to receive his just compensation in the protection which government affords to his life, liberty and property, and in the increase of the value of his possessions by the use to which the government applies the money raised by the taxes. When private property is taken by right of eminent domain, special compensation is made, for the reasons hereinafter stated. . . . Taxation exacts money or services from individuals as and for their respective shares of contribution to the public burthens. Private property is taken for public use by right of eminent domain, not as the owner's share of contribution to the public burthen, but in so much beyond his share. Special compensation is therefore to be made in the latter case because the government is a debtor for the property so taken; but not in the former, because the payment of taxes is a duty and creates no obligation to repay otherwise than in the proper application of the taxes. Taxation operates upon a community or upon a class of persons in a community, and by some rule of apportionment. The exercise of the right of eminent domain operates upon an individual, and without reference to the amount or value exacted from any other individual or class of individuals."

§ 185. *Powers as to property.*— A municipal corporation may, unless restrained by statute, purchase and hold all such real property as may be necessary to the proper exercise of any power specifically conferred, or essential to those purposes of municipal government for which it was created.[1] So when a municipal corporation has power to purchase "any property" in connection with a given object, it may purchase both real and personal property necessary to the object specified. The omission of the word "real" does not limit the power so as to exclude the purchase of real property from its exercise.[2] And it has been held that where a city council has power to "purchase a site for a city hall and lockup," the power was not exhausted by a single purchase; but that it appearing afterwards that a larger lot was necessary, it might be purchased, and the one first purchased turned in in part payment.[3] But a municipal corporation has no authority to purchase lands and erect buildings for any but municipal purposes.[4] So a charter authorizing a city to buy real estate and personal property "for the use, convenience and improvement of the city" does not authorize it to purchase land within the city limits for the benefit of an agricultural and mechanical association, and to give such association the "exclusive use of the premises" for holding its "annual fairs."[5]

[1] Dill. Mun. Corp., § 562; Ketchum v. Buffalo, 4 Kernan (N. Y.), 356; Le Couteulx v. Buffalo, 33 N. Y. 333; Paterson v. Mayor, 17 N. Y. 449; Perin v. Carey, 24 How. (U. S.) 465; State v. Madison, 7 Wis. 688; State v. Commissioner, etc., 23 N. J. L. 510; State v. Brown, 27 N. J. L. 13; Louisville v. Commissioners, 1 Duvall (Ky.), 295; Louisville v. University, 15 B. Mon. (Ky.) 642; Greeley v. People, 60 Ill. 19; People v. Harris, 4 Cal. 9; Konrad v. Rogers, 70 Wis. 492.

[2] De Witt v. San Francisco, 2 Cal. 289.

[3] Konrad v. Rogers, 70 Wis. 492.

[4] Sherlock v. Winnetka, 59 Ill. 389, 68 Ill. 531; Jackson v. Hartwell, 8 Johns. (N. Y.) 422.

[5] Eufaula v. McNab, 67 Ala. 588.

§ 186. *Powers concerning divided municipalities.*— Old municipalities may be divided under legislative regulation, and new ones incorporated out of such parts of the territory of those previously organized; and in enacting such regulations the legislature may apportion the common property and the common burdens, and may, as between the parties in interest, settle all the terms and conditions of the division of their territory, or the alterations of their boundaries, as fixed by any prior law.[1] The powers exercised in the division of public corporations being purely legislative, the power to prescribe the rule by which the property of the corporation shall be divided and the debts apportioned, being incidental to the power to divide the territory, must also be strictly legislative; and the courts have no authority over the subject, and can only construe the act of the legislature and see that the legislative will is carried into effect.[2] But where no regulation is made by the legislature for any apportionment of the property, in case of division the old corporation owns all the public property within her limits, and is responsible for all the debts of the corporation contracted before the act of separation was passed.[3] And where the charter of one corporation is vacated and rendered null, the whole of its territory being annexed to two others, if no legislative arrangements are made, the effect of the annulment and annexation will be that the two enlarged corporations will be entitled to all the pub-

[1] Mount Pleasant v. Beckwith, 100 U. S. 514.

[2] Barker Dist. v. Valley Dist., 20 Am. & Eng. Corp. Cas. (W. Va.) 11; Bristol v. Newchester, 3 N. H. 524; Overseers v. Overseers, 18 Johns. (N. Y.) 382; St. Louis v. Russell, 9 Mo. 507.

[3] Dill. Mun. Corp., § 189; Mt. Pleasant v. Beckwith, 100 U. S. 514; Laramie Co. v. Albany Co., 92 U. S. 307; North Yarmouth v. Skillings, 45 Me. 141; Greenville v. Mason, 53 N. H. 515; People v. Trustees, etc., 86 Ill. 613; Town of Depere v. Bellevue, 31 Wis. 120.

lic property and immunities of the one that ceases to exist, and they will become liable for all the legal debts contracted prior to the time when the annexation was carried into operation.[1]

§ 187. *Powers of extinguished municipalities.*— Extinguished municipalities neither own property nor have they any power to levy taxes to pay debts. Whatever power such municipality may have had to levy taxes when the act passed annulling her charter terminated, and from the moment the annexation of her territory was made to the new town, such power of taxation became vested in the proper authorities of the town to which the territory and jurisdiction were by that act transferred.[2]

[1] Thompson v. Abbott, 61 Mo. 176.
[2] Mt. Pleasant v. Beckwith, 100 U. S. 514; North Hempsted v. Hempsted, 2 Wend. (N. Y.) 109; Hartford Bridge Co. v. East Hartford, 16 Conn. 149.

CHAPTER XIV.

GENERAL POWERS AS TO CONTRACTS.

§ 188. Introductory — General rule as to contracts.
189. The mode prescribed must be strictly pursued.
190. *Ultra vires* contracts by officers.
191. Implied municipal contracts.
192. When estoppel not applicable.
193. When estopped to deny irregularity.
194. Ratification of *ultra vires* contracts.
195. Contracts of compromise and arbitration.
196. Limitation on contracting indebtedness.
197. Instances where increase denied.
198. Equity will enjoin illegal increase of debt.

§ 188. *Introductory — General rule as to contracts.* — A municipal corporation, unless in some way restrained by charter, has the same general powers with other corporations to make contracts in furtherance of the corporate objects.[1] It is elementary that under the law govern-

[1] Boone, Corp., § 289; Douglas v. Virginia City, 5 Nev. 147; Goodrich v. Detroit, 12 Mich. 279; Albright v. Town Council, 9 Rich. 399; Williamsport v. Comm., 84 Pa. St. 487; Bateman v. Mayor, etc., 3 Hurl. & N. 322; East St. Louis v. Gas Light Co., 98 Ill. 432.

In East St. Louis v. Gas Light Co., *supra*, Mr. Justice Walker says:

"The long and well-established doctrine of the law is that all acts performed without authority are void. This applies as well to corporate bodies as to natural persons. The most simple and elementary rules hold that corporate bodies derive all their powers from their creator, whether they be granted by the legislature or (as in England) by the executive department of government. They are by their charters endowed with all their franchises and faculties, and any attempt to exercise others is usurpation that the law

ing the acts of municipal corporations they may adopt all the ordinary means which may be necessary to the execution of the powers expressly given in their charters

can never sanction. Natural persons are born with faculties, rights and powers, but corporate bodies possess none but such as are conferred by law, in express terms, or by clear and unmistakable implication. These rules are so elementary that it is almost inexcusable to refer to them.

"If, then, this is true, how can it be said that a municipal or private corporation can enter into a valid contract which is prohibited by law, or one that is not in conformity with the requirements of the law, or where no authority is possessed to so contract? It would seem to be so clear that such a contract would be utterly void as to require no discussion to establish its truth. It must follow that if a contract by a corporate body is void for want of power to make it, such a body is equally powerless to ratify it, or to perform acts that would estop it from asserting its invalidity. There must be the same *quantum* of power to ratify a void as is required to enter into a binding contract. The stream can never rise higher than its source, and a contract void for want of power cannot be ratified or the body estopped where the power is only the same and no greater than when it was first executed. This would seem to be axiomatic; but I am fully aware that some courts of respectability have announced an opposite rule, and some text-writers have followed such decisions. But I can never indorse the doctrine, and dissent to it in its entire length and breadth.

"Who ever heard of its being claimed that, under the operation of the common law, a contract of a married woman, or a person *non compos mentis*, could be ratified, or they could be estopped during the continuance of the disability? So of the contract of a minor, which may be only voidable. I presume it was never urged that such a contract would be rendered valid by a further contract, or the infant be estopped by his acts before arriving at his majority. And this is so because of the want of power to bind himself at the time of making the contract, and therefore a subsequent agreement, or the performance of acts that otherwise would operate as an estoppel, cannot produce such results. And the same must be true, to its full extent, of corporate bodies acting without power. No well-founded reason or distinction can be taken. A rule that a party under disability, entering into a contract, may, during such disability, ratify it, or may so act as to become estopped, is not sanc-

or those which are incidental thereto.[1] The power to make contracts is usually conferred in general terms in the incorporating act. But where the power is conferred in this manner, it is not to be construed as authorizing

tioned by any rule, and is opposed to every well-founded legal principle; nor can any rule or principle be found that can sanction it as an exception.

"But if such an exception could be maintained against private corporations, what possible reason can be assigned for applying it to a public corporation? They are dissimilar in the purpose of their creation and in the powers with which they are endowed. The one class is created for business purposes, and the other as aids to the government in conducting public affairs. The one is endowed with a portion of the powers of natural persons, and the other with a portion of governmental functions. In this consists a broad difference between the two. If deemed necessary to make the exception against private corporations to enforce void contracts made in the course of their business, it does not, by any means, follow that the same exception should be applied to public corporate bodies. To sanction such an exception is to abolish all distinction between rightful exercise of power and action without power by such bodies, and if carried to its logical conclusion must destroy legislative power to limit and restrict these bodies by their charters. It would be to enable persons to procure a charter with specified franchises and powers, and to exercise all other enumerated franchises and corporate powers. Whilst it is desirable that contracts entered into by such bodies shall be protected and enforced, it is not desirable that all or any of the well-defined principles of the law should be overturned to accomplish the purpose.

"It may be that the general assembly has authority to empower a corporation to ratify a contract made by it without power, or to declare that certain acts performed by it shall operate as an estoppel to assert the want of power; but no proposition can be plainer than that the courts have no such power, and to exercise it is to infringe upon the powers and functions of the legislative department of government. If maintained, it will operate as judicial enactments that find no sanction in the fundamental law conferring judicial powers. The functions of the different departments must be

---

[1] See § 170, *ante.*

the making of contracts of all descriptions, but only such as are necessary and usual to enable the corporation to secure or to carry into effect the purposes for which it was created.[1]

§ 189. *The mode prescribed must be strictly pursued.*— Where the mode of procedure in respect to contracts of municipal corporations is prescribed by law, such mode

kept distinctly separate and well defined to avoid confusion and to carry out the purposes of the founders of our system of government.

"I, however, do not understand the main opinion to sanction or indorse this doctrine, but it refers to cases and text-books that do assert it, and I feel constrained to avoid even the semblance of its indorsement, as I regard the question of more than ordinary importance. The past generation has been prolific in creating these artificial bodies, and their number and extent are vast, and thus this question assumes importance.

"The courts have held that private or business corporations are artificial persons, endowed with rights that are entitled to the same protection as those of natural persons, and if natural persons under disabilities cannot bind or estop themselves, it may be asked why corporate bodies under like disabilities should not receive like protection? This is not a question of policy, but of right. But if it were, it is not for the courts, but the legislature, to inaugurate the policy."

[1] Ketchum v. Buffalo, 14 N. Y. 356; Douglas v. Virginia City, 5 Nev. 148; Indianapolis v. Ind. etc. Co., 66 Ind. 396; Goodrich v. Detroit, 12 Mich. 279; Chaffee v. Granger, 6 Mich. 51; Rae v. Mayor, etc., 51 Mich. 526; Bank of Columbia v. Patterson, 7 Cranch (U. S.), 299; Montgomery County v. Barber, 45 Ala. 245; Siebrecht v. New Orleans, 12 La. Ann. 412; Albright v. Town Council, 9 Rich. L. (S. C.) 399; Bateman v. Mayor, etc., 3 H. & N. 322; Williamsport v. Comm., 84 Pa. St. 487; Wells v. Atlanta, 43 Ga. 67; Rome v. Cabot, 28 Ga. 50; Lawrence v. Killam, 11 Kan. 512; Wyandotte v. Zeitz, 21 Kan. 649; Jones v. Richmond, 18 Grat. (Va.) 517; Miller v. Milwaukee, 14 Wis. 642; Brenham v. Water Co., 67 Tex. 542; Sturtevant v. Alton, 3 McLean (U. S.), 393; Robinson v. St. Louis, 28 Mo. 488; Royalton v. Royalton, etc. Co., 14 Vt. 311; Gregory v. Bridgeport, 41 Conn. 76; State v. Hammonton, 38 N. J. L. 430; Argenti v. San Francisco, 16 Cal. 255; Dill. Mun. Corp., § 443.

must be strictly pursued by the corporation in relation to the awarding and making of contracts or their subsequent ratification. If it is not done the contract will be void.[1] And this is so although the contract entered into relates to a subject-matter with respect to which the corporate authorities have capacity to contract. If the provisions of the charter as to the mode of entering upon such contracts be violated, the contract is void.[2] Illustrations of this doctrine are to be found in those cases in which it is required of the corporate body to put out the public work to the lowest bidder; for, as such a requisition is a circumscription of the power of the corporation, it has invariably been held that any other method of contracting is illegal, and consequently cannot be subsequently validated by a ratification.[3] Accordingly, where it is provided by statute that city contracts for work or material shall be given to the "lowest responsible bidder, under such regulations as shall be prescribed by ordinance," it is essential that an ordinance providing for the awarding of a contract should designate certain plans and specifications on which to bid, as otherwise there can be no competitive bidding.[4] So a contract let under an ordinance directing the paving of a street, without speci-

[1] Town of Durango v. Pennington, 8 Colo. 257; McBride v. Grand Rapids, 56 Mich. 95; Niles Water Works v. Niles, 59 Mich. 311; Keeney v. Jersey City, 47 N. J. L. 440.
[2] Gregory v. Jersey City, 34 N. J. L. 397; Brady v. City of New York, 20 N. Y. 312; Christopher v. Same, 13 Barb. (N. Y.) 557; Cowan v. West Troy, 43 Barb. (N. Y.) 48.
[3] Cory v. County of Somerset, 45 N. J. L. 445, and cases cited.
[4] Mazet v. Pittsburg, 137 Pa. St. 548; Wilkins v. Detroit, 46 Mich. 120; Detroit v. Hosmer, 79 Mich. 384; People v. Commissioners, 4 Neb. 150; Wells v. Burnham, 20 Wis. 112; Kneeland v. Milwaukee, 18 Wis. 411; Barber Asphalt Pav. Co. v. Hunt, 100 Mo. 22; Same v. Gogreve, 41 La. Ann. 251; Ely v. Grand Rapids, 84 Mich. 336; Coughlin v. Gleason, 121 N. Y. 631.

fying the kind of paving to be done, is illegal and void when no specifications for the kind of pavement contracted for were prepared, and the advertisement inviting bids referred bidders to specifications on file in a certain office, all of which related to other kinds of paving.[1] And again, where by statute the making and filing of plans and specifications of the work to be done are conditions precedent to the power of the commissioners to advertise for proposals and award contracts for such work, the due filing of full specifications of the work will not render such contracts valid, if the plans have not been made and filed as required by statute.[2] So where a municipal charter provides that contracts for work shall be let to the lowest responsible bidder, the officials authorized to let a contract may not arbitrarily reject the lowest bid and accept a higher, without any facts justifying it.[3]

§ 190. *Ultra vires contracts by officers.*—The officers, agents, or even city council, of a municipal corporation cannot bind it by any act or contract which transcends their lawful or legitimate power; and the municipal corporation may set up the plea of *ultra vires* or its own want of power under its charter, or statute under which it was organized, to enter into a given contract, or to do a given act in excess of its corporate power and authority.[4] A person contracting with public officers must take

[1] Mazet v. Pittsburg, *supra.*
[2] Kneeland v. Milwaukee, 20 Wis. 437; Walls v. Burnham, 20 Wis. 112.
[3] Coughlin v. Gleason, 121 N. Y. 631; Bigler v. Mayor, etc., 5 Abb. N. Cas. (N. Y.) 51.
[4] Dill. Mun. Corp., § 457; Mayor, etc. v. Cunliffe, 2 Comst. (N. Y.) 175; Marsh v. Fulton County, 10 Wall. (U. S.) 676; Thomas v. Richmond, 12 Wall. (U. S.) 349; Hayes v. Holly Springs, 114 U. S. 120; Knox County v. Aspinwall, 21 How. (U. S.) 539; East Oakland v. Skinner, 94 U. S. 255; Post v. Kendall Co., 105 U. S. 667; Bates Co.

notice of their powers; and he is charged with a knowledge of the law, and makes a contract in violation of the law at his own risk.[1] So where the law commands public officers, before entering into contracts, to advertise, and contract with the lowest bidder, a contract made without advertising and without competition is wholly void, and imposes no obligation upon the public body assumed to be represented.[2] So an offer of a reward for the arrest and conviction of thieves who robbed the treasury of the county and for the recovery of the money, made "by order of the board of supervisors, H. D. Lucas, chairman," is *ultra vires* of the county commissioners and void, nor are the commissioners themselves personally liable.[3]

v. Winter, 97 U. S. 83; Daviess Co. v. Dickenson, 117 U. S. 657; Carroll Co. v. Smith, 111 U. S. 556; Dixon Co. v. Field, 111 U. S. 83; Burrill v. Boston, 2 Cliff. (U. S.) 590; Seibreicht v. New Orleans, 12 La. Ann. 496; Fox v. New Orleans, id. 154; Mayor, etc. v. Reynolds, 20 Md. 1; Baltimore v. Eschbach, 18 Md. 276; Baltimore v. Musgrove, 48 Md. 272; Maupin v. Franklin Co., 67 Mo. 327; Perkinson v. St. Louis, 4 Mo. App. 322; Cheeney v. Brookfield, 60 Mo. 53; McCaslin v. State, 99 Ind. 428; Commissioners v. Cox, 6 Ind. 403; State v. Beyers, 86 N. C. 588; Yancey v. Hopkins, 1 Munf. (Va.) 419.

[1] Parr v. Greenbush, 72 N. Y. 463; Brady v. New York, 20 N. Y. 312; McDonald v. Mayor, etc., 68 N. Y. 23; Argenti v. San Francisco, 16 Cal. 255.

[2] Parr v. Greenbush, 72 N. Y. 463.

[3] Huthsing v. Bousquet, 2 McCrary (U. S.), 152, 156; Treadway v. Schnauber, 1 Dak. Ty. 236.

In Huthsing v. Bousquet, *supra*, the court say: "When an agent makes a contract in the name of his principal, but without authority, he binds himself, for the reason that if he (the agent) is not bound there is no one to respond to the third contracting party. If in such case the agent were not bound, his act in representing himself to have authority would operate as a fraud upon the other contracting party. But if in such case the agent were to tell the third contracting party that he had no authority to bind the principal, it would be the folly of the other contracting party to enter into such

§ 191. *Implied municipal contracts.*— Although it is a well-settled principle that *ultra vires* contracts of municipal corporations are void, and that those who have dealt with such corporation under a misapprehension have no standing to demand the fulfillment of such contracts, there are occasions when this principle is modified; the modification being spoken of as the "doctrine of implied municipal liability."[1] This doctrine applies to cases where money or other property of a party has been received under such circumstances that the general law, independent of express contract, imposes the obligation upon the city to do justice with respect to the same; that

a contract, and he could not claim to be defrauded. Neither could he count upon a contract against the agent, because that would be contrary to the very terms of the manifest intent of the contract. He would have to lie upon the bed which he had made for himself with his eyes open. The law aims to relieve a party against the consequences of his own folly. The case before us stands upon this principle. The board of supervisors had no authority by law to make the contract on which the plaintiff relies in this action. The plaintiff was bound to know the law, and we must proceed, therefore, upon the assumption that he did, when he accepted the offer and performed the services, know that the board had no authority to offer the reward. The offer was *ultra vires;* the plaintiff knew it; it was his own folly to accept such an offer, and the court cannot relieve him." And see McCurdy v. Rogers, 21 Wis. 197; Richards v. Warren Co., 31 Iowa, 389; Boardman v. Hayne, 29 Iowa, 339.

[1] Wheeler v. Chicago, 24 Ill. 105; Sangamon Co. v. Springfield, 63 Ill. 66; Moore v. New York, 73 N. Y. 238; State Board, etc. v. Railway Co., 47 Ind. 407; Louisiana v. Wood, 102 U. S. 294; Gas Co. v. San Francisco, 9 Cal. 453; Paul v. Kenosha, 22 Wis. 266; Bridge Co. v. Frankfort, 18 B. Mon. (Ky.) 41; Marsh v. Fulton Co., 10 Wall. (U. S.) 676; Adams v. Farnsworth, 15 Gray (Mass.), 423; Shrewsbury v. Brown, 25 Vt. 197; Gassett v. Andover, 25 Vt. 342; Maher v. Chicago, 38 Ill. 266; Bryan v. Page, 51 Tex. 532; State Board v. Aberdeen, 56 Miss. 518; McSpeden v. Mayor, etc., 7 Bosw. (N. Y.) 601; McCracken v. San Francisco, 16 Cal. 591; Pimental v. San Francisco, 21 Cal. 351; Dickinson v. Poughkeepsie, 75 N. Y. 65; Richardson v. Grant Co., 27 Fed. Rep. 495; Argenti v. San Francisco, 16 Cal. 255.

if the city obtains money of another by mistake or without authority of law, it is her duty to refund it, not from any contract entered into by her on the subject, but from the general obligation to do justice which binds all persons, whether natural or artificial; and that if the city obtains other property which does not belong to her, it is her duty to restore it, or, if used by her, to render an equivalent to the true owner from the like general obligation.[1]

§ 192. *When estoppel not applicable to municipal corporations.*— It is of the essence of an estoppel *in pais* that the party having the authority to act in the matter shall have knowingly done an act to influence the conduct of another, and that the other must have acted in the faith of that act.[2] A person having no authority to act cannot by his conduct estop others not responsible for his conduct. Accordingly, no estoppel can ordinarily arise from the act of a municipal corporation or officer done in violation of or without authority of law.[3] Every person is presumed to know the nature and extent of the powers of municipal officers, and therefore cannot be deemed to have been deceived or misled by acts done without legal authority.[4] So a city will not be estopped by the acts or promises of a committee of the city council, or the acts of the city attorney, such committee being known to have no power to do the act which is sought to be effected by estoppel.[5]

[1] Field, J., in Argenti v. San Francisco, *supra*.
[2] St. Louis, etc. R. Co. v. Belleville, 122 Ill. 376; Davidson v. Young, 38 Ill. 145; Schnell v. Chicago, 38 Ill. 382; Bigelow on Estoppel, 480.
[3] Bigelow on Estoppel, 480.
[4] Seeger v. Mueller, 133 Ill. 86.
[5] St. Louis, etc. R. Co. v. Belleville, 122 Ill. 376.

§ 193. *When estopped to deny irregularity.*—Although, as has been shown, a municipal corporation may set up as a defense to an action upon a contract alleged to have been made by it, its own want of power to contract, yet it may be estopped from availing itself of irregularities in the exercise of powers conferred.[1] Acts of the general governing body of a municipal corporation, within their general powers, which were published, represented and held out as valid, with invitations to individuals to enter into engagements and expend money and labor on the faith of them, may be assumed by those dealing with the municipal authorities to be as represented; and the corporation having received the fruits of contracts entered into on the faith of such representations will be estopped from alleging a mere irregularity, not of the substance of the power or jurisdictional in its character, to avoid them.[2]

§ 194. *Ratification of ultra vires contracts.*—As a municipal corporation has no authority to contract in excess of its chartered powers, therefore no ratification by it could validate such contracts; nor will ratification validate an abuse of authority by an officer where his act goes beyond the charter powers. An act which does not follow the requirements of a statutory enactment, under no circumstances binds the corporation.[3] So where the charter or statute binding upon the corporation has committed a

[1] Moore v. New York, 73 N. Y. 238; Knox County v. Aspinwall, 21 How. (U. S.) 539; Moran v. Commissioners, 2 Black (U. S.), 722; Bissell v. Jeffersonville, 24 How. (U. S.) 287; Marsh v. Fulton County, 10 Wall. (U. S.) 676.

[2] Moore v. New York, *supra;* Hitchcock v. Galveston, 96 U. S. 341; Dill. Mun. Corp., § 457.

[3] Paterson v. Mayor, 17 N. Y. 449; Brady v. Mayor, 17 N. Y. 312; Hodges v. Buffalo, 2 Denio (N. Y.), 110; Gates v. Hancock, 45 N. H. 528; Reilly v. Philadelphia, 60 Pa. St. 467; Withelm v. Cedar County, 50 Iowa, 524; Smith v. Newburgh, 77 N. Y. 130.

class of acts to particular officers or agents other than the governing body, or where it has prescribed certain formalities as conditions to the performance of any description of corporate business, the proper functionaries must act and the designated forms must be observed, and generally no act of recognition or ratification can supply a defect in these respects.[1] Persons dealing with a municipal corporation are bound to know the extent of its authority, and when the charter has not been complied with they are not in a position to set up a ratification.[2] While ratification is equivalent to previous authority, the assent of the municipality must be shown. So ratification may be inferred from acquiescence after knowledge of all the material facts, or where the acts of the corporation are inconsistent with any other supposition.[3]

§ 195. *Contracts of compromise and arbitration.*— It is well settled that a municipal corporation has power to

[1] Paterson v. Mayor, *supra.*
[2] Marsh v. Fulton County, 10 Wall. (U. S.) 676; Cowen v. West Troy, 43 Barb. (N. Y.) 48; Brown v. Mayor, 63 N. Y. 239; McDonald v. Mayor, 68 N. Y. 23; Horton v. Thompson, 71 N. Y. 513; Hague v. Philadelphia, 48 Pa. St. 528; Green v. Cape May, 41 N. J. L. 45; Sault Ste. Marie County v. Van Duzen, 40 Mich. 429; Jefferson County v. Arrighi, 54 Miss. 668; Nash v. St. Paul, 11 Minn. 174; McCracken v. San Francisco, 16 Cal. 591; Alexander v. Caldwell, 83 N. Y. 480; Union Township v. Gibboney, 94 Pa. St. 534; Parsons v. Monmouth, 70 Me. 262; Bryan v. Page, 51 Tex. 532.
[3] Wilson v. School District, 32 N. H. 118; People v. Swift, 31 Cal. 26; Blen v. Bear River County, 20 Cal. 602; Clark v. Lyons County, 8 Nev. 181; Howe v. Keeler, 27 Conn. 538; Emerson v. Newburgh, 13 Pick. (Mass.) 377; Mills v. Gleason, 11 Wis. 470; Backman v. Charleston, 42 N. H. 125; Trott v. Warren, 2 Fairf. (11 Me.) 227; Topsham v. Rogers, 42 Vt. 199; St. Louis v. Armstrong, 56 Mo. 298; Lamm v. Deposit Association, 40 Md. 233; Chouteau v. Allen, 70 Mo. 290; New Orleans v. South Bank, 31 La. Ann. 560.

effect the compromise of claims held against it.[1] So a city council has authority to compromise with a party against whom the city holds a judgment, by accepting, before the expiration of the time for appeal, one-half of such judgment and costs as payment in full.[2] And where a judgment had been obtained against a fire district for injuries resulting from the conducting of electricity into a house by means of one of the wires in the district's electric fire-alarm system, it was held that a settlement of the claim by compromise was not *ultra vires* or without consideration.[3] So, also, a municipal corporation, unless disabled by positive law, can submit to arbitration all unsettled claims, with the same liability to perform the award as would rest upon a natural person; but such power must be exercised by ordinance or resolution of the corporate authorities.[4] But where a way was laid out under what was termed the "betterment law," for determining the amount of the damages of the landowners by the laying out of a street under such law, an agreement by which a city undertook with the owners of land taken for a street to submit the assessment of damages and betterments to arbitration was held *ultra vires* and void, and the city could not maintain an action to enforce the award made under such submission.[5]

§ 196. *Limitation on contracting indebtedness.*—Constitutional provisions exist in many of the states of the

[1] People v. San Francisco, 27 Cal. 655; People v. Coon, 25 Cal. 648; Grimes v. Hamilton Co., 37 Iowa, 290; Mills Co. v. Burlington, 47 Iowa, 66; State v. Martin, 43 N. W. Rep. 244; Bean v. Joy, 23 Me. 117.
[2] Agnew v. Brall, 124 Ill. 312.
[3] Prout v. Inhabitants, etc., 28 N. E. Rep. 679.
[4] Shawneetown v. Baker, 85 Ill. 563; Kane v. Fond du Lac, 40 Wis. 495; Dill. Mun. Corp., § 478; Dix v. Dummerston, 19 Vt. 263; Paret v. Bayonne, 39 N. J. L. 559.
[5] Somerville v. Dickerman, 127 Mass. 272.

Union prohibiting municipal corporations from increasing their indebtedness beyond certain designated limits, the limit usually being fixed by reference to some specified per centum of the taxable property of the municipality. Therefore, where a city or other municipal corporation is so prohibited, when such municipality shall have reached the limit prescribed by the constitution it is prohibited from making any contract whereby an indebtedness is created, even for the necessary current expenses in the administration of the affairs and government of the corporation.[1] Such constitutional provisions cannot be evaded by contracting indebtedness to be discharged in the future out of taxes which are to be levied in the future, nor can a city by any device actually increase its indebtedness,— such increase above the limit fixed being illegal.[2] So if a contract is void because it creates a liability in excess of the limit of indebtedness, the municipality has no power to make any appropriation therefor, or to levy a tax to pay interest.[3] And if an action be brought against the municipal authorities to compel them to levy a tax for the payment of an indebtedness in excess of the constitutional limit, a taxpayer is entitled to intervene and defend if the municipal authorities refuse to set up the defense.[4] · All persons

---

[1] Price v. Quincy, 105 Ill. 138; Baltimore v. Gill, 31 Md. 375; Springfield v. Edwards, 84 Ill. 77; Weston v. Syracuse, 17 N. Y. 110; Hitchcock v. Galveston, 96 U. S. 341; United States v. Ft. Scott, 99 U. S. 152; French v. Burlington, 42 Iowa, 614; Council Bluffs v. Stewart, 51 Iowa, 385; Appeal of City of Erie, 91 Pa. St. 398; Buchanan v. Litchfield, 102 U. S. 278; Walsh v. Augusta, 67 Ga. 293.

[2] Springfield v. Edwards, 84 Ill. 626; Law v. People, 87 Ill. 385; Fuller v. Chicago, 89 Ill. 282; Fuller v. Heath, 89 Ill. 296; Garrison v. Chicago, 7 Biss. 480.

[3] Law v. People, *supra.*

[4] Richards v. Supervisors of Lyon County, 69 Iowa, 612.

are chargeable with notice of the constitutional limitation on the power of municipal corporations to become indebted.[1]

§ 197. *Instances where increase denied.*— If the municipal indebtedness has reached the constitutional limit, a city cannot enter into an agreement to pay a stated sum as rent for a market-house, if its annual revenues are insufficient, over and above the interest of its indebtedness and the ordinary expenses of the city, to meet the rent proposed to be paid.[2] In order to bring the indebtedness within the constitutional limit, however, it is not necessary that the debt contracted should be actually payable. Thus, where a city contracted for the construction of water-works, it was held that it became indebted at the time of making the contract, and not merely upon completion and acceptance of the work.[3] But a constitutional provision limiting the amount of indebtedness does not affect contracts made before the adoption of the provision.[4] It has been held in Iowa that a contract made by

---

[1] People v. May, 9 Colo. 404; Law v. People, 87 Ill. 385; French v. Burlington, 42 Iowa, 614.

In People v. May, *supra*, the court say: "The hardships and inconveniencies resulting from this construction are urged upon our attention. To such appeals the language of the courts is uniform. The province of the judiciary is not to make the law, but to construe it. The meaning of a constitutional provision being plain, it must stand, be recognized and obeyed as the supreme law of the land. It is not for us, but for those who made the instrument, to supply its defects. If the legislature or the court may take that office upon themselves, or under color of construction, or upon any other specious ground, they may depart from that which is plainly declared, the people may well despair of ever being able to set any boundary to the powers of the government."

[2] Appeal of City of Erie, 91 Pa. St. 398.

[3] Culbertson v. Fulton, 127 Ill. 30; Law v. People, 87 Ill. 385.

[4] County of Moultrie v. Bank, 92 U. S. 631; Davenport, etc. Co. v.

a city whose indebtedness has already reached the constitutional limit, by which a contractor agrees to construct a sewer, and to accept in payment of the contract price certificates assessing the benefits against the property benefited, does not create any liability on the part of the municipality, and is not within the constitutional prohibition.[1] Where the charter of a municipal corporation provided that the common council should have no power " to contract debts, incur liabilities, or make expenditures in any one year which shall exceed the revenue for the same year," a contract entered into without submitting the question to the tax-payers, for a supply of water for a term of years at a cost per year which would not exceed any such percentage as could be allowed in any one year, was held void, and there could be no recovery thereon for any water that had been furnished thereunder.[2]

§ 198. *Equity will enjoin illegal creation of debt.*— A municipal corporation will not be permitted to dispose illegally of corporate money or to illegally create a debt, and may be prevented by an application of resident taxpayers for an injunction.[3] " Of the right of resident tax-

Davenport, 13 Iowa, 229; Bound v. Wisconsin Cent. R. Co., 45 Wis. 543.

[1] Davis v. Des Moines, 71 Iowa, 500.
[2] Niles Water-works v. Niles, 59 Mich. 311.
[3] Crampton v. Zabriskie, 101 U. S. 601; Gifford v. Railroad Co., 10 N. J. Eq. 171; Baltimore v. Gill, 31 Md. 375; Wade v. Richmond, 18 Grat. (Va.) 583; Page v. Allen, 58 Pa. St. 338; Stevens v. Railroad Co., 29 Vt. 546; Webster v. Harrington, 32 Conn. 131; Terrett v. Sharon, 34 Conn. 105; Merrill v. Plainfield, 45 N. H. 126; Normand v. Otoe Co., 8 Neb. 18; Oliver v. Krightley, 24 Ind. 514; Drake v. Phillips, 40 Ill. 388; Grant v. Davenport, 36 Iowa, 396; Hooper v. Ely, 46 Mo. 505; Douglass v. Placerville, 18 Cal. 643; Patterson v. Bowes, 4 Grant (Canada), 170; West Guillimbury v. Railroad Co., 23 Grat. (Va.) 383.

payers to invoke the interposition of a court of equity to prevent an illegal disposition of the moneys of the county, or the illegal creation of a debt which they in common with other property holders of the county may otherwise be compelled to pay, there is at this day no serious question. The right has been recognized by the state courts in numerous cases, and from the nature of the powers exercised by municipal corporations, the great danger of their abuse, and the necessity of prompt action to prevent irremediable injuries, it would seem eminently proper for courts of equity to interfere upon the application of the tax-payers of a county to prevent the consummation of a wrong, in excess of their power, to create burdens upon property holders. Certainly in the absence of legislation restricting the right to interfere in such cases to public officers of the state and county, there would seem to be no substantial reason why a bill by or on behalf of individual tax-payers should not be entertained to prevent the misuse of corporate powers."[1]

[1] Field, J., in Crampton v. Zabriskie, 101 U. S. 601.

CHAPTER XV.

PARTICULAR POWERS AND LIABILITIES OF MUNICIPAL CORPORATIONS.

§ 199. Exclusive control over streets.
200. When estopped to deny existence of street.
201. Power to grade and improve.
202. Discretionary powers as to improvement.
203. Liability for consequential damages.
204. Liability for accidents upon streets.
205. Instances of liability for defective streets.
206. Notice to authorities required.
207. Sewers — General powers as to.
208. Discretion in selecting sewer system.
209. Duty to provide sewer outlet.
210. City not insurer of condition of sewer.
211. Liability for injury from defective sewer.
212. Power to abate nuisances.
213. Liability as to nuisances.
214. Powers as to quarantine regulations.
215. Powers as to public wharves.
216. Exclusive privileges to gas or water companies.
217. Contracts as to gas and water supply.
218. Power to regulate rates.
219. Liability for damages owing to inadequate water supply.
220. Doctrine of *respondeat superior*.
221. Distinction between public *quasi*-corporations and municipal corporations.
222. Not liable for damages arising from *ultra vires* acts of officers.

§ 199. *Exclusive control over streets.*—When the charter of a city does not confer upon it in express terms the exclusive power over its streets, it has not the control of them to the exclusion of the sovereign power of the state.[1]

[1] Grand Rapids Electric Co. v. Gas Co., 21 Am. & Eng. Corp. Cas. 270; Dill. Mun. Corp., § 547; State v. Coke Co., 18 Ohio St. 262; Gas

Nothing short of the whole sovereign power of the state can confer exclusive rights and privileges in public streets dedicated or acquired for public use, and which are held in trust for the public at large. It is the general doctrine that municipalities, under the power of exclusive control over their streets, may allow any use of them consistent with the public objects for which they are held.[1]

§ 200. *When estopped to deny existence of street.*— If the authorities of a city or town have treated a place as a public street, taking charge of it and regulating it as they do other streets, and an individual is injured in consequence of the negligence and carelessness with which this is done, the corporation cannot, when it is sued for such injury, throw the party upon an inquiry into the regularity of the proceedings by which the land became a street or into the authority by which the street was originally established.[2]

§ 201. *Power to grade, improve and alter streets.*— If the authorities of a municipal corporation are authorized by an act of the legislature to grade, improve, alter or

Co. v. Light Co., 115 U. S. 659; Cooley, Const. Lim. 38, 207, 208; Gas Light Co. v. Gas Co., 25 Conn. 19; Gas Light Co. v. Saginaw, 28 Fed. Rep. 529; Gas Co. v. Middleton, 59 N. Y. 228; East Hartford v. Bridge Co., 10 How. (U. S.) 511; Minturn v. Larue, 23 How. (U. S.) 435; Harrison v. State, 9 Mo. 530; Wright v. Nagle, 101 U. S. 796; Davis v. Mayor, 14 N. Y. 506; Railroad Co. v. Railway Co., 10 Wall. (U. S.) 52; Same v. Same, 12 Fed. Rep. 308; Parkersburg Gas Co. v. Parkersburg, 4 S. E. Rep. (W. Va.) 650.

[1] Grand Rapids Electric Light Co. v. Grand Rapids, etc. Gas Co., *supra.*

[2] Mayor v. Sheffield, 4 Wall. (U. S.) 189; James v. Portage, 48 Wis. 677; Bishop v. Centralia, 49 Wis. 609; Coates v. Canaan, 51 Vt. 131; Sewell v. Cahous, 75 N. Y. 45; Steck v. Lancaster, 57 N. H. 88; Manderchid v. Dubuque, 25 Iowa. 108; Aurora v. Cobshire, 55 Ind. 484; Phelps v. Mankato, 23 Minn. 277.

re-lay streets, such authority extends only to public streets or highways, and will not give authority to alter any road owned by other persons.[1] As a municipal corporation cannot contract in any other mode than is authorized by its charter, if the preliminaries to be observed, and the manner in which a contract for a local improvement shall be entered into, are prescribed by a mandatory charter provision or law, its directions must be complied with.[2] And if such contract be invalid when made for a failure to comply with the statutory requirements, its subsequent ratification by the corporation requires the observance of the same formalities and provisions necessary to be complied with in the making of a valid contract.[3] A general power to lay out and open streets in a city implies power to establish the grade of such streets;[4] and power to grade streets includes power to make contracts relating to the same, with respect to the work to be done and compensation to be paid.[5] Accordingly, when to make a contract for the improvement of a street, and to provide the funds to pay for it, the charter prescribed

[1] Quin v. City of Paterson, 27 N. J. L. 35; McGuire v. Rapid City, 43 N. W. Rep. 706.

[2] Terre Haute v. Lake, 43 Ind. 480; People v. San Francisco, 36 Cal. 595; Butler v. Charleston, 7 Gray (Mass.), 12; Zottman v. San Francisco, 20 Cal. 96; Brady v. Mayor, 20 N. Y. 312; Murphey v. Louisville, 9 Bush (Ky.), 189; Stecket v. East Saginaw, 22 Mich. 104; Taft v. Pittsford, 28 Vt. 286; Dill v. Inhabitants, 7 Met. (Mass.) 438; Bridgeport v. Railroad Co., 15 Conn. 475; Marsh v. Fulton Co., 10 Wall. (U. S.) 676; Horn v. Baltimore, 30 Md. 218; Steam Nav. Co. v. Dandridge, 8 Gill & J. (Md.) 248; Baltimore v. Eschbach, 18 Md. 276; Haynes v. Covington, 13 Sm. & M. 408.

[3] Town of Durango v. Pendleton, 8 Colo. 257.

[4] Smith v. Washington, 20 How. (U. S.) 135: Himmelmann v. Hoadley, 44 Cal. 213; Fish v. Mayor, 6 Paige (N. Y.), 268; Creal v. Keokuk, 4 Greene (Iowa), 47.

[5] Sturtevant v. Alton, 3 McLean (U. S.), 393; People v. Flagg, 17 N. Y. 584.

that it should *only* be done by local assessments on abutting property, this amounts to a direct inhibition against making any contract for such improvement only as such mode is pursued, and the failure or omission of the city to create the fund from the sources indicated to pay for such improvement, when made, will not subject the city to any general liability therefor.[1]

§ 202. *Discretionary power as to improvement.*—Where a city, by special charter or otherwise, is vested with the exclusive control of its streets and with power to regulate or improve the same, the manner in which they may

[1] Portland L. & M. Co. v. East Portland, 18 Oreg. 21.
In Portland, etc. Co. v. East Portland, *supra*, Lord, J., in discussing this question, said:
"The reason is plain. As the city is without any general power to contract for and provide the funds to pay for such improvements except by way of local assessment, it necessarily results that it cannot be subject to any general liability. To subject the city to a general liability there must be some general power under which it would be authorized to raise the funds to pay for such improvements. But when such general power is conferred, and an improvement is projected to be paid for out of funds to be derived from local assessments, and the city authorities upon whom is devolved the duty neglect or fail to take the requisite proceedings to create the lien which is to supply the funds to pay for such improvement, the improvement being within the scope of the general power of the corporation independent of the special mode by local assessments, such neglect or omission after the improvement is made will subject the city to a general liability to pay therefor. . . ."[1]

"A general liability is based upon the general power conferred to make such improvements and to defray the expenses thereof out of the general fund; for if the city has not such general power, but is confined exclusively in making and defraying the expenses of such improvements to the fund derived from local assessments upon abutting property, there would be no authority even though there was a failure to perform all the required acts intended to provide such fund, and to subject the acts to a general liability. It would be *ultra vires.*"

be improved must, in a large measure, be left to the discretion of the authorities; but when the discretion has been exercised and the street or improvement made, the duty of keeping it in repair is ministerial, and for neglect to perform such duty an action will lie.[1] So the authorities of a city may rightfully cause a street to be graded, and when the entire width is not needed for travel they may cause a strip in the center thereof to be sodded, instead of graveling the entire street, and provide for the payment of the cost thereof by special assessment upon the property benefited thereby.[2]

§ 203. *Liability for consequential damages caused by improvement.*—It is the general doctrine that persons appointed or authorized by law to make or improve a highway are not answerable for consequential damages if they act within their jurisdiction and with care and skill.[3] Accordingly, a municipal corporation is not liable for consequential damages where the act complained of was done by it or its officers under and pursuant to authority conferred by a valid act of the legislature, and

[1] Urquhart v. Ogdensburg, 91 N. Y. 67; Hines v. Lockport, 50 N. Y. 238; Mills v. Brooklyn, 32 N. Y. 489; Lansing v. Toolan, 37 Mich. 152; Marquette v. Cleary, id. 296; Darling v. Bangor, 68 Me. 112; Davis v. City Council, 51 Ala. 139; Campbell v. Montgomery, 53 id. 527; White v. Yazoo City, 27 Miss. 357; Hill v. Charlotte, 72 N. C. 55; Dewey v. Detroit, 15 Mich. 307; Carr v. Northern Liberties, 36 Pa. St. 324; Grant v. Erie, 69 Pa. St. 420; Western College v. Cleveland, 12 Ohio St. 375.

[2] Murphy v. Peoria, 119 Ill. 509.

[3] Transportation Co. v. Chicago, 99 U. S. 641; British Cast-plate Co. v. Meredith, 4 Durnf. & E. 794; Sutton v. Clarke, 6 Taunt. 28; Boulton v. Crowther, 2 Barn. & Cres. 703; Green v. Borough of Reading, 9 Watts (Pa.), 382; O'Connor v. Pittsburg, 18 Pa. St. 187; Callendar v. Marsh, 1 Pick. (Mass.) 418; Smith v. Washington, 20 How. (U. S.) 135.

there had been no want of reasonable care or want of reasonable skill in the execution of the power.[1] So a municipal corporation authorized by law to improve a street by building on the line thereof a bridge over or a tunnel under a navigable river where it crosses the street incurs no liability for the damages unavoidably caused to adjoining property by obstructing the streets or the river, unless such liability be imposed by statute.[2] Nor is a municipal corporation liable for consequential injury to abutting lots owing to a change in the grade of a street where such change is made under authority of law and with due care.[3] And if in the process of repairing or grading a street the walls of a dwelling-house or other building lose their support and in consequence fall, the owner cannot recover damages, provided due care has been used.[4] Where, however, the city, in grading the streets

---

[1] Dill. Mun. Corp., § 987; Transportation Co. v. Chicago, 99 U. S. 635; Smith v. Washington, 20 How. (U. S.) 135; Goszler v. Georgetown, 6 Wheat. (U. S.) 593; Tyson v. Milwaukee, 50 Wis. 78; Owens v. Milwaukee, 47 Wis. 461; Humes v. Mayor, 1 Humph. (Tenn.) 403; Nebraska City v. Lampkin, 6 Neb. 27; Stockford v. St. Louis, 4 Mo. App. 564; Hunt v. Boonville, 65 Mo. 620; White v. Yazoo City, 27 Miss. 357; Alden v. Minneapolis, 24 Minn. 254; Kaist v. St. Paul R. Co., 22 Minn. 118; Pontiac v. Carter, 32 Mich. 164; Reynolds v. Shreveport, 13 La. Ann. 426; Newport Bridge Co. v. Foote, 9 Bush (Ky.), 264; Noyes v. Mason City, 53 Iowa, 418; Quincy v. Jones, 76 Ill. 231; Fulla v. Atlanta, 66 Ga. 80; Dorman v. Jacksonville, 13 Fla. 538; Simmons v. Camden, 26 Ark. 276; Shaw v. Crocker, 42 Cal. 435; Trenton, etc. Co. v. Rabb, 36 N. J. L. 335; Carr v. Northern Liberties, 35 Pa. St. 324; Barritt v. New Haven, 42 Conn. 174; Simmons v. Providence, 12 R. I. 8; Hovey v. Mayor, 43 Me. 322.

[2] Transportation Co. v. Chicago, 99 U. S. 635.

[3] Smith v. City of Eau Claire, 78 Wis. 457; Dore v. Milwaukee, 42 Wis. 108; Dill. Mun. Corp., §§ 988, 990.

[4] Mitchell v. Rome, 49 Ga. 19; St. Louis v. Gurno, 12 Mo. 414; Pontiac v. Carter, 32 Mich. 164; Quincy v. Jones, 76 Ill. 231; Chambers v. Satterlee, 40 Cal. 297; Crossett v. Janesville, 28 Wis. 420.

and making public improvements, fails to exercise proper care and skill in the *selection of a plan,* and by reason thereof an injury to the owner of private property occurs, which by the exercise of reasonable care and skill could have been avoided, the city is liable for such injury.[1] No responsibility attaches, it has been held, for damages done by the diversion of surface water, where the diversion is merely incidental to and occasioned by the making or alteration of street grades.[2] But it has been held, on the other hand, that where a municipal corporation puts into execution a scheme of improvement by which surface water, collected from a large area, is prevented from following the grades of the street, and is carried by artificial means from where it would otherwise be discharged and made to flow onto the land of one person in ease of the lands of others, there an actionable wrong is committed.[3] And where the quantity of surface water sent to the point of discharge is increased by an enlargement of the area of drainage, but such enlargement results entirely from making the grade of the streets conform to the grade established by the proper authority, any injury resulting from the increase in the quantity of water discharged at that point is regarded in law as *damnum absque injuria.*[4]

§ 204. *Liability for accidents upon streets.*— A municipal corporation is not an insurer against accidents upon its streets and sidewalks, as seems to be quite generally supposed by the community at large, nor is every defect

[1] City of Valparaiso v. Adams, 123 Ind. 250; Derinzy v. Ottawa, 15 Ont. Rep. 712.
[2] Miller v. Norristown, 47 N. J. Eq. 62.
[3] Miller v. Norristown, *supra;* Field v. West Orange, 36 N. J. Eq. 118, 37 id. 600; Torrey v. Scranton, 133 Pa. St. 173.
[4] Miller v. Norristown, *supra.*

therein, though it may cause the injury sued for, actionable. It is sufficient if the streets are in a reasonably safe condition for travel in the ordinary modes by night as well as by day.[1] Accordingly, a city is not liable for injuries caused to a person by others while using the public streets for coasting.[2] Nor to a person injured by the discharge of a cannon by a crowd collected together for the purpose of firing the cannon for their amusement.[3] Nor for injury caused by the fall of snow and ice from a roof overhanging the sidewalk.[4] Nor by the fall of a weight attached to a flag suspended across the street.[5] But it has been held that where a city permits a wooden awning or roofing to be constructed over the sidewalk, it is liable for an injury occasioned by a defect therein, although it is not apparently in bad repair.[6] Nor is a city liable for injury done to property by a mob, unless it is so specially provided by statute.[7] But when it is shown that the city officers had actual knowledge of the defect, the city is liable for injuries sustained by a person falling into a sewer, owing to the displacement of a man-

[1] Dill. Mun. Corp., § 789.
[2] Faulkner v. Aurora, 2 Am. & Eng. Corp. Cas. 520; Pierce v. New Bedford, 129 Mass. 534; Ray v. Manchester, 46 N. H. 59; Schultz v. Milwaukee, 49 Wis. 254; Hutchinson v. Concord, 41 Vt. 271; Steele v. Boston, 128 Mass. 583.
[3] Borough, etc. v. Fitzpatrick, 94 Pa. St. 121.
[4] Norristown v. Thayer, 67 Pa. St. 355; Hutson v. Mayor, 9 N. Y. 163; Davenport v. Mayor. 37 N. Y. 568; Requa v. Rochester, 45 N. Y. 120; Hume v. Mayor, 74 N. Y. 264; Grove v. Ft. Wayne, 45 Ind. 429; House v. Montgomery Co., 60 Ind. 580; Drake v. Lowell, 13 Met. 292; Day v. Mitford. 5 Allen, 98; Merrill v. Portland, 4 Clif. C. C. 438.
[5] Hewison v. New Haven, 34 Conn. 136; Chicago v. Fowler, 60 Ill. 322.
[6] Dill. Mun. Corp., § 959, and cases cited; Louisiana v. New Orleans, 109 U. S. 285.
[7] Louisiana v. New Orleans, *supra.*

hole cover in the street;[1] and for injury to an ox which stepped into a hole in an embankment, when the street overseer had neglected to repair it or place a warning signal at its approach.[2]

§ 205. *Instances of liability for defective streets and sidewalks.*—It is the duty of a municipal corporation not only to keep its streets and highways unobstructed and in repair, but also to maintain its sidewalks free from obstructions and defects.[3] And a city is liable in damages for an injury resulting from such defects, although the sidewalk may not have been constructed by authority of the city.[4] For if a municipal corporation knowingly permits a way or walk constructed upon one of its streets by a private person, and designed for the use of pedestrians, to remain and be so used, the authorities by their official acts inciting and inducing such use, the duty devolves upon the corporation to keep the way in proper repair as a sidewalk.[5] The duty of a city to exercise reasonable care to keep its sidewalks in a safe condition does not extend to the removal of ice, which constitutes no other effect than slipperiness, there being no such accumulation of ice as to constitute an obstruction to travel, and no ridge or inequalities of such height, or lying at such inclination or angle, as would be likely to trip passengers

[1] Barr v. City of Kansas, 105 Mo. 550.
[2] Bradford v. Mayor, 8 So. Rep. 683.
[3] Reinhard v. Mayor, 2 Daly (N. Y.), 243; Higert v. Greencastle, 43 Ind. 574; Furnell v. St. Paul, 20 Minn. 117; Manchester v. Hartford, 30 Conn. 118; Hubbard v. Concord, 35 N. H. 52.
[4] Higert v. Greencastle, *supra;* Boucher v. New Haven, 40 Conn. 457.
[5] Graham v. Albert Lea, 50 N. W. Rep. (Minn.) 1108; Estelle v. Lake Crystal, 27 Minn. 243; Champaign v. McInnis, 26 Ill. App. 338; Weare v. Fitchburg, 110 Mass. 334; Saulsbury v. Ithaca, 94 N. Y. 27; City of Flora v. Nancy, 26 N. E. Rep. 645; Mansfield v. Moore, 124 Ill. 133.

or cause them to fall.[1] A municipal corporation is under no obligation to construct a street crossing on the same level as the sidewalk.[2] And it has been held that where a sidewalk was at an elevation of four inches above the level of the crossing, it was not such evidence of negligence in the construction of the crossing as to make the corporation liable for injury to a foot passenger sustained by striking her foot against the curbstone while attempting to cross the street.[3]

§ 206. *Notice to authorities required.*— But a city will not be held liable, as a general rule, for injuries from a defective sidewalk or street, unless the authorities have notice of the defect, or unless they have notice of such facts and circumstances as would, by the exercise of reasonable diligence, lead a prudent person to such knowledge.[4] Actual notice to the public authorities is not, in all cases, however, required, and it has been held that negligence may be inferred from the omission by the corporation to cause dangerous obstructions to be removed from the streets after sufficient time has elapsed to afford

[1] Henckes v. Minneapolis, 42 Minn. 530; Stanton v. Springfield, 12 Allen (Mass.), 566; Nason v. Boston, 14 Allen (Mass.), 508; Stone v. Hubbardston, 100 Mass. 49; Smyth v. Bangor, 72 Me. 249; Mekellar v. Detroit, 57 Mich. 158; Taylor v. Yonkers, 105 N. Y. 202; Chicago v. McGiven, 78 Ill. 347; Broburg v. Des Moines, 63 Iowa, 523; Cook v. Milwaukee, 24 Wis. 270; Buckley v. Prescott, 12 Ont. App. 637.

[2] Miller v. St. Paul, 38 Minn. 134.

[3] London v. Goldsmith, 16 Sup. Ct. Can. Rep. 231.

[4] City of Chicago v. Stearns, 105 Ill. 554; Centralia v. Krouse, 64 Ill. 19; Rapho v. Moore, 68 Pa. St. 404; Cleveland v. St. Paul, 18 Minn. 279; Doulson v. Clinton, 33 Iowa, 397; Mayor v. Sheffield, 4 Wall. (U. S.) 189; Portland v. Richardson, 54 Me. 46; Chicago v. Robbins, 2 Black (U. S.), 418; Johnston v. Charleston, 3 S. C. 332; McGinnity v. New York, 5 Duer (N. Y.), 674; Griffin v. New York, 9 N. Y. 456; Durant v. Palmer, 5 Dutch. (N. J.) 544; Sterling v. Thomas, 60 Ill. 264; Jeverin v. Eddy, 52 Ill. 189; Estelle v. Lake Crystal, 27 Minn. 243.

§ 207.] STREETS, SEWERS, ETC. 275

a presumption of knowledge of their existence and an opportunity to effect their removal.[1] And four hours has been held to be a reasonable time.[2]

§ 207. *Sewers — General powers as to.* — The authority to construct sewers is a general one, and resides in all municipal corporations, unless expressly denied to them by the legislature.[3] This authority is one which may be rightfully exercised upon any of the highways of the municipality, for it is invested with exclusive authority over all streets and highways within its limits.[4] Upon the principle that a grant of power carries with it, by implication, the right to use all means and instrumentalities necessary to a beneficial exercise of the power, the grant of a general power to construct sewers, without any restriction as to the mode in which they are to be built or operated, must be construed with reference to the situation and requirements of the district in which the sewers are to be constructed, and must be held to confer authority to construct them in such a manner and with such appliances as may be necessary to render them serviceable and effective.[5] So, where a system of sewerage of the ordinary kind cannot be used to advantage for want of sufficient fall to carry away the contents of the mains and pipes by the force of gravitation, villages and other municipal corporations under a general grant of power to

[1] Requa v. Rochester, 45 N. Y. 136.
[2] Bradford v. Mayor, 8 S. Rep. 683.
[3] Ft. Wayne v. Coombs, 107 Ind. 75; Leeds v. Richmond, 102 Ind. 372.
[4] Ft. Wayne v. Coombs, *supra*.
[5] Drexel v. Town of Lake, 127 Ill. 54; St. Louis Bridge Co. v. People, 125 Ill. 226; Cone v. Hartford, 28 Conn. 363; Fisher v. Harnsburg, 2 Grant Cas. (Pa.) 291; Stoudinger v. Newark, 28 N. J. Eq. 187; Glasby v. Morris, 18 N. J. Eq. 72; Trapshagen v. Jersey City, 29 N. J. Eq. 206; Michener v. Philadelphia, 118 Pa. St. 535.

construct main drains and sewers, etc., without any limitation or restriction as to the mode in which they shall be built or operated, will have the right to construct pumping works, to be used in the working and use of sewers.[1] But a city council has not the power, by calling in its ordinance a "sewer" a "street," to construct the one under the pretense of repairing the other, so as to lay a burden of taxation, which should have been borne by the public at large, upon a few adjacent property-holders.[2]

§ 208. *Discretion of city in selecting sewer system.*—The duties of the municipal authorities in adopting a general plan of drainage and determining when and where sewers shall be built, of what size and of what level, are of a *quasi*-judicial nature, involving the exercise of deliberate judgment and large discretion and depending upon considerations affecting the public health and general convenience throughout an extensive territory; and the exercise of such judgment and discretion in the selection and adoption of the general plan or system of drainage is not subject to revision by a court.[3] But the construc-

---

[1] Drexel v. Town of Lake, 127 Ill. 54.
[2] Clay v. Grand Rapids, 27 N. W. Rep. 695.
[3] Johnson v. District of Columbia, 118 U. S. 19; Child v. Boston, 4 Allen (Mass.), 41; Mills v. Brooklyn, 32 N. Y. 489; Radcliff's Ex'r v. Mayor, 4 N. Y. 195; Franklin Wharf Co. v. Portland, 67 Me. 46; Haskell v. New Bedford, 108 Mass. 208; Savannah v. Spears, 66 Ga. 304; Lynch v. New York, 76 N. Y. 60.

In Mills v. Brooklyn, *supra*, the court say: "The duty of draining the streets and avenues of a city or village is one requiring the exercise of deliberation, judgment and discretion. It cannot, in the nature of things, be so executed that in every single moment every square foot of the service shall be perfectly protected against the consequence of water falling from the clouds upon it. This duty is not in a technical sense a judicial one, for it does not concern the administration of justice between citizens; but it is of a judicial nature, for it requires, as I have said, the same qualities of deliberation and repair of sewers according to the general plan so adopted are simply ministerial duties, and for any negligence in so constructing a sewer, or keeping it in repair, the municipality which has constructed and owns the sewer may be sued by a person whose property is thereby injured.[1]

§ 209. *Duty to provide sewer outlet.*—It is the law that if a municipal corporation by its system of constructing sewers renders an outlet necessary, it must provide one.[2] The outlet is a necessary part of the sewer, and if the municipal corporation enters upon the work of constructing a sewer it assumes control over the entire work, and must construct and maintain it with ordinary care and skill. This obligation extends to the entire sewer, not merely to such parts of it as are on property owned by the city, and it cannot escape the consequences resulting from negligence by asserting that part of the sewer was constructed on private property.[3]

§ 210. *City not insurer of condition of sewer.*—A municipal corporation is not an insurer of the condition of its sewers, but it is bound to use ordinary care and skill in constructing and maintaining them, and for a failure so to do is responsible to a citizen who suffers loss from

---

tion and judgment. It admits of a choice of means, and the determination of the order of time in which improvements shall be made. It involves, also, a variety of prudential circumstances relating to the burdens which may be discreetly imposed at a given time, and the preference which one locality may claim over another."

[1] Johnson v. District of Columbia, *supra*.

[2] City of Evansville v. Decker, 84 Ind. 325; Crawfordsville v. Bond, 96 Ind. 236; Van Pelt v. Davenport, 42 Iowa, 308; Byrnes v. Cohoes, 67 N. Y. 204.

[3] Ft. Wayne v. Coombs, 107 Ind. 75; Commissioners v. City, 79 Ind. 491; Angell on Highways, § 216; Dill. Mun. Corp., §§ 656, 688.

such negligence. This care and skill requires the municipality to take notice of the liability of timbers to decay from time and use, and to take such measures as ordinary care and skill dictate to guard against a sewer becoming unsafe because of the decay of the materials used in its construction.[1]

§ 211. *Liability for injuries from defective sewer.*— Though a sewer is constructed with care and skill, a municipal corporation is liable for injuries for negligently failing to keep it in repair, and where it is suffered to remain out of repair for such a length of time as that it was the duty of the corporate authority to take notice of its condition, the law will charge the corporate officers with notice of its condition.[2] And though a city is not responsible because of any failure to provide proper sewerage, yet if the effect of the construction of one of its public works shall be to collect water and cast it upon the land of an individual where it would not overflow, the city is liable.[3] And where the property of private persons is flooded, either directly by water being set back, when this is the result of the negligent execution of the plan

---

[1] Indianapolis v. Scott, 72 Ind. 196; Board of Com'rs v. Legg, 93 Ind. 523; Indiana Car Co. v. Parker. 100 Ind. 181; Rapho v. Moore, 68 Pa. St. 404; Norristown v. Thayer, 67 Pa. St. 335; Todd v. Troy, 61 N. Y. 506.

[2] Fort Wayne v. Coombs, 107 Ind. 75; City of Madison v. Baker, 103 Ind. 41; Dill. Mun. Corp., § 1025.

[3] Buford v. Grand Rapids, 53 Mich. 98; Ashley v. Port Huron, 35 Mich. 296; Dixon v. Baker, 65 Ill. 518; Weis v. Madison, 75 Ind. 241; Indianapolis v. Tate, 39 Ind. 282; Ross v. Clinton. 46 Iowa, 606; Van Pelt v. Davenport, 42 Iowa, 308; Wilson v. New Bedford, 108 Mass. 261; O'Brien v. St. Paul, 25 Minn. 333; Thurston v. St. Joseph, 51 Mo. 510; Byrnes v. Cohoes, 67 N. Y. 204; Rhodes v. Cleveland, 10 Ohio, 159; Inman v. Tripp, 11 R. I. 520; Gillison v. Charleston, 16 W. Va. 282.

adopted for the construction of sewers, or of the negligent failure to keep the same in repair and free from obstructions, the municipality is liable, and this whether the land injured is below grade of street or not.[1] And it has been held that if a city constructs a sewer in such a manner that an additional flow of surface water into a lot is caused thereby, in other words, if the sewer gathered other than surface water, the owner of such lot may recover such damages as may have been caused by such increased flow.[2]

§ 212. *Power to abate nuisances.*—The power to abate nuisances is a portion of police authority necessarily vested in all municipal corporations and populous towns; and the legislature may invest a municipal corporation with power to abate nuisances summarily, without requiring resort to legal proceedings.[3] The power so conferred is for the public good and not for any private advantage, and for failure of its officers to properly exercise the power the municipality is not liable.[4] But, in the absence of authority, neither the board of health nor the city council of a city has any power to erect a dam on a person's land without his consent for the purpose of abating a nuisance existing on adjacent land.[5] But where a municipal corporation, however, is authorized by its charter or general laws to remove and prevent nuisances,

---

[1] Hutchins Bros. v. Mayor of Hurlburg, 20 Am. & Eng. Corp. Cas. (Md., 1887) 400; Lynch v. Mayor, 76 N. Y. 60; O'Brien v. St. Paul, 25 Minn. 333; Inhabs. W. Orange v. Field, 37 N. J. Eq. 600; Ashley v. Port Huron, 35 Mich. 296.

[2] Arn v. City of Kansas, 4 McCrary (U. S.), 558.

[3] Baumgartner v. Hasty, 100 Ind. 575; King v. Davenport, 98 Ill. 305; Kennedy v. Phelps, 10 La. Ann. 227; Dill. Mun. Corp., § 374.

[4] Armstrong v. Brunswick, 79 Mo. 319.

[5] Cavanagh v. Boston, 139 Mass. 426.

the only restriction upon that right is that what is done shall clearly be done for the public health, safety and convenience.¹ The mere declaration by the city council that a certain structure is an encroachment or obstruction does not make it so, nor can such declaration make it a nuisance unless in fact it has that character. That which is authorized by legislative authority cannot be declared a nuisance by a city corporation. "It is a doctrine not to be tolerated in this country that a municipal corporation, without any general laws either of the city or of the state within which a given structure can be shown to be a nuisance, can, by the mere declaration that it *is* one, subject it to removal by any person supposed to be aggrieved, or even by the city itself. This would place every house, every business and all the property in the city at the uncontrolled will of the temporary local authorities."²

§ 213. *Liability as to nuisances.*— It is the duty of a municipal corporation to provide wholesome laws within its sphere for the protection of the persons and property of its citzens, but it cannot guaranty them against the

[1] Dubuque v. Maloney, 9 Iowa, 450; Commissioners v. Worcester, 3 Pick. (Mass.) 462; Roberts v. Ogle, 30 Ill. 459; Commissioners v. Gas Co., 12 Pa. St. 318; Salem v. Railroad Co., 92 Mass. 431; Dingley v. Boston, 100 Mass. 544; Lake View v. Letz, 44 Ill. 81; Commissioners v. Goodrich, 13 Allen (Mass.), 546; Whyte v. Mayor, 2 Swan (Tenn.), 364; People v. Albany, 11 Wend. (N. Y.) 539; St. Paul v. Coulter, 12 Minn. 51; Williams v. Augusta, 4 Ga. 509; St. Louis v. Bentz, 11 Mo. 611; Collins v. Hatch, 18 Ohio, 523; New Orleans v. Phillipi, 9 La. Ann. 44; Peck v. Lockwood, 5 Day, 22; Taylor v. Carondelet, 22 Mo. 105; Phillips v. Allen, 41 Pa. St. 481; Mobile v. Yuelle, 3 Ala. 137; Baltimore v. Radecke, 49 Md. 217.

[2] Yates v. Milwaukee, 10 Wall. (U. S.) 497; Pieri v. Shieldsboro, 42 Miss. 393; Underwood y. Green, 42 N. Y. 140; Darst v. People, 50 Ill. 286; Miller v. Burch, 32 Tex. 209; Everett v. Council Bluffs, 46 Iowa, 66; Rye v. Paterson, 45 Tex. 312; Chicago v. Laflin, 49 Ill. 172.

infringement of such laws.¹ Accordingly, a municipal corporation is not liable in damages for a failure to abate a nuisance existing upon private property when not created by its agents, though such nuisance exists in violation of its ordinances.² Nor is a town liable for an act which results in creating a nuisance to the property of one of its citizens, when the act complained of is not within the scope of its corporate powers.³

¹ Levy v. Mayor, 1 Sandf. (N. Y.) 465.
² Kansas City v. Kiley, 13 Am. & Eng. Corp. Cas. (Mo., 1885) 446; Davis v. Montgomery, 51 Ala. 139; Levy v. New York, 1 Sandf. (N. Y.) 465; Heurson v. New Haven, 37 Conn. 475; Armstrong v. Brunswick, 79 Mo. 319.
³ Seele v. Deering (Me.), 10 Atl. Rep. 45.

In Seele v. Deering, *supra*, which was an action for damages for injuries to plaintiff's mill-pond, caused by the highway surveyor of the defendant town digging a ditch which turned the drainage from a tripe factory into the pond, thereby rendering the water unfit for use, the court say:

"To create a liability on the part of the town not connected with its private advantage, the act complained of must be within the scope of its corporate powers as defined by statute. If the particular act relied on as the cause of action be wholly outside the general powers conferred on towns, they can in no event be liable therefor, whether the performance of the act be expressly directed by a majority vote, or was subsequently ratified. . . .

"It is quite evident that a town, independent of any statutory authority, has no corporate authority to dig ditches across another's land. Such an act is *ultra vires;* and any express majority vote, based on a proper article in a warrant calling a meeting of the defendants, directing such acts, would create no liability on the part of the town. Cushing v. Bedford, 125 Mass. 526; Lemon v. Newton, 134 Mass. 476."

See, also, Morrison v. Lawrence, 98 Mass. 219; Brown v. Vinalhaven, 65 Me. 402; Small v. Danville, 51 Me. 359; Woodcock v. Calais, 66 Me. 234; Anthony v. Adams, 1 Met. (Mass.) 284; Estes v. China, 56 Me. 407; Franklin Wharf Co. v. Portland, 67 Me. 46; Proprietors, etc. v. Lowell, 7 Gray (Mass.), 223.

§ 214. Powers as to quarantine regulations.— It has been held that a town organized under general laws with the usual and ordinary powers has no power to establish a quarantine against property and persons, and a contract for services to be rendered in connection therewith is *ultra vires* and void.[1] In *New Decatur v. Berry, supra,* the court say: "How the power to prohibit persons from coming into the town under any circumstances can in any just sense be said to be incident to any one of the powers enumerated, we are unable to see. Every power conferred may be fully exercised and effected without the exercise of the power here claimed. No power conferred would in the slightest degree be aided by the exercise of the power claimed here. The power claimed is not expressly granted; it is not implied in or incident to any power granted; it is not essential to the declared objects and purposes of the corporation; it does not exist. The employment of the appellee by the corporate authorities as 'chief of the quarantine guard' cannot find justification or authorization under the power 'to establish night and day watches and patrols, and to appoint captains thereof.' The watches and patrols thus provided for are for the ordinary police of the town, charged with the conservation of the peace and good order and the enforcement of authorized ordinances of the municipal government. None of these duties were to be performed by the alleged quarantine guard, or the appellee as chief of that guard. He was employed, if at all, solely for the purpose of discharging functions with which the municipality had no power to clothe him, and rendering services which were not in furtherance of any municipal object or purpose."

[1] New Decatur v. Berry, 90 Ala. 432; Dill. Mun. Corp., §§ 89, 463–465.

§ 215. *Powers as to public wharves.*— In the absence of any special statutory authority a city has no power to lease a public wharf to private persons. When it undertakes to confer on a private individual such a right in streets or wharves as will produce a conflict between the public and the private use, the act is *ultra vires*.[1] So an ordinance giving to private persons the right to occupy a portion of the public wharf with a grain elevator for fifty years, without reserving the right to resume possession and regulate the charges, is void.[2] The use and control of public highways, such as streets and wharves, belonging to the city, cannot be surrendered by contract to a private individual to the exclusion of the public. Such highways are public property, intended for public use, and placed under the control of the city government for the benefit of the public; and any other disposition of such property, without special authority conferred by the law-making power, must be disregarded.[3] It is a doctrine which has often been decided and is settled law that a municipal corporation must at all times retain the full possession of its legislative powers so as at all times to be able to discharge its public duties.[4]

[1] Bateman v. Covington, 14 S. W. Rep. 361 (Ky., 1890); City of Louisville v. Bank, 3 B. Mon. (Ky.) 138; Dill. Mun. Corp., §§ 659-661.
[2] Illinois Canal Co. v. St. Louis, 2 Dill. C. C. 70.
[3] Bateman v. Covington, *supra*.
[4] Gale v. Kalamazoo, 23 Mich. 344; People's R. R. v. Memphis R. R., 10 Wall. (U. S.) 38, 50; Louisville Ry. v. Louisville, 8 Bush (Ky.), 415; Brooklyn v. City R. R., 47 N. Y. 475; Milhau v. Sharp, 27 N. Y. 611; Presbyterian Church v. Mayor, etc., 5 Cow. (N. Y.) 538; Smith v. Morse, 2 Cal. 524; Stuyvesant v. Mayor, 7 Cow. (N. Y.) 588; Saving Fund v. Philadelphia, 31 Pa. St. 175; Ex parte Mayor, etc., 23 Wend. (N. Y.) 277; Railroad Co. v. Mayor, 1 Hill (N. Y.), 362; Martin v. Mayor, 1 Hill (N. Y.), 545; Bryson v. Philadelphia, 47 Pa. St. 329; Dingman v. People, 51 Ill. 277; Brimmer v. Boston, 102 Mass. 19; Johnson v. Philadelphia, 60 Pa. St. 445; State v. Gas Co., 18 Ohio St.

§ 216. *Exclusive privileges as to gas and water supply.* It is perfectly competent, of course, for the legislature to confer upon an individual or a private corporation the exclusive right to furnish gas or water supply to the inhabitants of a city, and to erect works and lay pipes therefor within the limits of a municipal corporation.[1] But a municipal corporation has no power to grant such exclusive privileges without express authority conferred by charter so to do. No such authority can be derived by implication.[2]

262; Jackson v. Bowman, 39 Miss. 671; Oakland v. Carpentier, 13 Cal. 540; Bateman v. Covington, 14 S. W. Rep. 361.

In Bateman v. Covington, *supra*, the court say: "We perceive no authority in the city charter or any legislative enactment empowering the city to make such a contract, or to deprive the public of its use. The city has the power to impose certain duties upon those availing themselves of wharf privileges, and to make such regulations as may be necessary to keep the wharf in repair for public use; but it has no power to confer absolute control to an individual who leases it for his own private use. The city must control the use, and for this purpose may place the ground in charge of a wharf-master, or some agent who acts for the city, that the public may enjoy the use. A city has the exclusive control of its streets, and a like control over its wharves; and in appropriating the use of either for the benefit of a private person, to the exclusion of the public, it is going beyond its power, and such a contract is void. The city is a mere trustee for the public, and all have the right to use streets and wharves, one citizen having the same right as another."

[1] State v. Milwaukee Gaslight Co., 29 Wis. 454; New Orleans Gaslight Co. v. Louisiana Light Co., 115 U. S. 650; New Orleans Water Co. v. Rivers. 115 U. S. 674; St. Tamany Water Works v. New Orleans Water Works, 120 U. S. 64; Crescent City Gaslight Co. v. New Orleans Gaslight Co., 27 La. Ann. 138; Hovelman v. Kansas City, etc. Co., 79 Mo. 632; Memphis v. Water Co., 5 Heisk. (N. J.) 495; Broadway Co. v. Hankey, 31 Md. 346; Atlantic City Water Works v. Atlantic City, 48 N. J. L. 378; Citizens' Water Co. v. Hydraulic Co., 50 Conn. 1; Lehigh Water Co.'s Appeal, 102 Pa. St. 515; Louisville v. Weible, 84 Ky. 290.

[2] Tuckahoe Canal Co. v. Railroad Co., 11 Leigh, 42; Gaines v. Coates,

§ 217. *Contracts as to gas or water supply.*— Under a general authority to make all contracts necessary for its welfare, a city has the implied power to make contracts for water or gas supply.¹ And having the power to make a contract touching the matter, it may make it according to its own discretion as to its prudence or good policy, within the limits of its franchise.² And where the charter of the city provides that the city may establish water-works or contract for the furnishing of water for the city, it has the power to make a contract with a water company to furnish water for the city upon payment of a monthly rental therefor;³ or it may receive its water supply by leasing its own water-works to another company for that purpose.⁴

§ 218. *Power to regulate water, gas and telephone rates.* Municipalities may, under delegated legislative authority, regulate the rates at which water or gas supply may be furnished or telephone service enjoyed.⁵ But the power of regulating rates is not a power of confiscation, or to

51 Miss. 235; Mohawk Bridge Co. v. Railroad Co., 6 Paige (N. Y.), 554; State v. Cincinnati Gas Co., 18 Ohio St. 262; Norwich Gas Co. v. City Gas Co., 25 Conn. 20; East St. Louis v. Gas Co., 98 Ill. 415; Des Moines Gas Co. v. Des Moines, 44 Iowa, 505; Gas Co. v. Light Co., 115 U. S. 659; Gaslight Co. v. Saginaw, 28 Fed. Rep. 529; Gas Co. v. Middleton, 59 N. Y. 228; Parkersburg Gas Co. v. Parkersburg, 4 S. E. Rep. (W. Va., 1887) 650; Citizens' Gas Co. v. Elwood, 114 Ind. 332.

¹ Cabot v. Rome, 28 Ga. 50; Wells v. Atlanta, 43 Ga. 67; Atlantic City Water Works v. Atlantic City, 39 N. J. Eq. 367; McKnight v. New Orleans, 24 La. Ann. 412; Grant v. Davenport, 36 Iowa, 396; Hale v. Houghton, 8 Mich. 458.

² Indianapolis v. Gaslight Co., 66 Ind. 396.

³ Capitol City Water Co. v. Montgomery, 9 S. Rep. 343.

⁴ Los Angeles Water Co. v. Los Angeles, 55 Cal. 178.

⁵ State v. Gas Co., 18 Ohio St. 262; Norwich Gaslight Co. v. Gas Co., 25 Conn. 19; State v. Gaslight Co., 29 Wis. 452; Spring Valley Water Works v. San Francisco, 82 Cal. 286.

take the property of a company without just compensation. The municipal authorities have no right to fix rates arbitrarily without investigation, or without the exercise of judgment and discretion in determining what is a fair and reasonable compensation.[1] And where a city ordinance granting a franchise to a gas company and accepted by the gas company fixes the maximum price of gas, the city cannot subsequently reduce such price.[2] An ordinance of a city regulating water rates is not invalid because it fixes different rates for the consumers of the same class; one section providing that when there is a large consumption of waste water the company may apply a meter and collect a certain amount for certain quantities of water used, although another section of the ordinance fixes certain specific rates for the use of water according to the size of the house.[3]

§ 219. *Liability for damages owing to inadequate water supply.*— It is the general rule that, in the absence of an express statute so declaring, municipalities are not liable to actions for injuries occasioned by reason of negligence in using or keeping in repair the fire-engines owned by them, or furnishing them with an inadequate supply of water.[4] So a city making a contract with a water com-

[1] Spring Valley Water Works v. San Francisco, 82 Cal. 286; State v. Gas Co., 18 Ohio St. 262.
[2] State v. Gas Light Co., 102 Mo. 472.
[3] Sheward v. Citizens' Water Co., 90 Cal. 635; Shiras v. Ewing, 20 Pac. Rep. 320.
[4] Black v. Columbia, 19 S. C. 415; Wheeler v. Cincinnati, 19 Ohio St. 19; Eastman v. Meredith, 36 N. H. 284; Bigelow v. Randolph, 14 Gray (Mass.), 541; Hafford v. New Bedford, 16 Gray (Mass.), 297; Jewett v. New Haven, 38 Conn., 368; Og v. Lansing, 35 Iowa, 495; Elliott v. Philadelphia, 75 Pa. St. 347; O'Meara v. Mayor, 1 Daly (N. Y.), 425; Smith v. Rochester, 76 N. H. 506; Howard v. San Francisco, 51 Cal. 52; Maximilian v. Mayor, 62 N. Y. 160; Greenwood v.

pany to furnish water for fires is not liable to its citizens or residents on account of the failure of the company to furnish water or to perform the conditions of the contract. The contract in such case is between the city and the water company.[1] Nor is a city liable, it has been held, for its neglect in cutting water off from a hydrant, but for which the fire might have been extinguished.[2]

§ 220. *The doctrine of respondeat superior.*—The rule *respondeat superior*, though well recognized in fixing the liabilities of private corporations and natural persons, has been the source of much doubt and perplexity in its application to municipal corporations. It is now well settled, however, that such corporations, when acting in a certain capacity, are liable as superiors and employers for injuries to third persons resulting from the negligence and unskilfulness of their agents or servants while in the line of their employment.[3] And it has been said that

---

Louisville, 13 Bush (Ky.), 226; Pollock v. Louisville, 18 Bush (Ky.), 221; Fisher v. Boston. 104 Mass. 87; Hayes v. Oshkosh, 33 Wis. 314; Heller v. Sedalia, 53 Mo. 159; Bishmeyer v. Evansville, 29 Ind. 187; Western College of Medicine v. Cleveland, 12 Ohio St. 375; Grant v. Erie, 69 Pa. St. 420; New Orleans v. Crescent City Ins. Co., 25 La. Ann. 390; Davis v. Montgomery, 51 Ala. 139; Hill v. Boston, 122 Mass. 324; Tainter v. Worcester, 123 Mass. 311; Foster v. Lookout Water Co., 3 Lea (Tenn.), 42; Wright v. Augusta, 78 Ga. 241; Van Horn v. Des Moines, 4 Am. & Eng. Corp. Cas. 339.

[1] Becker v. Keokuk Water Works, 79 Iowa, 419; Davis v. Clinton Water Works, 54 Iowa, 59; Van Horn v. Des Moines, 63 Iowa, 447; Nickerson v. Bridgeport Hydraulic Co., 46 Conn. 24; Fowler v. Athens City Water Works. 83 Ga. 219; Vrooman v. Turner, 69 N. Y. 280; Weet v. Brockport, 16 N. Y. 161; Marvin Safe Co. v. Ward, 46 N. J. L. 19; Exchange Bank v. Rice, 107 Mass. 37.

[2] Tainter v. Worcester, 123 Mass. 311; New Orleans v. Insurance Co., 25 La. Ann. 390; Wheeler v. Cincinnati, 19 Ohio St. 19.

[3] Toledo v. Cone, 41 Ohio St. 149; Dill. Mun. Corp., § 974; Barnes v. District of Columbia, 91 U. S. 540; Rowell v. Williams, 29 Iowa,

under analogous conditions there seems to be no foundation in reason or public policy for exempting such public corporations any more than private individuals from liability for injuries inflicted on others through the negligence of their agents.[1]

210; Powers v. Council Bluffs, 50 Iowa, 97; Russell v. Mayor, etc., 2 Denio (N. Y.), 461; Tone v. Mayor, etc., 70 N. Y. 157, id. 459; Campbell v. Montgomery, 53 Ala. 527.

[1] Toledo v. Cone, *supra*.

In Toledo v. Cone, *supra*, the court say:

"While they (municipal corporations) act in a public character or capacity and exercise public powers, they may and do also act in a private capacity, like private corporations, and as such are held to a like responsibility. Thus, if a municipal corporation acquires real or personal property, and in the discharge of what may be deemed ministerial duties in respect to the same an individual receives injury through the negligence of its officers or servants, it should be held responsible to that individual. Though not liable for a defect of judgment or discretion while acting as a state instrumentality in the exercise of legislative functions, yet, having like a private corporation or natural person become the owner or obtained the control of property, it should not be relieved from the operation of the general maxim that one should so use his own as not to interfere with that which belongs to another. Thus, if a city neglects its ministerial duty to cause its sewers to be kept free from obstructions, to the injury of a person who has an interest in the performance of that duty, it is liable to an action for the damages thereby occasioned. Emery v. Lowell, 104 Mass. 13. So, if a city owns a wharf and has the exclusive control of it and receives wharfage or profit for the use thereof, it will be held liable to a private action for an injury suffered by an individual by reason of a defect in the structure. Pittsburg v. Grier, 22 Pa. St. 54. And the same rule applies in respect to a city's failure to keep its streets in a safe condition for public use, where this is a duty resting upon it.

"Of course, before a municipal corporation is subjected to liability for the misfeasance or neglect of its agents or servants, it becomes material and sometimes difficult to determine whether they are in fact the agents or servants of the corporation. It is said by an approved text-writer that if the municipal corporation appoints

§ 221. *Distinction between public quasi-corporations and municipal corporations.*— The authorities establishing the doctrine that a city is responsible for its mere negligence are so numerous that the law must be deemed to be settled in accordance therewith.[1] A distinction must be noted, however, between the liability of a municipal corporation made such by acceptance of a charter, and the involuntary *quasi*-corporations known as counties, towns, school districts, and especially the townships of New England. The liability of the former is greater than

or elects them and can control them in the discharge of their duties, can continue or remove them, can hold them responsible for the manner in which they discharge their trust; and if those duties relate to the exercise of corporate powers and are for the peculiar benefit of the corporation in its local or special interest, they must justly be regarded as its agents or servants, and the corporation will be held responsible for their acts within the scope of their employment. And in broad terms to the same effect, it is laid down in Wood on Master and Servant, section 459, that if an independent public officer, or some one whose duties are defined or specified by law, is in any measure subject to the discretion or control of a municipal corporation, and acts in obedience to its instructions, the relation of master and servant exists and the rule of *respondeat superior* applies. The rule is predicated upon the right of the employer to discharge and control the servant. Blake v. Ferris, 5 N. Y. 48."

[1] Barnes v. District of Columbia, 91 U. S. 551; Mayor v. Henley, 2 Cl. & Fin. 331; Mersey Docks v. Gibbs, 1 H. L. Cas. 93; Canal Co. v. Parnably, 11 Ad. & Ell. 223; Scott v. Mayor, 37 Eng. L. & Eq. 465; Weightman v. Washington, 1 Bl. 39; Nebraska v. Campbell, 2 Bl. 590; Robbins v. Chicago, 4 Wall. (U. S.) 658; Davenport v. Ruckman, 37 N. Y. 569; Requa v. Rochester, 45 N. Y. 129; Clayburg v. Chicago, 25 Ill. 525; Springfield v. Le Claire, 49 Ill. 476; Smoot v. Mayor, 24 Ala. 112; Jones v. New Haven, 34 Conn. 1; County Commissioners v. Duckett, 20 Md. 468; Pittsburg v. Greer, 22 Pa. St. 54; Erie v. Schwingle, 22 Pa. St. 388; Cook v. Milwaukee, 24 Wis. 270; Sawyer v. Coose, 17 Grat. (Va.) 241; Williams College v. Cleveland, 12 Ohio, 377; McCombs v. Akron, 15 Ohio, 476.

that of the latter, even when vested with corporate capacity and the power of taxation.[1]

[1] Barnes v. District of Columbia, 91 U. S. 551; Dill. Mun. Corp., §§ 10, 11, 13, 961; Elmore v. Drainage Commissioners, 135 Ill. 269.

In Elmore v. Drainage Commissioners, *supra*, the court say:

"That a private corporation formed by voluntary agreement for private purposes is held to respond in a civil action for its negligence or tort goes without saying, and yet, in deciding the mooted question at issue in this case, it seems convenient to restate that proposition. So, also, it is admitted law that municipal corporations proper, such as villages, towns and cities which are incorporated by special charters or voluntarily organized under general laws, are liable to individuals injured by their negligent or tortious conduct or that of their agents or servants in respect to corporate duties. In regard to public involuntary *quasi*-corporations the rule is otherwise, and there is no such implied liability imposed upon them. These latter, such as counties, townships, school districts, road districts and other similar *quasi*-corporations, exist under general laws of the state, which apportion its territory into subdivisions for the purpose of civil and governmental administration, and impose upon the people residing in the said several subdivisions precise and limited public duties and clothe them with restricted corporate functions co-extensive with the duties devolved upon them. In such organizations the duties and their correlative powers are assumed *in invitum*, and there is no responsibility to respond in damages in a civil action for neglect in the performance of duties unless such action is given by statute.

"The grounds upon which the liability of the municipal corporations proper is usually placed are that the duty is voluntarily assumed and is clear, specific and complete, and that the powers and means furnished for its proper performance are ample and adequate. . . . In such case there is a perfect obligation and a consequent civil liability for neglect in all cases of special private damages. The non-liability of public *quasi*-corporations, unless liability is expressly declared, is usually placed upon these grounds: that the corporators are made such *nolens volens*, that their powers are limited and specific, and that no corporate funds are provided which can, without express provisions of law, be appropriated to private indemnification. Consequently, in such case the liability is one of imperfect obligation, and no civil action lies at the suit of an individual for non-performance of the duty imposed."

§ 222. *Not liable if damages arise from ultra vires act of officer.*— Where the officers of a municipal corporation assume the power to do some act on behalf of the municipality which is *ultra vires* the corporation, no liability is in consequence imposed.[1] To establish the liability of a municipal corporation for damages resulting from the alleged negligence or want of skill of its agents or servants in the course of their employment, it is essential to show that the act complained of was within the scope of the corporate powers; if outside the powers of the corporation as conferred by statute or by special charter, the corporation is not liable, whether its officers directed the performance of the act or it was done without any express direction.[2] Or, to state the proposition in differ-

[1] Mayor, etc. v. Cunliff, 2 Comst. (N. Y.) 165; Browning v. Owen Co., 44 Ind. 11; Haag v. Commissioners, 60 Ind. 511; Smith v. Rochester, 76 N. Y. 506; Anthony v. Adams, 1 Met. (Mass.) 284; Baker v. Boston, 12 Pick. (Mass.) 184; Thayer v. Boston, 19 Pick. (Mass.) 511; Perley v. Georgetown, 7 Gray (Mass.), 464; Baltimore v. Eschbach, 18 Md. 276; State v. Mayor, 27 Md. 85; Railroad Co. v. Quigley, 21 How. (U. S.) 202; Cooper v. Atlanta, 53 Ga. 638; Sewell v. St. Paul, 20 Minn. 511; Aldrich v. Tripp, 11 R. I. 141; Chicago v. McGraw, 75 Ill. 566; Mead v. New Haven, 40 Conn. 72; Morrison v. Lawrence, 98 Mass. 219; Barbour v. Ellsworth, 67 Me. 294. *Cf.* Salt Lake City v. Hollister, 118 U. S. 256.

[2] Smith v. Rochester, 76 N. Y. 506.

In Salt Lake City v. Hollister, *supra*, a distinction has been drawn, and a rather fine one, it must be confessed, between the liability of a municipality for the wrongful acts of its agents and officers in the course of the corporate business and its liability on contracts which the law does not authorize it to make. That was a case where a suit was instituted by Salt Lake City to recover of Hollister a sum of money said to be illegally exacted by him as collector of internal revenue for the district of Utah from the city for a special tax upon spirits alleged to have been distilled by said city and not deposited in the bonded warehouse of the United States by plaintiff as required by law. The plaintiff, under threat of selling sufficient property of the city to pay said taxes, paid the sum demanded under

ent language: When individuals, although professing to act under color of authority from municipal corporations, do acts which are injurious to others, if the objects and

protest, appealed to the commissioner of internal revenue, who failed to refund the money, and after waiting six months brought suit. It was held that a municipal corporation cannot, any more than any other corporation or private person, escape the taxes due on liquor, whether distilled legally or illegally; and it cannot make the want of legal authority to engage in the business a shelter for the taxation imposed by the government on such business, by whomsoever conducted. Mr. Justice Miller, in delivering the opinion of the court, said:

"While it may be true that the rule we have been discussing may require a more careful scrutiny in its application to municipal corporations than to corporations for pecuniary profit, we do not agree that they are wholly exempt from liability for wrongful acts done, with all the evidence of their being acts of the corporation, to the injury of others, or in evasion of legal obligations to the state or the public. . . . The question of the liability of corporations on contracts which the law does not authorize them to make, and which are wholly beyond the scope of their powers, is governed by a different principle. In such case the party dealing with the corporation is under no obligation to enter into the contract. No force or restraint or fraud is practiced on him. The powers of the corporation are matters of public law, open to his examination, and he may and must judge for himself as to the power of the corporation to bind itself by the proposed agreement. It is to this class of cases that most of the authorities cited by appellant belongs — cases where the corporations have been sued on contracts which they have successfully resisted because they were *ultra vires*. But even in this class of cases the courts have gone a long way to enable parties who had parted with property or money on the faith of such contracts to obtain justice by recovery of the property or the money specifically, or as money had and received to their use."

Judge Dillon, in discussing this case in his valuable work on Municipal Corporations, in a note to section 973, observes:

"The opinion of the court in this novel case seems to assert the proposition that the city, although acting *ultra vires* in the strongest sense of that expression, *i. e.*, in respect of a matter *manifestly and necessarily* outside of the scope of its powers either general or spe-

§ 222.] STREETS, SEWERS, ETC. 293

purposes which they propose to accomplish are not within the scope of the corporate powers of the municipality, and not done in the execution of any corporate duty im-

cial, would be liable in tort, although perhaps not in contract, for the acts of its agents and servants in the course of such unauthorized business. But the action, viz., to recover back taxes actually though involuntarily paid, being equitable in its nature, the judgment of the court, which on the special facts was unquestionably sound (for the tax was a tax upon property and was justly due), need not necessarily rest upon so broad a basis as the one above indicated, and the observations of the court in the opinion must be limited accordingly. If not thus limited, and the court is to be understood as laying down the broad principle that the city would be liable in the conduct of such business to the same extent as if the business was *infra vires* (for example, that it would be liable in damages to the manager of the distillery for a negligent injury to him happening in the course of the business), it would be, as it seems to us, an extension of the doctrine of liability of municipal corporations for *ultra vires* acts beyond the limits heretofore and generally recognized, since such extended liability would appear to rest upon a supposed estoppel created by the mere fact of conducting an *ultra vires* business, and this in the face of the limitations imposed by the charter of the city upon its corporate powers. Such view, if sound as respects private corporations, would seem not to be so as respects municipal corporations, whose powers are defined and limited for the express purpose of protecting the inhabitants from just such liability. Cases within the apparent or possible powers of the municipality, where the other party acted in good faith and had no reasonable means of protecting himself from loss or damage, may stand upon different grounds."

Mr. Jones, in his recent work on Negligence of Municipal Corporations, in reviewing this criticism, remarks:

"This decision has been somewhat criticised by an eminent authority, and quite a limited construction is put upon the opinion in the case. But the learning of the justice who wrote the opinion, and his familiarity with the subject under discussion, as well as a recent reference to the case (Central Transp. Co. v. Pullman's Car Co., 139 U. S. 24, 46 — 1890), all give evidence that the opinion was a deliberate expression of the view of the court upon the general questions discussed. The effect of this decision is to broaden materially

posed upon the corporation by law, the city is not liable for the damages occasioned by such acts.

<blockquote>the view of liability of municipal corporations for torts, and it is a strong authority in support of the contention that these bodies should be liable for negligence in respect to their *ultra vires* acts. Following its reasoning it may be said that an individual who contracts with a corporation is under the obligation of ascertaining the powers of the particular body with which he assumes to deal. But when, as a member of society, he is acting within his own rights, and is not dealing with or interfering with other independent members of the community, he should not be without remedy when injured by an *ultra vires* act of a corporation done in violation of his right of personal safety. Such an act of the corporation is made doubly wrongful by the fact that it is in excess of the corporate powers, and for the damages resulting from it the corporation should respond."</blockquote>

CHAPTER XVI.

POWERS AND LIABILITIES AS TO MUNICIPAL SECURITIES.

§ 223. Power to issue bonds.
224. Purposes for which bonds may be issued.
225. Instances where power denied.
226. Formality in execution as affecting legality.
227. Irregularity as affecting liability.
228. Effect of recitals in bonds.
229. Who are *bona fide* holders.
230. Power to issue bonds not implied from power to borrow.
231. Limitation on indebtedness as affecting legality of bonds.
232. Invalid bonds cannot be ratified.
233. Liability cannot be avoided by reorganization.
234. Liability in *assumpsit* on invalid bonds.
235. Illegal issue of bonds may be enjoined.
236. Municipal-aid bonds.
237. Power must be specifically granted.
238. Power to subscribe to railroad stock.
239. Limitation on amount of subscription.
240. Levying tax to pay subscription.

§ 223. *Power to issue bonds.*—Municipal corporations, unless authorized by their charters, have no power to make and place on the market commercial paper, and all persons dealing in municipal bonds must see that the power to issue them exists.[1] There is no presumption

[1] Police Jury v. Britton, 15 Wall. (U. S.) 566; Claiborne County v. Brooks, 111 U. S. 400; Concord v. Robinson, 121 U. S. 165; Kelley v. Milan, 127 U. S. 139; Young v. Clarendon Township, 132 U. S. 340; Norton v. Dyersburg, 127 U. S. 160; Hill v. Memphis, 134 U. S. 198; Merrill v. Monticello, 138 U. S. 673; Hewitt v. School Dist., 94 Ill. 428; Harding v. Rockford, etc. R. Co. 65 Ill. 90; Wiley v. Silliman, 62 Ill. 170; Clark v. Hancock, 27 Ill. 305.

that such paper has been issued within the scope of their powers, as in the case of corporations created for business purposes, and even *bona fide* holders cannot recover upon bonds or their coupons where there was no authority to issue the bonds.[1]

§ 224. *Purposes for which bonds may be issued.*— Municipal bonds cannot be issued for other than public purposes, inasmuch as the taxation, from the proceeds of which the principal and interest must be met, can only be imposed for public purposes.[2] Accordingly a municipal corporation cannot, without legislative authority, issue bonds in aid of an extraneous object; and every person dealing in them must, at his peril, take notice of the existence and terms of the law which conferred the power to issue them, no matter under what circumstances he may obtain them.[3]

---

[1] Hewitt v. School Dist., *supra*, and cases cited.

In Hewitt v. School Dist., *supra*, the court say: "The fact, then, that the bond was not issued for an authorized purpose undeniably rendered it void. Municipal corporations are not usually endowed with powers to enter into traffic or general business, and are only created as auxiliaries to the government in carrying into effect some special governmental policy, and to aid in preserving the order and in promoting the well-being of the locality over which their authority extends. . . . Being created for governmental purposes, the borrowing of money, the purchase of property on time and the giving of commercial paper are not inherent or even powers usually conferred; and, unless endowed with such power in their charters, they have no authority to make and place on the market such paper, and persons dealing in it must see that the power exists."

[2] City of Eufaula v. McNab, 67 Ala. 588; Hanson v. Vernon, 27 Iowa, 47; Parkersburg v. Brown, 106 U. S. 487; Camden v. Allen, 2 Dutch. (N. J.) 398; Pray v. Northern Liberties, 31 Pa. St. 69; Sharpless v. Mayor of Philadelphia, 21 Pa. St. 147; Allen v. Inhabitants of Jay, 60 Me. 124; Loan Association v. Topeka, 20 Wall. (U. S.) 655; Curtis v. Whipple, 24 Wis. 350; Whiting v. S. & F. Ry. Co., 25 Wis. 167; Jenkins v. Andover, 103 Mass. 94.

[3] South Ottawa v. Perkins, 94 U. S. 260; Brenham v. German Am.

§ 225. *Instances where power to issue denied.*— It has been held that a city has no power to incur a debt and issue bonds to raise money to build a dam across a river within its limits, for the purpose of introducing the water of such river into the city, with the view of developing the natural advantages of the city for manufacturing purposes.[1] Nor has a municipal corporation power to authorize the issuance of bonds and levying of taxes in support of private manufacturing and mining companies;[2] nor to aid persons suffering from a great flood.[3] But bonds may be issued for the making and paving of streets,[4] to sustain public schools,[5] and to construct public buildings.[6]

Bank, 144 U. S. 173; Marsh v. Fulton County, 10 Wall. (U. S.) 676; East Oakland v. Skinner, 94 U. S. 255; Buchanan v. Litchfield, 102 U. S. 278; Hays v. Holly Springs, 114 U. S. 120; Daviess County v. Dickinson, 117 U. S. 57; Hopper v. Covington, 118 U. S. 148; Merrill v. Monticello, 138 U. S. 673.

[1] Mather v. Ottawa, 11 A. & E. Corp. Cas. 248 (Ill., 1885); Ottawa v. Carey, 108 U. S. 110.

[2] Commercial Bank v. Iola, 2 D ll. (U. S.) 353; Loan Association v. Topeka, 3 Dill. (U. S.) 376; s. c., 20 Wall. (U. S.) 655; Ohio Iron Works v. Moundeville, 11 W. Va. 1; Allen v. Jay, 60 Me. 124; Tyler v. Beecher, 44 Vt. 648; Bissell v. Kankakee, 64 Ill. 249; Brodhead v. Milwaukee, 19 Wis. 624; Cole v. Le Grange, 113 U. S. 1.

[3] Lowell v. Boston, 111 Mass. 454; State v. Osawkie Township, 14 Kan. 418.

[4] People ex rel. v. Ragg, 46 N. Y. 401; Lumsden v. Cross, 10 Wis. 282; Hammett v. Philadelphia, 65 Pa. St. 155; In re Washington Avenue, 69 Pa. St. 352; Rogers v. Burlington, 3 Wall. (U. S.) 654; People v. Mayor, 4 N. Y. 419.

[5] Harper v. Emery, 14 Me. 375; State v. McCann, 21 Ohio St. 198; Williams v. School District, 33 Vt. 271; Danielly v. Cabaniss, 52 Ga. 211; Gordon v. Cornes, 47 N. Y. 608; Read v. Plattsmouth, 107 U. S. 568; Merrick v. Amherst, 12 Allen (Mass.), 500; Hensley v. People, 84 Ill. 544; Marks v. Purdue University, 37 Ind. 155; Board of Education v. State, 26 Kan. 44; Bank of Sonoma County v. Fairbanks, 52 Cal. 196.

[6] Leavenworth v. Miller, 7 Kan. 749, and cases cited in note 5.

§ 226. *Formality in execution as affecting legality.*— When a statute authorizing the issue of bonds provides that the bonds shall be signed by the mayor, they must be signed by the person who is mayor of the city when they are signed, and not by any other person, and the city council cannot empower any other person to sign them. And where it affirmatively appears that the person who was mayor of the city at the time when the bonds were signed took no part in signing, delivering or issuing them, the city is not estopped from contesting the validity of such bonds upon the ground that they had not been signed by the mayor of the city as required by statute.[1]

§ 227. *Irregularity as affecting liability.*—Where municipal bonds are in the hands of a *bona fide* holder, and the recitals therein are to the effect that the same are lawfully issued, mere irregularities cannot be taken advantage of by the city in suits brought thereon against the municipality.[2] The persons who execute and deliver the bonds are the agents of the city authorizing their issue, and if these agents exceed their authority as to

---

[1] Coler v. Cleburne, 131 U. S. 162; Anthony v. County of Jasper, 101 U. S. 693; Bissell v. Spring Valley Township, 110 U. S. 162; Northern Bank v. Porter Township, 110 U. S. 608; Merchants' Bank v. Bergen Co., 115 U. S. 384.

[2] Rouede v. Jersey City, 18 Fed. Rep. 719; Knox Co. v. Aspinwall, 21 How. (U. S.) 439; Moran v. Miami Co., 2 Black (U. S.), 722; Supervisors v. Schenck, 5 Wall. (U. S.) 772; Gelpcke v. Dubuque, 1 Wall. (U. S.) 175; St. Joseph Township v. Amy, 16 Wall. (U. S.) 644; Pendleton v. Amy, 18 Wall. (U. S.) 297; Coloma v. Eavis, 92 U. S. 484; County of Randolph v. Post, 93 U. S. 502; Commissioners v. Thayer, 94 U. S. 631; Cass County v. Johnson, 95 U. S. 360; San Antonio v. Mehaffey, 96 U. S. 312; Nauvoo v. Ritter, 97 U. S. 389; Daviess Co. v. Huidekoper, 98 U. S. 98; Hackett v. Ottawa, 99 U. S. 86; Foote v. Pike Co., 101 U. S. 688.

form, manner, detail or circumstance, the loss must fall on those whom they represent, and not on those who deal with them.[1]

§ 228. *Effect of recitals in municipal bonds.*— The effect of recitals in municipal bonds is like that given to words of negotiability in a promissory note. They simply relieve the paper in the hands of a *bona fide* holder from the burden of defenses other than the lack of power growing out of the original issue of the paper, and available as against the original payee. If municipal bonds contain recitals which, upon fair construction, amount to a representation that the municipality's indebtedness, increased by the amount of bonds in question, is within the constitutional limit, the municipality will be estopped from disputing the truth of such representation as against a *bona fide* holder of its bonds.[2] And where legislative authority has been given to a municipality or to its officers to subscribe to the stock of a railroad company, and to issue municipal bonds in payment, but only on some precedent condition, such as a popular vote favoring the subscription, and where it may be gathered from the legislative enactment that the officers of the municipality were invested with power to decide whether the condition precedent has been complied with, their recital that it has been, made on the bonds issued by them and held by a *bona fide* purchaser, is conclusive of the fact, and binding upon the municipality.[3] But if the officers authorized to issue bonds upon a condition are not the appointed tri-

[1] County of Daviess v. Huidekoper, 98 U. S. 100.
[2] Buchanan v. Litchfield, 102 U. S. 278; Coloma v. Eavis, 92 U. S. 484; Orleans v. Pratt, 99 U. S. 676; Nesbit v. Riverside District, 144 U. S. 620.
[3] Coloma v. Eavis, 92 U. S. 484; Orleans v. Pratt, 99 U. S. 676; Buchanan v. Litchfield, 102 U. S. 278.

bunal to decide the fact which constitutes the condition, their recital will not be accepted as a substitute for proof. The grounds of the estoppel is that the recitals are the official statements of those to whom the law refers the public for authentic and final information on the subject.[1] So a recital in a bond that it was issued in accordance with authority conferred by an act, specifying it, and in accordance with a vote of a majority of the qualified voters, is sufficient to validate the bond in the hands of a *bona fide* holder, and the certificate of its regularity by the auditor of the state is conclusive upon the municipality.[2] And the recitals in a bond issued under an act of the legislature, authorizing counties to fund their debts, which show full compliance with the act but not the amount of issue, will estop the county from alleging, against a *bona fide* holder, that the bond was issued in violation of the constitutional limitation.[3] But when the bonds issued by a municipal corporation do not contain any recitals to the effect that the corporation is actually authorized to issue them, the corporation is not estopped from denying the authority of its supervisor and clerk to issue them.[4] From the foregoing it may be seen that the principle is well established that where the power exists by legislative authority to issue negotiable securities, and the local officers, who by the statute are invested with the duty to carry out or execute this power, issue the bonds with recitals that the right to issue them exists, or has arisen, and the bonds have passed into the hands of *bona fide* holders for value, they are not open to the defense of consideration or fraud on the part of the officers,

---

[1] Dixon County v. Field, 111 U. S. 83.
[2] Commanche County v. Lewis, 133 U. S. 198.
[3] Potter v. Commissioners of Chaffee Co., 33 Fed. Rep. 614.
[4] Concord v. Robinson, 121 U. S. 165.

or non-compliance with precedent conditions to the right to exercise the power.[1]

§ 229. *Who are bona fide holders.*— To be a *bona fide* holder, one must be himself a purchaser for value without notice, or the successor of one who was. Every man is chargeable with notice of that which the law requires him to know, and of that which, after being put upon inquiry, he might have ascertained by the exercise of reasonable diligence. As an essential preliminary to protection as a *bona fide* holder, authority to issue municipal bonds must appear. If such authority did not exist, the doctrine of protection to a *bona fide* purchaser has no application. This is the rule even with commercial paper purporting to be issued under a delegated authority. This delegation must be first established before the doctrine can come in for consideration.[2] So every dealer in municipal bonds, which upon their face refer to the statute under which they were issued, is bound to take notice of the statute and of all its requirements.[3] And all persons taking securities of municipal corporations having only special powers must see to it that the conditions prescribed for the exercise of the power existed. So it has been held that persons who purchase bonds issued under an unconstitutional act, upon the certificate of the municipal authorities that a majority of the voters had

[1] Carpenter v. Buena Vista Co., 5 Dill. (U. S.) 560; Knox v. Aspinwall, 21 How. (U. S.) 539; Moran v. Miami Co., 2 Black (U. S.), 722; St. Joseph Township v. Rogers, 16 Wall. (U. S.) 644; Grand Chute v. Winegar, 15 Wall. (U. S.) 373; Kennicott v. Supervisors, 16 Wall. (U. S.) 452; Lexington v. Butler, 14 Wall. (U. S.) 282; Northern Bank v. Trustees, 110 U. S. 608; Dixon County v. Field, 111 U. S. 83.

[2] Merchants' Bank v. Bergen Co., 115 U. S. 384; McClure v. Oxford Township, 94 U. S. 429; Ogden v. Daviess County, 102 U. S. 634; Hayes v. Holly Springs, 114 U. S. 120; Hackett v. Ottawa, 99 U. S. 86.

[3] McClure v. Oxford Township, *supra*.

voted for the issue, are not to be protected as innocent and *bona fide* purchasers without notice, being charged with knowledge of the illegal origin of the bonds.[1] And where the charter of a municipal corporation requires that bonds issued by it shall specify for what purpose they are issued, a bond which purports on its face to be issued by virtue of an ordinance, the date of which is given, but not its title or its contents, does not so far satisfy the requirements of the charter as to protect an innocent holder for value from defenses which might otherwise be made.[2]

§ 230. *Power to issue bonds not implied from power to borrow.*— The implied power of a municipal corporation to borrow money to enable it to execute the powers expressly conferred upon it by law, if existing at all, does not authorize it to create and issue negotiable securities to be sold in the market and to be taken by the purchaser freed from the equities that might be set up by the maker of it.[3] As a general rule, whether a municipal corporation possesses the power to borrow money and to issue negotiable securities therefor depends upon a true con-

[1] Duke v. Brown, 17 A. & E. Corp. Cas. (N. C., 1887), 336.
[2] Barrett v. Dennison, 145 U. S. 135, and cases there cited.
[3] Merrill v. Monticello, 138 U. S. 673; Brenham v. German Bank, 144 U. S. 173; Hill v. Memphis, 134 U. S. 198; Young v. Clarendon, 132 U. S. 340; Norton v. Dyersburg, 127 U. S. 139; Concord v. Robinson, 121 U. S. 165; Mayor v. Ray, 19 Wall. (U. S.) 478; Emery v. Mariaville, 56 Me. 315; Willey v. Greenbush, 30 Me. 452; Clark v. Des Moines, 19 Iowa, 199; School District v. Lombard, 2 Dill. (U. S.) 493; Keller v. Leavenworth Co., 6 Kan. 510; Goodwin v. Ramsay Co., 11 Minn. 31; Smith v. Chesire, 13 Gray (Mass.), 318; Andover v. Grafton, 7 N. H. 298; Mathes v. Cameron, 68 Mo. 504; People v. County, 11 Cal. 170; Chandler v. Bay St. Louis, 57 Miss. 327; Wall v. Monroe County, 103 U. S. 704; Ouachita Co. v. Wolcott, 103 U. S. 557.

struction of its charter and the legislation of the state applicable to it. It has no incidental or inherent authority under the usual grants of municipal powers as a means of discharging its ordinary municipal functions. Such authority may be inferred from special and extraordinary powers, which require the expenditure of unusual sums of money, when such appears to have been the legislative intent.[1]

§ 231. *Limitation on indebtedness as affecting legality of bonds.*— As a general proposition, all bonds issued by a municipality in excess of the constitutional or statutory limitation placed upon its indebtedness, even in the hands of a *bona fide* holder, are illegal and void. But, in cases of this kind, a municipal corporation's liability is usually dependent upon the peculiar circumstances governing the particular case. This branch of the question cannot be better explained than by giving instances where the question has arisen and been decided. Thus, where the indebtedness of a city was restricted to $50,000, an issue of bonds for $300,000 by such city was held to be invalid, notwithstanding the fact that the bonds were not payable for twenty years, and the yearly tax levied with interest upon them would not exceed $50,000 annually.[2] But it has been held that where the amended charter of a city authorized the city council to borrow money and issue bonds for an amount not to exceed $100,000, the bonded debt of the city is thereby limited to $100,000, and the city has authority for the public use of the corporation to issue bonds at any one time to the extent of $100,000.[3] Certificates of indebtedness issued to procure temporary loans

[1] Gause v. Clarksville, 5 Dill. (U. S.) 165; Dill. Mun. Corp., § 124.
[2] Coulson v. Portland, Deady (U. S.), 481.
[3] Mauldin v. Greenville, 31 A. & E. Corp. Cas. 604 (S. C., 1890).

of money for current expenses are *ultra vires* if, at the time they were issued, the debt of the municipality had reached the constitutional limit.[1] But generally only that part of the indebtedness incurred which exceeds the constitutional limitation will be held to be void.[2] And a judgment may be recovered for bonds first delivered up to the amount authorized.[3]

[1] Law v. People, 87 Ill. 385.

[2] McPherson v. Foster, 43 Iowa, 48; Culbertson v. Fulton, 18 N. E. Rep. 781; Stockdale v. Wayland School District, 47 Mich. 226; County of Daviess v. Dickinson, 117 U. S. 657; Hedges v. Dixon County, 37 Fed. Rep. 304.

[3] County of Daviess v. Dickinson, *supra*.

In the case of Hedges v. Dixon County it was held that, if a county contracts to issue bonds as a donation of a specific sum in aid of the construction of a railroad, the contract is to be deemed entire and indivisible, although the amount of the donation is represented by a number of bonds. The whole donation is therefore *ultra vires* and the whole bonds are void, and the jurisdiction of a court of equity cannot be invoked by the bondholders for the purpose of scaling down the donation in so far as it exceeds the constitutional limit. Mr. Justice Brewer, in delivering the opinion of the court in this cas⸱, said:

"'The contract in this case, in its inception, was, on the part of the county, a single and indivisible obligation; that is, an attempted donation of $87,000 to the railroad company. The bonds are merely evidences of the contract, the contract standing behind them, and, whatever separate and divisible obligations of the county exist after the issue of the bonds, the contract in the first instance was single and entire. Now, that was an attempted donation of $87,000 to the railroad company. Such donations the county had no right to make, and, after it had finished its action, nothing which the promisee, the other party to the contract, could do could give validity to the obligation of the county. It was either good or bad, dead or alive, when it left the hands of the promisor. Take this illustration: If, in a state where usury avoids the entire contract, a usurious note be given, the note is void, and no willingness of the payee, no act of his, can transform that invalid into a valid contract. Of course it would be very satisfactory if the promisee, by consenting to a reduction of the interest, could give validity to a void promise — va-

§ 232. *Invalid bonds cannot be ratified.*—As we have heretofore seen,[1] it is impossible to ratify a contract the original making of which was outside the scope of the corporate powers. So the express assent of all the inhabitants of a municipality will not validate bonds issued in excess of the constitutional limit.[2] Nor is the payment of interest on the whole bonds issued a ratification of those which have been issued beyond the lawful limit.[3] The inhabitants of a city are not estopped from contesting the validity of bonds by standing by in silence and permitting the bonds to be issued; nor is the municipality estopped by knowledge and long acquiescence in the act of the officers issuing them, and by the levy of taxes and the payment of interest.[4]

lidity to a dead contract. So here, if the promisee, the railroad company, could reduce the extent of the promise, it doubtless would be satisfactory, but it would thereby be making a contract, or attempting to make a contract, different from that which the promisor proposed. The fact that eighty-seven bonds were issued instead of one in no manner changes the primary obligation attempted to be assumed by the county."

To a casual reader the case just quoted from would seem to conflict with Daviess County v. Dickinson. In the last-named case, the county having authorized the issue of bonds to the amount of $250,000, the county officers issued $320,000; but the cases are not at all parallel. In the Daviess County case the principal had proposed a valid contract. It had done that which it had a right to do, and the wrong and misconduct of its agents was held not to invalidate that which the county had lawfully authorized. In the Hedges case the action of the principal was *ultra vires* and created no valid obligation.

[1] § 78, *ante.*
[2] McPherson v. Foster, 43 Iowa, 48; Dill. Mun. Corp., § 529; Buchanan v. Litchfield, 102 U. S. 278; Dixon County v. Field, 111 U. S. 83.
[3] County of Daviess v. Dickinson, 117 U. S. 657; Dill. Mun. Corp., § 548.
[4] McPherson v. Foster, 43 Iowa, 48; Dill. Mun. Corp., § 546.

§ 233. *Liability cannot be avoided by reorganization.*— Municipal corporations cannot extinguish their debts by changing their names, or reorganizing under new charters, or by failure to exercise their corporate powers. A debt once contracted by a municipal corporation will survive as a debt against whatever corporate entity is subsequently created to take its place and exercise its powers of local government over substantially the same people and territory.[1] Even if a municipal corporation can forfeit its franchise by non-user, such forfeiture will not operate to extinguish debts of the corporation contracted before the forfeiture was incurred or declared.[2]

---

[1] Broughton v. Pensacola, 93 U. S. 266; Mobile v. Watson, 116 U. S. 289; Laird v. De Soto, 22 Fed. Rep. 421; People v. Murray, 73 N. Y. 535; Hill v. City of Kahoka, 35 Fed. Rep. 32.

[2] Hill v. City of Kahoka, *supra*.

In Broughton v. Pensacola, *supra*, the court say: "Although a municipal corporation, so far as it is invested with subordinate legislative powers for local purposes, is a mere instrumentality of the state for the convenient administration of government, yet, when authorized to take stock in a railroad company, and issue its obligations in payment of the stock, it is to that extent to be deemed a private corporation, and its obligations are secured by all the guaranties which protect the engagements of private individuals. The inhibition of the constitution which preserves against the interference of a state the sacredness of contracts applies to the liabilities of municipal corporations created by its permission; and although the repeal or modification of the charter of a corporation of that kind is not within the inhibition, yet it will not be admitted, where its legislation is susceptible to another construction, that the state has in this way sanctioned an evasion of, or escape from liabilities, the creation of which is authorized. When, therefore, a new form is given to an old municipal corporation, or such a corporation is reorganized under a new charter, taking in its new organization the place of the old one, embracing substantially the same corporators and the same territory, it will be presumed that the legislature intended a continued existence of the same corporation, although different powers are possessed under the new charter, and different

§ 234. *Liability in assumpsit on invalid bonds.*— It is the settled doctrine that if a municipal corporation has received money for an authorized purpose, derived from the issue of illegal and void bonds, and has applied it to that purpose, an action will lie as for money had and received, although the corporation had no authority to issue the bonds.[1] So where money is borrowed by a municipal corporation without authority of law, but for a legitimate purpose, although warrants issued to the lender of such money may be *ultra vires* and void, yet the corporation is liable as on an implied *assumpsit* for money had and received; but this principle does not apply when there is an express prohibition of the power to borrow money.[2] And when negotiable certificates of indebtedness issued by a city have been sued upon by the payee, and declared invalid for want of power to issue negotiable instruments, the payee may maintain an action for money had and received, provided the city had power to make the contract out of which the indebtedness arose.[3] Where, however, bonds of a city are void because issued under a provision of the constitution of the state which declares that the general assembly shall not

officers administer its affairs; and, in the absence of express provisions for their payment otherwise, it will also be presumed in such case that the legislature intended that the liabilities as well as the rights of property of the corporation in its old form should accompany the corporation in its reorganization."

[1] Bangor Savings Bank v. Stillwater, 49 Fed. Rep. 721; Louisiana v. New Orleans, 102 U. S. 204; Chapman v. County of Douglas, 107 U. S. 348; Hitchcock v. Galveston, 96 U. S. 341; Norton v. City of Nevada, 41 Fed. Rep. 582.
[2] Allen v. La Fayette, 89 Ala. 641; Salt Lake City v. Hollister, 118 U. S. 256; Marsh v. Fulton County, 10 Wall. (U. S.) 676; Louisiana v. Wood, 102 U. S. 294; Chapman v. County of Douglas, 107 U. S. 348; Litchfield v. Ballou, 114 U. S. 190.
[3] Bangor Savings Bank v. Stillwater, *supra.*

authorize any city to loan its credit to any corporation unless two-thirds of the qualified voters assent thereto, the purchaser cannot maintain an action for money had and received to recover the amount paid to the city for such bonds, as, the city having no power to create the debt, no implied power can arise for its payment, notwithstanding the general statutes gave the board of trustees power "to borrow money for the improvement" of the town, the money having been borrowed in violation of the constitution, and not for the improvement of the town, but to buy a right of way and depot grounds for a railroad.[1]

§ 235. *Illegal issue of bonds may be enjoined.*— Any citizen and tax-payer may restrain the illegal issue and sale of bonds by a municipal corporation if there is no adequate remedy at law, if valid in the hands of an innocent purchaser for value.[2] But a tax-payer cannot enjoin the issue of bonds voted by a city which would be void even in the hands of a *bona fide* purchaser, since neither he nor the city could suffer injury from the issue.[3] It is not necessary for a person to wait until his liability is fixed before he can have redress. It is enough that he may be affected by an illegal ordinance or resolution to entitle him to a hearing, before any attempt has been made to

[1] Norton v. City of Nevada, 41 Fed. Rep. 582.
[2] Johnson County v. McClintock, 51 Ind. 325; Livingston County v. Weider, 64 Ill. 249; Allison v. Railway Co., 9 Bush (Ky.), 247; Bound v. Railway Co., 45 Wis. 543; Wright v. Bishop, 88 Ill. 302; Springfield v. Edwards, 84 Ill. 266; Flack v. Hughes, 67 Ill. 384; Winston v. Tennessee, etc. Ry., 1 Bax. (Tenn.) 60; State v. Montgomery, 74 Ala. 226; Lynch v. Eastern, etc. Ry., 57 Wis. 430; Wilkinson v. Peru, 61 Ind. 1; Meyer v. Porter, 65 Cal. 67; Hodgman v. Chicago, etc. R. Co., 20 Minn. 48; Redd v. Henry County, 31 Grat. (Va.) 695.
[3] Bolton v. City of San Antonio, 21 S. W. Rep. 64.

enforce it.¹ So courts of equity have jurisdiction to enjoin the board of supervisors of a municipal corporation from passing an ordinance which is not within the scope of their powers, where the passage of such ordinance would work irreparable injury.²

§ 236. *Municipal-aid bonds.*— Some twenty-five or thirty years ago a veritable railroad epidemic swept over this country, depositing its infectious germs in almost every county, township and city in the land. Under the influence of this frenzied excitement, the honest but enthusiastic tax-payer voted such an avalanche of indebtedness upon himself that in many communities he has scarcely yet recovered from the effects of his March-hare madness. He has learned a thing or two, however, and it would not be considered safe, or at least wise, for a sleek and smiling emissary of a proposed railroad corporation to again go through such rural districts soliciting aid for some gigantic enterprise the completion of which would certainly make every tiller of the soil rich beyond the wildest dreams of avarice.

§ 237. *Same subject—Power must be specifically granted.* The power of municipal corporations, when authorized by the legislature, to engage in works of internal improvements, such as building of railroads, canals, harbors, and the like, or to loan their credit in aid thereof, and to defray the expenses of such improvements by an exercise of the power of taxation, has always been sus-

[1] State v. City of Paterson, 34 N. J. 163; State v. Jersey City, 5 Dutch. (N. J.) 170.
[2] Spring Valley Water Works v. Bartlett, 61 Cal. 3. And see generally as to injunction, Dill. Mun. Corp., § 519; Union Pacific R. Co. v. Lincoln County, 3 Dill. (U. S.) 300; McClure v. Oxford Township, 94 U. S. 429; Portland, etc. R. Co. v. Hartford, 58 Me. 23.

tained on the ground that such works, by reason of the facilities which they afford for trade, commerce and intercommunication between different and distinct portions of the country, are indispensable to the public interests and public functions.[1] The power of municipalities to issue bonds in aid of such enterprises, however, does not exist unless specifically granted by the legislature.[2] And where the power does not exist, the bonds issued are void, no matter in whose hands they may be found.[3] A grant to a municipal corporation of power to appropriate money in aid of the construction of a railroad, accompanied by a provision directing the levy and collection of taxes to meet such appropriation, and prescribing no other mode of payment, does not authorize the issuing of negotiable bonds in payment of such appropriation.[4] Whilst a municipal corporation, authorized to subscribe for the stock of a railroad company, or to incur any other obligation, may give written evidence of such subscription or obligation, it is not thereby empowered to issue negotiable paper for the amount of indebtedness incurred by the subscription.[5] But municipal bonds issued without authority of law, and therefore void, may be validated by

[1] Hasbrouck v. Milwaukee, 13 Wis. 43.

[2] Mississippi, etc. R. Co. v. Camden, 23 Ark. 300; Pitzman v. Freeberg, 92 Ill. 111; Barnes v. Lacon, 84 Ill. 461; City of Aurora v. West, 22 Ind. 88; Dranesburgh v. Jenkins, 46 Barb. (N. Y.) 294; Taxpayer v. Tennessee C. R. Co., 11 Lea (Tenn.), 329; Wells v. Supervisors, 102 U. S. 625; Lewis v. Clarendon, 5 Dill. (U. S.) 329.

[3] Donovan v. Green, 57 Ill. 63; Clay v. County, 4 Bush (Ky.), 154; Weismer v. Douglas, 61 N. Y. 91; Police Jury v. Britton, 15 Wall. (U. S.) 566; Savings Association v. Topeka, 3 Dill. (U. S.) 376; Commercial Bank v. Iola, 2 Dill. (U. S.) 353.

[4] Concord v. Robinson, 121 U. S. 165.

[5] Hill v. Memphis, 134 U. S. 198; Police Jury v. Britton, 15 Wall. (U. S.) 566; The Mayor v. Ray, 19 Wall. (U. S.) 468; Claiborne County v. Brooks, 111 U. S. 400; Young v. Clarendon Township, 132 U. S. 340.

an act of the legislature passed for that purpose, if the legislature of the state could authorize the issuing of similar bonds.[1]

§ 238. *Power to subscribe to railroad stock.*— A municipal corporation cannot subscribe for stock in a railroad corporation unless it has the authority of the legislature for the act.[2] The legislature usually requires the approval of the electors of incorporated towns and cities, or other municipalities, at an election for that purpose, as a condition to such subscription, and when the sanction of a popular vote is required it must be obtained. So where an act of the legislature, authorizing a town to subscribe to the capital stock of a railroad company, provided that if a majority of the legal voters, voting at an election held for that purpose, shall be found to be in favor of such subscription, it shall be deemed and held that such town has taken stock in said company according to the proposals made, it was held that the statutes make such a majority vote equivalent to, and a substitute for, a subscription by the town upon the books of the company.[3] Accordingly where, upon the performance of certain conditions precedent, the issue of bonds to a railroad company by the proper officers of a municipality is authorized by law, the bonds when issued, if they recite such performance, are, in the hands of a *bona fide* holder for value, binding

[1] Deyo v. Otoe County, 37 Fed. Rep. 246.
[2] Town of East Oakland v. Skinner, 94 U. S. 255; Township of Elmwood v. Marcy, 92 U. S. 289; Gelpcke v. Dubuque, 1 Wall. (U. S.) 175; Thompson v. Lee County, 3 Wall. (U. S.) 327; Pine Grove Township v. Talcott, 19 Wall. (U. S.) 666; Loan Association v. Topeka, 20 Wall. (U. S.) 655.
[3] East Lincoln v. Davenport, 94 U. S. 801; Migret v. Supervisors, 19 Wall. (U. S.) 241.

upon the municipality.[1] And if a legislature has power to authorize a subscription to stock of a railroad by a township, and to provide, as a condition precedent to such subscription, that a majority of the legal voters of such township signify their assent thereto, it has the power to legalize an election held for that purpose before the passage of the act of authorization, and to validate a subscription so made.[2] Where the statute authorizing a county to subscribe to the capital stock of a railroad company declares that subscriptions should not be valid and binding until conditions precedent imposed by the vote should have been complied with, and a vote is had in favor of a subscription payable in county bonds, " said bonds to be issued upon the following conditions, and not until they are complied with," a condition that the road shall be commenced and completed within a specified time is a condition precedent, and if bonds are issued without a compliance therewith they are void.[3] So it has been held that if a county has voted an issue of bonds in aid of the construction of a railroad upon the condition that the road shall be constructed and in operation by a certain day, and that the company should locate their machine shops at a certain specified place, bonds issued by the county are invalid if the company has not fulfilled the conditions.[4]

§ 239. *Limitation on amount of subscription.*— Where the amount of the subscription fixed by the legislature

[1] Commissioners v. January, 94 U. S. 202; Commissioners v. Bolles, 94 U. S. 104.

[2] Anderson v. Township of Santa Ana, 116 U. S. 356; St. Joseph Township v. Rogers, 16 Wall. (U. S.) 644; Cowgill v. Long, 15 Ill. 202; Keithburg v. Frick, 34 Ill. 405; Fanning v. Schammel, 68 Cal. 428; People v. McCune, 57 Cal. 153.

[3] German Sav. Bank v. Franklin Co., 128 U. S. 526.

[4] Onstott v. People, 15 N. E. Rep. 34.

has been reached, any subscription beyond that amount and any issue of bonds therefor will be invalid.[1] So where the amount of subscription is properly limited in the submission, and the election results in favor of the proposition, this does not fix the amount of subscription, but vests in the proper authorities a discretionary power as to the amount of stock to be taken and bonds issued not to exceed the amount specified in the submission.[2]

§ 240. *Levying a tax to pay subscription.*— Where the law authorizes the donation of money by a municipal corporation to aid in the construction of a railroad, and provides *for levying* a tax to raise the amount to be donated, the officers of the corporation cannot adopt any other mode of paying the same, and bonds issued by them for the purpose of paying such indebtedness are void.[3] And where an act of the legislature gives to a town authority to vote a donation in aid of a railroad company, and *levy and collect taxes* to pay the same, the railroad company cannot be compelled to accept bonds issued by the municipality, because the road has only a claim for money and has no right to say how the money shall be raised.[4]

[1] Amey v. Allegheny City, 24 How. 364.
[2] Winter v. City Council, 65 Ala. 403.
[3] Town of Middleport v. Ætna Ins. Co., 82 Ill. 562.
[4] Chicago, etc. R. Co. v. St. Anne, 101 Ill. 151.

INDEX.

References are to sections.

A.

ABATEMENT OF NUISANCES (see NUISANCES).

ABUTTER:
>assessment on, for street improvements, 201.

ACCIDENTS UPON STREETS (see STREETS AND SIDEWALKS):
>liability of municipal corporation for, 204.
>city not insurer against, 204.
>not liable for injuries caused to person by others coasting on, 204.
>nor to person injured by discharge of cannon, 204.
>nor by fall of snow from roof, 204.
>nor by fall of weight attached to flag across street, 204.
>nor injury by mob, 204.
>but liable for injuries when officers have knowledge of defect, 204.
>liable for injuries from awning over sidewalk, 204.
>from injuries from falling in sewer, 204.
>for injuries from hole in embankment, 204.
>for injuries from defective sidewalk, 205.
>not liable for injuries from ice on sidewalk, 205.

ACCOMMODATION PAPER (see NEGOTIABLE INSTRUMENTS):
>liability of corporation on, to *bona fide* holder, 104.

ACKNOWLEDGMENTS:
>what certificate should state, 89.
>when no particular mode directed, 89.
>by officer who affixes seal, 89.

ACTIONS (see COURTS; EXECUTED CONTRACTS):
>on illegal contracts, general rule, 69.
>any undertaking to promote unlawful object will not maintain, 69, 74.

References are to sections.

ACTIONS (continued):
    no distinction between acts *malum in se* and *malum prohibitum* relative to, 69.
    courts will not assist in maintaining, on *ultra vires* acts, 69, 70.
    ultra vires as defense to, 70.
    no performance of *ultra vires* contract gives foundation for right of, 70, 72.
    court must be satisfied of legality of contract before, 71.
    no alleged estoppel can give right of, 71.
    on executed *ultra vires* contract, 72.
    in courts of equity and at law, 73.
    for relief on *ultra vires* contract, 74, 75.
    suing to recover as on *quantum meruit*, 74, 75.
    relief on *quantum meruit* and under statute of frauds compared, 75.

AGENTS (see OFFICERS AND AGENTS; DIRECTORS):
    acts of, confounded with corporate acts, 150.
    distinction between, 151.
    directors are, of corporations, 151.
    ultra vires acts of, not imputable to corporation, 151.
    test to distinguish acts of, from corporate acts, 152.
    what reasonably incidental to corporate business, 152.
    have no power to bind by contracts outside corporate business, 152.
    cashier of bank as, 160.
    liability of corporation for torts of, 162, 163.
    for negligence and omissions of, 162.
    for malicious prosecutions, libel, false imprisonment or false representations of, 162.
    doubt as to liability for slander, 162.
    defense of *ultra vires* for torts of, not allowed, 163.
    authority of in fixing liability, 164.
    acts must be connected with business for which employed, 164.

AID TO RAILROADS (see MUNICIPAL CORPORATIONS; BONDS; MUNICIPAL BONDS).

ALIENATION (see CONVEYANCES).

AMALGAMATION (see CONSOLIDATION AND AMALGAMATION; RAILROAD CORPORATIONS).

References are to sections.

ARBITRATION:
    municipal corporation may submit unsettled claims to, 195.
    power must be exercised by ordinance or resolution, 195.
    when assessment of damages may not be submitted to, 195.

ASSIGNMENT:
    directors may make, for benefit of creditors, 11, 155.
    insolvent corporations may make, 91.
    may not divert property from payment of debts by, 91.
    by president, is company's contract, 91.
    shares of stock may be assigned to creditors, 91.

ASSUMPSIT (see QUANTUM MERUIT).

B.

BANKS (see NATIONAL BANKS):
    may own and convey real property, 85. 157.
    but only for purposes prescribed in charter, 85.
    power to convey includes power to mortgage, 85.
    may make negotiable paper, 102.
    power to discount does not imply power to purchase, 103.
    power to increase capital stock, 111.
    directors' powers over affairs of, limited, 157.
    must exercise care and prudence in administration of affairs, 157.
    may commit affairs of to duly authorized officers, 157.
    directors are liable to, for wrong-doing resulting from gross inattention to business, 157.
    have no ownership in assets of, 157.
    when not chargeable with assets of, 158.
    not liable to, for misconduct of co-director, 158.
    president of, no more control of property than any other director, 158.
    acts of, outside official duties, not binding on, 159.
    cannot dispose of cash and credits of, to settle creditors' demands, 159.
    cannot release claim of, against any one, 159.
    personally liable for overdrafts allowed on, 159.
    cashier presumed to have necessary power to transact business of, 160.
    may indorse commercial paper of, 160.
    receive funds coming to and give certificates for, 160.

INDEX.

References are to sections.

BANKS (continued):
    collect debts owing to, 161.
    release debt secured by mortgage, 161.
    may borrow money for, and bind bank by promissory note, 161.
    may draw checks on funds of, 161.
    may transfer shares of stock of, 161.
    may deliver notes of to attorney for collection, 161.
    but may not compromise claims of, 161.
    nor transfer non-negotiable notes of, 161.
    nor discharge surety on note to, 161.

BEQUEST:
    corporation may take personal property by, 95.
    may take its own stock by, 95.
    of money to church, 95.
    to corporation, for education of students, 95.
    to city, of money for hospital, 95.
    to city, for relief of blind and lame, 95.

BORROWING:
    power of corporation as to, 96.
    incidental to every corporation, 96.
    but prohibition against must be obeyed, 96.
    not permitted by company constituted for special purposes, 96.
    test to determine if transaction is, 97.
    banks have implied power to, 98.
    power to borrow gives no right to issue irredeemable bonds, 98.
    benefit society no power without special authority, 98.
    where power to borrow gives right to secure loan, 98.
    instances where power allowed, 98.

BONDS (see MUNICIPAL BONDS; RAILROAD BONDS).

C.

CALLS (see CAPITAL STOCK):
    future calls as assets, 125.
    as to mortgage or pledge of, 125.

CAPITAL STOCK (see STOCK AND STOCKHOLDERS):
    definition of, 106.
    nature and purpose of, 106.
    as a trust fund, 107.
    unpaid stock as assets, 107.

References are to sections.

CAPITAL STOCK (continued):
   limitation on doctrine as trust fund, 108.
   only when corporation insolvent, 108.
   power to increase, 109.
   power may be conferred subsequent to grant of charter, 110.
   consent of stockholders necessary, 110.
   power of national bank to increase, 111.
   power to reduce not implied by power to increase, 113.
   fund cannot be increased or diminished without legislative license, 113.
   reduction of as dissolution of old corporation, 113.
   reduction of in England, 114.
   power to issue new stock, 115.
   as to special stock under Massachusetts statute, 116.
   ultra vires to issue shares at discount, 117.
   power to issue preferred stock, 118.
   must be expressly conferred, 118.
   liability on *ultra vires* issue of, 119, 127.
   dealing in own stock, 120.
   purchasing stock of another corporation, 121.
   may take in payment of debt, 121.
   declaring dividends, 124.
   liability on declared dividends, 126.
   as individual property of stockholder, 126.
   declaration of, discretionary with directors, 126.
   future calls as assets, 125.
   mortgage or pledge of, 125.

CHARTERS (see CONSTRUCTION OF CHARTERS):
   grant from sovereign power of state, 3.
   must be certified by directors and recorded, 8.
   what must specify, 3.
   powers in, which contravene statute, void, 3
   creates subscribers a corporation, 3.
   what acceptance of, implies, 4.
   general rule of construction, 8.
   to be strictly construed, 8.
   ambiguity in, vitiates grant, 8.
   province of court in construing, 12, 48.
   construction of, as to incidental powers, 13.
   not only grants rights, but imposes duties, 19.

320 INDEX.

References are to sections.

CHARTERS (continued):
  acceptance of rights is assumption of duties, 19.
  contract which binds both state and corporation, 19.
  when prescribes mode of contracting, must be strictly pursued, 52.
CITIES AND TOWNS (see MUNICIPAL CORPORATIONS).
CONDITIONS PRECEDENT (see MUNICIPAL BONDS).
CONSOLIDATION AND AMALGAMATION (see RAILROAD CORPORATIONS):
  definition of consolidation, 142.
  definition of amalgamation, 142.
  corporations can consolidate only with consent of legislature, 143.
  authority may be conferred by original charter, 143.
  or by general or special act of legislature, 143.
  or even by express sanction of unauthorized agreement, 143.
  agreement between directors to, *ultra vires*, 143.
  effect of variously stated, 144.
  effect of interstate consolidation, 145.
  of stock, does not constitute one corporation of both states, 145.
  subject to control of each state, 145.
  treated in each state as domestic corporation, 145.
  consolidated company has all rights and subject to liabilities of corporations of which composed, 146.
  may take advantage of all contracts and enforce all debts, 146.
  liable for all torts committed by various corporations, 146.
  newly-created company entitled to all property, 146.
  where indebtedness of old company has not ripened into lien, 146.
  stockholders not bound by, without consent, 147.
  stockholders of old entitled to withdraw shares, 147.
  where two corporations consolidate, exemption of one from taxation will not inure to the other, 148.
  when immunity of old corporation does not inure to new, 148.
  when exemption of shares of old passes into new, 148.
CONSTRUCTION OF CHARTERS (see CHARTERS):
  general rule of construction, 8.
  charters to be strictly construed, 8.
  ambiguity vitiates grant, 8.
  province of court in, 12, 48.

References are to sections.

CONSTRUCTION OF CHARTERS (continued):
of incidental powers, 13.
tendency to disregard statutory enactments, 18, 49.
intention of legislature should control, 49.
substitution of judicial for legislative will, 49.

CONTRACTS (see CORPORATIONS; ULTRA VIRES):
doctrine of *ultra vires* applied to, 47.
incidental powers as to, 50.
corporate contract is act of legal entity, 50.
irregularity no defense to liability on, 51.
officers cannot bind by, beyond charter limits, 52.
ultra vires and illegal; alleged distinction, 55.
prohibited contracts, illegal, 56.
courts cannot legalize by ignoring statutes, 57.
Morawetz on unauthorized and illegal, 57.
ultra vires contracts not enforceable, 69, 70, 71.
performance or part performance will not make valid, 70, 72.
as to performance by innocent party, 58, 61, 62.
as to relief on *ultra vires* contracts, 74, 75.
relief under statute of frauds compared with, 75.
general doctrine of ratification, 76.
effect of ratification, 77.
ultra vires contracts incapable of ratification, 78, 194.
promoters' contracts may be ratified, 79.
as to unauthorized contracts of directors, 151.
actions on illegal, 69.
action on executed *ultra vires* contracts, 72.
in courts of equity and at law, 73.
of municipal corporations, 188.
general powers as to, 188.
prescribed mode must be pursued, 189.
not bound by *ultra vires* contracts of officers, 190.
implied municipal contracts, 191.
of compromise and arbitration, 195.
limitation on indebtedness by, 196.

CONVEYANCES:
power to acquire implies power to convey, 83.
corporation may sell all property for lawful purpose, 83, 85.
power to convey implies power to mortgage, 84.
must be executed in corporate name under seal, 87.

21

References are to sections.

CONVEYANCES (continued):
may be made by agent having authority, 87, 89.
as evidence of title when made by agent, 88.
what certificate to should state, 89.
when no particular mode of acknowledgment directed, 89.
affixing corporate seal, 90.
invalid when officer executes in own name, 90.

CORPORATIONS (see DE FACTO CORPORATIONS; FOREIGN CORPORATIONS; MUNICIPAL CORPORATIONS; RAILROAD CORPORATIONS; POWERS OF CORPORATIONS):
a legal entity, 2.
general character and attributes, 2.
property and powers vested in, 2.
acts within chartered powers only affect, 2.
acts of officers beyond, not ascribed to, 2, 17.
confusion of with individuals composing, 2.
created only by virtue of legislative enactment, 3, 4.
no express words required to create, 3.
manner of creation prescribed by general laws, 3.
special acts of incorporation now generally prohibited, 3.
nature of not changed by organization under general laws, 3.
act of incorporation, enabling act, 21.
limited management and liability under legislative acts, 3.
charters of, to be recorded, 3.
specifications in charter which contravene statute, void, 3.
strict compliance with law required before *in esse*, 3.
powers of, depend on law of creation, 3, 19.
have no natural or inherent capacities, 19.
charter creates subscribers a corporation, 3.
creation of, based on theory of benefit to public, 4.
distinction between and natural persons, 5.
distinction between and partnerships, 6.
as organized under general and special laws, 7.
general powers possessed by, 7, 9, 13, 21, 22.
powers granted to be strictly construed, 8.
object of construction to protect public, 8.
construction not to defeat legislative intent, 8.
strict construction peculiarly applicable to organization under general laws, 10.
province of court in construing powers, 12, 18.
should not enlarge powers beyond limits of charter, 12.

References are to sections.

CORPORATIONS (continued):
  specific grant of powers implies inhibition of others, 12.
  what are incidental powers, 13.
  discretion in exercising powers, 14.
  when mode prescribed can be exercised in no other way, 14.
  miscellaneous incidental powers, 15.
  contracts of, disabling performance of duties, *ultra vires*, 19.
  acts under assumption of powers, void, 19.
  all persons bound to take notice of limits of powers, 53.
  if powers are exceeded, state may take away charter, 53.
  not liable on *ultra vires* contracts, 54.
  capacities of, analogous to those resting under legal disability, 60.
  performance of *ultra vires* contract by innocent party, 58, 61, 62.
  San Antonio v. Mehaffey, 63.
  Railway Co. v. McCarthey, 64.
  Hitchcock v. Galveston, 65.
  Jones v. Guaranty Co., 66.
  National Bank v. Mathews, 69.
  Central Trans. Co. v. Pullman Co., 68.

COURTS (see ACTIONS; CONSTRUCTION OF CHARTERS):
  province of in construing charters, 12, 18.
  tendency of to disregard statutes, 18, 49.
  substitution of judicial for legislative will, 49.
  will not enforce contract violative of statute, 69.
  or *ultra vires*, 70.
  must be satisfied of legality of contract, 71.
  and one over which accustomed to exercise jurisdiction, 71.
  no estoppel will induce to enforce *ultra vires* contract, 71.
  neither in equity nor at law, 73.
  difference between merely forms and remedies, 73.
  must accept contracts as they find them, 73.
  no power to make contracts for parties, 73.
  will grant relief on *ultra vires* contracts as on *quantum meruit*, 74.

D.

DEEDS (see CONVEYANCES).

DE FACTO CORPORATIONS:
  when estopped from denying legality of organization, 168.
  when person dealing with, also estopped, 168.

References are to sections.

DE FACTO CORPORATIONS (continued):
validity of organization cannot be impeached collaterally, 168.
acts of officers under color of election, binding on, 168.
effect of presuming to act before capital paid in, 168.
continuing to act after expiration of charter, 168.

DIRECTORS (see AGENTS; OFFICERS AND AGENTS):
confounding acts of with corporate acts, 150.
distinction between and corporate acts, 151.
acts of within limits of corporate powers, 151.
are agents of corporation, 151.
acts outside sphere of agency unlawful usurpations, 151.
acts of beyond prescribed corporate powers, not corporate acts, 151.
test to distinguish from corporate acts, 152.
to determine, charter must be consulted, 152.
bona fides not sole test, 152.
relation to stockholders as that of trustees, 153.
essential distinction between and trustees, 153.
general powers of, 154.
no power to bind outside corporate powers, 154.
not presumed to have powers corporation itself has not, 154.
cannot, as creditors, secure to themselves preference, 155.
may make valid assignment for benefit of creditors, 155.
declaration of dividends with knowledge of no profits, illegal, 155.
courts will enjoin *ultra vires* act approved by, 155.
cannot enforce contract made with co-director, 155.
resolutions by, to assume debts of rival corporation, *ultra vires*, 155.
general liability of, 156.
error of judgment will not subject to liability, 156.
personally liable for violation of charter, 156.
liable for want of good faith or wilful abuse of discretion, 156.
or gross negligence, 156.
personally liable for waste of corporate funds, 156.
powers of bank directors, 157.
may commit affairs of bank to duly authorized officers, 157.
liable for wrong-doing, when, 157.
have no title to assets, 157.
personally liable for issue of spurious stock, 158.
not chargeable with assets unless appropriated by, 158.
not liable for loss occasioned by fraud of co-director, 158.

INDEX. 325

References are to sections.

DIVIDENDS:
definition, 124.
declaration of, discretionary with directors, 124.
where right to fixed by contract, court will compel declaration, 124.
directors cannot discriminate between stockholders, 124.
after declaration of, belongs to stockholder, 126.
as to liability after notice of, 126.
as to liability if declared payable elsewhere than at office, 126.

E.

EMINENT DOMAIN:
definition, 183.
for what purposes may be exercised, 86, 183.
right not to be extended by implication, 86.
as to sale of real property acquired by, 86.
distinction between and taxation, 184.

ESTOPPEL:
the doctrine as applied to executed contracts, 58, 59, 60.
not applicable to unauthorized act of officer, 59, 192.
doctrine of, no more applicable to corporations than to persons under legal disability, 60.
powers of corporation and married woman compared relative to, 60.

EXECUTED CONTRACTS (see CONTRACTS; CORPORATIONS; ULTRA VIRES):
doctrine of *ultra vires* as applied to, 58–62.
as to alleged rule that doctrine should not be applied to, 58.
fallacy of alleged rule shown, 59, 60, 61, 62.
cases cited to support rule not applicable, 63, 64, 65, 66, 67, 68.
Taylor on alleged rule, 61.

F.

FOREIGN CORPORATIONS:
general rule as to powers of, 165.
powers depend on laws of sovereignty where exercised, 165.
can make no contract without sanction of such sovereignty, 165.
absence of prohibitory legislation relative to, presumes tacit adoption of foreign laws, 166.

References are to sections.

FOREIGN CORPORATIONS (continued):
individuals cannot complain because business is being done by, 166.
contractual powers similar to domestic corporation, 167.

FRANCHISES:
cannot be leased or transferred without legislative authority, 137.
lease of, *ultra vires*, 138.
cannot mortgage, 141.
cannot be levied upon by execution, 141.
mortgage or transfer of, may be ratified by subsequent enactment, 141.
alleged distinction between franchise to be a corporation, and as a corporation to operate railway, 141.

FUTURE CALLS (see CALLS).

G.

GAS COMPANIES (see MUNICIPAL CORPORATIONS):
as to exclusive privileges to, 216.
municipal corporations may contract with, for gas supply, 217.
rates of, may be regulated by city, 218.

GUARANTY:
railroad company no power to guaranty bonds of another without express authority, 136.
has power to guaranty bonds received in payment of debt due it, 136.
where guaranty *ultra vires*, stockholders estopped from repudiating, 136.

H.

HYPOTHECATION OF STOCK (see PLEDGE).

I.

ILLEGAL COMBINATIONS:
definition, 149.
how combination usually consummated, 149.
power of trustees under, 149.
dividends made from common fund, 149.

INDEX.

References are to sections.

ILLEGAL CONTRACTS (see CONTRACTS; ULTRA VIRES).
IMPLIED POWERS (see INCIDENTAL POWERS).
INCIDENTAL POWERS (see POWERS OF CORPORATIONS):
  definition of, 13.
  power to acquire real estate, 81, 85.
  power to borrow money, 96.
  to make negotiable paper, 100.
INCREASE OF CAPITAL STOCK (see CAPITAL STOCK).

J.

JURISDICTION (see ACTIONS; COURTS).

L.

LAND (see REAL ESTATE).
LEASE:
  road and franchises may not be transferred by without express authority, 137.
  denied on theory of duties to public, 137.
  instances where denied, 137.
  will not be set aside at suit of lessor, though *ultra vires*, 138.
  relief denied under rule *in pari delicto potior est conditio defendentis*, 138.
  affirmative relief denied unless executory, 138.
  when cannot lease real estate where power to sell exists, 139.
  when made by officers unauthorized, void, 139.
  where holders of majority of stock cannot lawfully authorize, 139.
LEVY:
  cannot be made on franchises in execution, 141.
LIABILITY OF CORPORATIONS (see CORPORATIONS; RAILROAD CORPORATIONS; MUNICIPAL CORPORATIONS):
  where irregularity of proceedings no defense to, 51.
  why not liable on *ultra vires* contracts, 54.
  on accommodation paper, 104.
  on *ultra vires* issue of preferred stock, 119, 127.
  on declared dividends, 126.
  for consequential damages, 203.
  for accidents upon streets, 204.

References are to sections.

LIABILITY OF CORPORATIONS (continued):
for defective streets and sewers, 205, 211.
as to nuisances, 213.
for damages for inadequate water supply, 219.
doctrine of *respondeat superior*, 220.
as to *ultra vires* acts of officers, 222.
general rule as to torts, 162.
for tortious acts of agents, 163.
authority of agent in fixing, 164.
irregularity in bonds as affecting. 227.
effect of recitals in, as affecting, 228.
limitation on indebtedness as affecting, 231.
cannot be avoided by reorganization, 233.
in *assumpsit* on invalid bonds, 234.

LIBEL:
corporation's liability for, 162.

LIEN:
where indebtedness of old company on consolidation has not ripened into, 146.

M.

MUNICIPAL BONDS (see MUNICIPAL CORPORATIONS):
power of municipality to issue, 223.
no presumption as to legality of, 223.
purposes for which may be issued, 224.
instances where power to issue denied, 225.
formality in execution as affecting legality, 226.
irregularities in issuing, no defense to liability on, 227.
recitals in, as affecting liability, 228.
who *bona fide* holders of, 229.
power to issue not implied from power to borrow, 230.
limitation on indebtedness as affecting legality, 231.
when invalid cannot be ratified, 232.
liability on, cannot be avoided by reorganization, 233.
liability in *assumpsit* on invalid issue, 234.
illegal issue of, may be enjoined, 235.
power to issue municipal-aid bonds, 137, 238.
limitation on subscription to, 239, 240.

MUNICIPAL CORPORATIONS:
general nature of, 169.
exercise of general powers of, 170.
manner of rests in their judgment, 170.
when not liable for defects in execution of powers, 170.
can exercise only such powers as granted them, 170.
no powers implied except essential to purposes, 170.
acts beyond powers of no effect, 170.
power requiring exercise of discretion cannot be delegated by, 173.
courts cannot interfere with discretionary powers of, 177.
ordinances of, definition, 171.
legislature may delegate power to enact, 171.
may be conferred upon any department of municipality, 171.
must be made in subordination to general laws, 172.
must be reasonable, 176.
but ordinances expressly authorized by legislature cannot be unreasonable, 176.
within limits of corporation have force of laws, 172.
power to pass includes power to make effectual, 172.
distinction between judicial and ministerial ordinances, 173.
effect of *ultra vires* ordinances, 174.
ordinance levying tax for purpose unauthorized, void, 174.
where power exists, but exercised in unauthorized manner, 174.
validity of cannot be questioned collaterally, 174.
when ordinance making appropriation *ultra vires*, 175.
instances of illegal and void ordinances, 175, 176.
courts may restrain *ultra vires* ordinances, 178.

Taxation —
power relating to, 179.
may be delegated by state, 179.
essential attribute to municipal government, 179.
power may be revoked, 180.
can be exercised only for public purposes, 181.
cannot levy taxes to aid private enterprises, 181.
or to aid sufferers by fire or flood, 181.
taxation and power to license distinguished, 182.

Eminent Domain —
power to exercise right of, 183.
distinction between and taxation, 184.
powers as to real property, 185.

330 INDEX.

References are to sections.

MUNICIPAL CORPORATIONS (continued):
 Eminent Domain (continued) —
  apportionment of between old and new municipality, 186.
  powers of extinguished municipalities, 187.
  powers revert to new town, 187.
 Contracts —
  powers as to, 188.
  usually conferred in incorporating act, 188.
  mode prescribed must be strictly pursued, 189.
  void, if mode prescribed violated, 189.
  for public work to lowest bidder, 189.
  advertisement and specifications, 189.
  officers cannot bind by *ultra vires* contract, 190.
  persons contracting with must take notice of powers, 190.
  contracts by, when law requires advertising, 190.
  as to implied contracts, 191.
  when estoppel not applicable, 192.
  no estoppel arises when act violative of law, 192.
  acts without authority not misleading, 192.
  when estopped to deny irregularity, 193.
  ratification of *ultra vires* contracts, 194.
  no act of can supply defect in, 194.
  may be inferred by acquiescence, 194.
  may make contracts of compromise, 195.
  or submit unsettled claims to arbitration, 195.
  but must be exercised by ordinance or resolution, 195.
  when submission to arbitration *ultra vires*, 185.
  limitation on contracting indebtedness, 196.
  when limit reached in, 196.
  cannot be evaded by future levies, 196.
  cannot make appropriation for indebtedness beyond, 196.
  all persons charged with notice of limitation on, 196.
  instances where increase beyond limit denied, 197.
  equity will enjoin illegal creation of, 198.
 Streets —
  powers as to, 199.
  exclusive control over, 199.
  whole sovereign power required to confer, 199.
  use of must be consistent with public objects, 199.
  when estopped to deny existence of, 200.
  power to grade, improve and alter, 201.

References are to sections.

MUNICIPAL CORPORATIONS (continued):
 Streets (continued) —
  power to open, implied power to grade, 201.
  to improve by assessment, inhibits any other mode, 201.
  manner of improvement discretionary, 202.
  duty to keep in repair, ministerial, 202.
  liability for consequential damages, 203.
  when not liable for, 203.
  instances of liability for, 203.
  liability for accidents upon, 204.
  not insurers against accidents, 204.
  instances of liability for accidents, 204.
  instances of liability for defective streets, 205.
  notice of defects in, required, 206.
 Sewers —
  authority to construct, 207.
  discretion as to mode, 207.
  discretion as to selection of system, 208.
  liability for negligence in construction, 208.
  duty to provide outlet, 209.
  not insurer of condition of, 210.
  liability for injuries from defects in, 211.
  liability for property flooded from, 211.
 Nuisances —
  power to abate, 212.
  power conferred for public good, 212.
  not liable for proper exercise of power by officers, 212.
  when not liable for failure to abate, 213.
  when not liable for act which results in, 213.
 Quarantine Regulations —
  powers as to, 214.
 Wharves —
  no power to lease to private persons, 215.
 Water and Gas Supply —
  exclusive privileges to, 216.
  no power to grant without express authority, 216.
  contracts for, 217.
  mode of furnishing supply discretionary, 217.
  power to regulate rates of, 218.
  ordinance regulating not invalid because different rates fixed, 218.
  liability for inadequate water supply, 219.

References are to sections.

MUNICIPAL CORPORATIONS (continued):
Respondeat Superior —
  doctrine of, 220.
  when liable, 220.
  distinction between public-*quasi* and municipal corporation, 221.
  not liable for *ultra vires* act of officer, 222.

N.

NATIONAL BANKS (see BANKS):
  power of to increase capital stock, 111.
NEGOTIABLE PAPER:
  may make for legitimate purposes, 100.
  corporation as indorsee of, 101.
  power of savings bank to make, 102.
  liability of corporation on accommodation note, 104.

O.

OFFICERS AND AGENTS (see AGENTS; DIRECTORS):
  are special agents of corporation, 52.
  when mode of acting by prescribed must be strictly pursued, 52.
  have no power except within limits of charter, 52.
  parties dealing with, charged with authority of, 52.
  execution of deeds by, 90.
  may prove corporate seal, 90.
President of Bank —
  powers and liability of, 159.
  control over corporate property as other director, 159.
  cannot settle demands of creditors without authority, 159.
  cannot release claims of bank, 159.
  may be invested with capacity to do acts not inherent in office, 159.
  having power to contract, may release same, 159.
  liable for indorsement in excess of paid-up capital, 159.
  and for overdrafts which he directed, 159.
  and loss caused by permitting securities to be carried away, 159.
Cashier —
  powers and duties of, 160.
  presumed to have necessary powers to transact business, 160.

References are to sections.

OFFICERS AND AGENTS (continued):
   Cashier (continued) —
      powers habitually exercised define powers as to public, 160.
      has authority to indorse paper of bank, 160.
      to receive funds and give certificates of deposit, 160.
      to collect debts owing to bank, 160.
      to release debt secured by mortgage, 161.
      to borrow money and bind bank by note, 161.
      to draw checks upon funds of bank, 161.
      to transfer shares of bank, 161.
      to deliver notes for collection, 161.
      but no power to compromise claims, 161.
      nor transfer non-negotiable paper, 161.
      nor to discharge surety on note, 161.
      nor indemnify officer for levying execution, 161.
   Torts —
      general liability of corporation for, 162.
      rule stated by Cooley, 162.
      liable for malicious prosecution of, 162.
      for libel, 162.
      for false imprisonment, 162.
      for false representation, 162.
      doubt as to liability for slander, 162.
      for conspiracy, 162.
      for assault by, 163.
      ultra vires no defense for tort, 163.
      authority in fixing liability, 164.
ORDINANCES (see MUNICIPAL CORPORATIONS).

P.

PLEDGE:
   power of corporation to, 105.
   where may contract debt, may pledge securities for payment, 105.
   call already made may be pledged, 125.
   proceeds of future call may not be, 125.
POWERS OF CORPORATIONS (see MUNICIPAL CORPORATIONS):
   to acquire real property under common law, 81.
   and under modern statutes, 81.
   limits on power generally prescribed by statute, 81.

References are to sections.

POWERS OF CORPORATIONS (continued):
    no power for purposes other than objects of creation, 81.
    power to acquire by eminent domain, 86.
    to take by devise, 82.
    by bequest, 95.
    power to dispose of property, 82.
    power to sell implies power to mortgage, 84.
    power of bank to hold and convey, 85.
    alienation by deed, 87.
    conveyance by agent, 88.
    to assign property for benefit of creditors, 91.
    to act as trustee, 92.
    must be within scope of powers, 93.
    to borrow money, 96.
    instances of implied power to borrow, 98.
    to loan money, 99.
    as to negotiable instruments, 100.
    to pledge securities, 105.
    to increase capital stock, 109.
    irregularity of exercising powers as affecting stockholders, 112.
    to reduce capital stock, 113.
    power to increase gives no power to diminish, 113.
    to issue new stock, 115.
    as to special stock, 116.
    to issue at discount, 117.
    to issue preferred stock, 118.
    to deal in own stock, 120.
    to purchase stock of another corporation, 121.
    instances where power denied, 122.
    of foreign to purchase stock of domestic corporation, 123.
    such purchase *ultra vires*, 123.
    to declare dividends, 124.
    discretionary with directors, 124.
    to mortgage future calls, 125.

PREFERRED STOCK (see CAPITAL STOCK).

PROMOTERS:
    no statutory authority to make preliminary contracts, 79.
    if ratified by corporation and within its powers, enforceable, 79.
    should be adopted in same way corporate contracts are made, 79.

PROPERTY (see REAL PROPERTY).

Q.

QUANTUM MERUIT (see ACTIONS):
relief against *ultra vires* contract on, 74.

R.

RAILROAD BONDS:
definition of, 132.
power to issue, 133.
formalities prescribed in issuing must be strictly pursued, 134.
negotiability of, 135.
usually payable to trustee named in mortgage, 135.
not strictly negotiable under law merchant, 135.
railroad company no power to guaranty bonds of another company, 136.

RAILROAD COMPANIES:
general power to make contracts, 128.
may not release itself by from public duties, 128.
may contract to carry beyond own lines, 129.
acceptance of goods where destination beyond own lines, 129.
American doctrine as to, 129.
traffic agreements between, 130.
contracts which prevent competition between, not necessarily contrary to public policy, 130.
powers as to pooling contracts, 131.
definition of pools, 131.
traffic and money pools, 131.
as to regulation of rates by railroad commission, 131.
bonds of, definition, 132.
for what purposes bonds may be issued, 133.
formalities prescribed should be strictly pursued, 134.
negotiability of railroad bonds, 135.
power to guaranty bonds of another company, 136.
power to lease road and franchises, 137.
power must be expressly conferred, 137.
where power to lease denied, 137, 139.
ultra vires lease not set aside at suit of lessor, 138.
power to mortgage road and franchise, 140, 141.
power to consolidate, 142, 143.

INDEX.

References are to sections.

RAILROAD COMPANIES (continued):
  definition of consolidation and amalgamation, 142.
  effect of consolidation, 144.
  effect of interstate consolidation, 145.
  rights and liabilities of consolidated company, 146.
  consolidation as affecting stockholders, 147.
  consolidation as affecting taxation, 148.

RAILWAY AID BONDS (see MUNICIPAL BONDS).

RATIFICATION:
  general doctrine stated, 76.
  to be binding must be act of corporate agency, 76.
  cannot arise from action of officer who had no authority to do original act, 76.
  nature and effect of ratification, 77.
  ultra vires contracts cannot be ratified, 78.
  by corporation of acts of promoters, 79.

REAL ESTATE:
  power of corporation to acquire, 81.
  special authority to acquire by devise, 82.
  power to acquire implies power to dispose of, 83.
  power to sell implies power to mortgage, 84.
  power of bank to hold and sell, 85.
  but only for purposes set forth in charter, 85.
  power to acquire by eminent domain, 86.
  to alienate by deed, 87.
  conveyance of, by agent, 88.
  acknowledgment of deeds to, 89.
  affixing corporate seal, 90.
  assignment of, for benefit of creditors, 91.

REDUCTION OF CAPITAL STOCK (see CAPITAL STOCK).

RESPONDEAT SUPERIOR (see MUNICIPAL CORPORATIONS).

S.

SALE OF ROAD AND FRANCHISES (see RAILROAD CORPORATIONS).

STOCK AND STOCKHOLDERS (see CAPITAL STOCK):
  stockholders not the corporation, 2.
  consent of, necessary to increase capital stock, 110.

STOCK AND STOCKHOLDERS (continued):
  stockholders who have accepted portions of increased stock cannot deny validity of, 112.
  powers as to new stock, 115.
  may issue if not cloak for watering, 115.
  powers as to special stock, 116.
  characteristics of, 116.
  issuing shares at discount, 117.
  issuing preferred shares, 118.
  power must be expressly conferred, 118.
  liability on *ultra vires* issue of, 119.
  power to deal in own stock, 120.
  power in many states regulated by statute, 120.
  purchasing stock of another corporation, 121.
  instances where power denied, 122.
  powers of foreign corporations as to, 123.
  power to declare dividends on stock, 124.
  stockholders may not be discriminated against in, 124.
  after declaration of, is individual property of stockholders, 126.
  stockholder cannot become member of company on illegal issue, 127.

T.

TAXATION (see MUNICIPAL CORPORATIONS):
  power may be delegated to municipal corporations, 179.
  is essential attribute of municipality, 179.
  but power may be revoked by legislature, 180.
  can be exercised only for public purposes, 181.
  power to license distinguished from, 182.
  distinguished from eminent domain, 184.

U.

ULTRA VIRES (see CONTRACTS; CORPORATIONS; POWERS OF CORPORATIONS, ETC.):
  legitimately applicable only to corporate acts, 1, 17.
  senses in which term used, 17.
  questions of to be decided by charter, 11.
  principles governing relations of trustee not properly applicable, 17.

References are to sections.

ULTRA VIRES (continued):
    principles of doctrine plain, 18.
    two propositions as to doctrine settled, 19.
    chronological review of doctrine, 20-45.
    principles supporting doctrine first enunciated in United States in 1804, 21.
    application of doctrine to contracts generally, 47.
    province of court in applying doctrine, 12, 18, 48.
    evolved to restrict corporations to granted powers, 48.
    estoppel as to defense of, 58, 59, 60.
    analogy of *ultra vires* acts of corporations to those of persons under legal disability, 60.
    defense of to actions, 70.
    actions on executed *ultra vires* contracts, 72, 73.
    relief on *ultra vires* contract, 74, 75.

W.

WHARVES (see MUNICIPAL CORPORATIONS).

www.ingramcontent.com/pod-product-compliance
Lightning Source LLC
Chambersburg PA
CBHW050851300426
44111CB00010B/1214